C000157195

For Using NetWare Administrator

To Do This	Enter Th...
Add a license certification	Tools | Ins...
Add a control access or public access NDPS printer	Object | C...
View status of all public access NDPS printers	Tools | NDPS Public Access Printers
Change multiple information and security for multiple users	Object | Details on Multiple Users
Recover deleted files	Highlight volume; then click Tools | Salvage

For Administering Z.E.N.works Starter Pack

To Do This	Enter This Command at the Workstation
Import a workstation into NDS	WSIMPORT [*context* | /T *tree* | /S[-] | /H | /?]
	T = Tree
	S = Subcontainers
	H = Hidden
	? = Help
	Default = default context and subcontainers
Register a workstation	WSREG32 (for Windows 95/98/NT)
	WSREG16 (for Windows 3.*x*)
Deregister a workstation	UNREG32 (for Windows 95/98/NT)
	UNREG16 (for Windows 3.*x*)
Display a Z.E.N.works version	ZENVER
Create a packaged Application object	SNAPSHOT

For Diagnosing and Repairing the Server

To Do This	Enter This Command at the Server
Repair a traditional NetWare volume	VREPAIR [*volume_name*] [*log_filename*]
Repair an NSS volume	NSS /rebuild=NSS [*volume_name*]
Repair Directory Services	DSREPAIR [-U]
	-U instructs DSREPAIR to run and exit without user intervention
Generate diagnostics reports for Directory Services	DSDIAG | Generate Report
Diagnose DHCP Server issues	DHCPSRVR -D*x*
	-D*x* turns on debug option level; possible values: 1,2,3 or none

For Using Common Command Utilities from the Server Console

To Do This	Enter This Command at the Server
Set parameters, view communication statistics, and identify performance issues with servers	MONITOR
Configure a protocol for the server	INETCFG | Protocols
Bring down a server and restart it	RESTART SERVER [-*parameter*]

Parameter	Description
-ns	Restart the server without executing the startup.ncf file
-na	Restart the server without executing the autoexec.ncf file

To Do This	Enter This Command at the Server
View all settings on your server	DISPLAY ENVIRONMENT
Run ConsoleOne on the server	STARTX | Novell | ConsoleOne
Send a message to all users connected to the server	BROADCAST {*message*}

For Server Hardware and Software Configuration Display Commands

To Do This	Enter This Command at the Server
Display a summary of the server's settings	CONFIG
Display processor information, including processor number, processor clock speed (in MHz), processor ID, etc.	CPUCHECK [*processor_number*]
Display processor speed only	SPEED
Display NLMs that are loaded	MODULES [*string*]

string displays a list of all NLMs with names identical to the string; wildcards (*) can be included

To Do This	Enter This Command at the Server
Display total amount of memory loaded on the server	MEMORY
Display amount of memory allocated to DOS and to the server	MEMORY MAP
Display volume information	VOLUME [*volume_name*]
Display and scan storage devices on the server and register new devices	LIST DEVICES
Display a list of registered storage adapters and the devices they drive	LIST STORAGE ADAPTERS
Show currently assigned hardware interrupts, interrupt handlers, and interrupt statistics	DISPLAY INTERRUPTS [*option*]

Option	Description
(no option)	Display all interrupts currently in use
n . . .	Display one or more interrupts by number
ALL	Display all interrupts
PROC	Display processor interrupt information
ALLOC	Display allocated interrupts
REAL	Display interrupts that occurred while the operating system was in real mode

Osborne's NetWare 5 Administration

Answers!
Tech Support

ABOUT THE AUTHORS

Billie Pierce

Billie is a senior trainer at RGI Education, based in Atlanta, Georgia, specializing in the Novell NetWare operating system. She is also a Certified NetWare Instructor (CNI), CNE, and MCNE. She was the founding president of the Network Professional Association (NPA) for the Provo, Utah, chapter and was formerly the managing editor of the Network News, a technical journal for network professionals. She has been in the networking industry since 1987.

Mark Pierce

Mark Pierce is a senior consultant at Whittman-Hart consulting in Atlanta, Georgia. He obtained his initial CNE in 1991 and his MCSE in 1996. His accomplishments include serving on the board of directors for the Network Professional Association (NPA) from 1991 to 1996 and founding the NPA Atlanta chapter. Mark recently has been involved in NetWare and Windows NT integration, in addition to enterprise resource planning (ERP) projects. He has been in the networking industry since 1984.

CONTRIBUTING AUTHORS

Jeff Dill

Jeff is a CNE-4, having received his original certification in July of 1991. He has over ten years experience in networking, working the past five years as a consultant. He has been a Senior Consultant with Whittman-Hart, Inc., for the past two and a half years, and is the lead Novell Engineer in the Dallas Branch.

Courtney Garrard

Courtney is a CNE and MCSE who has worked in the networking field for five years as a consultant. He is currently a Senior Consultant at Whittman-Hart, Inc., and has worked for the past year as a network design engineer in the Atlanta branch.

Osborne's NetWare 5 Administration

Answers!
Tech Support

Billie Pierce and Mark Pierce

Osborne/**McGraw-Hill**

Berkeley • New York • St. Louis • San Francisco
Auckland • Bogotá • Hamburg • London
Madrid • Mexico City • Milan • Montreal
New Delhi • Panama City • Paris • São Paulo
Singapore • Sydney • Tokyo • Toronto

Osborne/**McGraw-Hill**
2600 Tenth Street
Berkeley, California 94710
U.S.A.

For information on translations or book distributors outside the U.S.A., or to
arrange bulk purchase discounts for sales promotions, premiums, or fund-raisers,
please contact Osborne/**McGraw-Hill** at the above address.

Osborne's NetWare 5 Administration Answers! Tech Support

1234567890 DOC DOC 90198765432109

ISBN 0-07-211885-7

Publisher Brandon A. Nordin	**Technical Editor** Linda Yunashko
Associate Publisher and Editor-in-Chief Scott Rogers	**Proofreaders** Paul Medoff Linda Medoff
Acquisitions Editor Gareth Hancock	**Indexer** Valerie Robbins
Project Editor Emily Rader	**Computer Designers** Jani Beckwith Roberta Steele
Editorial Assistant Stephane Thomas	**Illustrators** Brian Wells Beth Young
Copy Editors Margaret Berson Paul Medoff Judy Ziajka Claire Splan	**Series Design** Michelle Galicia

To our son Christopher Allan Pierce, who was born on July 28, 1998. He has been a part of this book while in the womb and in the crib.

Contents @ a Glance

1   Top 10 Frequently Asked Questions   xx
2   What's New in NetWare 5   14
3   Server Installation   30
4   Managing the Server Environment   82
5   Managing Z.E.N.works and the Novell Client . 148
6   Managing Files and Directories 180
7   Managing Applications 228
8   Managing Network Printing 254
9   Managing the User Environment 298
10 Managing FastTrack Web Server 344
11 Managing DHCP and DNS Services 360
12 NDS and Tree Design 392
A   Web Resources 458

    Index 465

Contents

Acknowledgments   xiii
Introduction   xv

1 **Top 10 Frequently Asked Questions** . . . .   **xx**

   1. What is the difference between Microsoft Active
      Directory Services (ADS) and Novell Directory
      Services (NDS)?   1
   2. What is the difference between NetWare/IP
      and Pure IP?   6
   3. How do I migrate my Windows NT 4 server to
      NetWare 5?   6
   4. Is the Novell Client ready for the Year 2000? . . .   7
   5. Do my workstations need to have the latest
      Novell Client installed to access my
      NetWare 5 servers?   7
   6. What should I do before I upgrade a server to
      NetWare 5?   7
   7. I will be installing NetWare 5 into my NetWare
      4.x tree. What must be done prior to installing a
      NetWare 5 server into my NetWare 4.x tree? . . .   9
   8. What is the difference between Z.E.N.works and
      Z.E.N.works Starter Pack?   10
   9. I accidentally deleted my Admin user and have lost
      supervisor control of the tree. What can I do to get
      Supervisor rights back?   12
   10. What is Compatibility Mode?   12

2 **What's New in NetWare 5** **14**

   ? Hardware and Installation Enhancements   16
   ? Console Enhancements   17
   ? NDS and Licensing Changes   19
   ? Java Support   21

? Protocol Enhancements, Encryption, Internet,
and Web Services   21
? Printing and File System Support Enhancements . .   23
? Client and Application Support Enhancements   . . .   24
? Other Enhancements   27

3 **Server Installation** **30**
? Pre-Installation Issues   32
? Installation Basics   50
? PostInstallation Issues   73
? License Installation Issues   78

4 **Managing the Server Environment** **82**
? Server Maintenance   87
? Remote Server Management   88
? Novell License Service (NLS)   92
? ConsoleOne and GUI Server Management   93
? Protocol Management   96
? Virtual Memory   100
? Server Processors   102
? Troubleshooting the Server   104
? Optimizing the Server Environment   113
? Server Shortcuts   125
? Screen Savers   127
? Garbage Collection   128
? Storage Management and Backup   129
? Novell Encryption and Public Key Security   131
? Lightweight Directory Access Protocol (LDAP)
for NDS Services   134
? Service Location Protocol (SLP)   140
? Novell Internet Access Server (NIAS)   144

5 **Managing Z.E.N.works and the Novell Client** **148**
? Z.E.N.works Starter Pack   150
? Novell Client Installation and Upgrades   169
? Novell Client Functions   174
? Troubleshooting the Novell Client   176
? Communication Protocol Support   178

6 **Managing Files and Directories** **180**

? Novell Storage Services (NSS) 183
? Differences Between NWFS Volumes
and NSS Volumes 185
? Current Limitations of NSS 189
? NWFS Features 192
? NSS Components and Architecture 201
? Installing and Upgrading to NSS 207
? NSS Administration Utilities 212
? File System Security 220
? Maintenance 222

7 **Managing Applications** **228**

? Novell Application Launcher (NAL) Installation
and Tips 230
? Novell Application Launcher and
Application Objects 234
? Securing Novell Application Launcher 246
? Novell Licensing Service (NLS) 249
? Java Applications 251

8 **Managing Network Printing** **254**

? Queue-Based Printing 256
? NDPS Definition and Purpose 267
? Managing NDPS 269
? Migrating to NDPS 286
? Troubleshooting Network Printing 291

9 **Managing the User Environment** **298**

? User Administration 300
? Login Security 311
? Managing Groups of Users 317
? Login Scripts 319

10 **Managing FastTrack Web Server** **344**

? Overview 346
? Installation 349

? Administration 352
? Troubleshooting 356

11 Managing DHCP and DNS Services **360**

? DHCP Server Overview 362
? DHCP Installation 364
? Troubleshooting a DHCP Server 370
? DHCP Administration 372
? DNS Server Overview 377
? DNS Installation 382
? DNS Administration 388

12 NDS and Tree Design **392**

? NDS Basics 394
? Troubleshooting NDS 406
? Catalog Services 415
? WAN Traffic Manager 422
? Partition/Replica Management 427
? Schema Manager 432
? NDS Design 435
? Time Synchronization 445
? NDS Security 447

Appendix A Web Resources **458**

? Novell Sites 459
? NetWare-Related Magazines and Journals 460
? NetWare-Oriented Forum Resources 461
? Network Professional Associations 461
? Third-Party Backup Products for NetWare 461
? Other Third-Party NetWare Sites 462
? Operating System Service Pack and Patch Sites . . 463
? Useful Novell Shareware Program Sites 463

Index **465**

Acknowledgments

Words cannot express our deepest appreciation and respect for all the people at Novell who have assisted us in writing this book. Their inside knowledge and endless patience with our questions before and after the release of NetWare 5 has made this a great book. In particular, we wish to thank Novell's Eric Schmidt, Kim Eaves, Duane Bourgeious, Gary Hein, Steven Jones, Brad Dew, Todd Seager, and Marcie Shanty. These Novell representatives have gone beyond the call of duty with their normal day-to-day jobs to assist in producing this book for the typical network administrator.

We also would like to thank all of the people at Osborne/McGraw-Hill who kept us honest and articulate throughout the writing of the book. Gareth Hancock helped guide us through the triage of submissions, technical edits, and deadlines to get this book out and on the shelves. Stephane Thomas, who has received hundreds of e-mails from us regarding chapter revisions and additions, took the leadership in delivering the manuscript to the project editor. Emily Rader, who seemed to enjoy sending chapter copy edits to us in the wee hours of the morning, worked hard with holidays approaching to get this book into production. Thanks also to Jennifer Wenzel, who took over for Emily during her vacation and also helped during the final crunch; to Brian Wells and Beth Young, who assisted us in making sure our graphics were just right; and to Jean Butterfield in Production, who, along with Emily, worked a great deal of overtime during the holidays to get this book finished.

Linda Yunashko did an excellent job as technical editor. She caught our mistakes and turned them around quickly to meet our deadlines. William Payne, author of *The Complete Reference NetWare 5*, was helpful in sharing some of his technical resources with us.

Finally, we want to thank the network administrators that post issues to the Novell newsgroups. We have collected some of the issues in these groups and placed them in this book (along with the answers!).

Introduction

NetWare 5 is a major accomplishment for Novell. Extensive changes have been made to the product, from the redesign of the server kernel to expansion of functionality through server add-on products. It is no secret that Novell's biggest rival in the networking industry today is Microsoft. Therefore, Novell has stepped up to the plate in an attempt to beat Microsoft to the punch by bringing a state-of-the-art operating system to the market and keeping up with cutting edge technology. The key to Novell's success is to provide as much coexistence with Windows NT as possible. NetWare 5 provides a strong indication that this is the direction in which Novell is going.

As you read this book, you will discover that NetWare 5 is the most feature-rich operating system yet. Unfortunately, Novell's documentation does not give the product the justice it deserves. We feel confident that virtually any questions you have relating to NetWare 5 are answered in this book. Our objective is to answer questions about NetWare 5 that can arise both in a simple office environment and in the most complex corporate environment. You will notice that this book is not your typical question-and-answer book on a vendor product, but rather an extensive tool to help you integrate NetWare 5 with existing products in your environment. For example, we discuss topics that focus on Lightweight Directory Access Protocol (LDAP) configuration on a NetWare 5 server and then discuss how to configure a Microsoft Outlook Express client to access these services.

There are over 500 questions and answers in this book, and we have carefully considered each and every one for usefulness and accuracy in different network environments. We have a unique combination of network consulting and training experience that brings a special blend of knowledge to the book. The research for this book has also been extensive. We have interviewed several administrators and literally hundreds of consultants at Whittman-Hart about what they would like to see in a book of this format.

You will notice that we do not cover the DOS and Windows 3.1 environments as much as we do the Windows 95/98 and Windows NT environments, and that's not an accident. The obvious trend in the desktop arena is toward the 32-bit operating systems. Novell has intentionally slowed development on the older platforms because of lack of support and customer demand. However, as we focus on the 32-bit operating systems, you will quickly find out that they are more robust and have several nice features that the older operating systems cannot handle.

We also provide extensive coverage of Z.E.N.works, Novell Storage Services (NSS), Novell Distributed Print Services (NDPS), and much more. The new features of the operating system are numerous, and we attempted to concentrate on them while still giving attention to some of the tried-and-true features NetWare has had for years.

This book is not intended to give you "Novell" answers but rather answers that will work for you in your environment. We discuss third-party utilities that take some of the complexity out of NetWare 5, and we provide tips and tricks that are not mentioned anywhere in Novell's documentation or Web site.

We also provide troubleshooting and optimization techniques throughout the book, not only for NetWare but for Z.E.N.works, FastTrack, Public Key Infrastructure Services (PKIS), and several other add-on services as well. We want this book to be a lifesaver for you in time of need.

HOW THIS BOOK IS ORGANIZED

Osborne's NetWare 5 Administration Answers! Tech Support is divided into 12 chapters, each focusing on a major subject. Within each chapter, the questions and answers are further divided into subtopics. This structure, in addition to the table of contents and index, will assist you in finding your question quickly and easily. We also include an "@ a Glance" section at the beginning of each chapter, which summarizes what is covered in the main sections of the chapter.

Also included at the end of this book is an appendix that provides you with several excellent Web sites where you can find NetWare 5 patches, magazines, journals, and much more.

Command Card

At the front of this book, you will find an "Instant Answers!" reference card. This card contains useful information about the day-to-day administration of a NetWare 5 environment. We encourage you to tear out this card out and post it near your desk or in your cubical.

CONVENTIONS USED IN THIS BOOK

Osborne's NetWare 5 Administration Answers! Tech Support uses several conventions designed to make the book easier for you to follow:

- **Bold type** is used to indicate text you need to enter using the keyboard.
- Small capitals (for example, ENTER and SHIFT) indicate specific keys on the keyboard.

When you are expected to enter a command, you will be told to *press* the key(s). If you are told to enter text or numbers, you are told to *type* or *enter* them.

In addition to these conventions, we have also included symbols to draw your attention to important information. Here are the symbols and what they stand for:

 Note: *Notes are interesting tidbits or facts that help to further clarify the answers.*

 Tip: *Tips inform you of special conventions, shortcuts, and neat ways of configuring, administering, or troubleshooting NetWare 5.*

 Caution: *We use Cautions sparingly in the book, but when you encounter them, read them. They will help you to prevent possible data loss or misconfiguration.*

ONE WORD OF ADVICE

At the time of this writing, Novell has released Support Pack 1 for NetWare 5, which fixes several issues in virtually all areas of the operating system, including the server kernel. Therefore, we highly recommend that you install it as soon as possible. The Support Pack can be obtained on the Web at support.novell.com or ordered directly from Novell.

ARE YOU READY?

By now you are probably ready to dig into this book and have your questions answered. If you have a problem that you cannot solve with this book or something just does not seem clear, please drop us an e-mail at

Answers!@mindspring.com.

Be sure to include a detailed question, and include as much information as possible about your system.

Finally, we hope you enjoy reading this book as much as we enjoyed writing it. NetWare 5 is a proven product in the industry, and after reading this book you will better understand the benefits it has to offer and be able to use it to its fullest potential. Good luck, and enjoy the questions and answers.

Chapter 1

Top 10 Frequently Asked Questions

Answer Topics!

- Understanding the differences between Microsoft Active Directory Services (ADS) and Novell Directory Services (NDS)   1

- Understanding the differences between NetWare/IP and Pure IP?   6

- Migrating from Windows NT 4 to NetWare 5   6

- Understanding Year 2000 issues   7

- Working with older NetWare Clients running NetWare 5   7

- Preparing for your upgrade to NetWare 5   7

- Installing NetWare 5 in a 4.x tree   9

- Understanding the differences between Z.E.N.works Starter Pack and Z.E.N.works   10

- Recovering Admin rights   12

- Understanding Compatibility Mode   12

Top Ten FAQs @ a Glance

This chapter covers the most commonly asked questions about NetWare 5. Even if you have not raised these questions yet, the answers will provide you with the background information you'll need at some time in the not-too-distant future.

1. What is the difference between Microsoft Active Directory Services (ADS) and Novell Directory Services (NDS)?

The competition between Microsoft Active Directory Services (ADS) and Novell Directory Services (NDS) is fierce. At the time of this writing, ADS has not yet been released and is currently in its public BETA 2 testing cycle. Novell NDS has been widely used for over four years now and is fully functional and available to the public. Before we begin to answer this question, let us preface that these differences may change with the final release of ADS. Therefore, we will compare ADS versus NDS as it stands at the time of this writing.

What is ADS?

ADS can be considered a directory view of Microsoft Windows NT 4's domain architecture. It is designed to work well in any size installation, from a single server with a few hundred objects to thousands of servers with millions of objects. Windows NT 2000 will contain the first release of ADS to the general public. It is very similar to NDS in that it addresses objects in a hierarchical manner with containers and trees. ADS is also secure, distributed, partitioned, and replicated.

What is NDS?

NDS is a true X.500 directory service that provides hierarchical naming within the directory. NDS also has two major functions. First, NDS is a database of all network resources such as users, groups, containers, printers, servers, volumes, organizational roles, and so on. Therefore, whenever administrators add a new user or printer to the network, they are adding the user and/or printer to the NDS database. NDS has always been secure, distributed, partitioned, replicated, and extensible.

As you can see, ADS seems to be similar to NDS. However, this is far from the case. There are actually several differences, which this chapter will discuss, dealing with directory object naming, security, inheritance, object administration, catalog services, backup and restoration of directory services, client support, and attribute replication.

Object Naming

Currently, note that ADS is still Windows NT domain-based. Therefore, ADS is pretty much a flat domain name space. With this in mind, creating users with the same name but different organizational units must be considered. Currently ADS cannot handle duplicate names within organizational units as long as the fully distinguished names are unique. For instance, if you attempt to create a user named MikeM in the sales container (MikeM.Sales.Answers!) and then attempt to create a MikeM in the support container (MikeM.Support.Answers!), you will receive an error because MikeM is not unique.

NDS does allow identical names in different containers because it is not limited to the domain structure of NT.

Security

Another difference between how ADS works and the way NDS works involves security. ADS relies on security identifiers called SIDs that determine a user's access to resources. When a user authenticates to a directory, the user's SID is collected along with the SIDs of any group that the user is a member of, and a security token is created for that user. This is identical with the way Windows NT 4 security works today. This token will allow the user to access other resources on the network. The drawback of this method is that the user's security token is generated during the login to ADS. This means that if a user's rights are granted or revoked at any given time, the user *must* log out and log back in before these changes take effect.

NDS security is much different than ADS in that NDS users and groups are security principals that can have access to other directory objects or NDS resources such as NetWare

or NT file servers. In addition, NDS dynamically calculates a user's access rights without requiring the need to log out and log back in to the system.

Inheritance

Inheritance is the ability of directory management and resource rights to flow down a tree. ADS uses static inheritance to manage its directory and resource rights. This means that a user's management rights statically flow down to all subordinate objects by updating every subordinate object the user encounters along the way. This method allows the Active Directory database, which is a Microsoft Jet database, to grow quickly since redundant rights information is added to several objects.

On the other hand, NDS uses dynamic inheritance, which is updated at higher container objects, allowing management and resource rights to flow down without needing to update all other subordinate objects below them. This in turn does not cause that NDS database to increase in size. While both methods accomplish the same end result, ADS assigns more rights to more objects, which can slow down performance in a large network and increase the size of your database.

Object Administration

Microsoft Management Console (MMC) is the latest Microsoft effort to be the all-in-one program for administering a network. Unfortunately, MMC is really a front-end program to open several application windows using snap-in technology. Therefore, there is no single utility for managing the Active Directory. Novell uses NetWare Administration for all of its administration. Here's an example of how MMC is different from NetWare Administration: With ADS you must open different applications to view a file server log, create a user, manage directory replication, manage workstation policies, grant file system rights, and view directory trees. NetWare Administration allows you to do all of the previous functions with a single application.

Catalogs

A catalog is an index of select directory information to provide quick lookups for information such as phone

numbers, e-mail addresses, employee names, and other attributes. Catalogs can be used in various services such as Lightweight Directory Access Protocol (LDAP) and login services. For more information about catalogs, refer to "Catalog Services" in Chapter 12.

Although the feature is identical, catalogs in ADS are very different than in the NDS environment. Currently, ADS allows for only one catalog in a directory (domain), while with NDS there is no limitation. While both ADS and NDS do allow you to create a global catalog, ADS does not provide a scheduling activity to update its catalogs, nor does it give you the option to create custom catalogs for different departments. NDS does.

Backing Up and Restoring Directory Services

There is one major difference in how you can back up your Active Directory database versus an NDS database. Currently, the architecture of ADS with the JET database technology will not allow you to back up or restore portions of a tree such as a single user, group, or organization. Novell had this limitation in earlier versions of NDS but now supports the ability to back up and restore these individual objects.

Client Support

Currently, users who want to use ADS must depend primarily on Microsoft operating systems to access it. You should also note that Microsoft requires an Active Directory client software on every machine that logs into ADS. Unfortunately, Microsoft does not have any type of automatic upgrade for the client software, so administrators must allocate time to install the client on each PC or possibly use Storage Management Services (SMS) to upgrade the client. Novell has an automatic client upgrade utility, which is discussed in detail in Chapter 5. The following table lists the clients that are supported by ADS and NDS.

Operating System	ADS Access	NDS Access
DOS	No	Yes, but limited
Windows 3.1	No	Yes, but limited

Operating System	ADS Access	NDS Access
Windows for Workgroups	No	Yes, but limited
Windows 95/98	Yes, but limited	Yes
Windows NT 3.51	Not determined	Yes
Windows NT 4	Not determined	Yes
Windows NT 5	Yes	Yes
IBM OS/2	No	Yes
Apple Mac OS	No	Yes, Prosoft third-party support
Linux	No	Yes, Caldrea third-party support

Directory Attribute Replication

ADS and NDS replicate only the changed attributes of an object (for example, a user's phone number). However, ADS and NDS perform differently when the changes are actually applied.

In an ADS environment, attribute changes are performed on a timestamp basis. For instance, suppose that an administrator in ADS modifies a user's phone number, and five minutes later, another administrator modifies that same user's department location. When ADS synchronization occurs, ADS will discard the earlier change and implement the latest change. Therefore, the user's department location would be changed, but the phone number would not change.

In a NDS environment, attribute changes are performed at an attribute level. Therefore if different attributes are changed at different locations, the final object will include all attribute changes.

Conclusion

The major factor in regards to ADS and NDS is that NDS has gone through several generations of modifications and improvements over the years, and ADS has not. ADS will be a first-generation directory service when released. After reading this answer, you may think that we dislike ADS. This is not true: We believe ADS is a viable directory service and it is heading in the right direction. However, if the past could predict the future in regards to Microsoft's products, ADS will

have some growing to do just as NDS did when it was released. What's great about ADS is that when it is released, you should see a lot of sparks from Novell and Microsoft and some aggressive improvements and enhancement to directory services as a whole. As an administrator, you may be forced to make a decision on NDS or ADS in your network at some point. The best approach is to test ADS in a controlled environment and keep tabs on what Novell's and Microsoft's plans are about releasing a synchronization utility for NDS and ADS.

2. What is the difference between NetWare/IP and Pure IP?

NetWare/IP is IPX/SPX encapsulated with an IP wrapper around the protocol. Microsoft's TCP/IP environment within Windows NT 4 works similarly to NetWare/IP, with the exception that the NetBIOS protocol is encapsulated within IP.

Pure IP uses the TCP/IP suite for connectivity without any type of encapsulation. Pure IP supports the following standards:

- Dynamic Host Configuration Protocol (DHCP)
- Novell Directory Services (NDS)
- Domain Name Services (DNS)
- Service Location Protocol (SLP)
- WinSock2
- IP version 6
- Secure Sockets Layer (SSL)
- Network Time Protocol (NTP)

3. How do I migrate my Windows NT 4 server to NetWare 5?

Currently, Novell does not have an official way to migrate from NT 4 to NetWare 5. However, there is a way to do this by using Novell's NDS for NT 2. This product will allow you to import the NT database into an NDS tree. Its original purpose is to provide coexistence between NetWare and NT,

but it can be used as a migration utility as well. Using this program will migrate only users and groups from the NT database, but not file rights. For more information on this product, go to www.novell.com/products/nds/nds4nt/.

4. Is the Novell Client ready for the Year 2000?

Yes. The NetWare 5 Client has been fully tested and approved as Year 2000 (Y2K)–compliant. However, some operating systems that may be used within your NetWare environment may not be Y2K-compliant—such as Microsoft Windows NT 4, which requires NT Service Pack 4 for Y2K fixes.

5. Do my workstations need to have the latest Novell Client installed to access my NetWare 5 servers?

It really depends on how you configure NetWare 5. If your environment still runs IPX and you're not planning to move to IP any time soon, you should have no problem with running an earlier version of the Novell Client. However, if you decide to go to IP without Compatibility Mode, you must upgrade your client.

Note: *If you plan on using Z.E.N.works, you must upgrade to the NetWare 5 Client to take advantage of Workstation Manager, which allows you to kick off programs and set policies for the workstation.*

6. What should I do before I upgrade a server to NetWare 5?

The following is a list of pre-upgrade procedures:

❑ Back up and verify the NetWare 3.1*x*/4.*x* server (two backups are recommended); for NetWare 4.*x*, be sure to back up both the file system and the NDS.

Tip: *You should also back up the DOS directory containing the server startup files (C:\NWSERVER, C:\SERVER.312, and so on). You may need to restore this directory if the upgrade fails*

❑ Gather all pre-installation information. (For a pre-installation checklist, see the question "What items of information do I need before I begin the NetWare 5 installation or upgrade?" in Chapter 3.)

❑ Be sure to have sufficient NDS and file system rights.

❑ Clean up the file system (that is, delete unnecessary files).

❑ If you are upgrading from NetWare 4.*x*:

    ❑ Run an unattended full repair in DSREPAIR.NLM.

    ❑ Eliminate any NDS synchronization errors

    ❑ Eliminate time synchronization errors.

    ❑ Apply latest patches (go to support.novell.com).

❑ If you are upgrading to NetWare 3.1*x*:

    ❑ Delete unnecessary users, print queues, printers, and so on.

    ❑ Run BINDFIX.

    ❑ Eliminate duplicate names if migrating multiple NetWare 3.1*x* servers.

    ❑ Apply latest patches (go to support.novell.com).

❑ Upgrade the workstation client if necessary. The workstation must be running the NetWare 5 Client version 2.2 or higher for Windows 95/98 or 4.11 or higher for Windows NT 3.51 or higher.

✳ ***Note:*** *If the NetWare 5 Client is not installed, the Client will only be able to communicate with a NetWare 5 server running IPX.*

❑ Find out compatibility information if you are using third-party NLMs, LAN, or disk drivers. (Ask your Novell Authorized Reseller about compatibility issues.)

❑ Clear all connections prior to the upgrade.

❑ If necessary, add name space to the destination server.

❑ If the server being upgraded is running BorderManager 2.1, upgrade to BorderManager 3.

❑ If you're running ManageWise, comment out ManageWise lines from the server's AUTOEXEC.NCF file.

❑ Comment out all third-party NLMs from the STARTUP.NCF and/or AUTOEXEC.NCF files.

✚ ***Tip:*** *If you are installing LDAP Services for NDS, determine whether an LDAP catalog is available locally. If an LDAP catalog is available and you decide to keep it, do not install a new catalog during the installation/upgrade. Delete the LDAP catalog if you do not want to keep it.*

❓ 7. I will be installing NetWare 5 into my NetWare 4.*x* tree. What must be done prior to installing a NetWare 5 server into my NetWare 4.*x* tree?

● Install version 6 or above of NDS on all 4.11 servers in the tree prior to installing NetWare 5. The following three files must be copied to achieve the NDS upgrade: DS.NLM, ROLLCALL.NLM (version 4.10 or above), and DSREPAIR.NLM (version 4.59 or above). NetWare 4.10 requires DS.NLM 5.15 or above and DSREPAIR.NLM 4.59 or above. These files can be downloaded from support.novell.com.

● Correct any replica or NDS synchronization errors prior to installing NetWare 5.

✚ ***Tip:*** *You can use the DSDIAG.NLM utility that ships with NetWare 5 to get information about the state of NDS in a tree and NDS version information.*

✳ ***Note:*** *If you're using NDS Manager to update NDS, use NDSMGR.EXE version 1.25 or later. INSTALL.NLM can also be used.*

❗ ***Caution:*** *All servers not upgraded to NetWare 5 or NDS 6 and above will receive schema errors when the NetWare 5 server upgrade is complete.*

● Always make two backups if upgrading a server to NetWare 5.

● Time synchronization should be configured correctly.

 Note: *If you're upgrading from NetWare 4.1x to NetWare 5, always upgrade the server holding the Master replica of the [Root] partition first. This helps avoid schema conflicts in NDS.*

● If you plan to make the NetWare 5 server protocol IP only, the migration gateway (SCMD /G) must be loaded on the server with the Master replica. This allows NDS to communicate properly in a mixed protocol environment. Otherwise, an IPX server will not be able to connect. The Migration Agent can be set up at the Summary screen during the installation of NetWare 5.

● Install NetWare License Service (NLS) on one NetWare 4.*x* server in each partition of the NDS tree.

 Note: *Select a NetWare 4.11 server that has a Master or read/write replica of the partition. If you have old or existing licenses in the NDS tree, run SETUPNLS.NLM after upgrading the NetWare 4.11 server.*

● Install a NetWare 5 server directly into the 4.11 tree if the NetWare 5 server will have a read/write replica and the replica is in the NDS partition where the read/write activity will take place.

● If all servers in the tree will eventually be upgraded to NetWare 5, first upgrade servers in the lower portions of the tree. This allows NDS to cope with the NetWare 5 changes more easily than migrating from the [Root] directory and moving out.

 ### 8. What is the difference between Z.E.N.works and Z.E.N.works Starter Pack?

Z.E.N stands for Zero Effort Networks for users. The main difference between the two versions of Z.E.N.works is that

the Starter Pack, which is included in NetWare 5, gives the user a taste of what Z.E.N.works can do for your environment. With the Z.E.N.works Starter Pack, you can do the following:

- Update software seamlessly from your home or office.
- Distribute and update printer drivers on the fly.
- Schedule actions to occur on one or several workstations at specified times or intervals.
- Import workstation information in the NDS tree.
- Retrieve applications automatically on a workstation.
- Set workstation policies (perform desktop management), which enables administrators to enforce policies such as denying access to certain objects on the desktop as well as customize the standard look and feel of one machine or the entire corporate environment with wallpaper, sound, and other features of the Windows 95/98 and Windows NT operating systems.
- Customize the Novell Client configuration and registry on multiple workstations.

The full version of Z.E.N.works includes the preceding features, plus it also enables you to do the following:

- Create a hardware inventory, which stores information in NDS concerning the CPU, RAM, bus type, system BIOS, and other machine-specific items.
- Remotely control a workstation using IPX or IP.
- Use a help system with quick answers to questions by providing information about the user's specific setup.
- Scan workstation hardware, software, and data for Year 2000 bugs using a five-user version of the NDS-aware diagnostic tool called Check 2000.
- Experience improved integration with Novell's ManageWise 2.6.
- Track the number of software licenses distributed through Z.E.N.works and record the number of

individuals using a specific application at any time on the
network using Software Metering.

● Benefit from full support for Windows 98 (including the
option to control remotely).

9. I accidentally deleted my Admin user and have lost supervisor control of the tree. What can I do to get Supervisor rights back?

Several options are available to get your Admin rights back to
the root of the tree. The first option is to call Novell Technical
Services at (800) 858-4000. For security reasons, you will need
to supply proof that you are the administrator of your network.
The cost of this service is $200 at the time of this writing.

The second option is to obtain an NLM that is called
MAKESU.NLM, which will create a user in your tree with
Supervisory access to the [Root]. This program can be
purchased for $99 and can be downloaded from the Web at
www.dreamlan.com. If this utility creates a concern about
security in NetWare 5, you can always use the SECURE
CONSOLE command to prevent it from being loaded on the
servers. For more information about SECURE CONSOLE,
please refer to the question "How can I protect my NetWare
server from malicious tampering?" in Chapter 4.

! *Caution:* *This program is a third-party product and
inserts an object into your tree. Therefore, you should use it
with care.*

10. What is Compatibility Mode?

The Compatibility Mode driver (CMD) has two parts, one for
the server and one for the client. At the server, the CMD is
viewed as a network adapter. You can bind both IP and IPX
protocols to the CMD, and it acts like a router when IPX
packets need to be sent within the server. Otherwise, the
CMD patiently waits in the background, doing nothing and
using no resources.

At the workstation, the CMD is invisible because it
is an integral part of the new client. It provides the IP

communications link required by an IP client. If NetWare 5 is set up as pure IP, there is no need for IPX at the client.

The IPX Compatibility driver's task is to provide IPX connectivity over the IP network, allowing applications using the IPX stack for communications to function in an IP network. The IPX Compatibility driver also allows IP systems to communicate with IPX systems by using the services of Migration Agents. The IPX Compatibility driver treats the IP network as a virtual IPX network segment (CMD network segment), by encapsulating IPX datagrams inside UDP datagrams, and by resolving RIP and SAP requests through the use of the Service Location Protocol (SLP).

Chapter 2

What's New in NetWare 5

Answer Topics!

HARDWARE AND INSTALLATION ENHANCEMENTS 16

? Booting from a NetWare 5 CD

? Learning about PCI Hot Plug support

? Learning about I_2O support

? Learning about new disk driver support

? Counting the number of processors supported in NetWare 5

? Tracking kernel design changes in NetWare 5

CONSOLE ENHANCEMENTS   17

? Learning Netware 5's new console commands

? Learning Netware 5's additional SET commands

? Understanding changes in CDROM.NLM

? Learning what happened to SERVMAN.NLM

? Warm booting a NetWare 5 Server

? Learning about other server console changes

? Finding the screen saver

NDS AND LICENSING CHANGES   19

? Managing NDS traffic on a WAN

? Tracking NDS performance enhancements

? Managing TimeSync in an IP environment

? Finding NETADMIN and NWADMIN95

? Understanding Novell licensing changes

JAVA SUPPORT   21

? Learning about Java features in NetWare 5

PROTOCOL ENHANCEMENTS, ENCRYPTION, INTERNET, AND WEB SERVICES   21

? Supporting IP-only communications

? Migrating from IPX to IP

? Advertising services and SLP and SAP changes

? Finding Novell's Web Server

? Tracking DHCP and DNS changes

? Understanding encryption features

PRINTING AND FILE SYSTEM SUPPORT ENHANCEMENTS   23

? Learning about new printing features

? Tracking NetWare file system additions and enhancements

CLIENT AND APPLICATION SUPPORT ENHANCEMENTS   24

? Enhancing Client management

? Understanding new features in Novell Application Launcher (NAL)

? Learning about new features for the Novell Client

OTHER ENHANCEMENTS   27

? Adding Oracle 8 to Netware 5

? Saving server configuration in NetWare 5

? Backing up files in NetWare 5

What's New in NetWare 5 @ a Glance

Novell's NetWare 5 has undergone a very aggressive rewrite of its code bases. You will notice that this version of NetWare is very modular. This provides Novell an easy way to fix issues in different code bases as they are reported. This chapter will give a brief overview of several new features in NetWare 5. Once you digest all of these features, you can obtain greater knowledge in later chapters of this book. Here are the areas explored in this chapter:

Hardware and Installation Enhancements discusses enhancements to NetWare 5's hardware support and installation changes.

Console Enhancements covers new SET commands, console commands, and CD-ROM support enhancements.

NDS and Licensing Changes answers questions dealing with how Novell licenses NetWare and NDS enhancements made in NetWare 5.

Java Support discusses Novell's support of Java in NetWare 5.

Protocol Enhancements, Encryption, Internet, and Web Services answers questions dealing with NetWare's IP protocol support; new encryption capabilities; and enhancements with DHCP, DNS, and FastTrack server.

- **Printing and File System Support Enhancements** covers new printing functionality and additional file system support.
- **Client and Application Support Enhancements** focuses on Novell Application Launcher (NAL) changes, Z.E.N.works, and client support features.
- **Other Enhancements** answers questions about Oracle 8 and configuration-saving techniques.

HARDWARE AND INSTALLATION ENHANCEMENTS

Can I boot from the NetWare 5 CD to install the NetWare operating system?

Yes, the NetWare 5 CD will automatically boot from CD, create a DOS partition using DR-DOS, make it the active bootable partition, and format it with DR-DOS.

Does NetWare 5 provide PCI Hot Plug support?

Novell offers PCI Hot Plug support to allow administrators to replace a PCI network, storage, or other adapters without the need to take the system down.

Does NetWare 5 have I$_2$O *support?*

Novell has integrated I$_2$O support to allow the server's CPU to spend its time performing other functions and services that don't involve interrupt processing, increasing a server's I/O ability.

What new disk driver support does NetWare 5 provide?

Novell now supports .HAM and .CDM extensions and has eliminated support for .DSK drivers to provide more reliable driver support for third-party host adapters and storage devices.

 How many processors can NetWare 5 support?

The NetWare Kernel provides multiprocessor support for up to 32 processors— double the number that NetWare 4.11 could support—and can prioritize applications across multiple processors.

 What kernel design changes are included in NetWare 5?

Novell has made several changes in the design of the NetWare kernel:

● NetWare 5 now only uses one kernel instead of multiple kernels used in previous NetWare versions.

● NetWare 5 now uses memory protection for the NetWare kernel to run applications in protected mode.

● Applications running on the server can now swap to disk using virtual memory.

CONSOLE ENHANCEMENTS

 Are there any new console commands included with NetWare 5?

There are several new console commands to assist you in managing your servers. The following table describes the new commands:

Command	Description
ALERT	Allows you to manage NetWare alerts: enable or disable the logging and display of specifics, limit the amount of information displayed, and control other aspects of the alert messages
DISPLAY ENVIRONMENT	Displays the current search paths and values of the settable server parameters, along with their default values and range of valid values
DISPLAY INTERRUPTS	Allows you to display the assigned hardware interrupts, interrupt handlers, and interrupt statistics

Command	Description
DISPLAY MODIFIED ENVIRONMENT	Displays the set parameters that have been modified, showing the current values and default values
DISPLAY PROCESSORS	Displays the current number of processors in your server and the status of each processor
PROTECTION	Displays a list of protected address spaces and allows you to add or remove restart functionality to or from an existing address space
RESET ENVIRONMENT	Allows you to reset some or all of your settable variables to their default values
SWAP	Lets you move, increase, or decrease your swap file and displays its status
NCP ADDRESSES	Lists, in network protocol order, the protocols currently loaded on your server

What are the new SET commands in NetWare 5?

Novell has included several new SET command categories, including Multiprocessors, Service Location Protocol (SLP), and Licensing Service. For more information on these new SET commands, please refer to Chapter 4.

What changes have been made to NetWare's CD-ROM support?

NetWare 5's CDROM.NLM now automatically mounts your CD as an NSS volume.

What happened to SERVMAN.NLM?

SERVMAN.NLM is gone—it was merged into MONITOR.NLM, beginning with NetWare release 4.11.

How can I warm boot a NetWare 5 server?

Typing **RESET SERVER** at the server console will bring down the server, followed by a machine warm boot.

What other server console changes have been made to NetWare 5?

NetWare's LOAD command before loading an NLM is now optional. NetWare 5 also allows aliases for server console commands, giving administrators the ability to create shortcuts for commonly used console commands. An example of this is to assign MR to run MONITOR.NLM.

Is there a screen saver for NetWare 5?

Novell has included SCRSAVER.NLM, which replaced the screen saver functionality within MONITOR.NLM, to preserve the life of the monitor.

NDS AND LICENSING CHANGES

Does NetWare 5 include a method of managing NDS traffic over a Wide Area Network (WAN)?

There is a new feature called WAN Traffic Manager that allows administrators to manage traffic from NDS replication. For more information on WAN Traffic Manager, please refer to the question "What does WAN Traffic Manager do?" in Chapter 12.

What Novell Directory Services (NDS) performance enhancements have been added for NetWare 5?

The following table describes several NDS performance enhancements that have been made in NetWare 5:

Feature	Description
Transitive synchronization	This feature allows one replica to communicate with another replica without having to talk to all replicas, which helps reduce replication traffic on the network.
Randomized replica rings	NetWare 5 now randomizes the sequence in which replicas are processed. This reduces the chance of one server having to back off and attempt to resynchronize with a replica.
Caching of replica ring changes	Changes in objects are now cached, which increases the speed of searching and updating each replica and partition.

Feature	Description
Multiple objects per synchronization packet	You can now allow multiple changes to different objects in a single packet. Previous versions of NetWare only allowed changes for one object in a single communication packet.
Distributed reference links (DRL)	This is a new method, in conjunction with the backlink method in previous NetWare versions. DRLs store the partition name instead of the server name, which allows NetWare servers to resolve DRLs via NDS.
Restrict outbound synchronization from read-only replicas	NetWare 5 now does not assign a replica number to a Read Only partition. This does not allow Read Only partitions to replicate, making replication of the NDS tree more scalable.
No synchronization with subordinate reference replicas	The change in NetWare 5 with Transitive Synchronization means that the Subordinate References will not be a part of normal replica synchronization, greatly reducing traffic on a network.
Password Management Property	This will allow a user or group to manage user passwords without them having any other type of administrative rights to the network.
Inheritable ACL	Along with the Password Management Property, administrators now can assign users or groups to manage different parts of NDS, such as e-mail addresses, and phone numbers.

 ## How does NetWare 5 do time synchronization in an IP environment?

NetWare 5 now uses Network Time Protocol (NTP) RFC-1305 for IP time synchronization utility. Previous versions of NetWare used proprietary time synchronization through IPX. For more information on time synchronization, please refer to the following question in Chapter 12: "I set up a customized time synchronization strategy in my NetWare 4.11 environment. I am now migrating to a Pure IP environment with NetWare 5. How is time synchronization accomplished in a Pure IP or mixed IPX/IP environment?"

 ### What happened to **NETADMIN** and **NWADMN95?**

NETADMIN and NWADMN95 are no longer available in NetWare 5 and have been replaced by NWADMN32 located in the SYS:PUBLIC\WIN32 directory.

 ### How does Novell do its licensing in NetWare 5?

Novell uses Novell Licensing Services, which allows you to manage and monitor licenses on your network.

JAVA SUPPORT

 ### What Java features are included in NetWare 5?

NetWare 5 has an optional Java GUI Server console provided on the server that will allow administrators to run Java applications directly from the server. In addition, ConsoleOne—a Java application that can run on your NetWare 5 server or workstation—will allow you to execute file system functions. For more information on ConsoleOne with NetWare 5, refer to the section "ConsoleOne and GUI Server Management" in Chapter 4.

PROTOCOL ENHANCEMENTS, ENCRYPTION, INTERNET, AND WEB SERVICES

 ### Can NetWare 5 support IP-only communications?

NetWare 5 has the ability to have IP-only communications in NetWare without the need for any type of encapsulation of other protocols.

 ### Is there a way to migrate from IPX to IP?

Yes, Novell has included a Compatibility Mode gateway, which allows the transition from IPX to IP. For more information on Compatibility Mode please refer to the section "Protocol Management" in Chapter 4.

How does NetWare 5 advertise its services in the new IP environment?

NetWare 5 uses Service Location Protocol (SLP) in IP, which replaces the Service Advertising Protocol (SAP) used in an IPX environment. The IP environment also reduces broadcasting across a network by using Directory Agents. For more information on SLP, please refer to the section "Service Location Protocol (SLP)" in Chapter 4.

Where is Novell's Web server?

Novell's Web server has now been replaced by Netscape FastTrack server, which includes NDS, CGI, PERL, NETBasic, and ODBC support. For more information on Netscape FastTrack server, please refer to in Chapter 10.

What's new for Dynamic Host Configuration Protocol (DHCP) and Domain Name Server (DNS) NetWare 5?

NetWare 5 provides several new enhancements to DHCP and DNS, some of which are described here:

- Dynamic Domain Name Services (DDNS) allows for dynamic updates of host names based on changes in IP addresses.

- Dynamic Host Configuration Protocol (DHCP) is now included as part of NetWare with several new attributes to assign to a leased IP address.

- DHCP and DNS are now managed through NDS and the DNS/DHCP Management Console utility. For more information about the this utility, please refer to the question "How do I install the DNS/DHCP Management Console utility on my workstation?" in Chapter 11.

What type of encryption features are included in NetWare 5?

> Public Key Infrastructure Services (PKIS) is included in NetWare 5 and allows administrators to provide additional security to their networks using public key, private key, certificate authorities, and other security modules for LDAP and other authentication services.
>
> Secure Authentication Services (SAS) is also included in NetWare 5 and designed to provide support for new and evolving industry authentication mechanisms. The SAS design also includes a framework for distinguishing between authentication mechanisms of various qualities, as well as support for the introduction of third-party authentication services and includes LDAP support.
>
> For more information about NetWare's encryption, please refer to the section "Novell Encryption and Public Key Security" in Chapter 4.

PRINTING AND FILE SYSTEM SUPPORT ENHANCEMENTS

What are the new printing features in NetWare 5?

> Novell has redesigned it network printing strategy by using their existing queue-based printing and introducing NetWare Distributed Print Service (NDPS), which provides a new method of managing printers without the need for print servers, print queues, and print objects.
>
> In addition, printers can be configured as Public Access (no NetWare login required to use) or Controlled Access. For more information on NDPS, please refer to the question "What is NDPS?" in Chapter 8.

 Are there any changes in the NetWare file system?

Yes, Novell continues to use its traditional NetWare file system and has introduced Novell Storage Services. Novell Storage Services (NSS) gives administrators the ability to provide faster mount times, lower memory requirements, easy repair times, and support for the next generation of file storage services. You can now even load your DOS FAT partition as an NSS volume. In addition, when NetWare traditional volumes are created they are automatically set up with DOS and long filename support. For more information on NSS and its features, please refer to "Novell Storage Services" section in Chapter 6.

CLIENT AND APPLICATION SUPPORT ENHANCEMENTS

 What type of Client management does NetWare 5 provide?

Novell provides Z.E.N.works Starter Pack with NetWare 5. This new feature enables the administrator to control Windows profile deployment and application management. For more information on Z.E.N.works, please refer to the section "Z.E.N.works Starter Pack" in Chapter 5.

 What are the new features included with Novell Application Launcher (NAL)?

Novell Application Launcher (NAL) has been totally revamped to take advantage of the power of Z.E.N.works. Following is a table of new features included in NAL:

Feature	Description
Additional NAL startup options	NAL now includes additional parameters on startup for custom titles, behaves as a shell, hides application launcher, minimizes and maximizes NAL, and more.
Use of server time for schedule time	Scheduling for applications to be presented in NAL now locks the server time on the workstation where the user cannot change it.

Feature	Description
Nested macros	Macros now can contain other macros.
NAL copies files to local drive	NAL can copy necessary files on the local drive automatically.
Append INI values	You can modify .INI values.
No need to reboot for text files	You can now flag a text file so that a prompt to reboot does not show up.
Import and export of .AOT and .AXT files	You can now import .AOT and .AXT files. These are files that the snAppshot application uses to install and uninstall applications.
Synchronize and unsynchronize GUIs	This new feature is used for deployment of applications to verify that the proper applications are installed on a workstation.
Support for additional registry types	NAL now supports the following registry types: Expand String and Multi-Value String.
Wildcards for Copying and Deleting	Wildcards are now supported in the Application File property page.
Order configuration changes	You can now delete and create files automatically in the following order: Delete files Delete directories Create directories Create files You can also do this with .INI files.
Copy an application object	You can now create an application object based on an existing Application object.
Search for and replace an application object	You can now search and replace text fields within an Application object.
Import and export .INI and .REG files	You can import and export .INI and .REG files from the .INI files and registry setting property pages.
Launch closest application	You can launch an application based on the geographical location of a user, a nice feature for users who travel.

Feature	Description
Multi-Level Folders	You can specify and name a folder in which to display an application in NAL.
Terminate Application	Typically used in conjunction with a scheduled application, this feature allows NAL to terminate an application automatically after time has expired.
Update NT secure portion of registry	NAL includes a service module for Windows NT that can update the NT registry when a particular user logged into the station does not have rights to modify the registry.
Autogranting of file system rights	NAL automatically grants file system rights when an application object is associated with an Organization, Organizational Unit, User, or Group object.
Application launch/display priority	This feature allows you to sort applications in NAL by a priority number and force the installation of an application to a workstation.
Autoverify	If part of an application on a workstation is deleted, NAL presents a verification option to check to see whether files are missing and automatically send the missing file to the workstation.
Version checking	NAL can check the internal version number of .DLLs, executables, and other system files to make sure the workstation is up-to-date.
Prompt for distribution	You can prompt a user to install an application before the installation begins. This option must be checked in order to work.
Administration performance enhancements	NAL now loads much faster into memory than did previous versions of NAL.
Distribution performance enhancements	You can optimize the number of application calls to NDS and to the file system application distribution to run faster.

Feature	Description
Enhanced Launcher Configuration inheritance	You can set options in the Launcher Configuration above one level.
Dial-up connection detection	NAL automatically detects whether a user is dialing into a network and prompts the user before reading NDS. Accessing NDS over dial-up can be time-intensive.
Additional macros	Additional macros are now included with NAL for popular Windows directory locations such as the Startup Folder and Desktop Folder.
Enhanced snAppShot interface	The administrator can now select a Standard, Custom, or Express option when running snAppShot in order to create installable application objects.
Mapping up to 26 drives and capturing 9 ports	NAL can map up to 26 drives before launching an application and can capture 9 ports.

 ## What are the new Novell Client features with NetWare 5?

NetWare 5 now includes the following new features for the Novell Client:

- A contextless login that allows users to search for their username through the login prompt
- The Novell Desktop Manager, which allows the administrator or the user to schedule tasks and run with Z.E.N.works
- Location profiles, which allow users to manage the logins to different trees or environments.

OTHER ENHANCEMENTS

 ## What type of database ships with NetWare 5?

NetWare 5 includes Oracle 8 for NetWare (5 users), which provides the ability to run Oracle with NDS support.

? **Are there any new features for saving configuration information for either Technical Services assistance or documenting the system?**

NetWare 5 includes TECHWALK.NLM, which allows administrators to save server configuration information that is needed to send to Novell's Technical Services or for documenting a NetWare 5 server.

? **Are there any backup enhancements with NetWare 5?**

NetWare 5 includes a utility program called NWBACK32. NWBACK32 is protocol independent, adds multiple and repetitive scheduling, and supports a Windows 95 and Windows NT interface. It also allows the administrator to back up and restore a part of a tree rather than the entire tree.

Chapter 3

Server Installation

Answer Topics!

PRE-INSTALLATION ISSUES 32

? Upgrading to NetWare 5

? Using REXXWARE's Migration Tool versus Novell's Migration Wizard

? Determining hardware/software requirements

? Using the pre-upgrade/migration checklist

? Preparing for your upgrade to NetWare 5

? Setting up DOS partitions

? Using different versions of DOS

? Extending a DOS partition without deleting other partitions

? Finding DOS utilities

? Booting from the NetWare 5 CD

? Integrating NetWare 5 with existing IP and IPX networks

? Upgrading from NetWare 2

? Migrating passwords

? Understanding how login scripts migrate

? Migrating from Banyan to NetWare 5

? Determining the size of the SYS volume

? Installing numerous servers

? Understanding DS.NLM version upgrade requirements

? Using long filename support

? Performing a text-based NetWare 5 installation

? Using templates to migrate users to NetWare 5

? Installing NetWare 5 in a 4.x tree

? Migrating from Windows NT4 to NetWare 5

INSTALLATION BASICS 50

? Using keyboard Shortcuts for the GUI portion of the installation

? Solving problems with the CD-ROM not mounted for server-to-server installation

? Using .DSK files

? Installing or upgrading to the NetWare 5 server using the Novell installation program

? Naming Country objects

? Troubleshooting and loading hardware drivers

? Dealing with system hangs during GUI installation

? Responding to project creation error when using the Upgrade Wizard

? Solving File Copy issues with the Migration Wizard

? Customizing a registered IPX number during the installation

? Customizing volume block size, suballocation, and compression

? Loading the Migration Agent during the installation

? Customizing frame types during the installation

POST-INSTALLATION ISSUES   73

? Fixing Pre-NetWare 5 applications

? Uninstalling a Novell add-on product

? Reinstalling a Novell add-on product

? Installing a Novell Support Pack

? Disabling Compatibility Mode

? Seeing IPX servers with the Migration Agent

? Enabling IP client to access to IPX servers

? Changing the volume's block size after the installation

? Removing IPX from the network

? Fixing post-installation mouse problems

LICENSE INSTALLATION ISSUES   78

? Using utilities to install licenses

? Installing additional licenses

? Dealing with license errors

? Installing NLS on a NetWare 4.11 server

? Running out of licenses

Server Installation @ a Glance

What is the absolute best upgrade/migration path to NetWare 5 for your environment? Which method will provide a surefire, nonstressful upgrade? It's always better to answer these questions *before* you actually perform your NetWare 5 installation, or you may regret it during or soon after the installation. The goal is to have a very uneventful, easy installation. The following areas of this chapter help make this happen:

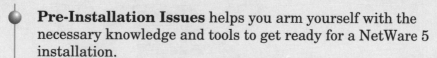

Pre-Installation Issues helps you arm yourself with the necessary knowledge and tools to get ready for a NetWare 5 installation.

Installation Basics provides detailed step-by-step instructions on successfully installing NetWare 5. You'll also find common installation problems and solutions.

Post-Installation Issues answers some common administrative concerns following a NetWare 5 installation.

License Installation Issues addresses all of the concerns administrators face when adding or installing NetWare licenses.

PRE-INSTALLATION ISSUES

 ## How do I upgrade from NetWare 4.*x* and/or 3.*x* to NetWare 5?

You can upgrade from an older version of NetWare in three ways:

- In-Place Upgrade (same server) / INSTALL.BAT
- Across-the-Wire Migration (different server) / Novell Migration Wizard
- REXXWARE Migration Toolkit (RMT)

In-Place Upgrades are performed when the same server hardware will be used following the upgrade. Only the server operating system is upgraded to a newer version of NetWare. The In-Place Upgrade uses the INSTALL.BAT installation program to upgrade NetWare 3.1*x* and NetWare 4.*x*, intraNetWare, and intraNetWare for Small Business servers to NetWare 5.

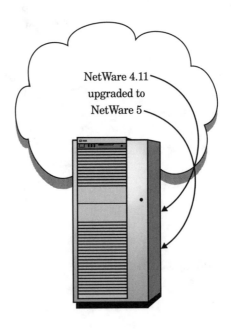

NetWare 4.11 upgraded to NetWare 5

 Note: *To upgrade a NetWare 4.11 server to NetWare 5, you can perform an In-Place Upgrade. However, do not perform an In-Place Upgrade if the 4.11 server has DHCP, NFS, NetWare AppleTalk File and Print Services, Novell Web Server, BorderManager, or NetWare/IP loaded. Instead, migrate this server to a new NetWare 5 system or retain the server as a NetWare 4.11 server in the NDS tree. Your NDS tree can contain both NetWare 4.11 and NetWare 5 servers.*

Across-the-Wire Migrations, shown in the illustration on the next page, are performed when both the NetWare 3.*x* server hardware and the operating system are replaced. Only the bindery, passwords, security, and file system are migrated to the NetWare 5 server and NDS tree. For example, you buy a new Pentium server for NetWare 5 to replace your old 486. An Across-the-Wire Migration can be used in this scenario. The file system (security, data, application files, and login scripts) and bindery (users, printers, groups, and so on) information will be migrated to the new NetWare 5 environment. Across-the-Wire Migrations use the Novell Upgrade Wizard to migrate a NetWare 3.1*x* server to NetWare 5. The Upgrade Wizard checks for possible conflicts and errors, such as NDS security, disk space limitations, and name conflicts, and presents options for resolution. Across-the-Wire Migration is probably the safest way to upgrade NetWare 3.1*x* to NetWare 5, since the 3.*x* source server is unchanged.

 Tip: *An Across-the-Wire upgrade should be performed with a workstation with a fast processor and the most RAM available. Be aware that later failures with NWADMN32.EXE, NDPS, and other servers can be expected if the minimum 64MB of RAM on the server has not been met.*

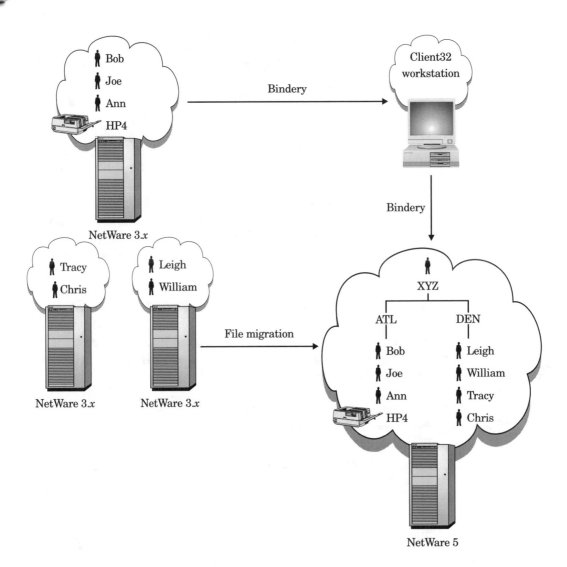

REXXWARE Migration Toolkit (RMT) is another server-based utility for Across-the-Wire upgrades. Novell has licensed RMT from Simware, Inc., and is offering it free of charge to customers who have an existing NetWare 3 server.

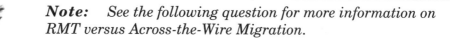

To obtain your copy of RMT, go to www.simware.com and complete the online registration form. You must provide the serial number of one of your registered NetWare 3.*x* file servers.

Note: *See the following question for more information on RMT versus Across-the-Wire Migration.*

How you upgrade your server may also depend on the features you want to implement in NetWare 5, such as suballocation, compression, and block size. For example, if you are upgrading from NetWare 3.12 and your server's block size was 4K, performing an In-Place Upgrade would not allow you to change the server's 4K block size to a larger, 64K block size during the upgrade process.

Note: *You cannot migrate individual files with the shipping version of the Novell Upgrade Wizard.*

Note: *NetWare 2.x servers cannot be upgraded using the In-Place or Across-the-Wire upgrade methods.*

Novell's Upgrade Wizard and REXXWARE's Migration Toolkit seem to perform the same upgrade tasks. How are they different?

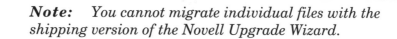

Novell's Upgrade Wizard will upgrade a NetWare 3.1*x* bindery, data, passwords, and printing environment, and is probably the easiest upgrade method. REXXWARE's Migration Toolkit (RMT) also migrates the bindery, data, passwords, and printing environment. The difference between the two is that RMT has more upgrade features than Novell's Upgrade Wizard. For example, RMT upgrades are faster and allow for customized modeling and reporting. They also provide the ability to restart and undo an upgrade and a checkpoint restart in case the file migration fails. A migration using RMT can also be performed from a workstation or from the server console using a Java-based

interface. The Upgrade Wizard can only be used from a workstation.

RMT is the recommended migration method if any of the following criteria are met:

- More than 15 servers migrating to NetWare 5
- More than 1,000 users
- More than 20GB
- Migration requires absolutely no risk
- Simultaneous server consolidation

Go to www.simware.com for your free copy of RMT and for more information.

 ## What are the hardware and software requirements for a NetWare 5 server?

It is always a good idea to verify that your hardware will support a NetWare 5 environment. Administrators *must* test older hardware in a lab environment before upgrading an existing NetWare 3.*x* or 4.*x* server. Novell recommends using Novell certified hardware manufacturers for a production environment. For a list of Novell certified hardware, go to developer.novell.com/netware5/hardware.htm.

- Pentium-level processor (100MHz or greater).
- 64MB RAM (128MB recommended to run Java-based applications).
- VGA or higher resolution display adapter (SVGA recommended).
- One or more network cards.
- A CD-ROM drive that is ISO 9660 formatted. Computers with bootable CD-ROM (to boot the server from the CD-ROM, the CD-ROM drive must fully support the EL-TORITO specification).
- SYS volume = 500MB minimum.

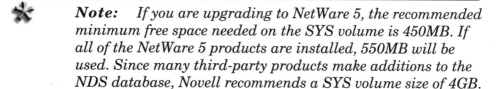

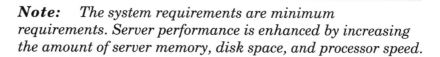 ***Note:*** *If you are upgrading to NetWare 5, the recommended minimum free space needed on the SYS volume is 450MB. If all of the NetWare 5 products are installed, 550MB will be used. Since many third-party products make additions to the NDS database, Novell recommends a SYS volume size of 4GB.*

- DOS Partition = 50MB minimum. The DOS partition should be increased to include enough space for the installed amount of RAM to allow for a core dump if needed for troubleshooting. For example, a 64MB RAM system should have 114MB in the DOS partition (64MB + 50MB = 114MB).

- Serial or PS/2 mouse recommended but not required.

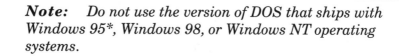 ***Note:*** *The system requirements are minimum requirements. Server performance is enhanced by increasing the amount of server memory, disk space, and processor speed.*

The following is a list of software requirements:

- DOS 3.3 or later. (DOS 7 is included on the NetWare 5 License disk.)

Note: *Do not use the version of DOS that ships with Windows 95*, Windows 98, or Windows NT operating systems.*

- DOS CD-ROM drivers (if you are installing from a CD-ROM drive in the server).
- NetWare 5 Operating System CD-ROM.
- NetWare 5 License disk.
- Novell Client for DOS and Windows 3.1x (optional; needed if you are installing from a network).

- NetWare 5 client to connect to an IP-only environment.
- Static IP address (optional).

 Note: *A static IP address is needed if the server will connect to the Internet. Contact your Internet service provider (ISP) for more information on obtaining a registered IP address.*

- Network board and hard disk device properties, such as the interrupt, slot, and port address. (For more information, contact your computer hardware manufacturer and/or documentation.)
- Update to DS.NLM if you are installing NetWare 5 in a NetWare 4.*x* tree. NetWare 4.10 tree needs DS.NLM 5.13 or later. NetWare 4.11 tree needs DS.NLM 6.00, ROLLCALL 4.10, and DSREPAIR 4.58 or later. Check for any DS patch kits available at www.novell.com. Install the latest Support Pack on NetWare 4 servers before upgrading them to NetWare 5.
- The CONFIG.SYS file should contain the following commands: FILES=40 and BUFFERS=30.

 Note: *Use LAN drivers certified after 11/1/97 to support the Virtual Memory feature in NetWare 5. Use the LAN drivers that come with NetWare 5 or go to the Web site developer.novell.com/infosys/mastr_02.htm. Otherwise, contact your vendor.*

 Tip: *For best results when installing multiple servers into the same tree, install the server that will hold the Master replica of [Root] first, and then install the remaining servers. This will ensure that the [Root] is fully installed and functioning for the remaining servers to access during installation. This is also true for upgrades to 4.x-based trees. Upgrade the server that holds the Master replica of the [Root] first, and then upgrade the remaining servers.*

What items of information do I need before I begin the NetWare 5 installation or upgrade?

The following is a detailed checklist of items to gather before the installation:

❏ NetWare 5 Operating System CD-ROM

❏ DOS CD-ROM drivers

❏ DOS 3.3 or higher disks

❏ Login Name _____ Password _____ (if you are installing NetWare 5 across the network)

❏ License disk

❏ Is this a new server installation or an upgrade from a previous NetWare version to NetWare 5?

   ❏ New Server   ❏ Upgrade

❏ If you're upgrading to NetWare 5 from a previous version of NetWare, what version are you upgrading from?

   ❏ NetWare 3.11   ❏ NetWare 3.12   ❏ NetWare 4.x

In what DOS directory does the current SERVER.EXE reside? _____

❏ Mouse type (that is, PS/2, Serial COM1...) _____

❏ Video type (that is, Standard or Super VGA) _____

❏ Regional settings (default regional settings are typically used):

   ● Country: Determines how dates or numbers are displayed. For example, country 001 (USA) displays dates as January 1, 1999. _____

   ● Code page: The code page determines which characters are valid for displaying and naming files and directories. _____

   ● Keyboard: Keyboards conform to a specific language and keyboard layout, which can vary by country or region. _____

❑ Will your server have multiple processors installed?

❑ No ❑ Yes

If yes, provide the name of the Platform Support Module (PSM) _____.

❄ ***Note:*** *It's a good idea to obtain the latest versions of PSMs to support your system's multiple processors.*

❑ Will your server support PCI HotPlug technology?

❑ No ❑ Yes

If yes, provide the name of the HotPlug Support Module (HSM) _____.

❄ ***Note:*** *It's a good idea to obtain the latest version of HSMs to support your system. For more information on PCI HotPlug technology, refer to the question "Does NetWare 5 provide PCI HotPlug support?" in Chapter 2.*

❑ What type of hard disk storage adapter(s) will be used in your server (that is, Adaptec 2920, IDEATA, Compaq Ultra/Fast Wide SCSI 2, and so on)?

_____

❑ Does the hard disk(s) installed in your server include hardware redirection as part of its interface, or will you need to use NetWare's Hot Fix feature?

  ❑ The hard disk will use NetWare's Hot Fix redirection feature.

  ❑ The hard disk will not use NetWare's Hot Fix redirection feature because the hard disk circuitry supports hardware redirection.

❑ What slot, port, and/or interrupt will your server's hard disk storage adapter use?

  Slot number: _____, interrupt: _____, port: _____.

❑ What type of network card(s) will be used in your server (that is, 3Com Fast Etherlink, Intel EtherExpress32, SMC EtherPower, and so on)?

_____

❑ What slot, port, and/or interrupt will your server's network card(s) use?

Slot number: _____, interrupt: _____, port: _____.

❑ Protocol(s) information:

   ❑ IP

      IP address: _____

      Subnet mask: _____

      Frame type: _____

   ❑ IPX

      IPX number (if registered IPX numbers are needed) _____

      Frame type: ❑ Ethernet 802.2 (default) ❑ Ethernet 802.3 ❑ Other _____

      Network number (if a partiular network number is needed) _____

❑ Time zone information (that is, United States Eastern, Central, and so on)

_____

❑ NetWare disk partition information:

     Size of the NetWare disk partition: _____

❑ Volume information:

     Size of the SYS volume: _____

✳ **Note:** *The SYS volume must be a traditional NetWare volume.*

❑ Other volumes to be created:

Name: _____ Size: _____
Volume type: ❑ NSS ❑ Traditional

Name: _____ Size: _____
Volume type: ❑ NSS ❑ Traditional

Name: _____ Size: _____
Volume type: ❑ NSS ❑ Traditional

❄ ***Note:*** *Only free space outside a NetWare partition can be used when an NSS volume is created.*

❑ Will this server be installed in a new NDS tree or into an existing NDS tree?

❑ New NDS tree

New NDS tree name: _____

Container(s)/context where new Server object will reside: _____

New Admin user password: _____

❑ Existing NDS tree

Existing tree name: _____

Existing or new container/context where server will be installed:

_____

Administrator or user name with needed supervisor rights to existing tree:

_____

Administrator password to existing tree: _____

❓ What should I do before I upgrade a server to NetWare 5?

The following is a list of pre-upgrade procedures:

❑ Back up and verify the NetWare 3.1*x*/4.*x* server (two backups are recommended); for NetWare 4.*x*, be sure to back up both the file system and the NDS.

✚ ***Tip:*** *You should also back up the DOS directory containing the server startup files (C:\NWSERVER, C:\SERVER.312, and so on). You may need to restore this directory if the upgrade fails.*

❑ Gather all pre-installation information. (For a pre-installation checklist, see the earlier question "What items of information do I need before I begin the NetWare 5 installation or upgrade?")

❑ Be sure to have sufficient NDS and file system rights.

❑ Clean up the file system (that is, delete unnecessary files).

❑ If you are upgrading from NetWare 4.*x*:

  ❑ Run an unattended full repair in DSREPAIR.NLM.

  ❑ Eliminate any NDS synchronization errors.

  ❑ Eliminate time synchronization errors.

  ❑ Apply latest patches (go to support.novell.com).

❑ If you are upgrading to NetWare 3.1*x*:

  ❑ Delete unnecessary users, print queues, printers, and so on.

  ❑ Run BINDFIX.

  ❑ Eliminate duplicate names if migrating multiple NetWare 3.1*x* servers.

  ❑ Apply latest patches (go to support.novell.com).

❑ Upgrade the workstation client if necessary. The workstation must be running the NetWare 5 Client version 2.2 or higher for Windows 95, or 4.11 or higher for Windows NT or higher.

✳ ***Note:*** *If the NetWare 5 Client is not installed, the Client will only be able to communicate with a NetWare 5 server running IPX.*

❑ Find out compatibility information if you are using third-party NLMs, LAN, or disk drivers. (Ask your Novell Authorized Reseller about compatibility issues.)

❑ Clear all connections prior to the upgrade.

- ❏ If necessary, add name space to the destination server.
- ❏ If the server being upgraded is running BorderManager 2.1, upgrade to BorderManager 3.
- ❏ If you're running ManageWise, comment out ManageWise lines from the server's AUTOEXEC.NCF file.
- ❏ Comment out all third-party NLMs from the STARTUP.NCF and/or AUTOEXEC.NCF files.

 Tip: If you are installing LDAP Services for NDS, determine whether an LDAP catalog is available locally. If an LDAP catalog is available and you decide to keep it, do not install a new catalog during the installation / upgrade. Delete the LDAP catalog if you do not want to keep it.

How do I set up the DOS partition?

The DOS boot partition will contain DOS and the NetWare startup and server files. The boot partition should be at least 50MB. The DOS partition may already exist and not need to be set up in environments where the server will be upgraded from an older version of NetWare to NetWare 5.

 Note: 50MB is the minimum size requirement for the DOS partition. Increase the size of the DOS partition if possible to allow for troubleshooting operations, such as core dumps, and management utilities.

Perform the following steps to create and format a boot partition:

1. Remove other operating systems, such as Windows, if installed.

 Note: You can maintain multiple operating systems on the computer by creating independent partitions for each operating system. For more information on how to create multiple partitions, consult your vendor's documentation.

2. Boot the computer using DOS 3.3 or above.

 Note: *DR-DOS is included on the NetWare 5 License disk and can be used to boot the computer.*

 Caution: *Do not use the version of DOS that ships with the Windows 95 or Windows 98 operating systems.*

3. Use FDISK to create a DOS partition of 50MB or greater. The DOS partition must also be made the active partition.

4. Format the server's new DOS partition by entering the command **FORMAT C: /S**.

5. Reboot the server.

 ### Can I use the DOS version that comes with Windows 95/98 or NT?

No. Do not use the version of DOS that ships with Windows 95 or Windows 98.

 ### I am upgrading to NetWare 5. I need to extend my DOS partition and don't want to delete any of my NetWare partitions. What can I do?

A program called ServerMagic from Powerquest will allow you to increase and decrease the size of your DOS and NetWare partitions without losing data. This utility is a must for administrators if you need to upgrade several servers. Further information about this program can be obtained at www.powerquest.com.

 ### I can't find the DOS utilities like DELTREE on my NetWare 5 Operating System disk. Where are they?

The DR-DOS 7.02 on the NetWare 5 Operating System disk contains only boot files, FDISK, and FORMAT. If you want to maintain a more complete set of DOS programs, use a full version of MS-DOS or DR-DOS.

 **I'm trying to boot my NetWare 5 server using the DOS found on the NetWare 5 Operating System CD-ROM, and it's not working. What can I do?**

If the CD fails to boot, the server is either not compliant with the EL-TORITO specification or requires that you alter your system's BIOS to adapt the boot sequence to try the CD-ROM device first.

It will take quite some time before my entire network is upgraded to NetWare 5. How do I integrate NetWare 5 with my existing NetWare/IP and IPX segments?

The Compatibility Mode driver must be installed on a server for an IP-only NetWare 5 node to communicate with an existing NetWare/IP network. See the first question in the "Post-Installation Issues" section, later in this chapter, for more information.

How can I upgrade a NetWare 2.2 server to NetWare 5.*x*?

There is no upgrade option from NetWare 2.*x* to NetWare 5. The only option is to upgrade your NetWare 2.*x* server to NetWare 3.1*x* and then perform an Across-the-Wire Migration or a Same Server upgrade.

Will I lose my passwords when I migrate?

No. The REXXWARE Migration Toolkit (RMT) and the Same Server installation will save passwords used in the NetWare 3.1*x* and 4.*x* environments.

Will login scripts migrate to NetWare 5?

Yes. System login scripts are placed in the container login script. Each line from the migrated script is treated as a

remark and does not execute. This allows the administrator to edit the script following the migration.

How large should my SYS volume be?

Novell recommends that the SYS volume be a *minimum* of 550MB. However, it is a good idea to have a SYS volume larger than 550MB. Keep in mind that NDS is stored on the SYS volume, so the more replicas you place on the server, the more SYS space is needed.

Several add-on products install files to SYS as well, such as Netscape FastTrack Web server, some backup programs, and so on. Correctly calculating how much disk space to allocate to the SYS volume is critical in your server environment. If the SYS volume becomes full, NDS will lock, making the network inaccessible.

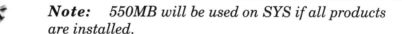

Note: *550MB will be used on SYS if all products are installed.*

I need to install 100 NetWare 5 servers. What is the best way to do this?

NWINST Automated Server Installation allows administrators to easily install numerous preconfigured servers. All it needs is a boot floppy and a CD. Companies from all over the world are using this system to roll out from 100 to over 1,000 servers. Go to consulting.novell.com/toolkit/iw_tools.html#nwinst for more information.

What version of DS.NLM do I need in a mixed NetWare 4.1*x* and 5.*x* environment?

Before you install NetWare 5 into your 4.1*x* tree, all 4.1*x* servers need to be updated with the appropriate version of DS.NLM. NetWare 4.10 requires DS.NLM v5.13 or above and DSREPAIR.NLM v 4.59 or above. NetWare 4.11 requires

DS.NLM v6.00 or above, and DSREPAIR.NLM v4.59 or above. These files can be downloaded from support.novell.com.

Are long filenames supported with Across-the-Wire Migration?

Yes, long filenames are supported with Across-the-Wire Migration.

Is it possible to perform a non-GUI installation of NetWare 5?

Yes and no. Although the current Installation Wizard does not support a non-GUI installation, NetWare 5 will support a non-GUI installation with a tool that will be made available at support.novell.com in the future.

Can I use a template to migrate my NetWare 3.12 users to NetWare 5?

Yes. You must use Novell's Migration Wizard if you would like to apply a template.

I will be installing NetWare 5 into my NetWare 4.*x* tree. What must be done prior to installing a NetWare 5 server into my NetWare 4.*x* tree?

- Install version 6 or above of NDS on all 4.11 servers in the tree prior to installing NetWare 5. The following three files must be copied to achieve the NDS upgrade: DS.NLM, ROLLCALL.NLM (version 4.10 or above), and DSREPAIR.NLM (version 4.59 or above). NetWare 4.10 requires DS.NLM 5.15 or above and DSREPAIR.NLM 4.59 or above. These files can be downloaded from support.novell.com.

- Correct any replica or NDS synchronization errors prior to installing NetWare 5.

Tip: *You can use the DSDIAG.NLM utility that ships with NetWare 5 to get information about the state of NDS in a tree and NDS version information.*

Note: *If you're using NDS Manager to update NDS, use NDSMGR.EXE version 1.25 or later. INSTALL.NLM can also be used.*

Caution: *All servers not upgraded to NetWare 5 or NDS 6 and above will receive schema errors when the NetWare 5 server upgrade is complete.*

- Always make two backups if upgrading a server to NetWare 5.
- Time synchronization should be configured correctly.

Note: *If you're upgrading from NetWare 4.1x to NetWare 5, always upgrade the server holding the Master replica of the [Root] partition first. This helps avoid schema conflicts in NDS.*

- If you plan to make the NetWare 5 server protocol IP only, the migration gateway (SCMD /G) must be loaded on the server with the Master replica. This allows NDS to communicate properly in a mixed protocol environment. Otherwise, an IPX server will not be able to connect. The Migration Agent can be set up at the Summary screen during the installation of NetWare 5.
- Install NetWare License Service (NLS) on one NetWare 4.*x* server in each partition of the NDS tree.

Note: *Select a NetWare 4.11 server that has a Master or read/write replica of the partition. If you have old or existing licenses in the NDS tree, run SETUPNLS.NLM after upgrading the NetWare 4.11 server.*

- Install a NetWare 5 server directly into the 4.11 tree if the NetWare 5 server will have a read/write replica and

the replica is in the NDS partition where the read/write activity will take place.

● If all servers in the tree will eventually be upgraded to NetWare 5, first upgrade servers in the lower portions of the tree. This allows NDS to cope with the NetWare 5 changes more easily than migrating from the [Root] directory and moving out.

How do I migrate my Windows NT 4 server to NetWare 5?

Currently, Novell does not have an official way to migrate from NT 4 to NetWare 5. However, there is a way to do this by using Novell's NDS for NT 2. This product will allow you to import the NT database into an NDS tree. Its original purpose is to provide coexistence between NetWare and NT, but it can be used as a migration utility as well. Using this program will migrate only users and groups from the NT database, but not file rights. For more information on this product, go to www.novell.com/products/nds/nds4nt/.

INSTALLATION BASICS

How do I move around in the GUI portion of the installation without using a mouse?

Use the following table for information on cursor movement without a mouse.

Key	Function
TAB	Move focus to next element
SHIFT-TAB	Move focus to previous element
ENTER	Select
UP ARROW (keypad 8)	Move cursor up
DOWN ARROW (keypad 2)	Move cursor down
RIGHT ARROW (keypad 6)	Move cursor right

Key	Function
LEFT ARROW (keypad 4)	Move cursor left
Hold SHIFT while pressing keypad	Accelerate cursor movement
Keypad 5	Select or click an object
Keypad 0	Lock a selected object (for dragging)
Keypad . (period)	Unlock a selected object (to drop)
Keypad + (plus)	Double-click an object
ALT-F7	Move to next window
ALT-F8	Move to previous window

 Note: *NUMLOCK must be on to allow cursor movements on the keypad.*

 I'm having a problem mounting the NetWare 5 Operating System CD-ROM when installing NetWare 5 from the CD mounted on another server. What could be wrong?

Do not use CDROM.NLM to mount the CD. CDROM.NLM uses NSS and does not support server-to-server installations. To use the Install CD-ROM in the source server, you must use the CDINST.NLM module. Using CDINST.NLM will allow you to mount the CD on the source server.

 During the NetWare 5 installation, I attempt to use a .DSK driver and it is not working. How can I get it to work?

NetWare 5 does not support the old .DSK standard. For a server to run NetWare 5, it must have a disk subsystem that has supported .HAM and .CDM modules. If supported .HAM and .CDM files are not found in the installation or in subsequent driver releases from Novell, you must either obtain them from the hardware vendor or install a new storage subsystem that supports the .HAM and .CDM drivers.

 How do I install or upgrade to NetWare 5 server using Novell's installation program?

You must consider several factors before upgrading to NetWare 5. It is essential that you make two backup copies of the 3.1*x*/4.*x* server before performing the upgrade. The following sections describe a comprehensive setup for upgrading your system.

Gather Necessary Pre-Upgrade/Migration Information

For the upgrade/migration checklist, refer to the earlier question "What items of information do I need before I begin the NetWare 5 installation or upgrade?"

Perform Pre-Upgrade Procedures

Refer to the earlier question "What should I do before I upgrade a server to NetWare 5?"

DOS Partition Setup

Refer to the earlier question "How do I set up the DOS partition?"

NetWare OS New Server Installation and Upgrade

If you are upgrading from NetWare 4.1*x* to NetWare 5, remember to upgrade the server holding the Master replica of the [Root] partition first. This helps avoid schema conflicts in NDS. Also, upgrade your server starting at the lower portions of the tree first. This allows NDS to cope with NetWare 5 changes more easily than migrating from the [Root] and moving out. The following are the steps for installing and upgrading your server:

1. Insert the NetWare 5 Operating System CD in the server to be installed or upgraded and change to the CD-ROM drive.

2. Type **Install** and press ENTER.

3. Press F10 at the Novell Terms and Conditions license information screen.

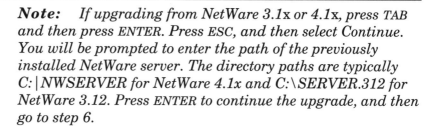

4. Highlight Continue, and press ENTER to accept both New Server and C:\NWSERVER default directory options.

> ❋ *Note:* *If upgrading from NetWare 3.1x or 4.1x, press TAB and then press ENTER. Press ESC, and then select Continue. You will be prompted to enter the path of the previously installed NetWare server. The directory paths are typically C:\NWSERVER for NetWare 4.1x and C:\SERVER.312 for NetWare 3.12. Press ENTER to continue the upgrade, and then go to step 6.*

5. Highlight Continue, and press ENTER to accept the default United States regional settings.

Mouse Setup

> ❋ *Note:* *Skip steps a–d if your server's mouse type is a PS/2.*

6. If the mouse connected to your server is not a PS/2 mouse type, perform the following steps:

   a. Press TAB to highlight the Mouse Type field, and press ENTER.

   b. Using the arrow keys, highlight the appropriate mouse type (PS/2, COM 1, and so on) that you have connected to your server, and press ENTER.

   c. Press TAB to return to the Options menu.

> ❋ *Note:* *The default video is Super VGA. Skip steps d–g if your server's monitor is a Super VGA. Perform the following steps if your server is using a Standard VGA monitor.*

   d. Press TAB again.

   e. Highlight the Video field and press ENTER. This will change the Video to Standard VGA.

   f. Press TAB to return to the Options menu.

g. When the correct mouse and video types are selected, highlight Continue and press ENTER.

 Note: *The installation program now copies the necessary startup files into the C:\NWSERVER directory.*

Hardware Device Driver Setup

7. The Device Types menu, shown here, allows you to select hardware device drivers.

```
NetWare Installation

The following device drivers were detected for this server.  Add, change, or
delete device drivers as needed.


  ┌ Device types ─────────── Driver names ──────────────────────┐
  │                                                              │
  │  Platform Support Module:    (optional)                      │
  │                                                              │
  │  HotPlug Support Module:     (optional)                      │
  │                                                              │
  │  Storage adapters:           AHA2940                         │
  │                                                              │
  └──────────────────────────────────────────────────────────────┘
                            ┌─────────────────┐
                            │     Options     │
                            ├─────────────────┤
                            │Continue         │
                            │Modify           │
                            └─────────────────┘

 Alt+F10=Exit  Esc=Back                                    F1=Help
```

 Note: *Skip to step u if all information displayed in the Device Types menu is correct.*

The Platform Support Module (PSM) is optional. Select a PSM only if you are running multiple processors in your server.

 Note: *Skip steps a–e if your server has only one processor installed.*

If your server has more than one processor, perform the following steps to select a PSM:

a. Press TAB.

b. Press ENTER and then INSERT for a list of PSMs.

c. Highlight the desired PSM module and press ENTER.

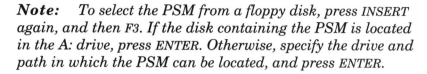

Note: *To select the PSM from a floppy disk, press* INSERT *again, and then* F3. *If the disk containing the PSM is located in the A: drive, press* ENTER. *Otherwise, specify the drive and path in which the PSM can be located, and press* ENTER.

d. Press ESCAPE two times.

e. Press TAB to return to the Options menu.

The PCI HotPlug Support Module (HSM) is optional. PCI HotPlug technology gives you the ability to add and remove PCI controller cards while your server is running and safeguards the system from the electrical effects of the replacement operation.

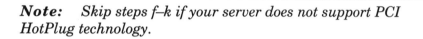

Note: *Skip steps f–k if your server does not support PCI HotPlug technology.*

If your server supports PCI HotPlug technology, perform the following steps:

f. Press TAB to move to the Device Types menu.

g. Press the DOWN ARROW to highlight HotPlug Support Module and press ENTER.

h. Press INSERT.

i. Highlight the desired HSM and press ENTER.

j. Press ESC two times.

k. Press TAB to return to the Options menu.

The Storage Adapter driver is *not* optional and must be selected for your server to operate its hard disk(s). NetWare 5 will attempt to autodetect the type of hard disk component(s) you have in your server; therefore, you may see the appropriate driver listed in the Storage Adapter field.

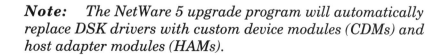

Note: *The NetWare 5 upgrade program will automatically replace DSK drivers with custom device modules (CDMs) and host adapter modules (HAMs).*

Note: *Skip to step u if the appropriate storage adapter was autodetected.*

If the storage adapter was not autodetected, you must perform the following steps to manually select the storage adapter:

l. Press TAB to move to the Device Types menu.

m. Using the DOWN ARROW keys, highlight the Storage Adapter field and press ENTER.

n. Press INSERT.

o. Using the arrow keys, highlight the appropriate adapter for your server and press ENTER.

p. Depending on the type of hard disk you have in your system, you will need to provide additional information, such as slot number, port, interrupt, and so on. Press TAB to move to the Properties menu.

q. Enter the needed information.

 Note: *This information will vary from one system to the next, depending on the type of hard disk installed. (That is, you'll need to provide a slot number if you have a PCI storage adapter, or an Interrupt and Port if you have an ISA storage adapter, and so on.)*

r. Once the required information is entered, press TAB, highlight Return to Driver List, and press ENTER.

s. Press TAB , highlight Return to Drive Summary, and press ENTER.

t. Press TAB to return to Options.

 Note: *Repeat steps l–t for each storage adapter you have installed in your server. You should see the name(s) of your server's storage adapter(s) listed under driver names.*

u. When the correct PSM(s), HSM(s), and storage adapter(s) have been selected for your system, highlight Continue and press ENTER.

8. You will see a summary of the storage adapter(s) you selected in the previous step under Driver Names. This gives you the opportunity to reselect or change the storage adapter(s) chosen in the previous step if necessary. If you need to change the storage adapter, press ESC and repeat steps l–u.

When you're installing a new server, you will need to enter a Network Boards driver, which is *not* optional—it must be selected for your server to operate its network interface card(s). NetWare 5 will try to autodetect the network card(s) installed in your server.

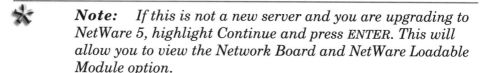

Note: *If this is not a new server and you are upgrading to NetWare 5, highlight Continue and press ENTER. This will allow you to view the Network Board and NetWare Loadable Module option.*

Note: *The installation may not be able to autodetect 16-bit network cards.*

Note: *Skip steps a–i if your network card(s) is shown in the Network Board Driver field.*

If your network card(s) isn't shown in the Network Board Driver field, you must perform the following steps:

a. Press TAB.

b. Using the DOWN ARROW key, highlight the Network Boards Driver field and press ENTER.

c. Press INSERT.

d. Highlight the appropriate network board installed in your server and press ENTER.

e. Press TAB to move to the driver Properties menu.

f. Enter the needed information. Depending on the type of network card you have in your system, you will need to provide additional information, such as slot, port, interrupt, and so on.

g. Press TAB, highlight Return to Driver List, and press ENTER when the required information is selected.

   h. Press TAB to highlight Return to Drive Summary, and press ENTER.

 Note: *Repeat steps a–h for each network card you have installed in your server. You should see the name(s) of your server's network board(s) listed under driver names.*

   i. Press TAB to return to the Options menu.

 Note: *The NetWare Loadable Modules field is optional and is needed only if your server supports Source Routing on a Token-Ring and/or FDDI network.*

   j. Highlight Continue and press ENTER when the correct Storage Device(s), Network Board(s), and NetWare Loadable Modules have been selected.

 Note: *If this is not a new server and you are performing an upgrade, skip to step 12.*

Partition and SYS Volume Setup
   9. Examine the default partition information displayed in the Volume SYS and Partition Properties menu. The SYS volume will contain all the necessary files for running the NetWare 5 operating system.

 Caution: *To avoid serious problems now and in the future, be sure that the SYS volume is large enough to store all necessary operating system files. NDS is locked and the server becomes inaccessible when the SYS volume runs out of disk space. Refer to the earlier question "How large should my SYS volume be?" for more information on your server's volume requirements. Volumes other than SYS are created later in the installation.*

 Note: *If this server will be set up as a Netscape FastTrack Web server, additional SYS volume space is necessary.*

   The NetWare Partition will contain the SYS volume as well as any other traditional NetWare volumes you want to create.

Note: *To avoid serious problems now and in the future, be sure the NetWare Partition is large enough to store desired traditional NetWare volumes.*

 Note: *Skip to step f if the default Volume and Partition Properties are satisfactory.*

If you would like to change the defaults, perform steps a–f:

a. Highlight Modify and press ENTER.

b. Type the desired size of the NetWare Partition and press ENTER.

 Note: *An NSS volume cannot be created from free space in a NetWare Partition. Be sure the NetWare Partition does not consume the entire space of your hard disk(s) if you intend to create NSS volumes on your server.*

c. Hot Fix is an optional feature of NetWare 5. Hot Fix prevents data from being written to the defective areas (bad sectors) of the hard disk by redirecting the information to a safe location. The Hot Fix Size field can be set to 0 if your hard disk supports hardware redirection as part of its circuitry.

 Note: *RAID devices include hardware redirection and do not need the Hot Fix data protection feature. Otherwise it's a good idea to keep the default setting.*

d. Enter the desired size of the SYS volume in the Volume SYS size (MB) field.

 Note: *If your server has more than one hard disk installed, use the Device field to change to the other hard disk and configure the SYS volume.*

e. Press F10 when all information has been correctly configured.

f. Highlight Continue and press ENTER.

10. Type the name you would like for your server in the Server Name field, and click the Next button.

File System Volume Setup

11. Examine the information displayed in the Configure File System window. Novell Storage Services (NSS) and traditional NetWare volumes can now be created. Refer to "What is Novell Storage Services?" in Chapter 6 for more information on NSS.

Note: *Skip to step g if the volume information displayed is satisfactory.*

If you would like to create additional volumes, perform steps a–g:

a. Click an available Free Space name and click Create.

b. Type a name for the new volume you are creating in the Volume Names field.

c. Click to select the radio button for Traditional or NSS, depending on the type of volume you would like to create.

Note: *The radio button for NSS will be inactive if the Free Space selected in step a was part of the NetWare partition. In order to create an NSS volume, you must select Free Space from a non-NetWare partition.*

d. Type the number of megabytes that this volume will occupy in the Space to Use field. Then click the Apply to Volume button.

e. Click OK. You should see the name of the new volume you created under Volumes Name.

f. Repeat steps a–e for each additional volume you would like to create.

g. Click the Next button when all desired volumes have been created.

 Note: *Skip to step 13 if SYS is the only volume that you have created.*

12. If additional volumes were created, you will be prompted to mount all volumes after the installation is complete. Click the radio button labeled No, Mount Volumes Now, which will mount all volumes now and allow you to install additional products to volumes other than SYS during the installation. Otherwise, you can keep the default, and volumes other than SYS will be mounted at the end of the installation, when the server reboots. Click Next when the desired selection is made.

Protocol Configuration

13. Examine the Protocols window, shown here, and find the server name you specified in step 10. Under the server name you will see the name of your network card driver. Click the name of your network card to make the Protocols portion of the window active.

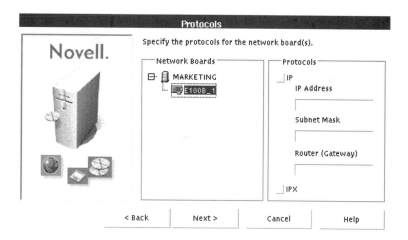

14. Depending on the protocols needed for this network segment, click the option box(es) for IPX and/or IP.

There are three possible setups: IP Only, IPX Only, or IP and IPX. Pure IP will be enabled if *only* the IP option box is marked. If the IP option box is checked, you will need to specify an IP address, subnet mask, and router (gateway).

 Note: *If you are upgrading from NetWare 4.1x, you will be prompted for the 4.1x Administrator name and password. Type the full name of the Admin in the Name field or browse to select Admin using the Browse button. Type the Admin password in the Password field and click Next. Skip to step 23.*

Be aware that if this is a new server installation and IP is the only protocol you selected, IPX Compatibility or Compatibility Mode is automatically loaded without binding IPX. Instead, IPX requests are encapsulated inside a UDP datagram, and resolution of RIP and SAP requests is performed via the Service Location Protocol (SLP). The IPX Compatibility Mode drivers use network resources only when needed by an application.

Compatibility Mode allows applications that require IPX to function on the network. Compatibility Mode is enabled at the server with SCMD.NLM and must be enabled at the workstation as well. Applications requiring IPX will encapsulate IPX requests in IP packets.

 Note: *Ethernet_II is the default Ethernet frame type installed for TCP/IP. Ethernet 802.2 is the default Ethernet frame type installed for IPX/SPX. The installation program will automatically bind the appropriate frame type to your network, such as Ethernet_II or Token-Ring_SNAP.*

15. Click the Next button when you have entered the desired Protocol information.

Server Time Configuration

16. Using the scroll bar, scroll down to select the correct time zone for your server.

17. Be sure a check mark is next to Allow System to Adjust for Daylight Saving Time if you would like the server to automatically adjust time for Daylight Savings Time.

18. Click Next.

Configuring NDS

19. Skip to step 20 if you are installing this server into an existing NDS tree. If this server will be installed in a new NDS tree, perform the following steps:

   a. Select the radio button for Create a New NDS Tree, and then click Next.

   b. Type the name of the new tree you are creating, as shown here:

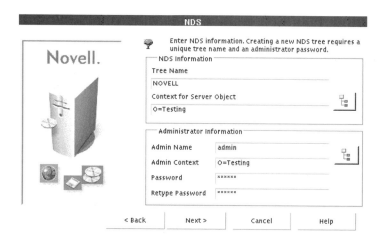

 Note: *The NDS tree name must be unique for your network. For example, the creation process will fail if you try to use the name XYZ_TREE twice on the same network.*

   c. Click the Browse button to select the context into which the server will be placed.

   d. Click the Add button to add a new container.

   e. Type the name of the container.

   f. Depending on the type of container you are creating, click the radio button for Organization, Country, or

Organizational Unit. For more information on containers, refer to Chapter 11.

Note: *If you want to place the Server object further down the tree, repeat steps e and f until you've created the desired container.*

g. Click OK.

Note: *If you created a Country container in step f, you must create an Organization container. Repeat steps d–g to create the Organization container.*

Caution: *If you are creating a Country container object, you must name the Country object according to the ISO 3166 standards. For example, CA is the standard for Canada.*

h. If you would like to create another Organizational Unit, perform steps d–g.

Note: *If the only container created is an organization, the installation program will place the Server object under the organization container.*

i. When all desired containers have been created and the container in which the Server object will reside is highlighted, click OK.

Note: *Skip to step 21 if you installed this server into a new tree.*

20. If you are installing this server into an existing NDS tree, perform the following steps:

a. Click the radio button for Install This Server into an Existing NDS Tree.

b. Click the Browse tree button.

c. Double-click the desired NDS tree in which this server will be installed.

d. The installation program will create a new Server object in the context you specify. Double-click the country or organization container to browse and expand the existing containers of the tree. Click the container in which you would like the new Server object to reside.

Note: Skip to step h if the container in which the new Server object will reside already exists and is selected.

If you would like to add a new container to the tree, perform steps e–h:

e. If the container you would like this new server to reside in does not exist, click the container in which you would like to create a new container, and then click Add.

f. Type the name of the new container.

g. Click OK.

h. When all containers have been expanded and/or created, click OK.

Note: Skip to step 21e if you performed step 20 and are installing this server into an existing NDS tree.

Note: If you performed step 19, this is the first server to be installed in a new NDS tree, and the installation program will automatically create user Admin. User Admin has supervisor rights to the tree. Unless otherwise specified, the installation program will place the Admin User object in the context designated in step 19.

21. To specify the placement of the user Admin object and password, perform steps a–d:

a. Type the desired fully distinguished context in the Admin Context field (for example, O=XYZ).

b. Type the desired password of the Admin user in the Password field.

    c. Retype the password in the Retype Password field.

    d. Go to step j.

 Note: *If this server is being installed into an existing NDS tree, perform the following to specify the existing Admin user.*

    e. Click the Browse tree button next in the Administrator Login portion of the screen.

    f. Double-click the container(s) in which the Admin user exists.

    g. Click the Admin user.

    h. Click OK.

    i. Type the Admin password in the Password field.

    j. Click Next.

22. You will receive a summary of the information you entered in steps 19–21 at the NDS Summary screen. You should write this information down for future reference. You will need the information later to authenticate the tree. Click Next to continue the installation.

 Caution: *You may be prompted to modify the schema if you are upgrading to NetWare 5. You will need to authenticate the tree with the Administrator name and password.*

Installation of NetWare License Services (NLS)

23. Place the NetWare 5 License disk into the A: drive and type **A:** in the License Location field. If the license is in a different location, you will need to specify the path where the license can be found. Or click the Install Without Licenses option box to install NetWare without a license.

24. When license information has been entered, click Next.

 Note: *If the Install Without a License option box is selected, only two connections will be available. The license can be installed after the installation using NetWare Administrator or NWCONFIG.*

Additional Product Installation

25. Click Next to continue the installation without installing add-on products at the Additional Products and Services screen.

 Note: *You can select the option boxes for each component you would like to install at the Additional Products and Services window. Use the scroll bar to view possible components and mark and unmark as needed.*

 Caution: *After you've upgraded to NetWare 5, some products will require additional configuration, or they will need to be completely reinstalled before they will perform properly.*

26. The Summary screen, shown here, displays a list of all selected components that are to be installed. Click Finish to complete the installation.

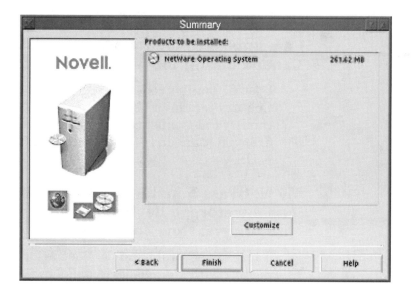

These installation steps will not be correct if additional products are selected.

 Tip: *Click Customize to modify any of the listed components and tailor your server's environment. For example, setting the IPX Internal Network Number, time synchronization, configuring block suballocation, compression, and enabling the Migration Agent can be performed via Customize.*

Final File Copy and Completion of Installation

27. Following the NetWare file copy, you will receive a confirmation that the NetWare 5 Installation is complete. Click Yes to restart the computer.

 Tip: *If you upgraded from NetWare 3.x/4.x to NetWare 5, you may want to remove IPX from the network. For instructions on how to do this, refer to this question, later in this chapter: "I upgraded my NetWare 4.x server to NetWare 5 and noticed that IPX is still bound to the network board, even though I only selected the IP protocol during the upgrade procedure. How do I remove IPX completely from this network?"*

I am unable to create a Country object called Canada during the NetWare 5 Installation. Why?

Specific country codes must be entered. In other words. a Country container object cannot be named just anything. The country codes must conform to the ISO 3166 standard. For example, Canada is CA, Mexico is MX, and the United States is US.

My NetWare 5 installation failed because I could not load my storage device (hard drive) and/or network card drivers. How can I get these devices to load?

There are several possible reasons for installation failures dealing with storage devices. Following is a list of troubleshooting tips that may solve your problem:

● Check for updated drivers from the manufacturer or at least an updated .DDI or LDI file. Create a directory on the DOS partition called \NWUPDATE. When you run

the installation program, it will check for the presence of this directory and search the directory for updated files.

- If the controller card is more than one year old, try another card temporarily. This will help you pinpoint whether the older hardware is the problem.

- Be sure that you are using DR-DOS 7.02, which comes with NetWare or DOS 3.3 or higher. Do not use the DOS that comes with Windows 95 or Windows 98. This DOS contains 32-bit code elements that will interfere with detection of more than 64MB or RAM as well as causing other conflicts.

- Make sure you are not using HIMEM, EMM386, or any other memory managers in the AUTOEXEC.BAT and CONFIG.SYS files, as these will conflict with NetWare.

- Load the NetWare client drivers in conventional memory when installing from the NetWare 5 Operating System CD-ROM that is mounted in the volume of another server. Be sure the CD-ROM is mapped with the MAP ROOT command. The DOS drivers become inactive once the NetWare server driver is loaded for the NetWare server controller. The installation copies additional files at this point, and you are prompted for a valid administrator name, context, and password. If more than 15 minutes pass before you enter this information, the watchdog on the server with the mounted CD-ROM will time out and you will lose your DOS connection. Therefore, be sure you are at the console at this point so that your connection is not lost.

- There is also a known problem with older adapters configured to use memory address 0A0000. This address conflicts with the server's new graphical splash screen when the server loads. To correct this problem, you should reconfigure the card to use a different memory address. Another option is to load the server using the SERVER -NL command.

- If your server installation has already failed, try initiating the server by typing **SERVER /NS /NA** from the

C:\NWSERVER DOS prompt. This command boots the server without using either the STARTUP.NCF or AUTOEXEC.NCF file and will give you the opportunity to try different driver/card combinations.

You will still see NetWare modules load. These modules are extracted from SERVER.EXE. Use the following syntax at the system console to enter the server name manually:

FILE SERVER NAME name of your server

Run the installation program again when you discover the correct drivers.

● Check your server's BIOS to be sure to turn off all shadowing, configuration for DOS support for drives larger than 1GB, and DOS translation for large drives.

My server hangs during the graphical installation. What is the problem?

One problem could be that you have accepted the default PS/2 mouse for the installation without having a mouse directly attached to the server. The only way to correct the problem is to restart the installation and select the No Mouse option.

Another possible solution is to unplug the mouse completely and restart the installation. You can also try to set up the mouse again after installation. For more information, refer to the question "My mouse was not installed correctly as COM 1 during the NetWare 5 installation. How do I fix this?" later in this chapter.

I get an error message when creating a project using the Novell Upgrade Wizard. Why?

You must have an IPX connection to both the NetWare 3.*x* and NetWare 5 servers. Check to see if the server has only the IP protocol bound to the client using the properties of Network Neighborhood.

If IPX is not bound, you must reinstall the client using the Custom installation option and select both IP

and IPX protocols. Also, edit the Protocol Preferences in Network Neighborhood Properties and select IPX as the preferred protocol.

Won't copying the contents of my NetWare 3.1*x* server's SYS volume to my NetWare 5 server's SYS volume with the Migration Wizard cause problems?

No, because the following directories are intentionally *not* copied using the Migration Wizard:

SYS:SYSTEM
SYS:LOGIN
SYS:DELETED.SAVE
SYS:ETC
SYS:PUBLIC

We use registered IPX network numbers at my company; but when I went through the NetWare 5 installation, I didn't see where I could customize the IPX number—so I configured the IPX number after the installation. Is it possible to customize the IPX network number during the installation?

Yes. Customization is available at the end of the installation program at the Summary screen where additional products are also installed. The Customize button at the Summary screen allows you to set the IPX number by selecting the Server Properties folder. (Language, ConsoleOne, license, and component properties can also be set here.) To access this folder, highlight NetWare Operating System, and then click the Properties button.

Where can the volume's disk allocation block size, block suballocation, and compression be set during the NetWare 5 server installation?

Block suballocation and compression can be disabled at the Summary screen during the NetWare 5 server installation. The Summary screen appears at the end of the installation and allows you to tailor the server's environment. Perform

the following steps at the Summary screen during the NetWare 5 server installation.

1. Click Customize | File System | Properties.
2. Click the volume where volume block size, block suballocation, and/or compression are to be set.
3. Click Modify.
4. You can set block size, suballocation, and compression by marking and unmarking the desired check boxes. Block size can be set by clicking the button next to Block Size and selecting the desired size for your volume.
5. Click OK when all items have been set.
6. Click OK twice.
7. Click Close.

 Note: *During the SYS volume creation, these advanced features can be manipulated by pressing F3.*

 ### Can I load the Migration Agent during the NetWare 5 server installation?

Yes. The Migration Agent can be loaded at the Summary screen during the NetWare 5 server installation. The Summary screen appears at the end of the installation and allows you to tailor the server's environment. Perform the following steps at the Summary screen during the NetWare 5 server installation.

1. Select Customize | Protocols | Properties; then click the IPX Compatibility tab.
2. Click the option box for Load the Migration Agent on This Server.
3. Click OK; then click Close.

 Note: *Both IP and IPX protocols should be configured on the server running the Migration Agent.*

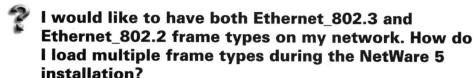 **I would like to have both Ethernet_802.3 and Ethernet_802.2 frame types on my network. How do I load multiple frame types during the NetWare 5 installation?**

Multiple frame types can be loaded at the Summary screen during the NetWare 5 server installation. The Summary screen appears at the end of the installation and allows you to tailor the server's environment. Perform the following steps at the Summary screen during the NetWare 5 server installation.

1. Click Customize | Protocols | Properties.
2. Click the name of the network card to be configured under the Network Boards field.
3. Click the option box(s) for the frame types you would like for this network in the IPX field.

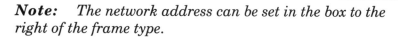 **Note:** *The network address can be set in the box to the right of the frame type.*

4. Click OK; then click Close.

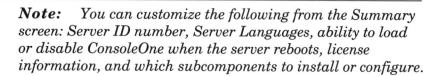 **Note:** *You can customize the following from the Summary screen: Server ID number, Server Languages, ability to load or disable ConsoleOne when the server reboots, license information, and which subcomponents to install or configure.*

POST-INSTALLATION ISSUES

One of my applications worked fine in the NetWare 3.1x and NetWare 4.1x environments; however, the application stopped working when NetWare 5 was installed. How can I fix this problem?

More than likely you will need to enable the Compatibility Mode driver. Compatibility Mode enables IPX and bindery-based applications to operate on an IP-only network.

There are three components to the Compatibility Mode technology. The first component, the Compatibility Mode drivers, enables applications using the IPX stack to function in an IP-only environment. The second component is the Migration Agent, which acts like a router to allow IP-only network segments to communicate with IPX-only network segments. The Migration Agent is enabled at the server by typing **SCMD /g** at the server console. The Migration Agent can also be executed to connect an IP-only backbone to IPX network segments by invoking **SCMD /bs**. The third component, the Bindery Gateway, enables backward compatibility to the NetWare 3 bindery.

 Note: *The Migration Agent can only be enabled at a server running IP and IPX protocols.*

 Tip: *This gateway must be loaded on the server with the Master replica for NDS to communicate properly. Otherwise, IPX-only servers will not be able to connect to the tree.*

Try enabling the Compatibility Mode drivers by loading **SCMD.NLM** on the server. In addition, the Service Location Protocol (SLP) must also be enabled to run IPX applications on your IP-only network. For more information on SLP, refer to the section "Service Location Protocol (SLP)" in Chapter 4.

 Note: *The IPX Compatibility Mode drivers are utilized only when the operating system uses an IPX application or if communication is needed between IP-only and IPX-only network segments. The Compatibility Mode drivers do not affect network communication when they are not in use.*

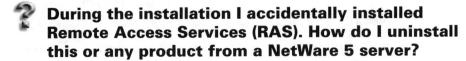 **During the installation I accidentally installed Remote Access Services (RAS). How do I uninstall this or any product from a NetWare 5 server?**

To uninstall the product, perform the following steps at the server console:

1. Type **NWCONFIG** and press ENTER.

2. Highlight Product Options and press ENTER.

3. Highlight View, then Configure, then Remove Installed Products, and press ENTER.

4. Highlight the product to be deleted, and press DELETE.

5. Highlight Yes to remove the product, and press ENTER.

How do I install or reinstall a product like RAS in NetWare 5?

Perform the following steps at the server console to reinstall a product:

1. Type **STARTX** to start up the GUI at the server console.

2. Click the Novell button in the lower-left corner of the screen.

3. Select Install. A list of all the installed products will appear.

4. Click the New Product button.

5. Enter the path to the root of the NW5 CD.

6. Place a check on the Products and Services that you want to install.

7. Click Next.

8. Log in as the Admin at the Novell Login page. Some products and services will ask additional questions that you will need to answer.

9. Click Finish.

Tip: *Products can also be installed using the NWCONFIG utility. Type* **NWCONFIG** *at the server console. Select Product Options. Press* INSERT *and provide the path to the CD-ROM. The difference between installing a product with NWCONFIG versus the GUI server interface is that default paths are used in NWCONFIG. You must enter the full path when using the GUI interface.*

 I'm having a problem with my NetWare 5 server that may be resolved by installing the latest support pack. How are the support packs installed?

NetWare Support Packs contain upgraded files that often fix problems you may encounter with your NetWare 5 server. When troubleshooting server problems, you should always upgrade the server with the latest patches first before calling Novell support. NetWare Support Packs can be downloaded from support.novell.com.

1. Create a directory on the server, for example, FS1\ SYS:SYSTEM\PATCHES.

2. Copy the Support Pack into the directory created in step 1. B2NW51.EXE is an example filename for the Support Pack.

3. Extract the files. You can do this from the DOS prompt by entering the name of the Support Pack filename. You can also use the Windows Run option. For example, browse to FS1\ SYS:\SYSTEM\PATCHES, and select the Support Pack's executable file. Using our example, the files are extracted to a subdirectory under FS1\SYS:\SYSTEM\PATCHES.

4. To complete the installation of the support pack, follow the instructions found in the test file within the Support Pack executable.

 I selected the IP protocol during the installation of my NetWare 5 server, and I would like to disable Compatibility Mode on the server. How can I do this after the installation?

You can disable Compatibility Mode by removing the LOAD SCMD command from the server's SYS:SYSTEM\ AUTOEXEC.NCF file.

 I am unable to see my IPX servers using the Migration Agent. Why?

The Migration Agent discovers IPX services through NLSP. Therefore, NLSP must be enabled in the IPX protocol setup

using INETCFG.NLM for all IPX servers that you want to be reported by the Migration Agent.

My Native IP clients cannot access IPX servers through the Migration Agent. Why?

The Migration Agent discovers IPX services through NLSP. Therefore, NLSP must be enabled in the IPX protocol setup using INETCFG.NLM for all IPX servers that you want the Migration Agent to report.

I noticed that the 4K volume block size did not change on my DATA volume when I performed an In-Place Upgrade on my NetWare 3.12 server. How can I change the block size to 64K?

One of the disadvantages of the In-Place Upgrade is that you cannot change the volume's block size during the upgrade. The only way to change the volume's block size is after the upgrade.

The first step is to make two backups of the volume. Then you must delete the volume and re-create it with the desired block size. The final step is to restore your files from the backup.

I upgraded my NetWare 4.x server to NetWare 5 and noticed that IPX is still bound to the network board, even though I only selected the IP protocol during the upgrade procedure. How do I remove IPX completely from this network?

The In-Place Upgrade does keep IPX bound to the network. In order to remove IPX, perform the following at the server console:

1. Type **INETCFG** and press ENTER.
2. Select Protocols from the Internetworking Configuration menu.
3. Highlight IPX and press DELETE.
4. Select Yes.
5. Exit INETCFG and reinitialize the server.

My mouse was not installed correctly as COM 1 during the NetWare 5 installation. How do I fix this?

Reconfiguring the mouse is performed at the server console. Execute the following:

1. Exit the GUI console if it is loaded.
2. Type **NETBASIC** and press ENTER.
3. Type **SHELL** and press ENTER.
4. Type **CD\SYS:JAVA\NWGFX** and press ENTER.
5. Type **REN MOUSE.CFG MOUSE.OLD** and press ENTER (this will rename MOUSE.CFG to MOUSE.OLD).
6. Type **EXIT SHELL** and press ENTER.
7. Type **STARTX** and press ENTER at the console prompt.
8. Type the serial COM port number of the mouse and press ENTER.
9. Move the mouse to test it, and click one of the mouse buttons.

Note: *A new MOUSE.CFG is created with Serial mouse configuration.*

LICENSE INSTALLATION ISSUES

Installing a license is very unclear in NetWare 5. How do you install a license?

You can install a license within NetWare 5 by any of the following methods:

- Open SYS:PUBLIC\WIN32\NWADMN32. Select the Tools menu. Click Install License, and then select Install Envelope. Enter the Path where your license files are located (typically A:\License). Select the appropriate license file and then click Open. Select OK.
- Open SYS:PUBLIC\WIN32\NLSMAN32.EXE. Select Tools. Select Install License, Install Envelope. Follow the instructions as stated in the preceding option.

Load NWCONFIG at the server console. Select License Options. Select Install Licenses. Enter the path where your license files are located. Highlight the appropriate license file and press ENTER. Press ESC, and close NWCONFIG.

How do I install additional licenses in NetWare 5?

Novell Licensing Services (NLS) manages licensing on your network. Perform the following steps at the server console to install additional licenses:

1. Type **NWCONFIG** and press ENTER.
2. Select License Options and press ENTER.
3. Highlight Install Licenses and press ENTER.
4. Place the NetWare 5 License disk in the A: drive and press ENTER.

 Note: *If the license *.NLF file is in a location other than the A: drive, press F3 and type in the correct path.*

5. Enter the administrator's complete name and password.
6. Highlight an envelope file at the Installable License screen and press ENTER.
7. Press ALT-F10 to exit NWCONFIG.

 Note: *NWCONFIG.NLM is one way to install additional licenses. In NetWare Administrator, select Tools, Install Licenses, and License Certificates to install additional licenses. NLS Manager can also be used.*

After I uninstall Directory Services using NWCONFIG and reinstall it on my NetWare 5 server, I'm unable to install my licenses. I get the error "Cannot install this license because licensing service is unavailable. (LICENSE_INSTALL-5-10)." Why?

You must set up the licensing service when trying to install the license. Licensing in NW5 uses the new NLS (Novell Licensing

Service). The NLS objects (certificates) need to be created and stored in the appropriate NDS context. Perform the following steps at the server console to create the NLS objects:

1. Type **SETUPNLS** and press ENTER.
2. Type the full distinguished name of Admin (for example, admin.xyz), and press ENTER.
3. Type the password and press ENTER.
4. Press ENTER.
5. Highlight Yes and press ENTER to allow the setup program to make modifications.
6. Press ENTER to continue.

With the NLS objects created, installing NetWare 5 license(s) with NWCONFIG should not generate any errors.

 Note: The NWCONFIG utility can also be used. Type **NWCONFIG** *and press ENTER. Select License Options and press ENTER. Highlight Set Up Licensing Service, press ENTER, and log in as Admin.*

 I will be installing a NetWare 5 server in my NetWare 4.11 tree. How do I install Novell Licensing Services (NLS) on my NetWare 4.11 server?

The Novell Licensing Services Installation Kit must be installed on your 4.11 server in order to extend the NDS schema as required by NLS. Configure at least one server in each partition to be a License Service Provider. Perform the following steps at the server console:

1. Type **LOAD INSTALL** and press ENTER.
2. Select Product Options and press ENTER.
3. Highlight Install a Product Not Listed and press ENTER.
4. Specify the path to the Novell Licensing Services Installation Kit. If the kit is located in a path other than A:, press F3 and BACKSPACE to remove the reference to

drive A:, and enter the correct path. For example: d:\products\411_upg\nlskit.

5. Select Novell Licensing Services (NLS) Installation Kit, and press ENTER.

6. Verify that the check box is checked, and press F10.

7. If SETUPNLS detects an old schema in the NDS database, the screen displays the following: "Old NLS Schema Extensions Detected. Convert Old NLS Objects?"

   a. Select Yes. If No is selected, the NetWare licenses (if there are any) may have to be reinstalled.

   b. If SETUPNLS detects an old schema, you are prompted to log in as administrator for the NDS tree. Otherwise, SETUPNLS prompts you to log in as administrator of the container. Enter the administrator's complete name (for example, admin.xyz) and password.

8. Select Yes to allow the setup program to make modifications.

9. SETUPNLS displays a dialog box containing the following question: "Do You Wish to Remove Old Schema Extensions?" If old NLS objects did not convert, select No. Otherwise, select Yes.

10. Press ENTER to complete the installation.

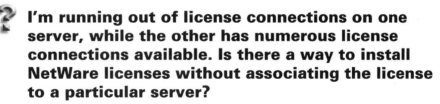

I'm running out of license connections on one server, while the other has numerous license connections available. Is there a way to install NetWare licenses without associating the license to a particular server?

Yes, if you install a Master License Agreement (MLA) instead of the traditional NetWare license. MLAs are container/tree-based, whereas traditional NetWare licenses are server/connection-based.

Chapter 4

Managing the
Server Environment

Answer Topics!

 **SERVER MAINTENANCE 87**

? Permanently removing a server
? Protecting the server

REMOTE SERVER MANAGEMENT 88

? Accessing the GUI interface for
  RCONJ.EXE
? Running RCONJ.EXE without mapping a
  drive
? Understanding the RCONSOLE Windows
  warning screen
? Using RCONSOLEJ
? Rebooting the server during a remote
  session
? Using RCONSOLE keys
? Using RCONAG6.EXE passwords
? Encrypting passwords
? Resolving RCONJ.EXE failures

NOVELL LICENSE SERVICE (NLS) 92

? Dealing with errors that indicate no license
  is installed
? Viewing Maximum License Connections
? Moving a license object
? Comparing Novell Licensing Service and
  Master License Agreement
? Installing Master License Agreements
  multiple times

**CONSOLEONE AND GUI SERVER
MANAGEMENT 93**

? Resolving ConsoleOne performance issues
? Using the mouse and screen saver with
  ConsoleOne
? Initializing ConsoleOne
? Updating the display in ConsoleOne
? Troubleshooting when ConsoleOne
  doesn't see the NDS tree

? Disabling GUI during server bootup

? Using Secure Console and ConsoleOne

? Running ConsoleOne on a workstation

? Troubleshooting ConsoleOne on a workstation

? Changing the GUI background

PROTOCOL MANAGEMENT 96

? Understanding Compatibility Mode

? Advertising services in a mixed IP/IPX environment

? Changing the protocol load order

? Comparing NetWare/IP and Pure IP

? Understanding iMac client support for Pure IP

? Understanding DOS client support for Pure IP

? Running NetWare 5 in IP without UDP

? Using the correct ports for NetWare 5

? Understanding TCP Defend Land and SYN Attacks

? Troubleshooting remote TCP/IP hosts

? Troubleshooting remote IPX routers

VIRTUAL MEMORY 100

? Understanding swap file location and size

? Learning how NetWare decides what to swap to disk

? Changing the swap file location

? Setting the size of a swap file

? Gauging performance issues relating to virtual memory swapping

? Understanding Virtual memory disk thrashing

? Resolving disk thrashing issues

SERVER PROCESSORS 102

? Supporting multiprocessors with NetWare 5

? Using NetWare 4.11 NLMs with NetWare 5

? Using server NLMs with multiple processors

? Defining I_2O

TROUBLESHOOTING THE SERVER 104

? Bringing down the file server when the server console screen hangs

? Handling a crashed NetWare 5 server

? Performing a core dump

? Saving a core dump

? Viewing a core dump

? Checking the patches on your server

? Obtaining configuration information on your server

? Understanding abends

? Troubleshooting abends

? Configuring your Server for a new mouse

? Installing a higher-resolution video card on a server

? Manually configuring your video card on a server

? Using the DISPLAY SERVERS and DISPLAY NETWORKS commands

? Loading NLMs with long pathnames

OPTIMIZING THE SERVER ENVIRONMENT 113

? Using the SET commands

? Viewing current memory on your server

? Changing SET commands to the default

? Viewing current SET commands on the server

? Editing configuration boot files

? Learning when to add more RAM to your NetWare 5 server

? Understanding Packet Burst Protocol

? Disabling Packet Burst Protocol

? Understanding Large Internet Packet (LIP)

? Enabling LIP on an Ethernet network

? Verifying memory space for specific NLMs

? Lowering processor utilization on a NetWare 5 server

SERVER SHORTCUTS 125

? Learning server console commands

? Creating shortcuts for console commands

? Automating the loading of remote management NLMs

? Recalling server commands

SCREEN SAVERS 127

? Locking the server keyboard

? Viewing current screen saver settings on server

? Initiating the screen saver immediately

? Using SCRSAVER.NLM without locking the keyboard

GARBAGE COLLECTION 128

? Forcing the garbage collection process

? Setting the garbage collection frequency

? Scheduling the garbage collection process

STORAGE MANAGEMENT AND BACKUP 129

? Understanding different types of backup strategies

? Backing up NetWare 5 with third-party support

? Understanding the rights needed to back up servers

? Understanding Novell SMS

? Understanding NWBACKUP features

? Understanding the NWBACKUP process

? Backing up DOS workstations with TSAs

? Communicating with the server

NOVELL ENCRYPTION AND PUBLIC KEY SECURITY 131

? Understanding what a Key Material object is

? Understanding applications that require Key Material objects

? Understanding certificate authorities

? Understanding Secure Sockets Layer

? Understanding RSA security

? Understanding the purpose of PKI Services

? Understanding the PKI process

? Using PKI Services features

LIGHTWEIGHT DIRECTORY ACCESS PROTOCOL (LDAP) FOR NDS SERVICES 134

? Understanding LDAP functionality

? Configuring LDAP on NetWare 5

? Supporting LDAP

? Configuring LDAP on Microsoft's Outlook Express

? Handling LDAP client errors

SERVICE LOCATION PROTOCOL (SLP) 140

? Understanding SLP functionality

? Comparing SLP and SAP

? Controlling SLP with server settings

? Understanding SLP Scope Container objects

? Setting SLP settings at the client

? Understanding scoping

NOVELL INTERNET ACCESS SERVER (NIAS) 144

? Using the correct multiport serial card

? Configuring NIAS for IP

? Using dialers with NIAS

? Monitoring NIAS

Managing the Server Environment @ a Glance

This chapter covers a wide variety of new and existing features in NetWare 5. We will discuss everything from maintaining servers to understanding how Service Location Protocol (SLP) works in replacement of Service Advertising Protocol (SAP). The topics in this chapter are particularly difficult to cover because they are so vast. However, this chapter will show you virtually everything you want to know about managing the server. The following topics will be discussed:

- **Server Maintenance** discusses removing a server from a tree to protecting your server from tampering.

- **Remote Server Management** explains the new features of RCONJ and how to secure remote control to your servers.

- **Novell License Service (NLS)** identifies the issues dealing with Novell License Service. Also, Chapter 7 gives more information on this service.

- **ConsoleOne and GUI Server Management** discusses the benefits and drawbacks of using ConsoleOne and GUI applications on a server. This section also discusses troubleshooting issues regarding ConsoleOne.

- **Protocol Management** assists you in answering questions about protocol prioritization, Compatibility Mode, and mixed-protocol environments. We will also cover the difference between NetWare/IP and Pure IP and discuss IP client support plus tips and tricks to optimize your IP environment.

- **Virtual Memory** explains how Novell literally redesigned its kernel to take advantage of disk swapping and memory optimization.

- **Server Processors** focuses on Novell's enhancements to its multiprocessing feature and limitations.

- **Troubleshooting the Server** offers tips and tricks to use to figure out what problems can happen with NetWare 5 and how to fix them.

Optimizing the Server Environment answers questions about optimizing your server with SET commands and understanding what to look for before performance degradation occurs.

Server Shortcuts covers how to create alias commands on the server and automate server tasks.

Screen Savers explains how to secure your console with the screen saver and the different loading options you can use for it.

Garbage Collection covers the garbage collection process and how to create a schedule for it. If you are a beginner in NetWare, you may think this is a strange section, but it is extremely useful in the NetWare environment.

Storage Management and Backup answers questions that relate to backing up your server with NWBACKUP or a third-party backup program as well as addressing the rights you need to back up your server.

Novell Encryption and Public Key Security explains the new security features in NetWare 5. These features are still going through a lot of development at this time; however, it can save you money, especially if you are thinking about doing electronic commerce or LDAP.

Lightweight Directory Access Protocol (LDAP) for NDS Services explains how to configure LDAP on your server and client as well as troubleshooting problems that can occur.

Service Location Protocol (SLP) describes the benefits of using SLP in an IP environment. We will discuss what the differences are between Service Advertising Protocol (SAP) and SLP, as well as multicasting versus broadcasting. Customers have complained to Novell about SAP, and Novell has answered with this solution.

Novell Internet Access Server (NIAS) explains how to configure your server to establish remote communication via IP. We will also discuss client support for NIAS.

SERVER MAINTENANCE

 I have an old 486 server that I would like to remove permanently from my NetWare 5 tree? What is the best way to do this?

Before bringing a server down permanently, it is important to maintain the integrity of NDS and properly remove any references to the server and its volumes. Perform the following steps at the server console:

1. Type **NWCONFIG** and press ENTER.
2. Highlight Directory Options and press ENTER.
3. Highlight Remove Directory Services from this Server and press ENTER.
4. After reading the warning, press ENTER.
5. Answer Yes to Remove Directory Services.
6. Log in to Directory Services as Admin. You need to provide a fully distinguished name for Admin in the Administrator Name field. Then type the Admin password in the password field and press ENTER.
7. Press ENTER to proceed with the removal of NDS from this server.
8. Press ENTER to confirm the fully distinguished name of the server Placeholder object.
9. Press ENTER to remove from the [Root] down.
10. Press ENTER at the confirmation screen telling you that Directory Services was successfully removed.
11. Press ALT-F10 to exit NWCONFIG and press ENTER.

 How can I protect my NetWare server from malicious tampering?

The best way to protect your server is to lock it up in a room with secure or limited access to users. The following are other ways to protect your server:

● Use the SECURE CONSOLE command. SECURE CONSOLE prohibits the loading of NetWare Loadable

Modules (NLMs) from any directory except the
SYS:SYSTEM directory. It also prevents unauthorized
users from changing the server's date and/or time.

● Use the SCRSAVER.NLM keyboard locking feature. Use
the SCRSAVER ENABLE LOCK feature so that anyone
trying to access the server console must provide Admin
name and password before access is granted.

● Be sure to add a secure password to RCONSOLE and
RCONAG6. The password is required whenever
remote access to the server console is attempted. You
can also generate an encrypted password to RCONSOLE
and RCONAG6.

REMOTE SERVER MANAGEMENT

I'm using RCONJ.EXE to remotely access my server and I can't get to the GUI interface. Why?

This is working as designed. When you're using RCONJ.EXE
or RCONSOLE.EXE, you will not be able to access the GUI
console screens.

Can I run RCONJ.EXE without having to map a drive to a server?

Yes. You need to copy all files and the SYS:PUBLIC\MGMT
directory and install the Java Runtime Environment (JRE)
on your PC.

Is there a way to remove the warning in Windows that comes up when using RCONSOLE?

RCONSOLE.EXE is launched through the RCONSOLE.PIF
file when it is started from within the NetWare
Administrator or Windows program. RCONSOLE.PIF is
programmed to warn administrators to exit Windows before
running, since RCONSOLE is a DOS executable program. To
configure the RCONSOLE.PIF file for the warning message
to go away, follow these steps:

1. Flag the SYS:PUBLIC\RCONSOLE.EXE file with a
read/write attribute.

2. View the properties of the RCONSOLE.EXE file using Windows Explorer.

3. Click the Program folder.

4. Click Advanced.

5. Click Prevent MS-DOS-Based Programs from Detecting Windows.

6. Unmark Suggest MS-DOS Mode as necessary.

7. Click OK twice.

8. An RCONSOLE.PIF is now placed in your Windows directory, and you can now execute RCONSOLE without the warning message.

 My workstation is set up as IP-only. Therefore I am unable to use RCONSOLE.EXE to remotely manage my server. How do I use RCONSOLEJ?

First, you must set up the server to allow RCONSOLEJ connections. At the server console, follow these steps:

1. Type **RCONAG6** and press ENTER.

2. Type the password that will be used to remotely access the server console and press ENTER. This password is case-sensitive.

3. Press ENTER to accept the default TCP port number 2034.

4. Press ENTER to accept the default SPX port number 16800.

Then, at the workstation, follow the steps in method 1 or method 2 next.

METHOD 1 There are several methods that can be used to remotely manage the server from an IP-only workstation. Using NWADMN32.EXE is one method. Log in as Admin and perform the following steps after NWADMN32.EXE is loaded:

1. Select Tools.

2. Select Pure IP Remote Console. (This will load RCONSOLEJ.)

3. Type the server IP address in the Server Address field.

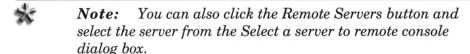

Note: *You can also click the Remote Servers button and select the server from the Select a server to remote console dialog box.*

4. Type the password in the Password field. This password is case-sensitive.

5. Click Connect.

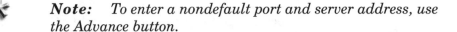

Note: *To enter a nondefault port and server address, use the Advance button.*

METHOD 2 Use SYS:PUBLIC\MGMT\CONMAN.EXE. Log in as Admin and perform the following steps after CONMAN.EXE is loaded:

1. Enter the IP address or the host name of the server in the Host field.

2. Enter the port in the Port field.

3. Enter the password in the Password field.

4. Click Connect.

Is it possible to bring the server down and have it reboot automatically during a remote session with NetWare 5?

Yes. You can have the server reboot by going to the server console screen, typing **RESTART SERVER**, and pressing ENTER. The RESTART SERVER command will down the server and then restart the server. You will temporarily lose your connection to the server until it is back up and running.

Tip: *You can prevent the execution of the AUTOEXEC.NCF by typing **RESTART SERVER –NA**. Prevent the execution of the STARTUP.NCF by typing **RESTART SERVER –NS**.*

You can also use RESET SERVER to cause the server to go down followed by a machine warm boot. However, the commands must be in the AUTOEXEC.BAT file to automatically initialize SERVER.EXE from the C:\NWSERVER directory.

Another method is to use the SHUTDOWN command from TOOLBOX.NLM version 2 or greater. You can download this utility (EBOX1.EXE or greater) from the Web at support.novell.com. Once TOOLBOX.NLM is loaded on the server, you simply type **SHUTDOWN** and press ENTER at the server console during a remote session.

What function keys are available during an RCONSOLE session?

The following table lists the function keys available in RCONSOLE:

Keys	Purpose
ALT-F1	Displays the Available Options menu
ALT-F2	Ends the RCONSOLE session
ALT-F3	Moves the display forward through the server console screens
ALT-F4	Moves the display backward through the server console screens
ALT-F5	Displays the network and workstation address for the server

Are passwords used with RCONAG6 case-sensitive?

Yes, passwords are case-sensitive in RCONAG6.

How do I encrypt passwords for RCONAG6?

Perform the following steps at the server console:

1. Type **LOAD RCONAG6 ENCRYPT**.
2. Type the desired password and press ENTER.
3. Type the TCP port number or accept the default TCP port, and press ENTER.
4. Type the SPX port number or accept the default SPX port, and press ENTER.

 Note: *If you want to run RCONAG6 with encryption via the command line, type* **LOAD RCONAG6 –E tcp port spx port** *and press* ENTER.

RCONJ.EXE fails if I do not have a drive mapping to the server. What is wrong?

If you do not have Java Runtime Environment (JRE) on the workstation, a drive letter mapping to the server is needed if you want to run RCONJ.EXE. This is working as designed.

NOVELL LICENSE SERVICE (NLS)

My server is beeping every second indicating that there is no license installed. I went into NWCONFIG and noticed that licenses are installed. What could be the problem?

The server base license may not be assigned to a server. Assign a server using the NLS Manager or NetWare Administrator utility.

Since Maximum License Connections is no longer on MONITOR's general information screen, how do I know what my maximum license connections are?

NetWare 5 prevents you from being able to view your license connections within MONITOR. Licenses are kept in NDS and must be viewed from the tree. Perform the following steps to view your license connections:

1. Open SYS:PUBLIC\NW32\NWADMN32.EXE.
2. Right-click the License object.
3. Select Details. (The General Informant window will give you all of the information about the license.)

 Note: *To find all information about your licenses, you can also run SYS:PUBLIC\WIN32\NLSMAN32.EXE.*

By adding the total of each installed connection license from each connection License object, you will get Maximum License Connections available for all NetWare 5 servers in the tree.

Can I move License objects?

Yes. License objects can be moved to another location using NWADMN32.EXE as long as the associated NLS_LSP_*servername* object is moved with it to the same destination.

What's the difference between an MLA license and an NLS license?

A Master License Agreement (MLA) can also be considered as a site license. These licenses are generic, nonrestricted licenses that allow administrators to install the license on multiple servers without the fear of any duplicate license messages. All NetWare servers in this environment report the same serial number.

Novell Licensing Service (NLS) licenses are restricted licenses that are more common in everyday environments. These licenses require a unique serial number for each server.

How many times can I install MLA licensing?

Licenses can be installed multiple times within a tree as long as the licenses do not conflict with each other.

CONSOLEONE AND GUI SERVER MANAGEMENT

Why is ConsoleOne so slow?

The minimum recommended memory for running the ConsoleOne management utility on the server is 128MB of server memory with at least 200 MHz of CPU power. Network management with ConsoleOne will be very frustrating if these requirements are not met.

In addition, ConsoleOne and the common GUI shell (known as the Graphical Console screen or the NetWare GUI) are written to disk to conserve physical memory and other server resources after 15 minutes of nonuse. If you are using the ALT-ESC keys to thumb through the server console screens, there may be a long pause when you pull up the Graphical Console screen. The reason for this is that the screen must first be reloaded into physical memory from the virtual memory swap file. Use CTRL-ESC instead of ALT-ESC to avoid this delay.

It may help to exit ConsoleOne when you are not using it, and reload it when needed.

The SCRSAVER.NLM kicks in and does not seem to detect my mouse movements when I am using ConsoleOne. Why?

Currently, this is working as designed. You can unload SCRSAVER.NLM if you are only using the mouse in the GUI screen.

How do I bring up ConsoleOne?

Type **C1START** and press ENTER at the server console. Another way to launch ConsoleOne is to type **STARTX** and press ENTER to load the server's GUI menu. Then select ConsoleOne from the Novell menu.

The files and directories I created after ConsoleOne starts fail to display in ConsoleOne. What can I do?

Press F5 to update the view.

ConsoleOne does not see the NDS tree. What can I do?

Add the statement **load SCMD.NLM** in the AUTOEXEC.NCF file after the LOAD and BIND statements for TCP/IP, and restart the server.

How do I disable the GUI screen from loading when the server is booted?

To disable the Graphical Console screen from loading when the server comes up, edit the AUTOEXEC.NCF file. Place a

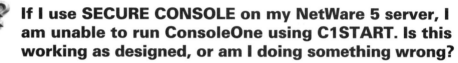

pound sign in front of the STARTX.NCF line to prevent the GUI Console splash screen loading at startup. The C1START.NCF line comes remarked out, preventing ConsoleOne from loading, as well as the GUI Console splash screen.

 Note: *The console screen will load for each Java application that needs it.*

Type **C1START** and press ENTER at the server console prompt whenever you want to load ConsoleOne.

If I use SECURE CONSOLE on my NetWare 5 server, I am unable to run ConsoleOne using C1START. Is this working as designed, or am I doing something wrong?

This is working as designed, since SECURE CONSOLE limits the loading of NLMs from SYS:SYSTEM only. The necessary ConsoleOne and GUI programs are located in the SYS:JAVA directory and its subdirectories.

How do I run ConsoleOne working on a PC?

To use ConsoleOne on your workstation, you have to run the CONSOLE1.EXE program from the SYS:PUBLIC\ MGMT directory.

You can also continue to run NWADMN32.EXE to administer your server. If you want to take over the server console from a workstation, you could load RCONAG6.NLM on your server and use RCONJ.EXE on your workstation to access the server and continue to administer ConsoleOne.

I can't get ConsoleOne to work on my workstation. What could be the problem?

Check to be sure the minimum requirements are met: ConsoleOne can run on Windows 95/98 or Windows NT client workstations. The workstation should have the NetWare 5 Client installed, a minimum of a 200 MHz processor, 64MB of actual memory, a 64MB swap file, 150 files allocated in the CONFIG.SYS file, and the monitor set to 800 × 600 resolution for easier screen manipulation.

 ## How do I change the server's GUI background to a background that I created?

You can change the server's GUI background by first copying your graphic file in XPM format to the SYS:JAVA\NWGFX\ PIXMAPS directory. Once the graphic file is copied, perform the following steps at the server console:

1. Click Novell.
2. Select Tools.
3. Click Backgrounds.
4. Select the desired background.
5. Click Test to display the background selected in step 4.
6. Click OK to change the background.

PROTOCOL MANAGEMENT

 ## What is Compatibility Mode?

The Compatibility Mode driver (CMD) has two parts, one for the server and one for the client. At the server, the CMD is viewed as a network adapter. You can bind both IP and IPX protocols to the CMD, and it acts like a router when IPX packets need to be sent within the server. Otherwise, the CMD patiently waits in the background, doing nothing and using no resources.

At the workstation, the CMD is invisible because it is an integral part of the new client. It provides the IP communications link required by an IP client. If NetWare 5 is set up as Pure IP, there is no need for IPX at the client.

The IPX Compatibility driver's task is to provide IPX connectivity over the IP network, allowing applications using the IPX stack for communications to function in an IP network. The IPX Compatibility driver also allows IP systems to communicate with IPX systems by using the services of Migration Agents. The IPX Compatibility driver treats the IP network as a virtual IPX network segment (a CMD network

segment), by encapsulating IPX datagrams inside UDP datagrams and by resolving RIP and SAP requests through the use of the Service Location Protocol (SLP).

In a mixed IP/IPX environment, when a service on the IP-only server, such as PSERVER, comes online, it takes five minutes for the service to be displayed on the Migration Agent's "DISPLAY SERVERS" table. During this time, no IPX servers know about the service and no IPX clients can browse the service. Why?

The Migration Agent is responsible for translating SLP information over to the IPX SAP/RIP table. It queries the SLP Service Agent to get all changes every five minutes. This interval is hard-coded and not configurable. The longest it can be is five minutes. The timing depends on when in the cycle the services come up. SLP and CMD clients and servers can see the service right away through an SLP query. Only the IPX servers and clients are affected.

I would like to have IP load first as my server boots, then IPX. How do I change the order in which protocols are loaded on my server?

Use the SET NCP PROTOCOL PREFERENCES command to change the order in which protocols are designated, no matter which protocol you bind first through the AUTOEXEC.NCF or INETCFG.NLM file. This setting will attempt to use the primary protocol assigned. If that protocol fails or does not respond, the server will switch to the secondary protocol.

A second method is to load the MONITOR utility at the server console. Select Server Parameters from the Available Options dialog box. Select NCP, highlight NCP Protocol Preferences, and press ENTER. Type in the order in which you want the protocols to be used by incoming service requests. Save this information to the NetWare Configuration file so it will be used each time the server is booted.

What is the difference between NetWare/IP and Pure IP?

NetWare/IP is IPX/SPX encapsulated with an IP wrapper around the protocol. Microsoft's TCP/IP environment within Windows NT 4 works similarly to NetWare/IP, with the exception that the NetBIOS protocol is encapsulated within IP.

Pure IP uses the TCP/IP suite for connectivity without any type of encapsulation. Pure IP supports the following standards:

- Dynamic Host Configuration Protocol (DHCP)
- Novell Directory Services (NDS)
- Domain Name Services (DNS)
- Service Location Protocol (SLP)
- WinSock2
- IP version 6
- Secure Sockets Layer (SSL)
- Network Time Protocol (NTP)

Can iMac clients use Pure IP?

Novell outsourced the Macintosh client to a company called Prosoft. Prosoft says that Pure IP support for iMac should be released in 1999. Prosoft's Web site can be found at www.prosofteng.com.

Can my DOS clients use Pure IP?

Currently there are no plans to support Pure IP on DOS clients. The workaround is to have both IPX/SPX and IP on your server until you can migrate to Windows 95/98 or Windows NT.

Can I run IP without any UDP traffic on my network?

Yes. To do this you must type **SET SLP TCP=ON** at your server. This will prevent your Service Location Protocol (SLP) from multicasting over the network. You must also use SLP for requests to Service Agents or Directory Agents directly. Please refer to the SLP section of this chapter for more information.

What TCP and UDP ports does NetWare 5 use?

Typically, administrators want to know what ports NetWare 5 uses so they can properly configure their firewalls to pass NetWare requests through. Here is a list of ports used by NetWare 5:

- **TCP 524 – (NCP requests)** Source port will be a high port (1024–65535)
- **UDP 427 – (SLP requests)** Source port will be the same (427)
- **TCP 427 – (SLP requests)** Source port will be the same (427)
- **TCP 2302 – (CMD)** Source port will be the same (2302)
- **UDP 2645 – (CMD)** Source port will be the same (2645)

Note: *All communication destined for an IPX device through a Migration Agent (MA) will use UDP packets. This means that running NetWare 5 with Compatibility Mode must require multicast UDP packets across your network.*

What do the TCP Defend Land Attacks and TCP Defend SYN Attacks do for me?

TCP Defend Land Attacks and TCP Defend SYN Attacks provide protection from hacks into the TCP/IP protocol, which can occur on *any* platform. Typically, these types of attacks can be configured through a firewall before an intruder even reaches the servers. Turn these settings off if your firewall provides this security feature.

How can I determine whether a remote TCP/IP host is available from my NetWare 5 server console?

Perform an echo test to see if the TCP/IP host is reachable by these following steps at the server console:

1. Type **PING** and press ENTER.

2. Type the remote TCP/IP host address in the Host Name field and press ENTER.

3. Type the number of seconds between each check in the Seconds to Pause Between Pings field.

4. Type the packet size to be transmitted in the IP Packet Size to Send in Bytes field.

5. Press ESC.

6. Check the received column for incoming echo reply packets.

How can I determine whether a remote IPX router is available from my NetWare 5 server console?

You can run an IPX Echo test to determine whether an IPX router is reachable from the NetWare 5 console with IPXPING.NLM. Perform the following:

1. Type **IPXPING** and press ENTER.

2. Type the target router address in the Network field and press ENTER.

3. Type the node address of the target router you want to ping, and press ENTER.

4. Press ESC to start pinging.

VIRTUAL MEMORY

How large is the virtual memory swap file and where is it stored?

Virtual memory allots a 2MB swap file that is located at the root of the SYS volume. The size of the swap file increases and decreases, depending on the number of server applications that are running and how much overall memory is needed by the system to maintain other server applications and users.

How does virtual memory decide what files will be swapped to disk?

NetWare swaps the least recently used (LRU) data out of physical memory onto the hard disk when it discovers memory resources are low. If the data is needed again, it is returned to physical memory.

Can I move the virtual memory swap file to a volume other than the SYS volume?

Yes. To move the swap file to the DATA volume, type the following command at the server console:

SWAP ADD DATA

To remove the SYS volume's swap file, type the following at the server console:

SWAP DELETE SYS

Then type **SWAP** at the server console and press ENTER to view the new swap file information.

Caution: *The swap file is deleted when a volume is dismounted. You must recreate the swap file when the volume is remounted. Use the AUTOEXEC.NCF file to automate this process each time the server is restarted.*

How can I set the size of the virtual memory swap file?

The SWAP command allows you to change the size of the virtual memory swap file. Suppose you wanted to change the minimum and maximum swap file size for the DATA volume. To set a minimum swap file size of 6MB and a maximum size of 1GB, enter the following at the server console:

SWAP PARAMETER DATA MIN = 6 MAX = 1000

Will I lose performance from applications written out to the disk with virtual memory?

If your system does not have enough physical memory to handle all of the needs of the programs you are running, parts of the program will be written out to the swap file, which does affect performance.

As a general performance guideline, it is recommended that applications should not page out to the swap file more than twice the physical memory that you have in the server.

What is virtual memory disk thrashing?

Disk thrashing occurs when server memory is extremely low and the system spends most of its time swapping memory to and from disk, therefore placing other server processes on hold. Virtual memory allows the server to keep running when memory is extremely low. However, the server is extremely slow when disk thrashing occurs.

What should I do if I notice that my server is experiencing disk thrashing?

Add more RAM when disk thrashing occurs. It's important to remember that virtual memory does not make up for a server's lack of memory. However, with adequate memory available, virtual memory can keep the server running and prevent server operation failures or abends.

SERVER PROCESSORS

I have a server with two processors. Does NetWare 5 support multiple processors?

Yes. NetWare 5 supports up to 32 processors per server. Future releases of NetWare 5 may support more processors.

I had several NLMs written to work with symmetrical multiprocessing (SMP) for my NetWare 4.11 server. Will I be able to use them in NetWare 5?

Yes. Server-based NLMs that have been written to work on SMP NetWare 4.11 will also work with NetWare 5's Multi-Processing Kernel (MPK) without modification.

How can I tell if a certain NLM will take advantage of the Multi-Processing Kernel?

If you have the Developer Option SET parameter set to ON (default is OFF), NLMs that don't take advantage of MPK multithreading capabilities will give the following information shown in green as they load on the server:

modulename does not have any XDC data.

What is I₂O?

Some redundant array of independent disks (RAID) controllers, Asynchronous Transfer Mode (ATM) controllers, and network boards support the Intelligent I/O (I₂O) Architecture Specification, which is an open architecture for developing device drivers that can offload considerable I/O processing from the main CPU(s). I₂O functions independent of operating systems, processor platforms, or the system I/O bus. I₂O allows the server's CPU to spend its time performing other functions and services that don't involve interrupt processing, increasing a server's I/O ability. NetWare 5 will automatically detect the server's I₂O hardware, such as I₂O-aware motherboards and network boards.

TROUBLESHOOTING THE SERVER

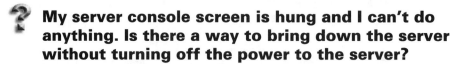**My server console screen is hung and I can't do anything. Is there a way to bring down the server without turning off the power to the server?**

Yes. You can use the CTRL-ALT-ESC key sequence to gracefully down the server if the server console is hung. You will see a screen that gives you the following two options:

● Down the file server and exit to DOS.

● Cancel the Volume Mount.

Type **1** and press ENTER to down the server. You will be asked again if you want to down the server and exit to DOS. Type **Y** and press ENTER.

My NetWare 5 server crashed and will not boot up anymore. What should I do now?

Perform the following steps to ensure that all other servers can synchronize properly until the crashed server can be reinserted into the NDS tree:

1. Be sure Time Synchronization is established on the network. Type **DSREPAIR** and press ENTER at the server console.

2. Highlight Time Synchronization and press ENTER. All servers should report that time is in sync.

3. Ensure that a Master replica exists for each partition in the tree. If the crashed server contained a Master replica of any partition, another server with a read-write replica must be selected for its read-write replica to become the new Master replica.

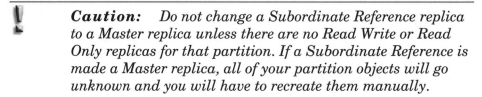

Caution: *Do not change a Subordinate Reference replica to a Master replica unless there are no Read Write or Read Only replicas for that partition. If a Subordinate Reference is made a Master replica, all of your partition objects will go unknown and you will have to recreate them manually.*

4. Delete the crashed Server object using NDS Manager. Deleting the Server object removes the server from the replica rings and from the tables each server maintains in the tree. Wait some time after deleting the Server object before executing step 5.

 Note: *Make sure you reinstall the server into the same context in which it previously existed.*

5. Check whether the server has been removed from each replica ring in which it was a member. This will ensure that each ring is consistent and valid. To check the replica ring:

    a. Type **LOAD DSREPAIR -A** and press ENTER at the server console.

    b. Select Advanced Options, and then select Replica and Partition Operations.

    c. Highlight each replica one at a time and press ENTER.

    d. Select View Replica Ring. If the crashed server name appears in the list of partition replicas and more than an hour has passed since you performed step 4, you should remove the server from the ring. To remove the server from the replica ring:

        1. Highlight the crashed server name and press ENTER. Select Remove This Server from the Replica Ring.

        2. Complete this step for each replica that the crashed server contained.

6. Using NWADMN32.EXE, delete the Volume objects corresponding to the crashed server. At this point, all references to the crashed server should be gone.

7. Make sure all remaining servers are synchronized. You can use DSREPAIR and the Report Synchronization Status option to make sure each server is synchronized within the last 30 minutes.

8. If necessary, reinstall NetWare and NDS on the crashed server.

 Note: *Recreate any print queues referring to this server's Volume object(s). User file system rights must be restored from backup. Otherwise you will need to reassign file system rights.*

What is a core dump?

Core dump, *image dump,* and *memory dump* are terms used to describe the process of downloading the contents of your server's memory to a file. The core dump file is used by Novell Technical Support to help analyze and troubleshoot various server problems.

You will need an open support incident with Novell Technical Support before sending the core dump. At that time you will be given a location to which to send your core dump file by FTP or an address where you can mail a tape.

 Note: *Do not automatically take a core dump. Wait until a Technical Support Engineer instructs you to do so. Be sure all patches have been installed on your server prior to performing a core dump.*

How do I save the core dump image? Can I send a core dump to another server?

You can save the core dump image to a floppy, a DOS partition of the server's hard disk, or to another server. You can also force a core dump, such as during a server abend, by using the OS internal debugger program. To break into the debugger, simultaneously press LEFT-SHIFT, RIGHT-SHIFT, ALT, and ESC. You can use the following commands in the debugger:

- **.c** Force a core dump
- **q** Quit to DOS
- **h** Help

Sending a core dump file to another server is usually the fastest way to perform a core dump. Use the NETALIVE.NLM file that comes with TABND2A.EXE. TABND2A.EXE can be downloaded from support.novell.com.

The problem server must have an additional Ethernet network card installed. This card enables the server to have a client connection to a second server. Boot the server as a client and log in to the other server, which becomes the destination for the image file. After connecting as a client, start the computer as a server.

Once the problem server is up, load NETALIVE and direct it to save the core dump to a location on the other server.

You can also use IMGCOPY.NLM, which also comes with TABND2A.EXE. Imgcopy (Image Copy) is used to transfer a core dump that has been initially copied to your server's DOS partition and then to a NetWare volume. This method usually allows you to bring your server up more quickly.

How can I view the results of a core dump?

Use the new VDB5.EXE file to look at the NetWare 5 core dumps.

Note: *The VDB for NetWare 4.x does not support NetWare 5.*

To get into the debugger, at the server console, press LEFT SHIFT-RIGHT SHIFT-ALT-ESC at the same time.

Caution: *All server activity is stopped when in debug mode.*

The following is a list of debugger commands:

- **h or .h**   Pull up Help
- **?**   Instruction pointer
- **Dds**   Dump the stack
- **Sw**   Perform a stack walk
- **L**   Write to the abend log
- **V**   View the different console screen states before the server crash
- **.m**   Display the modules and their versions

●   **.c**   Perform a core dump, with a new mini core dump feature added for times when you don't have enough disk space for a full core dump

Is there a quick way to determine what patches if any have been installed on my NetWare 5 server?

A quick way to assess the patches that have been installed on your NetWare 5 server is to type **PATCHES** and press ENTER at the server console. This will provide a list of installed patches and their version numbers.

Note: *If no patches are installed on the server, you will receive an error message of ??Unknown command?? when executing PATCHES at the server console.*

Is there a fast way to gather configuration information about my NetWare 5 server?

Yes. CONFIG.NLM is an invaluable tool for quickly collecting comprehensive data on your server's configuration. It is included in the TABND2.EXE or higher utility. TABND2A.EXE is used to troubleshoot server abends and can be downloaded from support.novell.com.

Once the TABND2A.EXE files are extracted, you can copy CONFIG.NLM to the SYS:SYSTEM directory. Then from the server console, type **LOAD CONFIG** and press ENTER. CONFIG.NLM will create the SYS:SYSTEM\ CONFIG.TXT file, which includes information about your server's configuration.

You can use CFGREADR.EXE (Config reader) version 2.66 or above or any text editor to view CONFIG.TXT information. CFGREADR.EXE can be downloaded from support.novell.com.

Tip: *CFGREADR.EXE also offers suggestions on how you can optimize your NetWare 5 server.*

What is an abend?

The term *abend* means any software or processor exception in which the server or a server process hangs or locks. Abend

stands for *abnormal end* of program. The primary reason abends occur is to ensure the stability and integrity of the internal operating system data. Therefore, abends protect the operating system against data corruption.

When an abend message appears on the server console, either NetWare or the server CPU has detected a critical error condition or fault. NetWare then displays the abend message on the server console.

What should I do if I receive an abend message on my NetWare 5 server console screen?

The following are a few troubleshooting steps you can perform to troubleshoot server abends:

- Most abends are corrected by installing all of the most current versions of the operating system (OS) patches, LAN, and disk drivers.

- NetWare OS patches can be downloaded from support.novell.com. An example OS patch name is NW5SP1.EXE (NW-NetWare 5, SP-Support Pack, 1-version 1). Install both the PT (pass test) and the IT (in test) OS patches.

- Download updated LAN and disk drivers from the respective vendors. It is very important to make sure you have the most current versions of all LAN and disk drivers installed.

- Look at the PATLST.TXT for NLMs that have been updated, and be sure to install all of the most current versions of NLMs on your server. PATLST.TXT can be downloaded from support.novell.com. Check with vendors other than Novell to update their NLMs as well.

- Read and decipher the abend message. An error condition, or fault, that is detected by the CPU is called a *processor exception*. An error condition that is detected by NetWare is called a *software exception*. Abend messages that are consistent sometimes indicate that software is at fault, while messages that are not consistent may indicate a hardware failure. Even though there is no rule about

abend messages, you want the data to point you in some troubleshooting direction.

● Look through all possible error logs and records you may be keeping about the server. Has new software or hardware (for example, new client software, backup programs, network boards, and so on) been added to the system?

● Perform a virus scan on all volumes linked to the server.

● Clean and reseat cards and cables. You might try adding one component at a time back to the system to eliminate potential conflicts. Use only hardware that you absolutely know works.

● Check SCSI ID, termination, interrupt, settings, and so on.

● Avoid interrupts 15, 2, and 9, in that order. The following is the order of interrupts from the highest priority to the lowest priority: 0, 1, (2/9), 10, 11, 12, 13, 14, 15, 3, 4, 5, 6, 7. Interrupt 0 is used for the system timer and 1 is used for the Keyboard Data Ready.

● Clean the system board and cards to remove dust and particles with antistatic air.

● Be sure the server fan is working properly.

● Can the abend be linked to any processes (for example, printing, database downloads, and so on) that were occurring at the time of the abend?

● Check ventilation and temperature in the server room. It should not be hot. Be sure static is not a problem.

● Use CONFIG.NLM to gather system configuration information quickly .

● Boot the server by typing **SERVER -NA** at the C:\NWSERVER prompt to prevent the AUTOEXEC.NCF from executing. Load each NLM manually, one at a time, to discover a possible offending NLM.

● Run the DSREPAIR utility, and/or the VREPAIR utility.

● Perform a core dump if instructed to do so by a Novell Technical Service Engineer.

● After all troubleshooting measures are exhausted, contact Novell Technical Services.

 Tip: *For a more comprehensive list of troubleshooting ideas, download TABND2A.EXE or higher from support.novell.com.*

 ## I had to purchase a new mouse for my server because the old mouse stopped working. How do I configure the server to use the new mouse?

The server must redetect your mouse. Depending on video card architecture, enter one the following commands at the server console:

VESA_RSP
DEF_RSP

VESA_RSP sets up for VESA SVGA video mode if possible; VGA16 video is default mode. Mouse probing is done. DEF_RSP sets up for default VGA16 video mode followed by mouse probing.

Note: *VESA_RSP and DEF_RSP also redetect your server's video driver. The video driver will be set back to the default resolution setting after executing VESA_RSP or DEF_RSP.*

 ## I purchased a new, higher-resolution video card for my server. How do I set it up on my NetWare 5 server?

Use the VESA_RSP command at the server console to redetect your VESA video card.

Note: *The VESA driver supports resolutions greater than 640 × 480; however, they must be configured manually.*

Default resolution for video cards conforming to VESA 1.2 or greater is 640 × 480 with 256 colors. A resolution of 640 × 480 with 16 colors is the default for video cards that do not conform to VESA 1.2 or greater.

Use the DEF_RSP command at the server console for default VGA16 video mode.

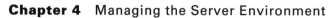 ### How do I manually configure the resolution for my server's video card?

If both the monitor and video card support resolutions higher than 640 × 480, you can use the display properties in the NetWare GUI to configure the resolution manually. Perform the following steps at the GUI server console:

1. Click Novell.
2. Select Tools.
3. Select Display Properties.
4. Select the desired resolution from the list of available resolutions.
5. Click Test.
6. Click OK to test the resolution mode.
7. Click OK if the test pattern displays properly.
8. Click OK to restart the GUI in order for the changes to take effect.

When I use the DISPLAY SERVERS and/or DISPLAY NETWORKS console command, why do I get the message "??? Unknown command ???"?

The DISPLAY NETWORKS and DISPLAY SERVERS console commands are IPX/SPX commands and function only when IPXSPX.NLM is loaded.

When I load NLMs with long pathnames, NetWare can't find the NLM. Why?

To emulate Windows 95/NT environments, NetWare 5 has changed the way it handles long filenames. You now have to

place a ~1 after an 8.3 filename instead of truncating the directory as you would have done in NetWare 4.*x*. Here is an example loading of an NLM in the PUBLIC\ RUNTHISNLM\ directory:

```
NetWare 4.x = LOAD \PUBLIC\RUNTHISN\RUNME.NLM
NetWare 5.x = LOAD \PUBLIC\RUNTHISN~1\RUNME.NLM
```

OPTIMIZING THE SERVER ENVIRONMENT

 I would like to optimize my NetWare 5 server. How do I know which SET parameters need adjusting on my server?

NetWare is self-tuning. Several server parameters are constantly adjusted on an as-needed basis by the operating system (for example, packet receive buffers, file cache buffers, directory cache buffers, service processes, and load balancing for multiple processors).

NetWare 5 defaults were chosen to provide high server performance and work in most environments. The file MONITOR.NLM can be used to track and log server statistics. MONITOR's General Information window provides the most important statistics that you can use to diagnose server performance.

Collecting daily server performance statistics will help you to better interpret the information in MONITOR. Sometimes understanding the data you've collected will require you to find out from other sources if what you are seeing is normal. For example, it is common for the server's utilization to stay at 100 percent for a few seconds or even a few minutes, or more. It is often only through experience that you will determine whether what you're seeing is normal or if it indicates a problem. To help you determine what is normal in your environment, you can determine your server's baseline (or average performance) through daily monitoring of your server. You can then adjust SET parameters as needed. It is important to establish what is normal for your environment so that you can accurately determine when you have a real problem and when the hardware and/or software is the real limitation and/or problem.

SET parameters should be adjusted from their default values in order to

- Optimize and tune the server.
- Correct weaknesses in the server's environment (for example, not enough resources are being allocated to handle incoming workstation requests to the server).
- Compensate temporarily for an inadequate subsystem, such as a slow hard disk. For example, you can use SET commands to boost the server's write ability to the disk temporarily .

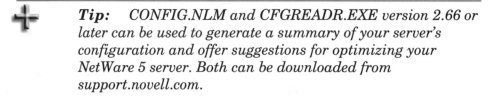

Tip: *CONFIG.NLM and CFGREADR.EXE version 2.66 or later can be used to generate a summary of your server's configuration and offer suggestions for optimizing your NetWare 5 server. Both can be downloaded from support.novell.com.*

How can I see how much memory is being recognized by NetWare?

Type **MEMORY** and press ENTER at the server console prompt to see how much memory is currently registered by NetWare.

Is there a way to change all SET parameters back to their default values quickly?

Yes. To change SET parameters back to their default values, type **RESET ENVIRONMENT** and press ENTER at the server console. You will be asked whether you want to change the value of each SET parameter back to its default value.

I would like to see what SET parameters have been configured on my NetWare 5 server. How can I do this?

Type **DISPLAY ENVIRONMENT** and press ENTER at the server console.

This command displays the current search paths and the current values of the SET parameters for the server. The name of the SET parameter(s) is displayed in white with the current value yellow. This command displays only SET parameters that are not marked as Hidden. To have this information saved to a file, type **SAVE ENVIRONMENT** *filename.ext* and press ENTER. The file will be stored at the root of the SYS volume.

You can also type **SET** and press ENTER at the server console. This displays a menu of settable configuration parameter categories. Select one of the categories, such as Communication, to view the corresponding SET parameters and values, along with a short description of the SET command.

To view SET parameters that have been changed from the default value, type **DISPLAY MODIFIED ENVIRONMENT** and press ENTER at the server console. You will see both the current setting as well as the default value. To have this information saved to a file, type **SAVE MODIFIED ENVIRONMENT** *filename.ext* and press ENTER. The file will be stored at the root of the SYS volume.

 ### How do I edit my server's configuration boot files?

NetWare 5 provides several tools to edit the AUTOEXEC.NCF and STARTUP.NCF files, such as NWCONFIG.NLM, ConsoleOne, and EDIT.NLM.

 Note: *The configuration files can also be edited with any text editor such as Notepad.*

To use ConsoleOne, perform the following steps at the server console:

1. If necessary, load ConsoleOne from the server's GUI interface by selecting Novell, then ConsoleOne.

2. Double-click the My Server icon.

3. Click Configuration Files in the left pane.

4. Double-click the configuration file to be edited in the right pane.

5. Once edits have been made, save changes by selecting File, and then Save from the menu bar.

To use NWCONFIG.NLM, perform the following steps at the server console:

1. Type **NWCONFIG** and press ENTER.
2. Highlight NCF Files Options and press ENTER.
3. Highlight either Edit AUTOEXEC.NCF File or Edit STARTUP.NCF File Options and press ENTER.
4. Make the necessary changes.
5. Press ESC.
6. Highlight Yes to save changes, and then exit NWCONFIG.

To use EDIT.NLM, perform the following steps at the server console:

1. Type **Edit AUTOEXEC.NCF** at the server console and press ENTER.
2. Make the necessary changes.
3. Press ESC.
4. Highlight Yes and press ENTER to save changes.
5. Press ESC, highlight Yes, and press ENTER to exit EDIT.NLM.

How do I know if I need to add more RAM to my server?

A slow network can often indicate that more RAM is needed in the server. However, this is not always the case. The following list describes a few items that you can check in MONITOR:

● **Long-term and short-term cache hits (on the General Information screen)** The percentage of long-term and short-term cache hits should not fall below 90 percent. If it does, you should add more RAM.

● **Least recently used (LRU) sitting time (select Disk Cache Utilization from Available Options)** The LRU sitting time should not drop below 15 minutes. If it does, you may need to add more RAM. Use the following table to assess your server's LRU as it relates to server RAM:

Above 40 minutes	Excellent.
20-40 minutes	Satisfactory to good (depending which number you're closer to).
Below 20 minutes	Below average. Keep an eye on it.
Under 5 minutes	Critical. There is definitely a problem with the server (unless it just came up 5 to 10 minutes ago, or if a heavy I/O operation just completed).

● **Cache buffer memory (select System Resources from Available Options)** If the amount of cache buffers drops below 40 percent, you should add more RAM to the server. You can also divide the total cache buffers by the original cache buffers (statistics found on the General Information window in MONITOR). The percentage can be used to assess cache buffer memory. Use the following table to assess your server's cache buffers percentage as it relates to server RAM:

Above 70%	Excellent. You're in good shape with the server memory.
50%–70%	Satisfactory.
40%–50%	Below average. Keep an eye on it. You may need to add memory to the server.
Below 40%	Critical. Add more memory. Adding memory should be your number one priority if this is your situation. Servers encounter high utilization, abends, lockups, and damage to data when memory is this low. Some programs are known to take server memory until it is depleted. When a server is below 40 percent cache buffers, RAM disappears fast, and data can be corrupted if the server abends.

 ## What is the Packet Burst Protocol?

The Packet Burst Protocol speeds up the transmission of large file reads and writes, resulting in a more efficient network. This is how Packet Burst works. A message is first broken up into fragments. As an example, suppose that the entire message consists of ten fragments. The transmitter then sends the ten fragments to the receiver. The fragments do not necessarily arrive in sequence; therefore the receiver must resequence the fragments into the original message as they arrive. An End of Message flag is received, and the receiver sends an acknowledgment to the sender. This acknowledgment includes a list of the fragments the receiver has not yet received. Let's say that fragment 7 was not received.

When the transmitter receives the acknowledgment, it retransmits only the message fragment(s) that the receiver claims are missing. In our example, only fragment 7 would be resent. This process continues until the receiver acknowledges that the complete message has been received.

Without Packet Burst, an acknowledgment would have to be sent for each fragment received. Therefore, there would be ten acknowledgments for ten fragments. Packet Burst can boost network performance up to 300 percent by eliminating the ping-pong effect and requiring only one acknowledgment for each burst of fragments.

Packet Burst is enabled by default at both the server and client in NetWare 5.

Can I disable Packet Burst from my server?

Yes. Novell Technical Services has a module called PBRSTOFF.NLM that will disable Packet Burst from the server. Go to support.novell.com to download the file PBRSTOFF.NLM. Without this file, you would need to disable Packet Burst from the client, since it is enabled at both the server and workstation by default.

What is Large Internet Packet (LIP)?

Large Internet Packet(LIP) is a feature that allows the workstation and server to communicate using the largest or maximum packet size that can be transmitted on a network with routers.

Token Ring networks allow packet sizes up to 4,202 bytes, while Ethernet networks will allow packet sizes up to 1,514 bytes. Therefore, network architecture determines the maximum allowable packet size. LIP enhances throughput on networks with routers by allowing the administrator to specify the largest allowable packet size.

However, if the server detects a router on the network, the packet size is set to a smaller 512 bytes. LIP overcomes this limitation by ignoring the router check during the packet size negotiation between the workstation and server.

LIP is automatically enabled at both the server and workstation.

I have an Ethernet network and I would like to enable Large Internet Packet (LIP) on my NetWare routers. How is this done?

Use the following SET command to enable LIP on your NetWare Router:

SET MAXIMUM PHYSICAL RECEIVE PACKET SIZE=1514

This command can be placed in the STARTUP.NCF file to ensure that it takes effect each time the server is booted. You will need to restart the server to implement this change. The SET command should be implemented on all servers in the network.

Note: *The default for Maximum Physical Receive Packet Size is 4,202 bytes. 4,202 bytes is the largest allowable packet size for Token Ring networks.*

I want to run a new NLM on my server, but I'm not sure I have sufficient memory to run it. How can I find out how much memory an NLM will require?

In general, memory needed for loading an NLM is more or less the same as the file size of the NLM. For precise memory information, you can use MONITOR to check the amount of memory before and after the NLM is loaded. Perform the following steps *before* loading the new NLM:

1. Type **MONITOR** and press ENTER.

2. Select System Resources and press ENTER.

3. Look at the percentage in bytes next to Cache Buffer Memory and write down the percentage value.

4. Now load the NLM in question.

5. Go back and check MONITOR's cache buffer memory percentage in System Resources.

The difference before and after loading the NLM is the approximate size of the NLM.

 Note: *Some NLMs will not load until other prerequisite NLMs are loaded. Therefore more memory is needed to load both the NLM and its prerequisite NLMs.*

 Note: *Some NLMs require more memory to be allocated as they are running. It's a good idea to test the NLM in a nonproduction environment to determine whether there are any potential NLM conflicts.*

 I've noticed that my NetWare 5 server is experiencing long periods of high utilization. What can I do to lower processor utilization?

Troubleshooting high utilization often requires patience, skill, and a little luck in some cases. Novell has released several Technical Information Documents (TIDs) that outline items to be checked when troubleshooting high utilization on your network. In addition, you can download HIGHUTL1.EXE (or later) for a comprehensive look at troubleshooting high utilization.

Server utilization in NetWare is measured as the amount of processor utilization. Processor utilization is the percentage of time the CPU is currently active. It can be normal for utilization to peak at 100 percent in some environments for short periods of time. The following conditions indicate that high utilization is indeed a problem

on your network and that performance will decline considerably. Check the following:

- Utilization peaks at 100 percent for 15 to 20 minutes or longer, possibly causing users to be disconnected from the server.
- User logins take a very long time.
- File copies take a very long time to complete.
- Applications fail or stop working.
- Switching screens at the file server console takes a long time.

Your server's utilization may be normal if you are not experiencing these signs.

The following items outline some of the most common solutions to problem high utilization:

- Load all current patches. Ensure that you are running the most current OS patches on your server. All LAN and disk drivers must also be current. LAN and disk drivers can be obtained from their respective hardware vendors.
- Reduce the number of printers using bindery emulation. A lot of bindery emulation can increase utilization. The following list gives some printing recommendations:

  - Make sure that no more than about 40 traditional NetWare printers are serviced from one server.

  - Make sure that third-party printing devices such as Intel's Netport and Hewlett Packard's JetDirect are set to be NDS-aware and that the firmware is current.

- Determine your server's baseline (average) performance to discover what is normal in your environment.
- Identify and remove any problem third-party NLMs. You can accomplish this by returning the server to a vanilla environment. Boot the server with the SERVER –NA command and load each NLM manually to see if a

particular module spikes processor utilization. Also use MONITOR to identify which NLMs are using the most processing power. Select Kernel from MONITOR's Available Options menu. Select Applications from the Kernel Options window. Select NetWare Applications and then press F4 to view the busiest threads. NLMs using the most processing power will display at the top of the screen.

- Ensure that there is adequate cache memory.
- Update client software version(s) (Client32, VLMs) to the latest available.
- Ensure that sufficient packet receive buffers (at the client) and service processes (at the server) are allocated for the conditions of your network.

 Note: *As network packets arrive from workstations, or disk reads or writes are done, there should be a buffer (a packet receive buffer) available to store the incoming request. Once the request is placed in a packet receive buffer, a service process must be available to take action on the request. Running out of packet receive buffers or service processes for more than a brief period will cause high utilization on the server, increased traffic on the network, and delay for the users.*

Modify the SET parameters as shown in the following table to reflect Novell's recommendations:

SET MINIMUM PACKET RECEIVE BUFFERS	2–3 per connection (the number of user connections, including other server and application connections, usually attached to that server—not the NetWare user license number on that server). This value can range from 10 to 2,000, with the default being 128.
SET MAXIMUM PACKET RECEIVE BUFFERS	4000. This value can range from 50 to 4294967295, with the default being 500.
SET MINIMUM DIRECTORY CACHE BUFFERS	2–3 per connection. This value can range from 10 to 4294967295, with the default being 150.

SET MAXIMUM DIRECTORY CACHE BUFFERS	4000. This value can range from 20 to 200000, with the default being 500.
SET DIRECTORY CACHE ALLOCATION WAIT TIME	0.5. This value can range from 0.1 to 120 seconds, with the default being 2.2.
SET MINIMUM SERVICE PROCESSES	1 per connection. This value can range from 10 to 500, with the default being 100.
SET MAXIMUM SERVICE PROCESSES	1000 (the maximum number allowed). This value can range from 500 to 1000, with the default being 500. If the server does not require an additional service process, it will not allocate more.
SET NEW SERVICE PROCESS WAIT TIME	0.3. This value can range from 0.3 to 20 seconds, with the default being 2.2.
SET UPGRADE LOW PRIORITY THREADS	Off.
SET PHYSICAL PACKET RECEIVE BUFFERS	Receive buffers are used to store incoming packets from each of the networks attached to a NetWare server. The Maximum Physical Receive Packet Size should be set according to the kind of network it is on. In most cases, this is 1524 bytes for Ethernet segments, 4540 bytes for Token Rings and FDDI, and 618 bytes for Arcnet and LocalTalk.

 Note: *The preceding guidelines are only general recommendations and may need to be adjusted to fit your server's usage baseline. For example, a server that has a large number of hits to the hard disk (for example, updating a database) may need more directory cache buffers.*

● Compression is set to run during the night between 12:00 A.M. and 6:00 A.M.. File compression and decompression will cause server utilization to peak. Directories that are flagged IC (immediate compress) can cause excessive compression and decompression during production hours. High utilization also occurs with compression if a volume is nearly full. To determine whether compression is the cause of high utilization, type **SET COMPRESS SCREEN=ON** at the console command line and watch the number of lines that are scrolling on the compression

screen. The lines per second indicate how busy compression is. The memory used by compression/decompression divided by 106K can tell you how many concurrent threads are compressing files currently. The number of concurrent compression threads can be adjusted with a SET parameter. Also, you can use the command SET DELETED FILES COMPRESSION OPTION = 2 to cause the immediate compression of files that have been deleted.

● Efficient tree design, partitioning, and replication are essential to avoid utilization problems. The size, type, and number of partition replicas can cause utilization problems if not managed properly. Check the total number of NDS objects residing in the partitions of that server. (Novell recommends no more than 3,000 to 5,000 objects in a partition.) NDS needs to keep synchronization among all servers in the replica ring. The more replicas there are of any partition, the more traffic there will be on the wire. (Novell recommends having at least three strategically placed replicas of each partition in the tree. This provides fault tolerance and allows for recovery of NDS if a database becomes corrupt.) Be sure the latest version of DS.NLM is running on all NetWare servers on the network. To troubleshoot possible NDS problems, load the server without directory services by typing **SERVER -NDB** at the C:\NWSERVER prompt. If directory services are causing the problem, type **LOAD DSREPAIR** and repair the database on this server.

   Tip: *DSREPAIR can be run on a SYS volume in which NDS is not opened or being used.*

● Adequate free blocks on your server's volumes are essential. A file that is deleted and purged leaves free space. A minimum of 1,000 free blocks on each NetWare volume should be maintained. To check how many free blocks your server has, go into MONITOR and select VOLUMES. Highlight the volume and then look at the statistic—FREE BLOCKS. You will need to press the TAB key to display the full statistics screen. If there are not at least 1,000 free blocks on the volume, run a PURGE /ALL command from the root of the volume from a client workstation. This will increase your volume's free space. If the server's utilization is so high that no one can log in, dismount the volume and run VREPAIR, selecting the Purge All Deleted Files option.

! *Caution:* *Purging deleted files will prevent the recovery of the files through the use of the Salvage feature in the NetWare Administrator utility.*

- If suballocation is in use on a volume, it should have a block size of 64K. The fastest and most efficient block size for volumes with suballocation enabled is 64K. You should also keep a minimum of 10–20 percent of the volume space free to prevent suballocation from going into aggressive mode.

- Check your disk subsystem statistics. If dirty cache buffers are consistently at or above 70 percent of the total cache buffers, upgrade to faster disk components if necessary.

- Ensure that the server has adequate RAM installed.

SERVER SHORTCUTS

I'm trying to learn all of the server console commands but sometimes I forget some of them. Is there a way to get help on console commands from the server console?

Yes. Type **HELP** and press ENTER at the console prompt for an alphabetical list of available console commands. For additional help on a particular console command like CONFIG, type **HELP CONFIG** and press ENTER.

Is there a way to create shortcuts for the console commands I use most of the time?

Yes. The ALIAS command allows you to create shorter and more easily remembered names for your most used console commands. Type **ALIAS** and press ENTER at the server

console prompt to see a list of the console commands that have already been given alias names.

The ALIAS command also allows you to set up your own shortcuts. Let's say you frequently use the DISPLAY SERVERS command and would like to use DSRV as a shortcut to invoke this command. To set up this shortcut, type the following at the server console:

ALIAS DSRV DISPLAY SERVERS

This will invoke the DISPLAY SERVERS command.

Caution: *Do not create an alias to call another alias. You may receive an UNKNOWN COMMAND ??? error if you try the command after downing the server.*

I would like to automate the loading of remote management NLMs using a batch file. Is it possible to create "batch-type" files for the server?

Yes. NetWare 5 server batch files must end with a .NCF extension. They can be created at the server console with the following commands:

1. Type **EDIT** *batch_ filename***.NCF** and press ENTER. For example, you could create a batch file named Remote by typing **EDIT REMOTE.NCF**. NCF files are stored in SYS:SYSTEM.
2. Highlight YES to create the new file and press ENTER.
3. Type the necessary commands.
4. Press ESC.
5. Highlight YES and press ENTER to save the NCF file.
6. To execute the NCF file, type the name of the NCF file you created in step 2 and press ENTER.

Is there a quick way to recall commands I've entered at the server console?

Commands you type at the NetWare server console are stored in the server's command queue so that you can recall them later and not have to retype lengthy strings of characters.

Once you've entered a command at the console screen, simply press the UP ARROW key to recall the previous console command at the prompt. Previous commands are shown each time the UP ARROW key is pressed. The DOWN ARROW will go backward if you skipped past the command with the UP ARROW. Once the command is displayed on the screen, you can use the LEFT and RIGHT ARROW keys, CONTROL-RIGHT and CONTROL-LEFT arrows, and HOME and END keys to modify the command.

SCREEN SAVERS

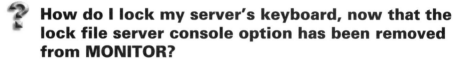 **How do I lock my server's keyboard, now that the lock file server console option has been removed from MONITOR?**

Lock the server keyboard by executing SCRSAVER.NLM as follows at the server console prompt:

SCRSAVER ENABLE LOCK

Enter multiple options on the same line by using semicolons to separate parameters. For example:

SCRSAVER ENABLE LOCK; DELAY=2

To know more about each setting/option, enter **SCRSAVER HELP** *[option]*.

Is it possible to view the screen saver's current settings on my NetWare 5 server?

Yes. To view the server's current screen saver settings, type **SCRSAVER STATUS** and press ENTER at the server console.

How can I initiate the server's screen saver immediately?

To activate the screen saver, type **SCRSAVER ACTIVATE** and press ENTER at the server console.

 **Can I use the screen saver without having to lock the keyboard?**

Yes. Enter the following at the server console prompt:

SCRSAVER ENABLE; DISABLE LOCK

GARBAGE COLLECTION

Is it possible to force the garbage collection process?

Yes. Load MONITOR from the server console. Select Virtual Memory, then Address Spaces. You can free address space memory with F4.

How often does the garbage collection process run?

Garbage collection runs every five minutes. Change this value by using the following SET command:

SET GARBAGE COLLECTION INTERVAL = *value in minutes*

Place this command in the STARTUP.NCF file to have it take effect each time the server boots.

Should I change how often garbage collection runs on my server?

Novell recommends leaving garbage collection parameters at the default values unless an NLM requires a specific change.

Garbage collection SET parameters are global, and a change will affect all NLM garbage collection. An adjustment for one NLM to improve its performance may adversely affect another NLM. For this reason, caution should be used in changing the default parameters for garbage collection.

STORAGE MANAGEMENT AND BACKUP

 What are the different backup strategies I can use to back up my server(s)?

The following table outlines the different backup strategies:

Full backup each day	Backs up all server data
Full backup with incremental backups	Backs up files that have been changed since the last backup, whether it was a full or incremental backup
Full backup with differential backups	Backs up files that have been changed since the last full backup

 Note: *Do not combine incremental with differential backups.*

The following tables are examples of weekly backups using the different types of backup methods.

Full Backups at Each Backup Session

SUN	MON	TUES	WED	THUR	FRI	SAT
Full	Full	Full	Full	Full	Full	Full

Full Backup Once a Week, Incremental Remaining 6 Days

SUN	MON	TUES	WED	THUR	FRI	SAT
Full	Incremental	Incremental	Incremental	Incremental	Incremental	Incremental

Full Backup Once a Week, Differential Remaining 6 Days

SUN	MON	TUES	WED	THUR	FRI	SAT
Full	Differential	Differential	Differential	Differential	Differential	Differential

 What third-party backup programs work with NetWare 5?

Go to developer.novell.com/npp to see a list of NetWare 5 certified backup products.

 What rights do I need to have in order to back up my server?

To back up the NetWare server file systems, you need Read and File Scan rights to the files. To restore files or the NDS tree, you must have Create rights as well. To back up NDS, you need the Browse object and Read property rights to the entire NDS tree.

The user must also know the target server and target workstation passwords.

 What is Novell's SMS?

SMS stands for Storage Management Services. SMS allows data to be stored (backed up) and retrieved (restored).

What does NWBACKUP allow you to back up?

You can back up the following with NWBACKUP:

- NetWare server's file system and DOS partition
- The NDS database
- GroupWise databases
- Windows 95 and Windows NT workstation files

How does the NWBACKUP process work?

NWBACKUP is comprised of a host server (the NetWare server on which the backup program resides) and a target (the NetWare server or workstation that contains the data to be backed up). A workstation is used to configure backup sessions using the NWBACK32 client-based utility.

NWBACKUP is comprised of a series of NLMs that run on the host server, which communicates with Target Service Agents (TSAs) on the target devices. NWBACKUP reads the information from the target and sends it to a storage device.

 What TSA do I use to back up my DOS workstation using the NetWare 5 NWBACKUP utility? I tried TSASMS.COM but received the following error: "TSASMS ERROR: Unable to load TSASMS. Unable to locate Server or unable to communicate with Server."

There is no NetWare 5 support for DOS workstation backup. You can use TSADOSP to back up the DOS partition of the NetWare Server.

NOVELL ENCRYPTION AND PUBLIC KEY SECURITY

 What is a Key Material object?

A Key Material object is a security object in NDS that contains a public key, private key, certificate, and certificate chain. The private key encodes a message to a NetWare server. The server then issues a public key to decode the message that was sent. This process allows the keys to be virtually unbreakable, since neither the keys nor the user's passwords are sent across the network. All keys that are created on the server remain on the server and cannot be transferred or modified. The following example shows how public and private keys work.

Suppose John wants to identify himself to a server. The server sends a random number, which John scrambles using his unique private key. The server then unscrambles the message using John's public key and compares it to the original random number it sent out. If the numbers match, the server has identified John.

 What applications require Key Material objects?

Currently, BorderManager, Lightweight Directory Access Protocol (LDAP) services for NDS, and Secure Sockets Layer (SSL) require the Key Material object to provide their security.

 ## What are certificate authorities (CAs)?

Certificate authorities are used to verify a person's identity or organization, as well as issue key pairs. CAs are used in conjunction with public and private keys to provide an additional level of security. These certificates can be internal to an organization or external. The following are some reasons why internal certificates (within NDS) would be used:

- Internal CAs are free and are managed internally without the need to pay a third-party vendor to manage them.
- An internal CA is compatible with other applications that are used within NDS, such as BorderManager and LDAP (mentioned later in this chapter).
- The network administrator can manage internal CAs.

External certificates can be used as follows:

- They can be compatible with other applications that are *not* NDS-compliant.
- They can carry liability protection.

Both types of CA can be used simultaneously in the NetWare 5 environment.

 ## What does Secure Sockets Layer (SSL) do?

The Secure Sockets Layer (SSL) protocol is installed when you select the Secure Authentication Service during the NetWare 5 installation. Its primary function is to exchange information between two devices using public key encryption. This protocol was drafted primarily by Netscape engineers in an effort to secure the Internet from tampering, eaves-dropping, and forgery between servers and clients. Therefore, SSL is available only for applications that are SSL-enabled across the Internet or intranet.

What is RSA security?

RSA (Rivest-Shamir-Adleman) is an algorithm used in a pair of encryption keys, so that output from one key can only be reversed by the other key.

What is the main purpose of using Novell Public Key Infrastructure Services (PKIS)?

The main function of PKI Services is to allow you to develop applications that require a high level of security, data encryption, and privacy, as well as to provide additional security if your server is exposed to the Internet or other open environments with great possibility of hacking.

How does PKI Services (PKIS) work?

PKI Services uses a matching pair of encryption and decryption keys to implement its security. Each key performs a one-way communication of data. Everyone has access to the public key, and the private key resides on each workstation. For more information on PKI Services keys, please refer to the question "What is a Key Material object?" earlier in this section.

What does PKI Services (PKIS) provide?

PKI Services allows administrators to enable public key encryption and certificate authorities (CAs) across their NetWare servers. Following are some of the features that PKI Services provides:

- Ability to integrate public key and certificate authorities through NDS.

- Certificate authorities generated by PKI Services are standardized to the X.509 version 3 standard, which is recognized internationally as providing public key and identity ownership.

- Ability to use a local certificate authority within NWADMN32.

- Ability to manage private keys through server applications.

LIGHTWEIGHT DIRECTORY ACCESS PROTOCOL (LDAP) FOR NDS SERVICES

 ## Why should I use LDAP?

The Lightweight Directory Access Protocol (LDAP) is becoming the standard directory service in the Internet community. Typically, many administrators use LDAP for their users to perform lookups of departmental phone numbers, e-mail addresses, and virtually any other type of user personal information located in NDS. For more information on LDAP, please refer to Chapter 10.

 ## How do you configure LDAP on a NetWare 5 server?

Configuring LDAP with security requires several objects to be created and assigned. The security objects mentioned in this question are described in detail earlier in this chapter.

To install LDAP, you must first have installed Secure Authentication Service and Novell PKI Services as mentioned previously in this chapter. You must also create a "proxy" user that your users would query NDS with. To create your LDAP services, follow these steps:

1. Log in as Admin and launch NWADMN32.

2. Right-click the Security object and select Create.

 Note: *The Security object is located at the top of the tree. If it is not present, Secure Authentication Services was not installed.*

3. Select the certificate authority and click OK.

4. Click Next to accept Standard, as shown next.

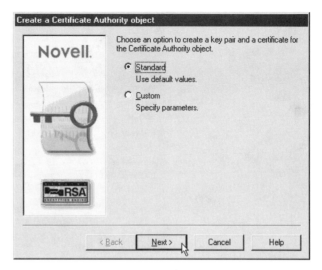

5. Now give the object a name, assign the server that will be the certificate authority, and click Finish.

   Now you must create a Key Material object:

6. Right-click the container that has LDAP objects and select Create.

7. Select the Key Material object and click OK.

8. Choose the Standard option and click Next.

9. Enter a unique name in the Key Pair Name field, verify that the server is correct, and click Finish.

10. Click OK to verify that the Key Material object has been created.

11. Refresh your screen and verify that your key is present.

    Getting closer to the end, now you must create an SSL certificate:

12. Double-click the LDAP server object in your container.

13. Click the Browse button next to the SSL Certificate field, select the key you created previously, and click OK, as shown next.

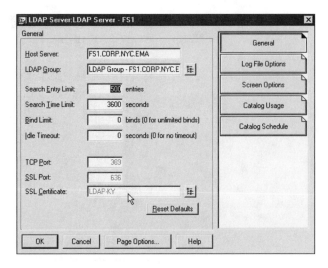

14. Double-click your LDAP Group object, which was created when you installed LDAP support.

15. At the Suffix entry, click the Browse button, select the container that will be searched, and click OK.

16. Next, go to the Proxy Username field, select the user that will be the secure user to log in as, and click OK.

 Note: *Make sure that this proxy user has no password restrictions. If a proxy user is not selected, any user can query NDS anonymously without the need of a username or password.*

---

17. Right-click the container where the objects are to be queried, select Trustees of This Object, and add the proxy user to the list.

18. Grant the proxy user Browse and Create object rights and Read property rights, as shown in the next illustration. Click OK when done.

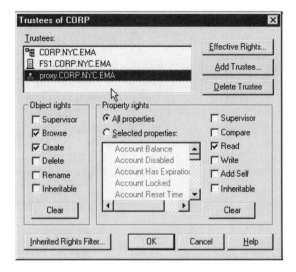

19. At this point your LDAP configuration is completed. Go to your NetWare 5 server and load NLDAP to initialize your new settings.

 What software supports LDAP?

Several software products on the market today support LDAP technology. The most popular ones are current versions of Microsoft Outlook, Netscape Communicator, and Novell GroupWise.

 My users have Outlook Express. How can I configure Outlook Express to look at my LDAP server?

Configuring your clients to search your LDAP server is quick and easy. The process of setting up LDAP configurations for one type of software can also be used with other types of LDAP client software. To configure Outlook Express, do the following:

1. Launch Outlook Express on the client.

2. Highlight the Tools menu and select Accounts.

3. Click your Directory Service tab, select Add, and then select Directory Service, as shown in the next illustration.

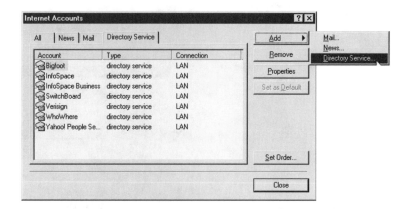

4. Type your host name or the IP address of the LDAP server you want to connect to.

5. Check the My LDAP Server Requires Me to Log On option and select Next.

Note: *If you have chosen not to utilize user security for LDAP, do not check this box; proceed to step 7.*

6. Enter the logon name and password that you created when configuring your LDAP on the server.

7. If you want to have Outlook Express verify addresses to e-mails used via LDAP, click Yes. Otherwise, select the default and click Next.

8. Enter the name you want your LDAP server to be known as, click Next, and then Finish.

9. Now you have to change the advance setting in your LDAP entry to point to the container you want to search. To do this, highlight your directory service and click Properties.

10. Click the Advanced tab, shown in the next illustration, enter the context in which your users are located, and click OK.

Note: *When entering your context, you must use commas, not periods, to separate your organizational units.*

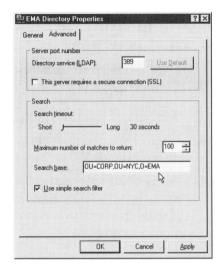

You now have configured your client. The procedures that follow will assist you in testing the client.

1. Select Edit from the main menu of Outlook Express and highlight Find People.

2. Select your LDAP directory from the Look In drop-down list box, type the name of the person you want to search. Click Find, then Find People, as shown here:

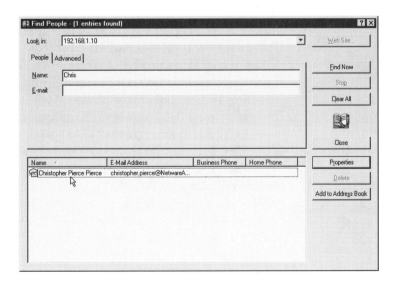

 Note: *You can type part of a name, and LDAP will perform a wildcard search for all names similar to your search.*

 I am getting errors on my LDAP client when I search NDS. What is wrong?

Here are a few troubleshooting tips that you can follow to verify that LDAP is working on your client:

● Verify that the host name or IP address is correct.

● Remove your security logon from your LDAP object group within NWADMIN32, and remove security from your client.

● Verify that your context is correct at your client. Working with Novell's NDS standards sometimes creates a habit of using periods to separate objects, but LDAP requires commas.

SERVICE LOCATION PROTOCOL (SLP)

 How does SLP work in the NetWare 5 environment?

The Service Location Protocol (SLP) is defined as a protocol that discovers and registers services automatically in an IP environment. SLP is much more refined than the Service Advertising Protocol (SAP) in the IPX environment. More specifically, SLP uses *multicast* technology, which allows SLP to send information to a group of nodes rather than broadcasting to all nodes. Multicast can route across other subnets, as long as the routers are configured to support the Internet Group Management Protocol (IGMP). Multicast uses 224.x.x.x in IP, and SLP uses 244.0.1.22 specifically to multicast. SLP is actually optional but required if you are running in Compatibility Mode or want to browse Network Neighborhood. SLP can use three types of agents. These agents include user agents (UAs), service agents (SAs), and directory agents (DAs).

SAs advertise service handles and are mandatory. SAs reside on every NetWare 5 server and client. Applications running on the server or client can advertise themselves by using SAs. One key point to remember about SAs is that they do *not* communicate with other SAs to build a list of services on the network. SAs respond only to requests that apply to services running on their machines.

UAs acquire service handles for user applications and are also mandatory. In relation with SAs, UAs also reside on every NetWare 5 server and client. When a client wants to discover a service, it will submit a request to the UA for the service. This request can contain certain attributes of the service or the type of service or name. The UA request will be sent as a multicast to the SAs. In turn, any SA on the local segment or routed across a network would respond to the UA. This is all that is needed for a client to discover services on the network but could cause network traffic issues when several SAs respond to the UA. You can use SLPINFO on your client to see your client SLP settings.

DAs collect service handles and act as repositories. DAs are optional and can be considered a link between SLP and NDS. DAs are used when IP multicast is not routed or cannot be used. Administrators must load SLPDA.NLM to enable DAs on the server. UAs can be configured to look for DAs through the Dynamic Host Configuration Protocol (DHCP).

A DA agent can be created using NetWare Administrator, and it defines the agent's scope, configuration, and security. DAs are responsible for processing these SLP messages:

- **Service registration**   Registration occurs when attributes are being modified or updated. This register contains URL, attributes, language indicator, and a time-to-live setting. An example of this is an NDPS-active printer on the network that advertises to the directory agent that it is available or has changed status. These messages are forwarded by a service agent to a directory agent.

- **Service deregistration**   Deregistration occurs when an object is no longer available such as an NDPS printer going down. A service agent also forwards these messages to the directory agent.

- **Service request**   A service request occurs when a user agent sends a request to the directory agent when it is looking for services. In exchange for the service request, the directory agent returns only services with a valid time to live.

● **Service type request**   This is a request that is sent from a user agent to a directory agent to request all service types or all service types in a specific name authority.

● **Attribute request**   A user agent sends this request to the directory agent for a specific URL or group of URLs.

By far, directory agents are the most active in an SLP environment for large networks that are sensitive to IP multicasting. In a small network environment (under 25 servers) that does not have extensive WAN links, SLP can run effectively in an IP multicast environment using user agents and services agents.

How does SLP differ from the Service Advertising Protocol (SAP)?

SLP is a much more advanced protocol than SAP. Here are the differences between the two:

● SAP maintains a global database by broadcasting advertisements across the network every 60 seconds. SLP uses user, service, and directory agents to register and deregister itself from the network on an as-needed basis.

● SLP allows the client to request network service information or use the NDS database to find the services.

What type of server setting can I use to control SLP?

There are several server commands that you can use to control how SLP works. The following table defines typical SLP settings and a description of what SLP does:

SLP DA Discovery Options = *value*	This setting specifies the use of multicast DA advertisements.

Bit 0x01	Use Multicast Directory Agent advertisements.
Bit 0x02	Use DHCP discovery.

Bit 0x04	Use the static file SYS:ETC\SLP.CFG. Note: You must first change the SET parameter to something else and then back to static to reread SLP.CFG.
Bit 0x08	Scopes required.
	A value of zero disables all DA discovery.
SLP TCP = *value*	The default setting is OFF and uses UDP. Turning this option on allows you to use TCP (host-to-host), which may degrade performance in large networks.
DISPLAY SLP SERVICES	This setting shows all services registered in SLP. Service types are described in TID 2943611 at support.novell.com.
DISPLAY SLP DA	This setting shows all directory agents and their status.
SET SLP Broadcast = *value*	The default setting is OFF and is set to multicasting SLP. Changing this value will allow SLP to act similarly to SAP and cause more traffic on the network.
SET SLP Multicast Radius = *value*	The default is 32 (max) and specifies an integer describing the multicast radius.
SET SLP DA Event Timeout = *value*	The default is 5 and the range is from 0–429. This parameter sets the number of seconds to wait before timing out on a DA request.
SLP Scope list = *value*	This setting specifies a comma-delimited scope policy list.

 ## What is an SLP Scope Container object?

An SLP Scope Container object is a storage container that contains information about SLP services. This scope collects its information when an SA forwards a service record to a DA within a specific scope. The scope then is mapped to the Scope Container object using the name attribute within the container. This object can also be moved to different locations within the tree and must contain read, write, and browse access to the container.

What SLP settings can I set at the client?

There are several settings that can be set at the client. For a full description of each setting, please refer to the September 1998 AppNote on page 8. The AppNote can be found at developer.novell.com/research/appnotes.htm.

What is the status of scoping? Can users use more than just the unscoped scope? Can servers belong to more than one scope?

The client side of scoping works fine with the shipping version of NetWare 5. A client can be configured to look to multiple scopes for a directory agent. On the server side, however, scoping was not finished with the shipping version of NetWare 5. A server can only be included in one scope. In a future upgrade, servers will be able to register in multiple scopes.

NOVELL INTERNET ACCESS SERVER (NIAS)

What type of multiport serial cards should I use for NIAS?

There are several multiport serial cards you can use for NIAS. Some of the more popular ones include serial cards from Digiboard, Equinox, Newport, and Netaccess.

How can I configure NIAS for the IP environment?

Once you have installed your multiport card and decided what protocol you are going to use, you are ready to configure NIAS. To configure, do the following:

1. Load NIASCFG.NLM. You will be prompted to copy your drivers; press ENTER to copy them.
2. Select Configure NIAS.
3. Select Remote Access.
4. Select No to bypass instructions.

5. NIAS will now step you through setting up the access server. Press ENTER at the message screen.

6. For this example, select No for Synchronous Adapters.

7. If no Asynchronous Input/Output (AIOs) are defined, press ENTER to begin AIO configuration.

8. Select the serial adapter you want to install. For this example, select Serial Port (COMX).

9. Name your serial board and accept the default. Press ESC and select Yes to save changes.

10. Press ENTER to confirm that your driver loaded successfully, and then select No when prompted to add additional AIO drivers.

11. Press ENTER for NIAS to do an automatic search of your modem.

12. If NAIS was successful in identifying your modem, press ENTER and continue to step 13. If not, press ENTER to continue, and press ENTER again to select your modem manually .

13. Select PPPNS and press ENTER.

14. Select IP and press ENTER.

15. Enter your unique IP address and press ENTER.

16. Set your subnet mask (for example, 255.255.255.0).

17. Select Yes for Header compression.

18. Select Yes and enter the range of addresses to be used by your remote clients. Do not enter a secondary client address range. These addresses should be excluded from your DHCP server.

19. Press ESC and select Yes to save your changes.

20. Press ESC and select Yes to answer the prompt "Do You Want to Start This Service Now?"

21. Your configuration is almost done. The final step is to go into NWADMN32. Select the user(s) you want to access the server remotely, and set their security as shown in the following illustration.

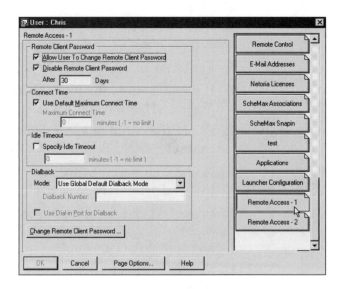

What dialers are supported for NIAS?

NIAS supports the following dialers:

- Windows 95/98 Dial-Up Networking
- Windows NT 3.51 Remote Access Service
- Windows NT 4 Dial-Up Networking
- DOSDIAL
- LAN Workplace 5
- Novell Mobile Services (for Windows 95 and Windows 3.1)
- Windows Dialer

How can I monitor my NIAS activity?

Novell has a 16-bit application called NetWare ConnectView, which monitors ports, connections, and traffic usage of NIAS. To install ConnectView, go to SYS:\PUBLIC\CVIEW\NLS\ENGLISH\DISK1 and type **SETUP.EXE**.

Chapter 5

Managing Z.E.N.works and the Novell Client

Answer Topics!

● **Z.E.N.WORKS STARTER PACK   150**

? Understanding the differences between Z.E.N.works Starter Pack and Z.E.N.works

? Understanding hardware and software requirements

? Installing Z.E.N.works Starter Pack on SFT III servers

? Using Z.E.N.works with MetaFrame, WinFrame, and Microsoft Terminal Server

? Creating a policy

? Registering using login scripts

? Automating tasks using WSIMPORT

? Updating workstations

? Importing workstations

? Troubleshooting workstation registration

? Setting user policies to perform virus scans

? Using Z.E.N.works to log virus infections within NDS

? Exporting data from NDS

? Preventing corruption of the Network

? Troubleshooting user policies

? Securing the desktop with Z.E.N.works

? Printing with Z.E.N.works

? Reducing LAN traffic with Z.E.N.works

? Determining what version of Z.E.N. works you are using

? Understanding effective policies

? Uninstalling Z.E.N.works

● **NOVELL CLIENT INSTALLATION AND UPGRADES   169**

? Understanding Novell operating system support

? Understanding Year 2000 issues

? Understanding the differences between the Microsoft Client for NetWare Networks and the Novell Client

? Automating the upgrade of the Novell Client

? Troubleshooting upgrade failures

? Using MSBATCH to install the
Novell Client

? Uninstalling the Novell Client

? Understanding Novell Client
version details

NOVELL CLIENT FUNCTIONS   174

? Changing passwords on NT and Novell
networks

? Printing from the client

? Understanding Location Profiles

? Setting up current trees and preferred
servers

? Understanding Contextless Login

**TROUBLESHOOTING THE
NOVELL CLIENT   176**

? Resolving Pure IP issues

? Resolving NDS and bindery login issues

? Responding to Novell Client failure

? Resolving time synchronization issues

**COMMUNICATION PROTOCOL
SUPPORT   178**

? Installing and configuring IP at the client

? Understanding slow network issues

? Understanding SLP

Managing Z.E.N.works and the Novell Client @ a Glance

Managing workstations in a network environment is much more difficult than it was five years ago when the only common operating systems were DOS/Windows, OS/2, and Macintosh. Many environments now use Windows NT Server, Windows NT Workstation, Windows 95, Window 98, and Windows for Workgroups, plus OS/2 and Macintosh. Novell has introduced a product that can help manage these operating systems: Z.E.N.works. This chapter discusses the use of Z.E.N.works along with enhancements and troubleshooting tips for the Novell Client. You will notice that this chapter does not provide details about Novell's DOS/Windows 3.1 Client; Z.E.N.works was written mainly for the 32-bit operating systems, and its features are not implemented in DOS/Windows 3.1. This chapter also focuses on questions dealing with new enhancements to the Novell Client, and the DOS/Windows Client has not changed dramatically from version 4.*x* to 5.*x*.

Here are the topics covered in this chapter:

Z.E.N.works Starter Pack answers questions about the purpose of this package and how to optimize printing and policy enforcement and how to query the data you import. Troubleshooting tips are also included.

Novell Client Installation and Upgrades answers questions ranging from automatic upgrading of the Novell Client without user intervention to the differences between the Microsoft NetWare Client and the Novell Client.

Novell Client Functions discusses how to perform time synchronization for your workstations and servers, change passwords in Novell and Windows NT networks, and print with the client.

Troubleshooting the Novell Client discusses issues concerning Pure IP, NDS, bindery login, client connect failure, and much more.

Communication and Protocol Support answers questions on how to address slow networks with IP and the new Service Location Protocol (SLP), which replaces SAP in the IPX world.

Z.E.N.works STARTER PACK

What is the difference between Z.E.N.works and Z.E.N.works Starter Pack?

Z.E.N stands for Zero Effort Networks for users. The main difference between the two versions of Z.E.N. is that the Starter Pack, which is included in NetWare 5, gives the user a taste of what Z.E.N.works can do for your environment. With the Z.E.N.works Starter Pack, you can do the following:

● Update software seamlessly from your home or office.

● Distribute and update printer drivers on the fly.

● Schedule actions to occur on one or several workstations at specified times or intervals.

● Import workstation information in the NDS tree.

● Retrieve applications automatically on a workstation.

● Set workstation policies (perform desktop management), which enables administrators to enforce policies such as denying access to certain objects on the desktop, as well as customize the standard look and feel of one machine or the entire corporate environment with wallpaper, sound,

and other features of the Windows 95/98 and Windows NT operating systems.

- Customize the Novell Client configuration and registry on multiple workstations.

The full version of Z.E.N.works includes the preceding features, plus it also enables you to do the following:

- Create a hardware inventory, which stores information in NDS concerning the CPU, RAM, bus type, system BIOS, and other machine-specific items.
- Remotely control a workstation using IPX or IP.
- Use a help system, with quick answers to questions by providing information about the user's specific setup.
- Scan workstation hardware, software, and data for Year 2000 bugs using a five-user version of the NDS-aware diagnostic tool called Check 2000.
- Experience improved integration with Novell's ManageWise 2.6.
- Track the number of software licenses distributed through Z.E.N.works and record the number of individuals using a specific application at any time on the network using Software Metering.
- Benefit from full support for Windows 98 (including the option to control remotely).

What are the hardware, software, and administrative requirements for installing the Z.E.N.works Starter Pack?

Before you attempt to install and use the Z.E.N.works Starter Pack, you must make sure you have the appropriate hardware and software, and you must know what administrative rights you are going to grant on your tree. Here is what you need to run Z.E.N.works:

- 70MB of memory
- 205MB of hard disk space

> ***Tip:*** *Even though Novell says 205MB of hard disk space is enough, this should be considered a minimum. This minimum does not take in consideration the additional objects created in your NDS tree. Therefore, a server that has Z.E.N.works Starter Pack installed should have a SYS partition of at least 1GB available. Administrators can refer to Chapter 12 or go to Novell's Web site at www.novell.com / coolsolutions / zenworks / basics.html for information on NDS design for Z.E.N.works.*

- Administrator rights to the NetWare Server in which you are going to install Z.E.N.works Starter Pack
- Administrator rights to the NDS container in which you are going to install Z.E.N.works Starter Pack
- Novell Workstation Manager Client software loaded on each client machine (included with the Novell Client software)

Can I install Z.E.N.works on a server running SFT III without any interruption?

Yes, since Z.E.N.works does not require any NLMs, your NetWare Server need not be interrupted.

Will Z.E.N.works run successfully in a WinFrame, MetaFrame, or Microsoft Terminal Server environment?

Yes and no. The Z.E.N.works Starter pack that ships with NetWare 5 has several problems with these products. You must download the Z.E.N.works 1.01 patch from the Web at support.novell.com/cgi-bin/search/download?/pub/updates/nw/nw5/zw101p1.exe to have these products run properly.

 How do I create a Workstation object in my NDS tree and begin to import my workstations?

To create a Workstation object, you must first create a user policy. For this example, you will register a Windows 98 workstation in the tree. To do this, you must open NetWare Administrator and do the following:

1. Create a user policy by right-clicking your organization unit and then clicking Create.

2. Select Policy Package for your new object.

3. Select WIN95 User Package.

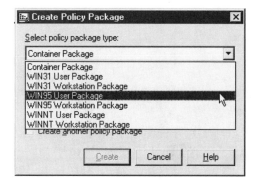

4. Type a name for your object (for example, User_WIN95/98).

5. Check the Define Additional Properties box and click Create.

6. Go to Workstation Import Policy and check the box.

7. Click the Associations tab and then click Add.

8. Select the organization unit from the Available Objects list and click OK.

9. At this point, you have successfully associated this policy with all users in your organization unit who have Windows 95/98 workstations. Click OK to confirm this change.

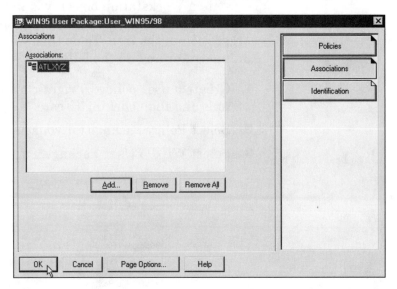

10. From the main menu of NetWare Administrator, choose Tools, select Workstation Utilities, and then select Prepare Workstation Registration.

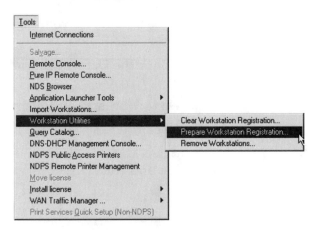

11. Select your container to grant rights to the users to register their workstations. For this example, select the organizational unit ATL.XYZ. Verify that Include Subcontainers is checked. Click OK.

Note: *WSRIGHTS.EXE in the SYS:PUBLIC\WIN32 directory will also perform the same function as step 11.*

12. Log in to a file server within the organization unit to which you granted registration rights. Make sure that the workstation is running the Novell 5 Client and that Workstation Manager was selected during installation.

13. After login succeeds, go to the NetWare Administrator, right-click your organizational unit, and select Details.

14. Scroll down to Workstation Registration and note that your user and computer names are now present in the Workstation Registration window.

15. Select Import; a progress indicator will show the progress of the import process. When the import process is complete, click OK and then close the Details menu.

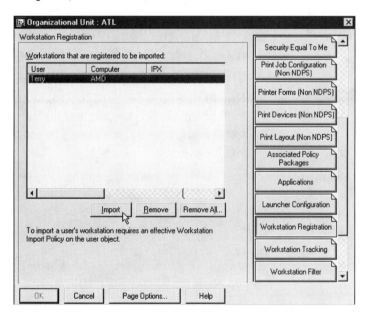

16. Refresh NetWare Administrator and note that your new object is now created in your organization unit.

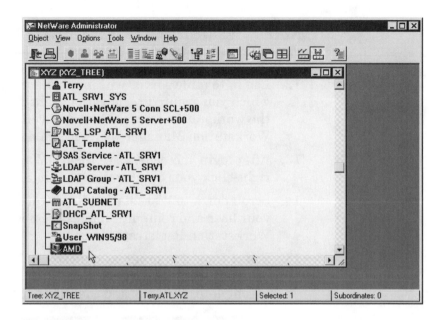

I don't have the Novell Workstation Manager loaded on my clients. Can I register my workstations using a login script?

Novell does not require Novell Workstation Manager to be loaded for the Z.E.N.works Starter Pack to work. Here are some examples of login scripts you can use to register your workstations:

Platform	Login Script
Windows NT and Windows 95/98 workstations	```If "%PLATFORM"="WNT" or "W95" then begin #WSREG32.exe end```
Windows 3.x workstations	```If "%PLATFORM"="WIN" then begin #WSREG16.exe end```
MS-DOS	```If "%PLATFORM"="MSDOS" then begin #WSREG16.exe end```

 I have over 1,000 users on my network and I am tired of manually importing workstations into my NDS. How can I automate this task?

The best way to import workstations automatically is to use the WSIMPORT.EXE program in the SYS:PUBLIC\WIN32 directory with a set of parameters. Here is an example of a command-line specification for updating NDS: WSIMPORT /T=*tree* /S=*subcontainer* /H (where H indicates the No User Interface status). You can use WSIMPORT within a login script or in the Z.E.N.works scheduler to automatically import your objects.

 How can you schedule a WSIMPORT operation automatically with the Z.E.N.works scheduler?

Once you have created your command-line entry, you can schedule WSIMPORT to run in whatever time scenario you like with the Z.E.N.works scheduler. To set up this schedule, you must use the Novell Client for Windows NT and not the Novell Client for Windows 95/98. When you use NT, Workstation Manager can run as an NT service, and users do not have to be logged in to the network for a scheduled action to occur. The only requirement is that the power for the workstation must be on. The following steps show how to schedule a WSIMPORT action to run once an hour.

1. On the Novell Client for Windows NT, right-click the scheduler located in the system tray and click Display Schedule.

2. Click Add to insert an action.

3. In the Action Properties window, give your action a name (for example, WSIMPORT) and select the Items tab.

4. Click Add to search for the WSIMPORT program. Browse through the directory structure in your network and select WSIMPORT.EXE.

5. Insert the necessary parameters for WSIMPORT to run in an unattended mode (for example, /T=*tree* /S=*subcontainer* /H). Then click OK.

6. Select the Schedule tab and click the Daily button. Choose the day and time when you want your action to run. Also make sure that the time in the Repeat the Action Every box is set to one hour.

7. Click Apply, and you're done.

How often should I update my workstation information in the NDS tree?

The answer depends totally on the size of your environment. Remember that additions and removals of Workstation objects take effect in NDS only when you import workstations with the new data. As a rule, you should import workstations when the following occurs:

● You want to generate a report of workstations for management.

● Workstations are added, moved, or removed from the network.

● Network cards are replaced. (This is especially important for workstations running IPX because the replacement cards will have new network numbers.)

● New containers are added to the NDS tree after Z.E.N.works has been installed.

My workstations are not being registered in my NDS tree. What's going on?

There are several possible reasons why you cannot register a workstation in your NDS tree. Here are some:

● The workstation may already be registered in another tree.

● The workstation does not have the rights needed for registration.

● The Workstation Manager is not loaded on the client.

To determine whether a workstation has been registered, look in the root of the workstation's C: drive for a file called WSREG32.LOG. This is a plain ASCII file that can be read in NOTEPAD.EXE, detailing the success and failure of workstation registration. If the log contains errors or gives false messages like "WSREG –v 1.00," the workstation may be successfully registered even though you cannot import it. Try this troubleshooting method:

1. Run UNREG32.EXE, found in the server's PUBLIC directory. This program will unregister and clean up any corruption or misinformation in the workstation registry.

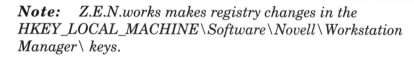

Note: *Z.E.N.works makes registry changes in the HKEY_LOCAL_MACHINE\Software\Novell\Workstation Manager\ keys.*

2. Shut down the workstation.

3. Open NetWare Administrator and delete the Workstation object in NDS, if present.

4. Restart the workstation

5. Log in to the workstation, right-click the Workstation Manager icon, and select Run Registration Agent Now.

Tip: *You also can run WSREG32.EXE in the server's PUBLIC directory to accomplish step 5 if you do not have the Z.E.N.works client installed.*

6. Review WSREG32.LOG in the root of drive C: and verify that the registration was successful.

7. Go to NetWare Administrator, choose Tools, and select Import Workstations.

Tip: *These same steps can be applied to the Windows 3.x Client, with the exception that you will need to run the DOS/Windows versions of UNREG16.EXE and WSREG16.EXE.*

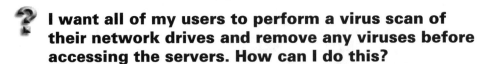

I want all of my users to perform a virus scan of their network drives and remove any viruses before accessing the servers. How can I do this?

You can easily accomplish this task with Z.E.N.works. The steps listed here show you how to configure Z.E.N.works to run a virus scan using Network Associate's Virus Scan program on all Windows 95/98 workstations during the server login process. You must have Virus Scan loaded on each machine before creating this policy.

1. Run NetWare Administrator and create a policy package.

2. Select WIN95 Workstation Package as the policy package type, name the package **Windows 95/98 Workstations**, and check Define Additional Properties.

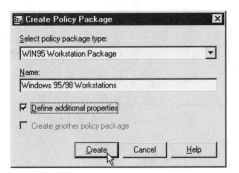

3. A dialog box appears, listing the policies you can enable. For this example, select Add Action and name the scheduled action **Virus Scan for Windows 95/98**. Then click Create.

4. You should now see a new policy created called Virus Scan for Windows 95/98, and it should have a check mark next

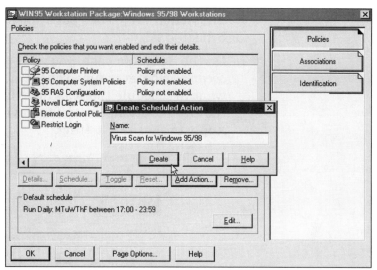

to it. The current schedule is set by default to 17:00-12:59 hours. You want to change the schedule to set this action to run at login. To do this, select Virus Scan for Windows 95/98 and click Details.

5. This screen should show the Schedule setting for the action you created. Set the scheduler to ignore the default schedule by checking Ignore Package Default Schedule and Use These Settings. Then click Details in the lower-right corner of the screen.

6. The Action Properties page appears. Click to the Schedule tab.

7. On the Schedule page, you can schedule your action to occur at whatever time you want. For this example, you want to schedule the scan to occur during an event. Click the Event button. The default event is User Login. Click Apply to save this setting.

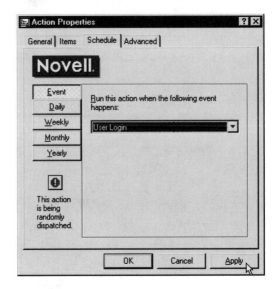

8. The schedule is set. Now tell Z.E.N.works where the program is and how it should be executed. Select the Items tab in the Action Properties window and click Add to create an executable action.

9. Now you need to point to the executable for the action on the user's hard disk or network drive and also set parameters to make the virus program scan automatically. For this example, keep the priority on Action Default, as shown in the next illustration, and click OK when you have finished.

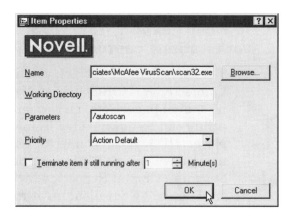

10. You should now see a new item in the Action window. Select the General tab and then click Apply to save the changes. You want to save the default settings of the General tab since the user is going to be interacting with the desktop during the scan process. Click Close to return to the Schedule Action page. Review the changes to the action, and then click OK.

11. The action is complete. The final step is to associate the action with a group of users in your tree. To do this, select Associations and click Add.

12. For this example, select the ATL organization unit to have all ATL users scanned for viruses. Once the object is selected, click OK twice to return to the main NetWare Administrator menu.

13. You're done! Log in to the tree where your policy is assigned.

 Can Z.E.N.works log virus infections within NDS when a workstation is infected?

Currently, Z.E.N.works does not have the ability to log virus checks within NDS.

 ### How can I export from NDS the information from my workstations captured from Z.E.N.works?

To export data from NDS, you need to use an Open Database Connectivity (ODBC) driver. Novell offers an ODBC driver at no charge to perform queries on your NDS database. This utility can be downloaded from developer.novell.com. The Novell NDS ODBC connector enables you to run reports using any type of ODBC-compliant report generator, such as Seagate's Crystal Reports, which you can use for a 30-day trial period by downloading it from www.seagate.com.

 ### Some of my users like playing with Windows 98's Control Panel and changing their protocols and services in the Network settings. How can I prevent them from corrupting their configurations?

To prevent your users from changing their network configurations, you can enable User System Policies within NetWare Administrator and then either completely remove the network icon from the Control Panel or just disable certain areas in the Network window. To remove the network icon, do the following:

1. Run NetWare Administrator, create a Windows 95 user policy, and check Define Additional Properties if a policy does not already exist.

2. Check 95 User System Policies and click Details.

3. Click Control Panel to expand the tree, and then click Network to open this window.

4. Check Restrict Network Control Panel, check Disable Network Control Panel, and then click OK, as shown in the following illustration.

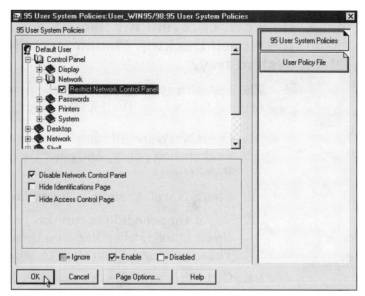

5. If this is a new user policy, click Associations and then click Add to assign the object you want to be active for the policy.

 Note: *All policies flow down the tree. Therefore, if you assign the [Root], then your entire tree will be affected.*

As you can see, you can be very specific with restrictions on Z.E.N.works.

 I enforced a Windows 95 User system policy to prevent users from accessing Network Neighborhood and later disabled (unchecked) the system policy. My users still can't get into Network Neighborhood. What is the problem?

Disabling and enabling policies does not release any restrictions you set on your clients. To enable users to access Network Neighborhood again, uncheck the restriction for Network Neighborhood and leave the policy enabled. Next time the users log in, the change will take effect. Once the change is complete, you can disable the policy.

 How can I prevent my users from accessing the Novell Desktop Management icon in the system tray?

The easiest way to do this is through a workstation policy using Z.E.N.works. Do the following:

1. Open NetWare Administrator, create a Windows 95 workstation policy, and click Define Additional Properties.

2. Check Novell Client Configuration and click Details.

3. To set the schedule to run this policy at network login, check Ignore Policy Package Default Schedule and Use These Settings. Then click Details.

4. Go to the Schedule tab and click Event. Verify that User Login is selected and then click Apply.

5. In the Schedule window, select the Settings tab. This tab will show all the configurations for Novell Client32. To turn off the scheduler, expand the client tree and click Client.

6. When the Novell Client Configuration window appears, click Advanced Settings, scroll down to Show Scheduler System Tray Icon, and turn off this option, as shown here:

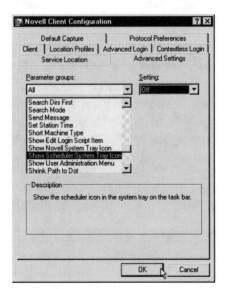

7. Click OK to exit the Advanced Settings window and click OK again to return to the Policies page.

8. Click Associations and click Add to assign the object you want to use with this package.

 ### Can I use Z.E.N.works to automatically assign and download printer drivers for my workstations?

Yes, Z.E.N.works allows an administrator to copy a printer driver to the network; whenever a user logs in to a specific container, the printer driver will automatically be downloaded and configured without any user intervention. Follow these steps:

1. Assign Read and File Scan rights to the SYS:PUBLIC directory. This is where the printer drivers will be stored.

2. Create or edit a Workstation package and check the 95 Computer Printer (or the NT Computer Printer if you are using an NT Workstation package).

3. Click Details and check Ignore Policy Package Default Schedule and Use These Settings.

4. Select the Printer tab and click Add.

5. Choose the Printer object you want your users to use and click OK.

6. Now you must assign a printer driver to the printer. Click New Driver and then click Select Printer Model.

7. Choose the desired printer driver you want the users to use and click OK. At this point, the drivers should be copied into the PUBLIC directory. Click OK when the copy operation is complete.

8. Set your policy schedule to whatever preferences you want and click OK.

 ### How can I reduce my LAN traffic with Z.E.N.works?

When you create and associate policy packages with NDS objects, you may increase your network traffic because of the

way Z.E.N.works searches the tree for associations between policy packages and objects. Minimizing your searches will reduce the network traffic. Do the following:

1. Create a Container policy package, name the policy, and check Define Additional Properties.

2. Check Search Policy and click Details.

3. In the Search for Policies Up to field, select Partition and then click OK. This will limit the number of directory levels searched for associations between the policy package and objects.

4. Click the Association tab and assign this object to the container to which you want to apply the search policy.

How can I tell what version of Z.E.N.works I am running?

A program called ZENVER.EXE, located in the SYS:PUBLIC directory, tells you what version of Z.E.N.works you are currently running.

What are effective policies in Z.E.N.works and how do they work?

Effective policies are the collection of all enabled policies and all policy packages associated indirectly or directly with an object.

Effective policies in the Z.E.N.works product are similar to effective rights in NDS. As in NDS, effective policies flow down the tree unless there is a direct object association with the policy package, such as an association with a User object. The flow of effective policies starts with all policy packages assigned to an object and then moves up the tree to associations with the parent container.

How can I uninstall the Z.E.N.works Starter Pack from my NetWare 5 Server?

To uninstall Z.E.N.works, do the following:

1. Go to the workstation that originally installed the Z.E.N.works Starter Pack.

2. Choose Control Panel and then select Add/Remove Program.

3. Select Z.E.N.works and click Add/Remove.

> **!** **Caution:** *If you installed Z.E.N.works with the NWAdmin32 files selected, the uninstall operation will delete your NetWare Administrator files, and you will have to reinstall NetWare Administrator. In addition, your extended schema will not be removed.*

NOVELL CLIENT INSTALLATION AND UPGRADES

? What Novell operating systems does the Novell Client support ?

Novell supports NetWare 3.*x*, 4.*x*, and 5.*x*.

? Is the Novell Client ready for the year 2000?

Yes. NetWare 5 has been fully tested and approved as Year 2000 (Y2K)–compliant. However, some operating systems that may be used within your NetWare environment may not be Y2K-compliant—such as Microsoft Windows NT 4, which requires NT Service Pack 4 for Y2K fixes.

? Do I really need to upgrade my Microsoft Client for NetWare Networks to the Novell Client?

No, but to use all of Novell's features and ensure that your environment is fully supportive, it is essential that all users upgrade to the Novell Client. You will not lose any features of the Microsoft operating system, and you will gain many features the standard Microsoft Client does not have. Following is a table listing some of the ways in which the Novell Client differs from the Microsoft Client for NetWare Networks.

Feature	Microsoft Client for NetWare Networks	Novell Client
Automatic client update	No	Yes
Z.E.N.works support	No	Yes
Native IP support	No (Microsoft uses NetBIOS with TCP/IP)	Yes

Feature	Microsoft Client for NetWare Networks	Novell Client
Login to multiple NDS trees	No	Yes
Extended attribute support	No	Yes
Packet signing	No	Yes
Complete NDS login script processing	No	Yes
32-bit native IPX/SPX API support	Some	Yes
Packet Burst Protocol	No	Yes

 ### Can I automate the upgrade of the Novell Client for all my users?

Yes, Novell provides a function called Automatic Client Upgrade (ACU) to upgrade previous versions of the Novell Client and to upgrade the Microsoft Client for NetWare Networks. To set up an upgrade, do the following:

1. Log in to the server as Admin.

2. Create a folder on a volume that users will access to upgrade and grant rights to all users that need to upgrade their clients.

3. Copy the Novell Client files to the folder you created. The files are located on the Z.E.N.works CD-ROM in \PRODUCTS\WIN95\IBM_ENU. If this is a Windows NT upgrade, the path is \PRODUCT\WINNT\I386.

Note: *If you are copying using Windows Explorer, you will be copying the read-only attributes from the CD.*

4. Once the copy of the client is complete, run NCIMAN.EXE (Novell Client Install Manager) located in the \WIN95\IBM_ENU\ADMIN directory of the client CD-ROM or in SYS:PUBLIC\WIN95\IBM_ENU\ENU or SYS:PUBLIC\WINNT\I386\ADMIN if you

installed the client files on the server. This program allows you to create a template for several workstations that can later be used in an unattended install operation. Set the options you want (Preferred Tree, Server, Context, and so on) and click File and Save As. Save this file in the directory where the client resides.

 Note: *There are two versions of NCIMAN.EXE. One is for Windows 95/98, and the other is for Windows NT, which is located in the ADMIN directory within the Windows NT installation client directory.*

5. Create a login script to execute a client upgrade. Here are examples of login scripts for an upgrade:

Platform	Login Script

Windows NT	`If "%PLATFORM" = "WNT" then begin`
	`#\\servername\sys\public\client\winnt\i386\setupunw.exe`
	`/ACU /u:unattend.txt`

Windows 95	`If "%PLATFORM" = "W95" then begin`
	`#\\servername\sys\public\client\win95\ibm_enu\setup.exe`
	`/ACI /u:unattend.txt`

Windows 3.x and MS-DOS	`IF OS = "MSDOS" then begin`
	`   IF PLATFORM <> "WIN" THEN BEGIN`
	`      WRITE " Updating the Novell Client`
	`               for DOS and Windows 3.1x with`
	`               the DOS install."`
	
	`      MAP y:=\\server1\sys\public\client\`
	`      #y:adm32\ibm_enu\dos_acu\nwdetect.exe`
	`      client32_version 2.5.0`
	`      IF ERROR_LEVEL = "1" THEN BEGIN`
	`         #y:doswin32\install.exe`
	`         IF ERROR_LEVEL = "0" THEN BEGIN`
	`            #y:adm32\ibm_enu\dos_acu\nwstamp.exe`
	`            client32_version 2.5.0`
	`            #y:adm32\ibm_enu\dos_acu\nwlog.exe`
	`            /f z:\doslog\dosacu.log`
	`            #y:adm32\ibm_enu\dos_acu\reboot.com`
	`      ELSE`
	`         WRITE "Error running installation (%ERROR_LEVEL.`
	`                  Contact your network administrator"`

Platform	Login Script

```
                    #y:adm32\ibm_enu\dos_acu\nwlog.exe
          /f z:\doslog\failed.log
     END
     ELSE
     WRITE "The Novell Client
                                   for DOS and Windows 3.1x
                                   was up to date."
   END
   EXIT
 ELSE
   WRITE "Updating the Novell Client
         for DOS and Windows 3.1x
         with the Windows install."
   MAP y:=\\server1\sys\public\client\
   #y:adm32\ibm_enu\dos_acu\nwdetect.exe
   client32_version 2.5.0
   IF ERROR_LEVEL = "1" THEN BEGIN
      #y:adm32\ibm_enu\dos_acu\nwstamp.exe
      client32_version 2.5.0
      @y:doswin32\nls\english\setup.exe /acu
      END
      EXIT
   END
 END

 WRITE "OS %OS not supported by ACU"
 WRITE ""
```

What happens if automatic upgrade fails for some of my Windows 95/98 clients?

The Novell Client's SETUP.EXE program has a parameter called rollback (/RB) that backs up the current client configuration to the NOVELL\CLIENT32\NWBACKUP directory. When the new client is installed and the workstation is rebooted, the rollback parameter will enable the Novell Client to check and see if the upgraded client is able to connect to the network. If the upgrade was successful, the rollback parameter will delete the backup in the NOVELL\CLIENT32\NWBACKUP directory. If the upgrade was not successful, the rollback parameter will restore the previous configuration. This option is especially useful when

you are upgrading a large number of clients on your network; it is available only for Windows 95/98 clients.

Can I use MSBATCH to install the Novell Client?

As of this writing, support for MSBATCH and the NetWare 5 Win95/98 Client is not available. This functionality is currently under development.

How can I safely uninstall the Novell Client for Windows 95/98?

There are two methods for uninstalling the Novell Client. The first method is to open the Control Panel, click Network, select the Novell Client, and click Remove. You must also remove the Novell ODINSUP and IPX 32-bit protocol for the Novell Client the same way. Then reboot your system.

Note: *The preceding method does not clean up all the information in the Registry. This is not a bug in the code, but gives you the option of preserving your client settings if you should want to reinstall the Novell Client at a later time.*

The second method is to run the Novell program UNC32.EXE found on the Z.E.N.works CD in the folder \PRODUCTS\WIN95\IBM_ENU\ADMIN. This file can also be found in the SYS:PUBLIC directory if you copied the client to the server. If you want to remove any ODI drivers installed on the workstation, check the Remote Novell 32-bit ODI Adapter box and click Continue. This method is good for administrators who have user profiles on Windows 95 workstations with no Control Panel option for their users.

Caution: *Once you start the removal of the client with UNC32.EXE, you cannot cancel it. Doing so could corrupt the registry of the workstation. If this does occur, just run UNC32 again, and you can properly uninstall the client.*

 How can I find out what version of the Novell Client I am running?

It is critical that you keep up with the latest client version for NetWare. You can view the version of the client by doing the following:

1. Open the Control Panel.

2. Click Network.

3. Select the Novell NetWare Client and click Properties. The Client version information appears at the bottom of the screen.

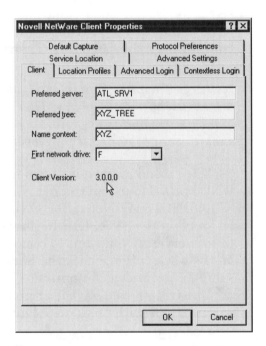

NOVELL CLIENT FUNCTIONS

 How can I change my Novell password and change it on my Microsoft NT servers as well?

There are two methods of changing your password on Novell and Microsoft networks at the same time. The first method is to open the Control Panel and click Passwords. Click Change Windows Passwords on the Change Passwords page and click OK. Then enter your new password information and click OK.

The second method is to click the Novell icon in the system tray, select User Administrator, and enter your new password. This method is for users who do not have access to the Control Panel at their workstations.

I want to print to a specific Novell networked printer that I do not usually use. How can I print to this printer?

To find a printer on the network, do the following:

1. Go to Network Neighborhood.

2. Navigate to the organization, organizational unit, or server to see the available printers.

3. Select the printer you want to use.

4. If this is the first time you are setting up the printer on your workstation, you will be prompted to select the manufacturer and model of the printer from a list provided. Follow the prompts, and your printer will automatically be set up.

What is a Location Profile?

A Location Profile allows a workstation to save login information for users. This is particularly useful if users travel from place to place. A user can have a profile for the office, for the home, and for traveling. Location Profiles can also be set up to log in to bindery services only or to NDS services only.

How do I set up my current tree and preferred server?

To set up your current tree and preferred server, do the following:

1. Right-click Network Neighborhood and select NetWare Login.

2. When the NetWare Login screen appears, click the Advanced button.

3. In the Tree field, enter the name of the tree you want to set.

4. In the Server field, select your server.

What is Contextless Login?

Contextless Login allows users to browse through a catalog within one or more organizational units. NetWare uses catalogs to browse through the tree. Catalogs and Contextless Login setup are explained in Chapter 12.

TROUBLESHOOTING THE NOVELL CLIENT

I am running the Novell NetWare 5.x Pure IP environment. Since I started using this environment, some of my client-server applications have stopped working. What is wrong?

Unfortunately, some older versions of software use IPX/SPX-specific calls to the Novell server. In an IP environment, you can choose IPX Compatibility Mode when you install the client. IPX Compatibility Mode allows IPX applications to run on IP-only networks. IPX Compatibility mode depends on the Service Location Protocol (SLP). Another quick workaround for this problem is to install IP and IPX support on your client. If this is unacceptable to your environment, contact the software vendor to see what enhancements may be available for the application.

My NetWare environment has a mixture of NDS and bindery services. When I installed my client, I had to choose between NDS and bindery services, not both. How can I enable login to both environments?

Because of the vast differences between NDS and bindery services, Novell forces you to choose NDS or bindery. However, you can create a shortcut on your Windows desktop that points to the LOGINW32.EXE and add /B to set up your

client to log in to a bindery server. You can also use Location Profiles to accomplish the same task, as described in the preceding section, "Novell Client Functions," in the question "What is a Location Profile?"

 I installed the Novell Client for Windows 95. The splash screen appears, but the login screen never appears, and when I click Network Neighborhood, the window is empty. What's wrong?

When you do not see the Novell login screen, this usually indicates that the client could not find a file server. Here are a few troubleshooting tips that can assist you in fixing this problem:

- Verify that LOGINW95.EXE is located on the local drive on the client workstation.
- Verify that your frame type is correct. This can be done as follows:
  1. Open the Control Panel and click Network.
  2. Select IPX 32-bit Protocol for the Novell NetWare Client.
  3. Click the Advanced IPX tab and verify that Use All Detected Frame Types is enabled.
- Verify that your network card is working properly.
- Check your network connection.

 My workstation's clock is out of synch with the network. How can I fix this?

The cause of this problem may be a simple setting in your Novell Client configuration. To synchronize your workstation with the network, do the following:

1. Open the Control Panel and click Network.
2. Select Novell NetWare Client and click Properties.
3. Click the Advanced Settings tab and look for the Set Station Time parameter. Verify that the station time is set to On.

COMMUNICATION PROTOCOL SUPPORT

When should I install the IP-only feature of the Novell Client?

Novell recommends that if your network in running only NetWare 5.x, then installing the IP-only feature is appropriate. However, if you have a version of NetWare earlier than NetWare 5.x, then you must install the Novell Client with the IPX-only option. In addition, if your environment includes a mixture of NetWare 4.x and NetWare 5.x, then you should install IP and IPX support or the Compatibility Mode driver on your server, depending on your protocol migration strategy.

I am connecting to my NetWare 5 server via a virtual area network (VAN) and I keep losing my connection to the server. How can I fix this?

Typically, VSAT and VAN connections are slow, and the NetWare Client will timeout from the server. To get around this problem, you need to increase the Minimum Time to Net parameter to 10,000 in your Novell Client configuration and enable Packet Burst on your client and your server.

What is SLP?

SLP, or Service Location Protocol, was developed as part of a joint venture between Novell and Sun Microsystems. This protocol provides a way for discovering and registering network services automatically in an IP environment. In the NetWare environment, it allows a user to search for NDS trees, NetWare servers, printers, and any other device that is SLP enabled. It can be considered the replacement for the Service Advertising Protocol (SAP) in the IPX/SPX environment, with the benefit of a significant reduction in broadcasts. For more information on SLP, refer to Chapter 4.

Chapter 6

Managing Files and Directories

Answer Topics!

**NOVELL STORAGE
SERVICES (NSS) 183**

? Defining Novell Storage Services

? Understanding capabilities of NSS

? Improving system performance with NSS

? Learning the requirements for an
NSS volume

**DIFFERENCES BETWEEN NWFS
VOLUMES AND NSS VOLUMES 185**

? Comparing NWFS and NSS

? Understanding CD-ROM changes with NSS

? Making a CD-ROM show up as a volume

? Converting servers to take advantages of NSS

? Handling print queues in NSS

? Handling name spaces in NSS

? Turning on Salvage volume by volume
in NSS

? Running FILER and similar programs in NSS

? Using NDIR, MAP, FLAG, and RIGHTS
with NSS volumes

CURRENT LIMITATIONS OF NSS 189

? Understanding SYS volume's
incompatibility with NSS

? Considering NWFS features that are
currently not available with NSS

? Calculating the minimum size for a
SYS volume

? DOS directory performance issues
and NSS

? Mounting a DOS partition as an
NSS volume

NWFS FEATURES 192

? Using user space limits

? Controlling user space limits in NetWare 5

? Understanding block suballocation

? Accessing long filenames in NetWare 5

? Using file compression with certain
file types

? Affecting server performance with
file compression

? Checking compression statistics

? Changing compression settings

? Disabling compression on a SYS volume

**NSS COMPONENTS AND
ARCHITECTURE   201**

? Comparing components that make up NSS
with those of NWFS

? Understanding the architecture setup of
NSS components

? Allowing for future storage types

**INSTALLING AND UPGRADING
TO NSS   207**

? Choosing upgrade options

? Transferring data from an NWFS volume
to an NSS volume

? Knowing which disk driver to use

? Allocating free space during installation

? Creating an NSS volume after installation

? Knowing which NSS volumes are added
in NDS

? Adding volumes to the NDS tree

? Removing volumes from the NDS tree

? Increasing and decreasing NSS
volume size

NSS ADMINISTRATION UTILITIES   212

? Managing NSS volumes

? Mounting NSS volumes

? Mixing NWFS free space with
unpartitioned free space

? Running NSS commands outside of the
NSS Administration utility

? Optimizing cache buffers for NSS

? Deleting a storage object or volume

FILE SYSTEM SECURITY   220

? Comparing Trustee rights and Inherited
Rights Filters (IRFs)

? Blocking the Supervisor right

? Calculating effective rights

? Granting rights in an NDS tree

MAINTENANCE   222

? Choosing backup support for NSS
volumes

? Verifying that your backup software works
with NSS

? Using VREPAIR in NetWare 5

? Recovering from a corrupted NSS volume

Managing Files and Directories @ a Glance

One of the more significant changes between NetWare 4.*x* and
NetWare 5 is apparent in the options for storage services. The
traditional NetWare File System (NWFS) is still available, but a new
powerful storage service called NetWare Storage Services (NSS) has
many advantages. NSS volumes mount faster while using less RAM,
they are beneficial for systems with large volumes, and they can
recover from errors more efficiently.

The majority of this chapter will focus on NSS—its benefits,
differences, administration, and architecture. We will discuss the
features included in NWFS, but not yet available in NSS. We will

also touch on file security and the command-line utilities for file and directory attributes; but, due to the fact that the administration commands for NSS volumes are new, we will spend more time in that area.

The topics for this chapter will be grouped into sections as follows:

- **Novell Storage Services (NSS)** defines NSS and provides information on the specifications, capabilities, and requirements of this totally new storage system.

- **Differences Between NWFS Volumes and NSS Volumes** compares the differences and benefits of NSS to NWFS.

- **Current Limitations of NSS** explains the limitations of NSS and the reasons the NWFS must still be used.

- **NWFS Features** covers unique features of the NetWare file system that are not currently available in NSS such as file compression, block suballocation, and user space limits.

- **NSS Components and Architecture** explains what the NSS components are and how they fit together. The architecture of NSS is new, and we will answer questions on that subject.

- **Installing and Upgrading to NSS** defines the components of NSS volumes described in the previous section. We will provide the steps required for installing or upgrading a volume to NSS.

- **NSS Administration Utilities** explores NetWare 5's use of new NSS utilities for management of NSS volumes. We will describe the use and syntax of these utilities.

- **File System Security** covers the security features of the file and directory system and discusses how Inherited Rights Filters (IRFs) work.

- **Maintenance** explores the procedures for backup, restore, and recovery of an NSS volume.

NOVELL STORAGE SERVICES (NSS)

 What is Novell Storage Services?

Novell Storage Services is a 64-bit indexed storage system that eliminates previous limitations on file number and size, and improves access to volumes through faster volume mounts and repairs. This service is offered in addition to the traditional NetWare file system (NWFS) on NetWare 5 servers.

 What new capabilities are provided by NSS?

NSS provides increased capacity for storage, with up to 8TB (8 terabytes) file sizes and up to 8 trillion files in a single volume. Not only does NSS support large files, but it offers extremely fast access. Large files can be opened in the same amount of time as smaller ones. Also, you can have up to a million files open at the same time.

Up to 255 NSS volumes can be mounted per NetWare 5 server. Add to that the SYS volume, which must be an NWFS volume, and you have a maximum number of mounted volumes of 256. If all volumes are NWFS volumes, the limitation is 64. You can actually have an unlimited number of NSS volumes on a server, but only 255 of them may be mounted at a time. Also, any unused free space, either in NetWare volumes or unpartitioned space, can be pooled for use by an NSS volume. Even unused space on the DOS partition can be added to a storage pool for an NSS volume.

Want to enable Salvage on NSSVOL1, but not NSSVOL2? NSS volumes can have Salvage set by volume, instead of by server.

With previous versions of NetWare, each name space added would create an additional directory entry for each file. Since each NWFS volume has a maximum of 16 million

directory entries, having two name spaces loaded would reduce the maximum to 8 million. Three name spaces would cut the maximum to 4 million. This could cause problems with the server running out of available directory entries. With NetWare 5, additional name spaces on NSS volumes share the same storage space. In fact, NSS volumes automatically load DOS, MAC, NFS, and LONG name spaces by default.

How will NSS improve my system performance?

Volumes mount extremely fast with NSS, yet utilize less RAM. Remounting a volume of any size can be counted in seconds rather than minutes, while still maintaining a footprint of only 1- to 2MB of RAM.

CD-ROMs are mounted as NSS volumes by default, providing faster mounting and access speeds. They also mount automatically upon inserting the CD into the drive. This has clear advantages for CD-ROM towers.

Finally, if you ever run into problems with your NSS volume, it can recover quicker, provide better error logging, and even rebuild itself with only a little help from you. You don't even have to use VREPAIR.

What are the requirements for creating an NSS volume?

To create an NSS volume, you will need NetWare 5, at least 10MB of free disk space, and NSS.NLM loaded on your server. You will use 1.5MB of RAM loading the NSS.NLM, and you will need a minimum of 1MB for the NSS cache buffers.

 Note: *Each cache buffer is a 4K block, and the default minimum number of cache buffers used when the NSS.NLM is loaded is 512. A quick calculation tells you that the default minimum amount of RAM used when the NSS.NLM is loaded is 2,048K, or 2MB. The absolute minimum setting for NSS cache buffers is 256 (1MB). NSS cache buffers are normally created using 10 percent of the total available cache buffers on the server.*

We will discuss the commands and syntax to change the number of cache buffers later in this chapter in the section "NSS Administration Utilities."

DIFFERENCES BETWEEN NWFS VOLUMES AND NSS VOLUMES

 How does NSS differ from NWFS?

We have touched on some of the differences between NSS and NWFS. However, it would be a good idea to compare them side by side. Table 6-1 details the file system features and how NWFS and NSS handle them differently.

Feature	NetWare File System (NWFS)	Novell Storage Services (NSS)
Partitions	Uses a standard partition type tied to physical devices	Uses a logical partition type not tied to physical devices
Volumes	Allows up to 64 mounted volumes	Allows up to 255 mounted NSS volumes
	Allows up to 32 segments per volume	Has no limit on the number of segments per volume
	Allows volume sizes up to 1TB	Allows volume sizes up to 8TB
Data capacity	Has lower limits on the number of volumes, files, and directories allowed	Allows much larger volumes, directories, and files than NWFS
Objects	Limits the size of objects such as files and volumes	Allows almost unlimited object sizes and supports almost any number of objects
Files	Has a 32-bit file system, which limits file sizes to 4GB	Has a 64-bit file system, which allows file sizes up to 8TB
	Allows up to 16 million files per server (actual limit is 16 million directory entries, which can mean even fewer files if additional name spaces are loaded)	Allows up to 8 trillion files per volume (dependent on a data limit of 8TB)
	Allows up to 100,000 open files per server	Allows up to 1,000,000 open files per server
Directory tree depth	Is limited to 100 directory levels	Is limited only by the client

Table 6-1   Differences Between NetWare File System and Novell Storage Services

Feature	NetWare File System (NWFS)	Novell Storage Services (NSS)
Mount time	Depends on volume size	Mounts large volumes in seconds
	In the event of an error, may take hours to repair and retrieve data	In the event of an error, recovers data faster and remounts volume faster
Storage administration	May require administration of volumes from several locations	Administers volumes from one location, even though volumes can reside on different devices
	Limits storage capacity according to the physical storage on a device	Does not limit storage availability to a single device
		Can recognize and use free space on various devices
Resources	May need more memory to support larger drives	Requires only 1MB of RAM, regardless of volume sizes
DOS partitions	Supports DOS partitions, but they can't be added as a volume	Allows DOS FAT partitions to be mounted as NSS volumes
CD-ROM support	Uses the old CDROM.NLM which has a slow indexing system	Mounts all CD-ROMs as NSS volumes
	Mounts CD-ROMs manually	Mounts CD-ROMs immediately and automatically
	Does not support non-DOS CD formats	Supports ISO 9660 and Macintosh HFS formats
Backup	Uses TSA, SMS, and enhanced SBACKUP	Requires the current version of TSA
Salvage	Can turn Salvage on and off only for the entire server	Can turn Salvage on and off by volume or by server
International languages	Uses ASCII double-byte characters	Uses UNICODE characters for complete internationalization
Extended attributes	Allows up to 16 attributes and 10 data streams	Allows unlimited attributes
File compression	Supports file compression	Does not support file compression*
Block suballocation	Supports block suballocation	Does not support block suballocation*
Transaction Tracking System (TTS)	Supports TTS	Does not support TTS*
SYS volume	Requires TTS and must reside on a NetWare file system volume	Cannot reside on an NSS volume*

* To be supported in the near future.

Table 6-1 Differences Between NetWare File System and Novell Storage Services *(continued)*

Have the CD Volume commands changed?

The CDROM.NLM is totally new, and mounts CDs automatically upon inserting them into the drive. Also, all CDs are mounted as NSS volumes. There is no need to remember any CD commands, because there are none. They have been removed, because there is no purpose for the commands to mount, dismount, or index the CD-ROM volumes.

 ## I have a CD-ROM disk in my server, but it's not showing up as a volume. What could be wrong?

CD-ROMs are automatically mounted as volumes as long as the appropriate CD-ROM drivers are running on your server. If you are having problems, try the following:

● Type **CDROM** at the server console to ensure that all necessary drivers for NSS ISO 9660–compliant CD-ROM support are loaded.

❋ *Note:* CDROM *will not load until NWPA disk NPA drivers are loaded.*

● Type **CDHFS.NSS** and press ENTER at the server console to load HFS support.

❋ *Note:* *To unload 9660 CD-ROM support, type* **unload CD9660.NSS** *at the server console. To unload HFS CD-ROM support, type* **unload CDHFS.NSS** *at the server console.*

 ## Do I have to convert all of my servers to take advantage of NSS?

No, NSS is optional and can be loaded or not on a server-by-server basis. It is not affected by the existence of NetWare 4.*x* server in your network or NDS tree.

 ## Can print queues exist on NSS volumes?

Yes, they are handled just as they would be on an NWFS volume.

Do additional name spaces still require an extra directory entry?

No, NSS volumes support DOS, NFS, MAC, and LONG name spaces without a separate directory entry for each name space type. As mentioned previously, all of the above name spaces are loaded automatically, by default on NSS volumes. NSS is designed to provide the capability to define new name space types, as well.

If you have one or more name spaces loaded on an NWFS volume on your NetWare 5 server, each name space loaded will still require an additional directory entry for each file on that volume.

Can I turn on Salvage by volume with NSS?

Yes, you have the choice of turning Salvage off for the entire file system or for each NSS volume individually. Any NWFS volumes would be controlled by the setting for the entire file system.

The commands and syntax for disabling or enabling Salvage on NSS volumes are covered in the section "NSS Administration Utilities," later in this chapter.

Do traditional applications such as FILER.EXE still work?

Yes, FILER is essentially the same as previous versions.

How do I use NDIR, MAP, FLAG, and RIGHTS?

Check your NetWare 5 documentation for the command syntax on these utilities, or enter the command at the DOS prompt with /? to get help with the syntax. In addition, with the new Novell Client, many of the functions performed by these utilities can be performed from within the Windows 95 Explorer, Network Neighborhood, or the new "N" utility in the Systray.

```
                                          NetWare Login...
                                          NetWare Connections...

            Personal Information...        Novell Map Network Drive...
            Work Information...            Disconnect Network Drive...
            Mailing Information...
            Edit Login Script...           Novell Capture Printer Port...
            Login Account Information...   Novell End Capture...
            Novell Password Administration...   Send Message...
            Group Memberships...
                                          User Administration for EMA_TREE  ▶
                                          Browse To                         ▶

                                          Configure System Tray Icon...
                                          Novell Client32 Properties...
```

CURRENT LIMITATIONS OF NSS

I heard NSS is incompatible with the SYS volume and the NDS database. Is this true?

Yes. NDS requires TTS, and TTS is not currently supported on NSS volumes, the SYS volume must be in NWFS format. Novell expects to release an update in the near future to allow SYS volumes to use the NSS format.

What features previously available are not available with NSS?

The following features are not currently available on NSS volumes:

- User space limits
- Block suballocation
- File compression
- Disk mirroring and duplexing
- NFS support

Novell expects to support these features in the next release of the NSS product. They are still supported on NWFS volumes. We have more information on these features in the next section of this chapter, "NWFS Features."

 If my SYS volume must have TTS and not be an NSS volume and I want to make it as small as possible, how should I calculate the minimum size for my SYS volume?

The minimum amount of space needed on the SYS volume depends on three questions:

● What portion of the operating system files will you install?

● How large is your NDS database on the server, and how much is it expected to grow?

● What amount of space will you need for data such as patches, NAL files, or queues?

The amount of space needed on SYS for the operating system is defined as follows:

● Volume minimum (OS only): 350MB

● All OS files without documentation: 375MB

● All products: 550MB

The NDS database is stored in a hidden subdirectory on the SYS volume. Therefore, it is very important to include the size of the NDS database in your calculations. To check the current size of your NDS database, RCONSOLE into the server, and from the Available Options screen, choose Directory Scan. For the directory to scan, type **sys:_netware**. You will see a list of the hidden files and their sizes.

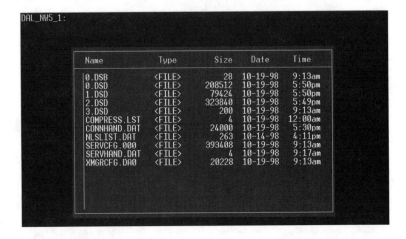

```
DAL_NW5_1:


  Name          Type      Size     Date       Time

  0.DSB         <FILE>        28   10-19-98    9:13am
  0.DSD         <FILE>    208512   10-19-98    5:50pm
  1.DSD         <FILE>     79424   10-19-98    5:50pm
  2.DSD         <FILE>    323840   10-19-98    5:49pm
  3.DSD         <FILE>       200   10-19-98    9:13am
  COMPRESS.LST  <FILE>         4   10-19-98   12:00am
  CONNHAND.DAT  <FILE>     24000   10-19-98    5:30pm
  NLSLIST.DAT   <FILE>       263   10-14-98    4:11pm
  SERVCFG.000   <FILE>    393408   10-19-98    9:13am
  SERVHAND.DAT  <FILE>         4   10-19-98    9:17am
  XMGRCFG.DA0   <FILE>     20228   10-19-98    9:13am
```

A third-party NLM utility, called NDSDIR, can display the name and sizes of all the NDS-related files from the SYS:_NETWARE directory. It is available from DreamLAN Network Consulting Ltd. at www.dreamlan.com. It also allows you to back up the NDS database in a single-server environment.

Allow space on your SYS volume for future patch files, additional NLM-based utilities, and third-party products you might plan to install.

Tip: *With the severe problems that can occur when you run out of space on SYS, most administrators place the print queues on volumes other than SYS, eliminating the print queues as a factor. Place NAL AOT files and the NAL Appfiles directory on a volume other than SYS for the same reason.*

Once you have all of this information together, try to err on the side of having too much space. You never want to run out of space on SYS, and you always can allocate some of the free space on your SYS volume to an NSS volume.

Use NWPRV.NSS to utilize extra space on SYS for other NSS volumes. To load NWPRV.NSS, change the NSS startup command line in the AUTOEXEC.NCF to include NWPRV as follows:

```
NSS NWPRV
```

This can only be done on startup of the NSS module.

Note: *Novell recommends that free space created from available space within an existing NWFS volume not be combined with unpartitioned free space on a hard disk or disk array, as unpredictable results may occur.*

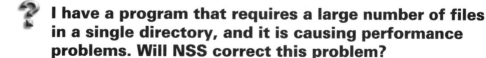

I have a program that requires a large number of files in a single directory, and it is causing performance problems. Will NSS correct this problem?

No, this is a DOS-related problem and is not resolved by NSS.

 NSS allows the administrator access to the DOS partition as a mounted volume. Have there been any problems reported with that scenario?

Yes, a problem was reported with DOS volume mount using DOSFAT.NSS, and a server ABEND. An interaction problem between the DOS volume mount and the debugger would not allow the debugger to do a diagnostic core dump or log the machine state to the ABEND.LOG file.

A workaround to this problem has been discovered. If you have the Auto Restart After Abend parameter set to 0, the debugger will function properly. If you have the parameter set to anything other than 0, you should not use the DOS volume mount feature.

✳ *Note:* *To load your local C: DOS partition, type* **NSS DOSFAT** *at the server prompt before loading any other NSS volumes.*

NWFS FEATURES

 Why are user space limits important?

The user space limit is another tool for the administrator of a NetWare network to proactively minimize problems on the servers. Viruses, malicious users, inexperienced users, or malfunctioning programs are all problems that can be limited by enabling user space limits on your server volumes.

 How are user space limits controlled in NetWare 5?

User space limits can be set for NWFS volumes only. NSS volumes do not allow this feature at this time. If you have NWFS volumes for which you want to set user space limits, you can use the NetWare Administrator. Follow these steps:

1. Load the NetWare Administrator.

2. Right-click the NWFS volume on which to place limits and select Details.

3. Click the User Space Limits button.

4. Select the search context and the list of users in that context who will populate the window.

5. Click the user for which you wish to set or modify a limit.

6. Click the Modify button and enter the limit in kilobytes.

7. Click the OK button.

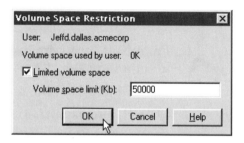

 Note: *You will notice that the window also displays the amount of disk space in use by the user.*

To set user space limits on multiple users you must approach the setting in the NetWare Administrator from the User object. Here are the steps required:

1. From within NetWare Administrator, select the users to set limits for from the tree.

2. Click Object from the menu and select Details on Multiple Users.

3. Click Volume Space Restriction.

4. Click the Add button and select a volume.

5. Enter the size limit in kilobytes and click the OK button.

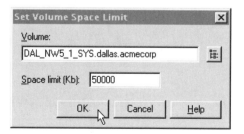

 Tip: *The easiest way to set volume space restrictions for your users is to set the limit in the template you use to create the users.*

One final note on space limits: space limitations can also be set by directory. This is helpful when you have a shared directory for a group of users, and you want to limit the amount of space they have available to them in that directory.

1. From NetWare Administrator, select the directory to set a limit for.

2. Click Object from the menu and select Details.

3. Click the Facts button.

4. Click the Restrict size check box.

5. Enter the limit for the directory in the Limit box.

6. Click the OK button.

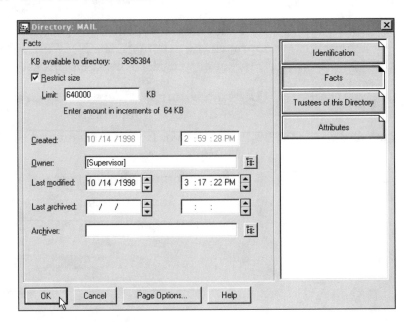

 What is block suballocation?

Block suballocation is a feature introduced in NetWare 4.10 that allows faster and more efficient use of space in a volume than previously available. Before block suballocation, each file would be stored in a separate block, and that block could not be shared with other files. For example, if you had a block size of 4K on your volume and you created a file 1K in size, that file would require an entire 4K block. Also, if you had a 17K file, it would use five 4K blocks. This feature was not very efficient, and the problem was only compounded if your volume was created with larger block sizes.

With suballocation, if a file is created that is larger than the size of your block size, or larger than an even multiple of your block size, the suballocation routine will break the remainder into the smallest number of chunks possible. The chunk sizes must be 512 bytes, 1K, 2K, 4K, 8K, 16K, or 32K. The routine then places these file chunks into preassigned blocks, which have only those size chunks already in them. Therefore, the disk is comprised of a limited number of fragmented and partially filled blocks. The result is a maximum of 511 bytes of wasted space per file.

As an example, let's say our volume has a block size of 64K and we have created a file 129.5K in size. This file would use two 64K blocks completely, with 1.5K left over. The balance would be placed in one 1K chunk and one 512-byte chunk. These chunks would then be inserted into blocks, which have the appropriate size chunks in them. Blocks containing partial file chunks are created as needed. If we still had 64K block sizes without suballocation, this one file would have used three complete blocks and wasted 62.5K!

Novell recommends a 64K block size with disk block suballocation for all volumes. NWFS is optimized to use 64K blocks with suballocation. Also, because you have fewer blocks with 64K block sizes, FAT tables are smaller.

 Note: *Once an NWFS volume is created, the block size is set and cannot be changed without re-creating the volume. We recommend that you use the 64K block size unless you have hardware constraints that do not allow block sizes that large.*

In NetWare 4.11, I could access long filename directories by shortening the name of the directory to eight characters. Why can't I do the same in NetWare 5?

The long 8.3 name generation algorithm was changed in NetWare 5 to emulate how Windows 95 and Windows NT create short names from long names. For example, in NetWare 4.11, you could access the \users\johnsmith directory by typing **\users\johnsmit**. However, in NetWare 5, you have to add a tilde, so that the preceding directory would be entered as **\users\johnsm~1**.

Does file compression work the same on all types of files?

No. The amount of space saved by compression can vary greatly for different file types. The average space saved per file by compression is between 60 and 70 percent. If you include files that cannot be compressed, the efficiency falls to about 50 percent. Novell reports the following average percentage gains for compression by file type:

File Type	Percentage of Space Gained
Executable	40 to 60%
Text	60 to 80%
Fonts	40 to 60%

Doesn't file compression slow down file reads and writes?

Not usually. With regard to writes, compression is a low-priority thread that is done in the background. Therefore, it does not have a noticeable impact on performance.

 Note: *If a file is set for Immediate Compression, performance can be affected. We recommend the use of this option sparingly.*

When reading files, decompression is a high-priority thread, so that files will be decompressed quickly when they are accessed. The decompression speed is 1MB per second.

Also, data is made available as soon as it is decompressed, even when the entire file has not yet been decompressed. This means that if a user tries to access data stored in the first bytes of a large file, those bytes will be available as soon as they are decompressed, while the rest of the file continues to be decompressed.

How can I check the compression statistics?

Compression statistics for a volume can be checked in the NetWare Administrator.

1. Select the volume in the NDS tree.
2. Right-click and select Details.
3. Click the Statistics button.

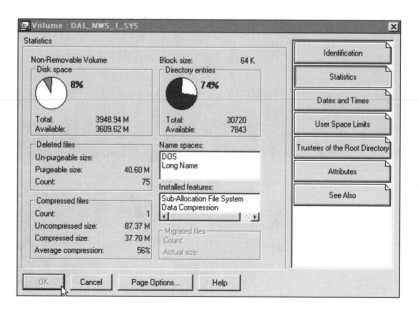

You can check the compression statistics by file using the FILER utility.

1. Load the FILER.EXE program in SYS:PUBLIC.

2. Select Manage Files and Directories and press ENTER.

3. Search through the directories for the file, highlight it, and press ENTER.

4. Select View/Set File Information and press ENTER.

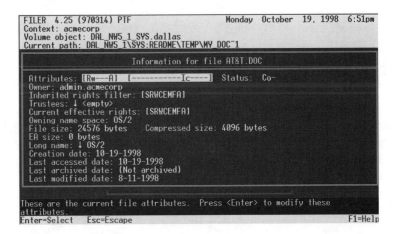

You can also check to see if a file has been compressed (Co status) by typing the **NDIR /COMP** or **FLAG** *command*, but you cannot display statistics on compression efficiency.

To check compression for a volume using NDIR, type **NDIR /VOLUME** at a DOS prompt.

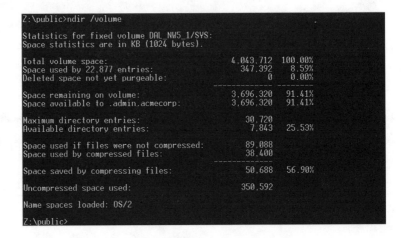

 ## What commands should I use to change the compression settings?

Compression is controlled by SET parameters and by file attributes set using the FLAG command-line utility.

For a list of the SET parameters that affect file compression, (see Table 6-2).

The FLAG command-line utility can be used to set file compression attributes on individual directories or files. The

Parameter	Description	Default
Compression Daily Check Starting Hour	The hour when you want to start scanning for files that need to be compressed.	0 (midnight)
Compression Daily Check Stop Hour	The hour when you want to stop scanning for files that need to be compressed.	6 (6:00 AM)
Minimum Compression Percentage Gain	The minimum percentage a file must compress in order to remain compressed.	20
Enable File Compression	The ON setting turns on file compression for a server.	ON
Maximum Concurrent Compressions	The maximum number of files that can be actively compressed at one time.	2
Convert Compressed to Uncompressed Option	The 0 setting means the files will always be left compressed. The 1 setting means to leave compressed if only accessed once in the Days Untouched parameter. The 2 setting means to always decompress.	1
Decompress Percent Disk Space Free to Allow Commit	The percentage of free disk space required on a volume for file decompression to permanently change compressed files to decompressed.	10
Decompress Free Space Warning Interval	The time between alerts when the file system is not changing compressed files to decompressed files because of insufficient disk space.	31 minutes and 18.5 seconds

Table 6-2   SET Parameters That Affect File Compression

Parameter	Description	Default
Deleted Files Compression Option	The 0 setting means deleted files will not be compressed. The 1 setting means to compress deleted files the next day. The 2 setting means to compress immediately.	1
Days Untouched Before Compression	The number of days the system waits after a file was last accessed before it is compressed.	14

Table 6-2 SET Parameters That Affect File Compression *(continued)*

attributes are Immediate Compress (IC) and Don't Compress (DC). The syntax statements are as follows:

- **FLAG *path* +IC**   Set the file or directory to Immediate Compress.
- **FLAG *path* +DC**   Set the file or directory to Don't Compress.
- **FLAG *path* -IC**   Remove Immediate Compress setting.
- **FLAG *path* -DC**   Remove Don't Compress setting.

These options can also be set using NetWare Administrator.
FLAG can also be used to check the status of a file or directory. For example,

- **FLAG *path***   Look for indicators: Cc = Can't Compress; Co = Compressed.

 Note: *Remember, file compression is not possible on NSS volumes at this time.*

 I currently have file compression enabled on my SYS volume, and I want to disable it. How can I do that?

You cannot disable file compression without re-creating the volume and restoring the data.

NSS COMPONENTS AND ARCHITECTURE

 What are the components that make up NSS, and how do they differ from NWFS?

NSS consists of NSS partitions, storage groups, NSS volumes, directories, and files. NWFS consists of NetWare partitions, volumes, directories, and files. The differences between NSS and NWFS are the storage group component in NSS and the distinction between NSS and NWFS partitions.

NSS scans each of your storage devices to find free space for NSS to use and lists each free space as a separate storage deposit. From this pool of storage deposits, you can select how much space you want NSS to claim ownership of. When NSS claims the free space on a device, it becomes an NSS managed object. Then, from the NSS managed objects, you can create storage groups and NSS volumes. The space on each storage device that is owned by NSS is an NSS partition.

 Note: A storage group *is a pool of free storage space that represents logical space owned by NSS. Once NSS claims this free space, it becomes a managed object, which can be divided into other storage groups and NSS volumes.*

For example, let's say you have two 1GB drives in a server, and you create two NWFS partitions on the first drive and leave the second drive unpartitioned. If you load NWCONFIG and scan the devices for free space, the second drive will display as available free space. This is a *storage deposit*. Once you claim ownership for this space, it becomes a *managed object,* and an NSS *partition* is created on the disk. Next, if you create a *storage group* with this managed object, you can configure one or more NSS volumes in the storage group as shown in Figure 6-1.

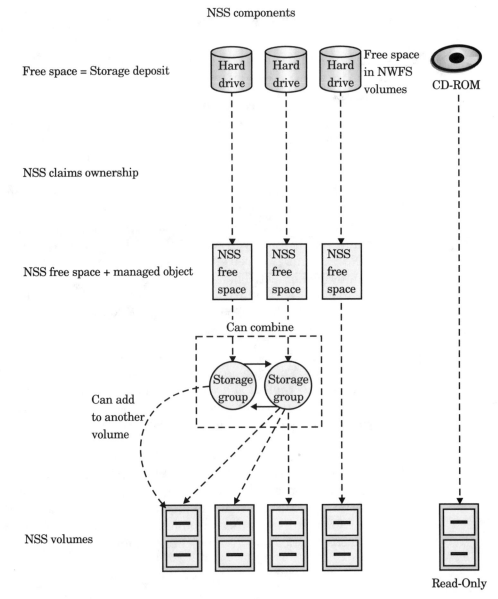

Figure 6-1 NSS components drawing

 I understand the components of NSS, but how does all of this work architecturally?

The NSS architecture, shown in Figure 6-2, consists of the following layers:

- Media Access Layer (MAL)
- Loadable Storage Subsystem (LSS)
- Object Engine
- Common Layer Interface (CLI)
- Semantic Agent (SA) layer

The *Media Access Layer* (MAL) provides connection to and communication with storage devices such as hard drives and CD-ROMs. It lets the network administrator create storage groups and volumes through the MAL managers that view and manage the storage capabilities of servers as a quantity of storage deposits.

The storage object bank is the central layer of the MAL and is responsible for the registration of the storage manager and storage objects. The registered provider in the MAL places storage deposits in the object bank. Each registered storage object in the object bank has a deposit type. In turn, each storage deposit type is tagged with attributes, such as Read-Only for a CD-ROM drive.

Storage managers are divided into two types: consumers and providers. They are the managers you select when setting up or changing the NSS configuration.

 Note: *Although designed to support a variety of storage devices, NSS currently only recognizes hard drives and CD-ROM storage devices. In the future, NSS will support other storage device types through the storage provider modules.*

Providers query the server's storage devices for free space. They find, manage, and register storage objects, such as NWFS volumes, DOS partitions, or CD-ROMs in the object bank. Providers can recognize partition types.

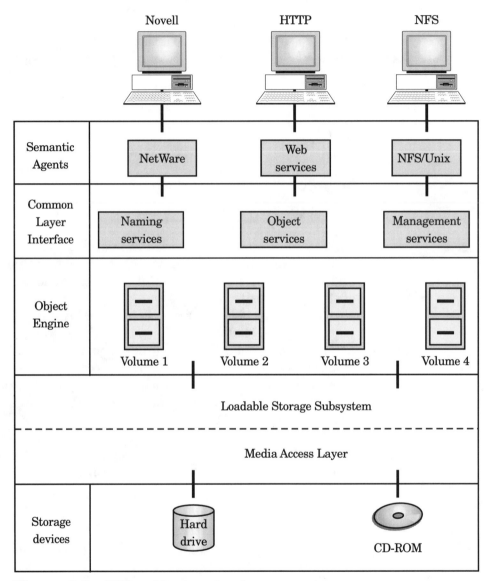

Figure 6-2 NSS architecture drawing

Providers perform four functions:

- Locating partitions or NWFS volumes
- Determining whether they are in use

- Constructing storage objects if they are not already created
- Depositing the storage objects as storage deposits in the object bank

When adding new media, you choose a provider to scan and recognize the device for NSS configuration.

Consumers are attached to the file system and help create the file input/output path. They configure and take ownership of the storage deposits that have been placed in the object bank by the provider. Consumers register themselves with the object bank so they can control storage deposits that are owned. The consumers take NSS ownership of the free space for storage group and NSS volume creation. NSS consumers cannot own NWFS partition space, but they can consume free space inside an NWFS volume.

The *Loadable Storage Subsystem* (LSS) contains the loadable file system types that various devices understand. The file system types currently supported include DOS FAT for local hard drives, ISO 9660 and Macintosh HFS for CD-ROMs, and the NSS file system. The LSS recognizes all of these formats as NSS volumes.

The LSS communicates with the MAL about the storage devices it recognizes. The MAL returns information to the LSS about what storage devices it identifies and registers an NSS volume on the storage devices with NSS. The LSS then receives information from the MAL about the NSS volume and passes the information up to the *Semantic Agent (SA) layer*, so the volume can be viewed at the client workstation.

The *Object Engine* is the NSS object store. This is the layer that allows higher levels of volume, directory, and file efficiency. The Object Engine uses sophisticated and efficient mechanisms to manage the objects it stores, achieving high levels of performance, scalability, robustness, and modularity.

The Object Engine stores objects on disk in balanced trees, called *B-trees*, to achieve better performance. The compact B-trees guarantee that the system can retrieve an object from disk in no more than four input/output cycles. They also allow the system to locate an object anywhere in storage without loading the entire directory entry table into memory.

The ability to share name spaces is another feature provided by the Object Engine.

The Object Engine provides greater scalability in using a 64-bit interface. This allows a much greater number of objects and objects of much larger size than in NWFS. Objects for the Object Engine are defined as volumes, directories, and files.

Rapid recovery from error is made possible by the Object Engine and LSS. LSS maintains a log of all transactions written and waiting to be written to disk. The Object Engine defines the interface, which allows the LSS to implement journaled management recovery. NSS does this by referencing the journal, noting the incomplete transaction, and reprocessing the incomplete transaction or backing it out completely.

The modularity of the Object Engine lets the administrator define new storage objects and add them to the storage system as they are needed. An update for NSS has already been released that add support for Digital Video Disc (DVD) as a storage device. Other future technologies like DVD could be plugged into the engine without affecting other pieces of the software.

The *Common Layer Interface (CLI)* contains a set of Application Protocol Interfaces that define the interfaces the Semantic Agent uses to access the Object Engine for NSS naming, object, and management services. They are defined as follows:

- *Naming services* consist of basic object naming and lookup operations, as well as name space and context management services.

- *Object services* provide the creation, deletion, storage, and definition of objects.

- *Management services* provide registration, file locking, transactions, and management of storage groups and NSS volumes.

The Semantic Agent layer contains loadable software modules that define client-specific interfaces available to stored NSS objects.

 ## How will the architecture help with future storage devices and clients?

As we mentioned before, the modularity of the Object Engine is designed to accept storage objects from new types of storage devices as they become available. Also, semantic agents that implement an HTTP interface can be created, allowing Web browser access to data stored by the Object Engine. Other semantic agents could be created to provide as-yet-unknown client types access to data stored by the Object Engine.

INSTALLING AND UPGRADING TO NSS

 ## What are my upgrade options?

If you choose the option to perform a server upgrade during NetWare 5 installation, all of your existing partitions, volumes, and data will be retained. The partitions will remain in NWFS format.

Once the file server is upgraded, you can perform an In-Place Upgrade to NSS volumes. Remember that the SYS volume must remain an NWFS volume. The requirements for an In-Place Upgrade are as follows:

● A server running NetWare 5

● One or more NWFS volumes other than SYS to convert to new NSS volumes

● A good verified backup of your data

● Enough free space for your NSS volume

✚ ***Tip:*** *Make sure that you take into consideration that NSS does not support file compression and suballocation. You will need to allow for extra space on your NSS volume to compensate.*

The In-Place Upgrade is initiated at the server console. You can only do this between volumes on a single server. The current version does not allow you to move or copy the volumes between two servers.

When you use this utility to move or copy volumes, the NSS volume is created automatically.

You can execute the command in three ways:

- ipcu *NetWare-volume_name*

  This command *moves* an existing NWFS volume to a new NSS volume. The old NWFS volume still exists, but the contents are empty, except for the NSS volume (it is recognized as a file). The new NSS volume resides inside the old NWFS volume. (This is the main difference between this option and the third option.)

- ipcu *NetWare_volume_name NSS_volume_name*

  This command *copies* an NWFS volume to a new NSS volume. The contents in the NWFS volume remain intact. The name of the new volume is *volume_name*_nss.

- ipcu –d *NetWare-volume_name NSS-volume_name*

  This final command option moves an NWFS volume from a specific location to the new NSS volume. The old NWFS volume still exists, but the contents are empty except for NSS.

Tip: *If you delete the NWFS volume when an NSS volume is created from free space inside an NWFS volume, the NSS volume is deleted as well.*

I don't want to use the In-Place Upgrade. How else can I transfer the data from an NWFS volume to a new NSS volume?

The best alternative would be to create a new NSS volume and restore the data from the backup. You *must* test your restore to an NSS volume prior to trying this method. It is also important that you set the data to be backed up as uncompressed. Otherwise, you will not be able to restore the files to your NSS volume. In ArcServe, use the Force Decompression of Compressed Files option in Global Backup Options.

Once again, you must allow extra space for the data on the new NSS volume because it does not support file compression or block suballocation.

 What disk drivers must I use?

NetWare 5 requires the use of HAM drivers. DSK drivers are no longer supported. Contact the manufacturer of your controller adapter if the driver you need is not included with NetWare 5.

 What happens if I don't create an NSS volume during installation?

You are not required to create an NSS volume. It would be a good idea to have a plan if you want to add one after the server installation is complete. You wouldn't want to allocate all available free space to NWFS volumes and determine later that you wanted to create NSS volumes from half of that space. In that scenario, you would need to remove one or more NWFS volumes to achieve your objective.

 How can I create an NSS volume after installation?

We will discuss this subject in more detail in the next section, but here are the steps:

1. At the server console, type **NWCONFIG** and press ENTER.
2. Select NSS Disk Options.
3. Select Storage.
4. Select Assign Ownership and choose space from the listing of Available Free Space. Enter the Size in megabytes and confirm the action by selecting Yes.
5. Press ESC to return to the Available NSS Options, select NSS Volume Options, and log in as an administrator.
6. Select Create and choose Storage Group.
7. Select a managed object to create a storage group and confirm by selecting Yes.
8. Choose NSS Volume.
9. Select a managed object to create the volume. Name the volume, and select Yes to confirm. You should see

confirmation that the volume has been created and added to NDS.

10. Note that the volume is not yet mounted. You can return to the server console and type **MOUNT** *volume_name*.

 Note: *NSS volumes can also be created using the NSS Administration utility.*

Are NSS volumes automatically added to NDS?

It depends. NSS volumes are automatically added to the NDS tree if the NSS volume is created using the NWCONFIG utility and NDS is loaded on the server.

If you created your NSS volume using the NSS Administration utility, you must add the volume to NDS using NWCONFIG, or the NetWare Administrator.

 Note: *CD-ROMs are not added to NDS automatically. Use NWCONFIG to add them.*

How do I add my NSS volume to the NDS tree?

Using NWCONFIG, make sure the volume is mounted, then follow these steps:

1. From the server console, type **NWCONFIG** and press ENTER.

2. Select Directory Options.

3. Select Upgrade mounted volumes into the directory.

4. Log in to the NDS tree. (You must have appropriate rights to create a volume.)

5. Select your NSS volume from the list.

Using the NetWare Administrator, also make sure the volume is mounted; then do the following:

1. Log in to the network at a client workstation.

2. Run the NetWare Administrator program for your type of workstation.

3. Click the container in the tree in which the NSS volume is to be located.

4. Press INSERT or click the New Object icon.

5. Select Volume as the object type and click OK.

6. Enter the NDS volume name and server, and select the NSS volume from the list of physical volumes.

7. Click Create.

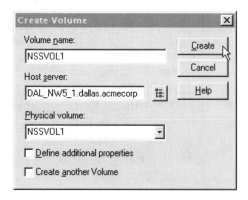

 Tip: *If you rename a volume using NWCONFIG, you will need to rename the volume in NDS using the NetWare Administrator.*

How do I remove an NSS Volume object from the NDS tree?

Use the NetWare Administrator to remove the Volume object from NDS. Load the NetWare Administrator; then highlight the Volume object and press DELETE. This will remove the volume from the NDS, but will not remove the volume itself.

Can volumes be expanded? Can they decrease in size?

NSS volumes can be increased in size. NWFS volumes can be expanded by adding new segments to the volumes with the following limitations:

● The maximum number of segments per volume is 32.

- The maximum number of segments you can create on one hard drive is 8.
- The maximum number of volumes per server allowed is 64.

Both NSS and NWFS volumes can only be decreased in size by removing them and re-creating the volumes with the new size parameters.

NSS ADMINISTRATION UTILITIES

 What utility is used to manage NSS volumes?

There are actually two utilities used to manage NSS volumes, with some feature overlap between the two. The first means of configuration is the NWCONFIG utility, and the second is the NSS Administration menus. The general recommendation is to use NWCONFIG to create your initial NSS volumes. Then use the NWCONFIG or NSS Administration menus to do maintenance work as needed.

Use NWCONFIG instead of the NSS Administration menus to create NSS storage groups and volumes. It is convenient if you are also managing NWFS volumes and are familiar with the standard NetWare menu-based utilities.

NWCONFIG does not have all of the features of the NSS Administration menus, but once you are comfortable with the two utilities, you should be able to move between the two without confusion. Here are the features not available with NWCONFIG:

- The ability to use the REBUILD command to rebuild the NSS volume
- The ability to use the VERIFY command to verify the NSS volume

The following list provides the basics regarding the configuration of NSS volumes with NWCONFIG. To load NWCONFIG and configure NSS, follow these steps:

1. Type **NWCONFIG** and press ENTER at the server console. (NSS will automatically load with NWCONFIG if it is not loaded already.)

2. Choose NSS Disk Options.

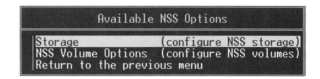

3. Select Storage. (This allows the administrator to view and prepare free space for NSS configuration.) Storage provides the following options:

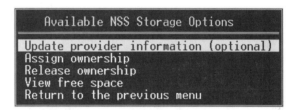

4. Press ESC to return to the Available NSS Options menu, and then select NSS Volume Options.

5. Authenticate to the NDS tree with administrator rights. The Available NSS Volume Options menu is shown here:

- If you want to create a single NSS volume from a single device, select Create from the NSS Volume Options menu, select a managed object designated as Single, and enter a name for your volume.

- If you want to create multiple NSS volumes in one storage group, create the storage group by following these steps:

   a. Select Create from the Available NSS Volume Options menu.

    b. Select Storage Group and press ENTER; then select Yes in the Confirm Action window.

    c. Select Create from the NSS Volume Options menu, and then select a managed object designated as Group.

    d. Enter the size you wish to make your volume and enter the volume name.

    e. Repeat this procedure until you have created the number of volumes desired or until you use all of the space in your storage group.

6. Load the NSS Administration menu (shown here) from the server console by typing **NSS MENU** at the server console.

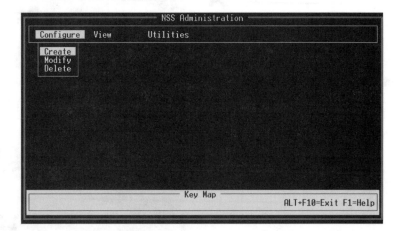

The NSS Administration menu contains all of the features related to NSS volumes that are provided in NWCONFIG. There are three drop-down menus on this page:

- **Configure** Allows you to configure NSS storage groups and NSS volumes

- **View** Allows you to view free space, NSS storage groups, and NSS volumes

- **Utilities** Contains the REBUILD and VERIFY utilities

> *Note:* *NSS must be loaded before the NSS Administration menus are loaded. Also, remember that if you create an NSS volume using the NSS Administration menus, you will need to add the volume to the NDS tree using the NetWare Administrator or NWCONFIG.*

How do I mount my NSS volumes? Is it any different than mounting an NWFS volume?

NSS volumes can be mounted by typing the **MOUNT ALL** or **MOUNT** *volume_name* command from the server console. If the volume does not mount, check to see if it is active by typing **NSS VOLUMES** from the server console.

If the volume is not active, type the following command at the server console: /Activate=*volume_name*.

Can I mix a storage object created from free space in an NWFS volume with regular unpartitioned free space storage objects to create a single NSS volume?

Yes and no. You actually can do that, but Novell recommends against it, stating that "unpredictable results may occur."

Can NSS commands be issued outside of the NSS Administration utility?

Yes, in addition to NWCONFIG and the NSS Administration menus, you can manage NSS volumes from the server console with NSS command-line utility commands.

NSS Command-Line Utilities

SALVAGE In NSS, you can turn Salvage on or off for each NSS volume. If the Immediate Purge of Deleted Files SET parameter is turned on, Salvage is disabled for all volumes on the server, including all NSS volumes. The NSS commands to configure the Salvage options are as follows:

NSS /Salvage=all enables SALVAGE on all NSS volumes.

NSS /Salvage=*volume_name* enables SALVAGE on the NSS volume you specify.

NSS /Nosalvage=all disables SALVAGE on all NSS volumes.

NSS /Nosalvage=*volume_name* disables SALVAGE on a specific NSS volume.

Caution: *If Salvage is turned off for an NSS volume by using /**Nosalvage** or by using the SET parameter, all deleted files are automatically purged from the NSS volume and can no longer be salvaged.*

INFORMATION ONLY Other NSS server console commands are used for information purposes. The next commands display information only:

NSS /Modules lists the providers, loadable storage subsystems, and semantic agents.
NSS /Status lists the current NSS status.
VOLUMES lists all mounted NWFS and NSS volumes, including NSS_Admin.
NSS Volumes lists all the NSS volumes, including NSS_Admin.
NSS Exit unloads the NSS modules.
NSS Help or **/?** allows you to access Help for the NSS commands.

NSS LOAD COMMANDS The following commands control the loading of NSS modules and the NSS Administration menus:

NSS /Menu opens the NSS Administration menus for NSS configuration management.
NSS /(No)SkipLoadModules prevents autoloading of all the NSS modules. This lets you load only the NSS modules you need.

DOS FAT COMMANDS The next list of commands control the settings for the File Allocation Table (FAT):

NSS /(No)FATInMemory loads the entire FAT into memory for faster access, regardless of its size. The default is OFF.
NSS /(No)FATLongNames enables long filenames on FAT volumes. The default is ON.

NSS /(No)FATLazyWrites performs lazy writes of FAT. If set to ON, data that is written will be kept in memory for a specified period of time before it is also written to FAT. This increases performance. The default is ON.

NSS /FATLazyWriteDelay=value sets the FAT lazy write delay (in seconds). When (No)FATLazyWrites is set to ON, you specify how many seconds you want data kept in memory before it is written to FAT. The default is 60. The range is 5–180.

NSS /FATPartition=*partition_type_number* supports up to three additional partition types containing 16-bit FATs, such as /FATPartition=12,13.

OTHER NSS COMMANDS   These commands control miscellaneous settings for NSS volumes:

NSS /Activate=*volume_name* activates an NSS volume.

NSS /Deactivate=*volume_name* deactivates an NSS volume.

NSS /Maintenance=*volume_name* switches the specified NSS volume to maintenance mode.

NSS /ForceActivate=*volume_name* forces an NSS volume to become active.

NSS /RebuildVolume=*volume_name* rebuilds the specified NSS volume.

NSS /VerifyVolume allows you to select an NSS volume from the menu to verify the volume's physical integrity.

NSS /RebuildVolume allows you to select an NSS volume from the menu for rebuild.

NSS /AutoVerifyVolume=*volume_name* allows you to verify an NSS volume at startup.

NSS /StorageAlarmThreshold=*value* allows you to set the threshold for a low storage space warning. The default is 10. The range is 0 to 1,000,000.

NSS /StorageResetThreshold=*value* allows you to reset the threshold for a low storage space warning. The default is 10. The range is 1 to 1,000,000.

NSS /(No)StorageAlertMessages turns ON or OFF the low storage message to users. The default is ON.

NSS /NumWorkToDo=*value* sets the number of WorkToDo entries that may be concurrently executing. NSS uses WorkToDo entries for tasks such as flushing file metadata to disk in the background. Increasing the

number of WorkToDo entries might be useful on a system that is heavily used. NSS always reserves 20 WorkToDo entries. The default is 40. The range is 5 to 100.

NSS /FileFlushTimer=*value* sets the flush time for modified open files in seconds. Increasing this number might reduce the number of writes to disk; however, it increases the amount of data that will be lost if the system crashes. The default is 10 seconds. The range is 1 to 3,600 seconds.

NSS /OpenFileHashShift=*value* sets the size of the Open File hash table (in powers of 2). If many files are used concurrently on the server, we recommend that you increase this number. The default is 11. The range is 8 to 20.

NSS /ClosedFileHashShift=*value* sets the number of closed files that can be cached in memory. The default is 512. The range is 1 to 100,000.

NSS /MailBoxSize=*value* sets the size of your mailbox. The default is 228. The range is 64 to 256.

How can I optimize the cache buffers setting for NSS?

We discussed at the beginning of this chapter the way that NSS uses cache buffers (see "What are the requirements for creating an NSS volume?"). The settings are controlled by the NSS command-line utility. The default cache buffers can be modified at the server console with the following commands:

- **NSS /MinBufferCacheSize** sets the minimum buffer size. The default is 512. The range is 256 to 1,048,576. When NSS is loaded, it requires at least 512 cache buffers.

- **NSS /MinOSBufferCacheSize** sets the minimum size for NetWare. The default is 1,024. The range is 1,024 to 1,048,576. We do not recommend that you set this value below 1,024.

- **NSS /NameCacheSize** sets the number of Name Cache entries. NSS keeps a cache of file and directory entry names it has recently looked up. This speeds up opening files and path searches. The default is 2,111. The range is 3 to 65,521.

- **NSS /(No)NameCache** sets Name Cache to ON or OFF. The default is ON.

- **NSS /(No)CacheBalance** sets the buffers to percentages, rather than integers, for dynamic balancing of free memory for the buffer cache. The default is ON. Use this switch with /MinBufferCacheSize.

- **NSS /CacheBalance** sets the percent of free memory NSS uses for its cache buffer. The CacheBalance percentage determines how many cache blocks NSS will take from the traditional NetWare file system for its own cache. If this number is too large, some NLMs may be difficult to load. If you use NSS extensively, the default should be changed. The default is 10 percent. The range is from 1 to 99 percent.

- **NSS /CacheBalanceTimer** sets the cache balance timer in seconds. NSS checks the total number of cache buffers in the system and determines whether or not the CacheBalance percentage is met. NSS then gives or takes the appropriate number of cache buffers. The default is 30. The range is 1 to 3,600.

- **NSS /AuthCacheSize** sets the number of Authorization Cache entries. If many trustees have been set on different files and directories, we recommend that you increase this number. The default is 1,024. The range is 16 to 50,000.

- **NSS /BufferFlushTimer** sets the flush time for modified cache buffers in seconds. The default is 1 second. The range is 1 to 3,600 seconds.

- **NSS /CacheStats** shows the buffer cache statistics.

 Note: *You can set the buffers in percentages rather than integers.*

 ## What happens when I delete a storage object or volume?

When you delete or remove an NSS volume, a storage group, or NSS ownership, the related objects are affected differently, depending on which link in the chain you remove:

 When you delete an NSS volume, the data and volume are removed, but the storage group remains.

 When you delete a storage group, the NSS volume, the data on the volume, and the storage group are removed, but the NSS ownership remains.

 When you release NSS ownership, the NSS volume, the data on the volume, and the storage group are removed, and the storage deposit returns to free space.

FILE SYSTEM SECURITY

What is the difference between trustee rights on files and directories that are granted, and rights that are filtered with an Inherited Rights Filter (IRF)?

Trustee rights can be granted, but IRFs can only filter, or block, rights. In fact, trustee rights can be used to revoke previously granted rights similar to IRFs. If a User object GeorgeW has [RWCEMF] rights to directory APPS, a new trustee assignment on the subdirectory NOTES of [R F] for GeorgeW would supercede the rights granted at the higher directory level of APPS. The effective rights would be essentially the same as an IRF, which filtered all of the rights except R and F.

Note: *If you add a trustee to a subdirectory with no rights in order to block all rights, the rights will be blocked just like an IRF; but, if you open the Details window in the NetWare Administrator for the Trustee object, the Rights to Files and Directories window will not show a trustee assignment for the revoked rights. The effective rights are correct, but the Rights to Files and Directories window will only display granted rights. If you check the trustee rights from the directory object, the trustee will display correctly. The bottom line is that using trustee access rights to filter rights can make the file system security more difficult to manage, because to find all of the trustee settings created in this manner requires checking the trustee rights directory by directory.*

 ## What happens if you want to block the Supervisor right?

You cannot block the Supervisor right with trustee settings at a lower level in the directory or with an IRF. You can only remove the Supervisor right from the trustee setting where the Supervisor right was granted.

 ## How do I calculate the effective rights for a User object when I have rights granted by a container and the user, and an IRF is in place?

If you have a complicated situation with trustee rights granted at a higher level in the directory, an IRF at a lower level, and trustee rights also granted at the lower level, it may be easier to create a table to calculate the rights. See the example shown here. (For this example, assume GeorgeW is a member of the Sales Group.)

Directory	Rights Assigned	Object	Rights Granted or Filtered
VOL1:\APPS	Group Trustee Rights Granted	Sales (Group)	+ [RWCEMF]
VOL1:\APPS\ GRPWISE	IRF [SR - - - - F -] (list before trustee rights granted)		– [WCEM A]
	Inherited Rights		= [R F]
	User Trustee Rights Granted	GeorgeW (User)	+ [WCE]
	GeorgeW's Effective Rights		= [RWCE F]

The table takes the rights granted at a higher level and removes rights filtered at the current level or higher. The result is the inherited rights. Add to the inherited rights those explicitly granted at the current level to determine the effective rights at the current level.

 ## How should I grant rights to the objects in my NDS tree to manage trustee assignments efficiently?

To limit the effort needed to administer the rights, you should assign rights to objects in the following order:

1. [Public]

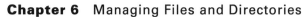

2. Container objects

3. Group and Organizational Role objects

4. User objects

5. Security equivalence (for temporary use only)

To make your file system security efficient, you must plan the trustee assignments. Try to assign the rights as high as possible on the list, while allowing access where needed and denying access where it is not desired. However, there are few practical situations where rights should be granted to [Public].

MAINTENANCE

 What backup programs can I use with NSS?

Storage Management Services (SMS) and Enhanced SBACKUP can perform backups and restores to and from your NSS volume. SMS is a collection of programs shipped with NetWare 5. Enhanced SBACKUP is one of those programs and is referred to as a Storage Management Engine. The Target Service Agent (TSA500) version shipped with NetWare 5 is required for backing up NSS volumes.

 How can I be sure if my third-party backup software will work with NetWare 5 or NSS?

Make sure that you are using the latest version of the TSA500, and then call the manufacturer of your backup software.

 Does VREPAIR still work in NetWare 5?

For NSS volumes, VREPAIR has been replaced by the REBUILD and VERIFY NSS administration commands. However, VREPAIR is still required for repairing NWFS volumes.

VREPAIR is used to repair data errors caused by hardware problems, power failures, or mirroring errors. It also can be used to remove name spaces, which are no longer needed. If a volume fails to mount as the server is booting, VREPAIR will load automatically and try to repair the volume. If VREPAIR loads automatically, it will use the default options.

In order to run VREPAIR, the volume must be dismounted, and the corresponding NLM for extra name spaces must be in the SYS:SYSTEM directory. The NLM for the LONG name space would be V_LONG.NLM, and the NLM for the MAC name space would be V_MAC.NLM.

Tip: *Copy VREPAIR.NLM and the NLM for the appropriate name spaces to the DOS partition of your server. This will allow you to run VREPAIR if SYS is the volume having a problem mounting.*

The basic procedures for running VREPAIR are as follows:

1. At the server console, type **DISMOUNT *volume_name*** (if the volume is already mounted).

2. Type **VREPAIR**.

3. Review the VREPAIR options. Choose Set VRepair Options and press ENTER.

4. Once you are satisfied with the settings, press ESC or type **5** to return to the first level of the VREPAIR menu.

5. Begin the repair process by selecting Repair A Volume, and select Option 4 to continue. If you did not specify the volume name while loading VREPAIR and there is more than one volume dismounted, you must select the volume to be repaired.

6. Monitor the server console screen for messages.

7. If you want to change the error settings during the repair process, press F1 from the VREPAIR Status screen to modify the current error settings.

8. After the repair process is complete, answer **Y** to write repairs to the disk.

9. If VREPAIR has found errors, run the process again until VREPAIR finds no errors.

10. If you are unable to mount the volume after running VREPAIR several times, you must delete the volume and re-create it using NWCONFIG.

 ## What is the procedure for recovering from a corrupted NSS volume?

NSS volumes can recover from software failures using the REBUILD utility. This is only useful for software failures, not hardware failures. The REBUILD utility takes much less time to recover an NSS volume than an NWFS volume using VREPAIR.

REBUILD verifies and uses the existing leaves of an object tree to rebuild all the other trees in the system. While the volumes are being verified and rebuilt, they are placed in maintenance mode. The NSS volumes are not usable until the process is completed and the volume is remounted.

REBUILD creates an error file at the root of SYS named VOLUME_NAME.RLF. That means that the error file for a volume called NSS_VOL1 would be NSS_VOL1.RLF. Each time REBUILD is run, it overwrites this file. If you want to keep previous copies of the error file, you should move the file to another location.

REBUILD can be run from the server console or from the NSS Administration menu. Your NSS volumes can be mounted or dismounted, but remember that they are placed in maintenance mode during the process. REBUILD is not available in NWCONFIG.

To use REBUILD from the server console, follow these steps:

1. Type **LOAD NSS** and press ENTER.

2. Choose one of the following commands:

   - **NSS /Rebuild** This command will display a list of volumes available for rebuilding that you can select from to begin the rebuild process.

   - **NSS /Rebuild=nss_volume_name** This command will begin the rebuild process on a single volume.

   - **NSS /Rebuild=nss_volume_name1, nss_volume_name2, ...** This command begins the rebuild process on more than one volume at once.

You can rebuild up to five NSS volumes at one time. You can switch to the monitor screen for each by pressing ALT-ESC.

3. View the output screen to monitor the time elapsed, time remaining, number of objects, and other information.

4. Verify the rebuilt NSS volume using one of the following commands:

   ● NSS /Verify=nss_*volume_name*

   ● NSS /Verify=all

   ● NSS /Verify (select a volume from the list)

5. Mount the volume, if necessary.

To use REBUILD using the NSS Administration menu, follow these steps:

1. Load NSS.

2. Open the NSS Administration menu by typing **NSS Menu**.

3. From the Utilities menu section, select Rebuild NSS Volume.

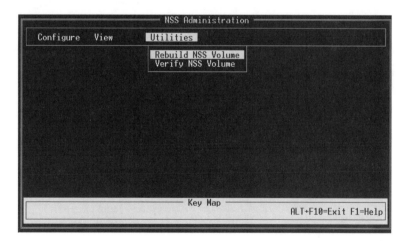

4. Select the volume to rebuild from the list.

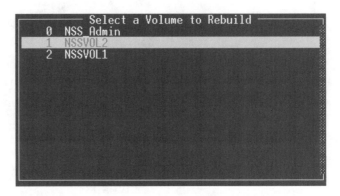

5. After rebuilding, select Verify NSS Volume from the Utilities option to check the volume's integrity.

6. Mount the volume, if necessary.

Chapter 7

Managing Applications

Answer Topics!

● **NOVELL APPLICATION LAUNCHER (NAL) INSTALLATION AND TIPS   230**

? Using commands to load NAL on different platforms

? Importing earlier NAL applications into NetWare 5 NAL

? Comparing Novell Application Launcher and Novell Application Explorer

? Using ADDICON

? Troubleshooting SHELL32.DLL

? Customizing the NAL title bar

? Mapping drives before launching applications

? Importing and exporting registry entries through NAL

? Including NAL in a Windows Start menu

? Understanding the differences between application fault tolerance and application load balancing

? Understanding roaming profiles support

? Trying to suppress the [ALL] icon

? Hiding the Application Launcher welcome screen

? Trying to change the NAL background

? Installing applications with NAL services

? Using NTFS rights with NAL

● **NOVELL APPLICATION LAUNCHER AND APPLICATION OBJECTS   234**

? Distributing applications on Windows 98 machines

? Displaying the Control Panel print folder through NAL

? Setting schedules in NAL

? Removing mapped drives

? Setting NAL to prompt users

? Preventing deletion of .DLL and .EXE files

? Creating a snapshot

? Distributing and installing applications

? Preventing users from running applications at certain times

? Forcing an application to run at login

? Detecting DOS SET variables

? Checking versions in NAL

? Deleting registry keys in NAL

? Uninstalling an application with NAL

● **SECURING NOVELL APPLICATION LAUNCHER   246**

? Securing desktops

? Customizing a secure desktop

● **NOVELL LICENSING SERVICE (NLS)** 249

? Understanding Novell Licensing Service

? Generating reports

? Upgrading licenses

● **JAVA APPLICATIONS** 251

? Understanding the types of Java applications that come with NetWare 5

? Understanding the advantages of Java over C++

? Understanding Java platforms

? Trying to view the server GUI in Java

? Understanding Java performance issues

? Obtaining Java run-time environments

? Obtaining development kits

? Understanding what is needed to run Java on your server

Managing Applications @ a Glance

This chapter focuses on several new features in NetWare 5. Novell has added so many enhancements to the Novell Application Launcher (NAL), which comes with the Z.E.N.works Starter Pack, that NAL merits coverage in its own chapter, separate from the Z.E.N.works chapter. The NAL enhancements are Novell's latest effort to provide a secure and fault-tolerant desktop without making you spend more money on additional software. Just imagine having the ability to make thousands of desktops totally secure in less than six steps!

Here are the topics discussed in this chapter:

● **Novell Application Launcher (NAL) Installation and Tips** focuses on the configuration and installation of NAL in your workstation environment.

● **Novell Application Launcher and Application Objects** addresses questions regarding the distribution of applications to workstations. This section also focuses on the installation and uninstallation of applications when users log in to the network.

● **Securing Novell Application Launcher** discusses different ways to lock down a workstation in different Windows environments.

● **Novell Licensing Service (NLS)** covers issues related to the licensing of applications on the server. Such applications include BorderManager 3, GroupWise, and other Novell-oriented programs.

● **Java Applications** explores various types of Java applications that can run in a NetWare environment and addresses performance issues that administrators may face when running these types of applications.

NOVELL APPLICATION LAUNCHER (NAL) INSTALLATION AND TIPS

What command do I use to load NAL for Windows 95, Windows 98, Windows NT, and Windows 3.*x*?

Just run NAL.EXE. This executable will automatically detect what Windows platform you are running and load either NALWIN32.EXE or NALW31.EXE.

How can I import NAL 1.0 Application objects from earlier versions of NAL into the latest version of NAL?

NAL has a built-in function for importing NAL 1.0 Application objects into the current version of NAL. Just select your Application object that needs to be imported, choose Tools, select Application Launcher Tools, and select Migrate Application Objects.

What is the difference between Application Launcher and Application Explorer?

Application Launcher is a standard window that appears when you run NAL.EXE from the SYS:PUBLIC directory. Application Launcher can run on Windows 3.*x*, Windows 95, Windows NT 3.*x*, and Windows NT 4. Application Explorer uses Windows namespace extensions, loaded automatically when you run NALEXPLD.EXE. Application Explorer runs only on Windows 95 and Windows NT 4.

How can I add NAL to the Startup group for a Windows 3.*x* machine?

NAL includes a utility called ADDICON that adds an icon item anywhere in a Windows 3.*x* group. To add NAL to the Startup group, use the following login script example:

```
If member of "Windows 3.x Group" then
      #addicon exe=nal.exe
end
```

> ❊ **Note:** *The default group for ADDICON is the Startup group. To see more options, type **ADDICON /H** at the DOS prompt.*

My Application Explorer keeps giving me a Dr. Watson message on SHELL32.DLL on my Windows 95 machine. What is going on?

Application Explorer needs a newer version of SHELL32.DLL. This file is part of Microsoft Windows 95 Service Pack 1; you can download it from the following site:

www.microsoft.com/windows/software.servpak1/sphome.htm

How can I customize my title bar in NAL?

To customize your title bar, insert the following command to launch NAL in your login script:

```
#NAL /c="Personal Menu for %FULL NAME%"
```

How many drives can I map before launching a NAL-assigned application?

You can map up to 26 drives.

Can I import and export .INI and .REG files with NAL?

Yes; you can automatically import and export .INI and .REG files when your applications require them.

You can also create an Application object that can just insert a registry or .INI settings change. This would be useful for creating a secure shell for Windows 95/98 and Windows 3.*x*, as will be discussed later in this chapter in the section "Securing Novell Application Launcher."

How can I include NAL as part of my Windows 95/98 Start menu?

To add NAL to the Windows 95/98 Start menu, do the following:

1. Log in as Admin.
2. Launch NWADMN32, right-click the container, and select Details.

3. Select the Applications tab and click the programs you want to include in your Start menu by checking the Start Menu box for each application.

4. Click OK when you have finished.

Have the users within the container log out and then back in to their workstations and run NALEXPLD.EXE. This will cause Z.E.N.works to send the users a new policy that lets them see Application objects within the Start menu.

Note: *This procedure works only for Windows 95 / 98 and Windows NT.*

 ### What is the difference between Application Fault Tolerance and Application Load Balancing?

Application Fault Tolerance allows a user to run a network application, such as a spreadsheet, with the assurance that if the server that is running the spreadsheet software is down, a backup server with the same application will automatically take over the application.

Application Load Balancing is the ability of NetWare to dynamically switch between different servers with the same application based on the load on an individual server.

Does NAL support roaming profiles?

Yes. NAL supports roaming profiles by linking your profile with your assigned Application objects and downloading the program needed to run your NAL-delivered applications.

Can I display only the NDS Tree icon and folders without displaying the [ALL] icon in the NAL window?

At the time of this writing, NAL does not support this approach.

How can I hide the Application Launcher welcome screen when it loads?

At the time of this writing, the Novell documentation states that using NAL.EXE /H will hide the Application Launcher welcome screen. Unfortunately, the /H parameter does not

work properly. However, Novell offers this workaround: type **NAL.EXE :H**, and the Application Launcher welcome screen will be hidden successfully.

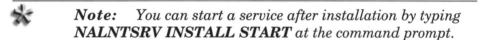 ## Can I change the background of NAL?

At the time of this writing, you cannot change the background of the NAL menu.

NAL doesn't allow me to install some applications when the user has restricted rights on a Windows NT Workstation. If I give the user administrative privileges, everything works fine, but I can't do this for security reasons. What can I do?

Z.E.N.works allows you to register Application Launcher as a service. This service will allow you to change the Registry without granting administrative rights to the server. To do this, follow these steps:

1. Log in to Windows NT as Administrator on your local box.

2. At the command line, type **NALNTSRV INSTALL**. This will create an NT service that will start when the system is rebooted.

Note: *You can start a service after installation by typing* ***NALNTSRV INSTALL START*** *at the command prompt.*

Caution: *Do not use the Start option when installing the service from Novell Workstation Manager 1.0.*

I have a Windows NT environment with NTFS on all my partitions, and I have restricted access to my C: drive to read-only. NAL is not working. What's wrong?

NAL needs some access to the C: drive, though not total access. NAL needs write access to the C:\TEMP directory and write access to \WINNT\PROFILES because NAL creates a directory to hold all of the user configuration sets in an NT User Policy object.

NOVELL APPLICATION LAUNCHER AND APPLICATION OBJECTS

 **I want to distribute an application on only Windows 98 systems. Does NAL 2.5 support Windows 98?**

Currently, NAL 2.5 does not support Windows 98, but it nevertheless seems to work just fine. In fact, Novell has a workaround for application distribution: since Windows 98 is actually Windows 95 version 4.10, you can set up a system requirement to look for that version.

I want to display the Control Panel Printers folder in NAL. How can I do this?

Use a utility called NCCPPR32.EXE, which can be found at consulting.novell.com/toolkit/zen.html. Create an Application object and point to this executable. This utility will bring up the Control Panel Printers folder without using the Start menu.

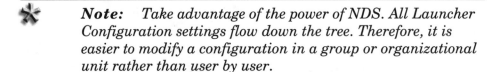 **I have set a schedule for users to access Netscape at a certain time, but they have to refresh the screen to see the icon. How can I automate the refresh operation?**

You need to configure Launcher Configuration at the Container or Leaf object level to perform automatic refreshes of the users' desktops.

Note: *Take advantage of the power of NDS. All Launcher Configuration settings flow down the tree. Therefore, it is easier to modify a configuration in a group or organizational unit rather than user by user.*

Follow these steps:

1. Right-click your container, group, or user and select Details.
2. Select the Launcher Configuration tab.
3. Click Edit.

4. Change the Enable Timed Refresh setting to Yes.

5. Change the Set Refresh Frequency setting to Custom and assign 120 seconds.

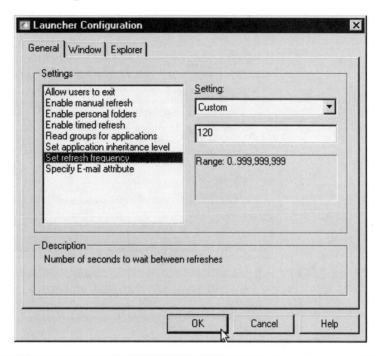

Caution: *Frequent refreshes of large numbers of users can increase network traffic.*

I have several mapped drives and captured ports scripted in my Application object when it runs. What is the easiest way to remove these?

The best way to remove these changes is to do the following:

1. Right-click your desired Application object and select Details.

2. Select Environment.

3. Make sure Clean Up Network Resources is checked; then click OK.

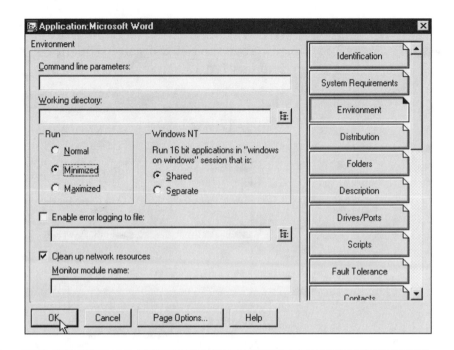

 Note: *Clean Up Network Resources is checked by default.*

 I am upgrading an application for my accounting department. Can I set NAL to prompt my users by asking whether they want to upgrade now or at a later time?

Yes. You can set up NAL to prompt users before distributing the upgrade. This prompt can also tell users ahead of time how long it will take to deliver the application and what will be done. To set up a prompt, do the following:

1. Right-click your desired Application object and select Details.

2. Select the Distribution tab.

3. Select Prompt Before Distribution.

4. Click OK.

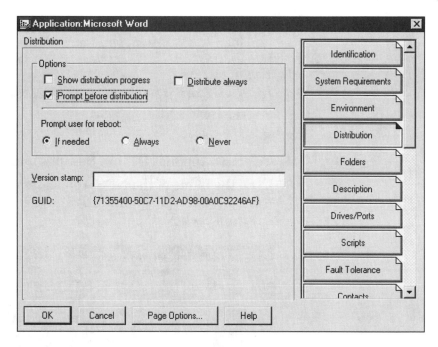

When my users get low on disk space, they start deleting files on their workstations. Unfortunately, sometimes users accidentally delete their application .DLL and .EXE files. How can I prevent this?

Users are going to do what they want with their workstations, but NAL does provide a new feature called Auto Verify. This feature will copy any missing files that belong to a specific application with little user intervention. The only requirements for this feature to work are these:

- The application must be controlled by NAL.

- The application must have a snapshot on the server. Snapshots are discussed in the next question.

How do I create a snapshot of Netscape Navigator?

To create a snapshot of Netscape Navigator, you must have a workstation with just the Novell Client installed. You will want to keep the environment as clean as possible to avoid

any conflicts during the imaging of the application. Therefore, on your clean workstation, you must do the following:

1. Log in as Admin.

2. Go to SYS:PUBLIC\SNAPSHOT and run the program SNAPSHOT.EXE.

3. Select Custom.

4. Select SnAppShot Default Settings and click Next.

5. Type the name of the NDS Application object (for example, **Navigator Install**) and the application icon title and click Next.

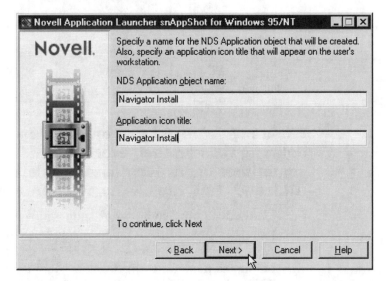

6. Enter the location where SnAppShot can store files (.FIL) for fault tolerance. Use a network drive. Then click Next.

7. Enter the path in which you want the application installation to reside and then click Next. SnAppShot will create an .AOT file, which is a set of instructions that tells NAL what files to install.

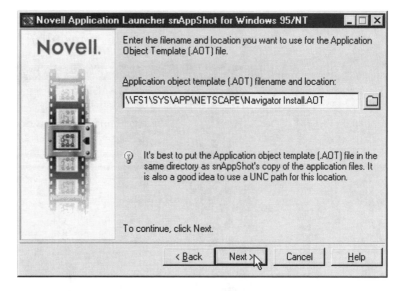

8. Accept all scan options and click Next.

9. Select C: as the drive for the Netscape Navigator installation and click Next.

10. Review the settings and click Next.

11. After the scan has taken place, click Run Application Install, go to the Navigator Install directory, and click Open.

12. Perform the Netscape Navigator installation as you would any other installation.

 Note: *If Netscape Navigator prompts you to reboot the system, select "No, I will reboot my system later."*

13. Go to the Novell Application Launcher SnAppShot for Windows 95/NT and click Next.

14. This page sets the defaults for your .AOT file. For this example, select the default settings and click Next.

15. Select the application's INSTALL directory, in which the application has just been installed.

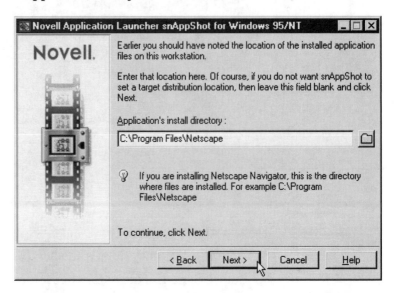

16. Review your target path and click Next.

 Note: *You can add macros on this page, such as usernames, to be placed in unique installation fields.*

17. Once a template has been created, click Finish to end the snapshot.

 I would like to distribute and install Netscape Navigator with NAL for several users. How can I do this?

You just created a snapshot of Netscape Navigator; now you need to create an Application object to install it. Do the following:

1. Log in as Admin and run NWADMN32.

2. Select the organization in which you want to create an Application object. Right-click the organization and click Create.

3. Select Application.

4. Choose Create an Application Object with an .AOT/.AXT File and click Next.

5. Browse to the application .AOT location, select the .AOT file, and click Next.

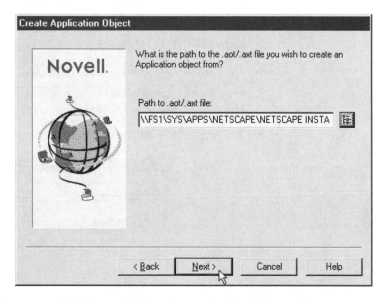

6. Verify the object name, source path, and target path, and click Next.

7. Check Display Details after Creation and click Finish.

8. Verify that the Install Only option is selected and click Run Once.

9. Click System Requirements and select the machine types on which you want to install the application; then click OK.

 I would like to prevent users from accessing Netscape Navigator during normal working hours. How can I do this?

NAL provides a scheduling feature that allows only certain icons to be displayed on the NAL menu at different times of the day. The example here assumes that an Application object has been created and associated.

 Tip: *For this feature to work properly, you must secure the users' desktops with Z.E.N.works and prevent them from accessing Run and Windows Explorer. You also need to have Netscape controlled by NAL.*

1. Log in as Admin.

2. Run NWADMIN32.EXE.

3. Double-click the Netscape application.

4. Go to the Schedule tab and select Range of Days from the Set Schedule In drop-down menu.

5. Set your date range from Today to 12 months from Today.

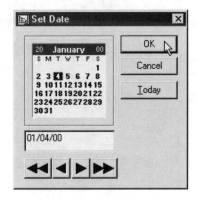

6. You want to invoke this policy for every day, so the default date range is fine.

7. Set the schedule time from 17:00 to 23:59.

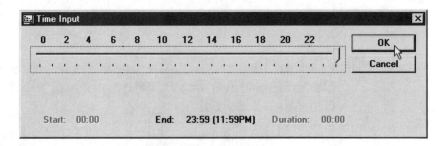

 Tip: *If you have workstations in other time zones, you need to check "Use this schedule in GMT for all clients." This will restrict workstations in different time zones at 5:00 P.M. their local time. Otherwise, NAL will use your local time.*

8. Click OK.

 How can I install an application immediately after invoking NAL?

NAL lets you perform a forced run of an application after NAL is up and running. For instance, suppose you want to install Netscape Navigator upon login and want to run it only once, and you have already set up a snapshot Application object to install Navigator. Here is what you need to do:

1. Log in as Admin.

2. Run NWADMIN32.EXE.

3. Right-click the organizational unit, group, or user you want to force Navigator to install, and select Details.

4. Select Applications Files.

5. Click the Add button and add your Netscape Install Application object.

6. Select the Force Run check box.

7. Click OK when you have finished.

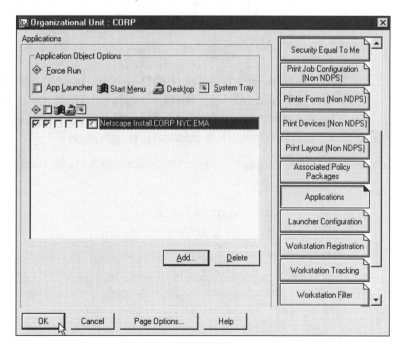

8. From the main Administrator screen, right-click your Application object, select Details, and review the Identification tab. Make sure that the radio button for Execution is set to Install Only and that the Run Once box is checked.

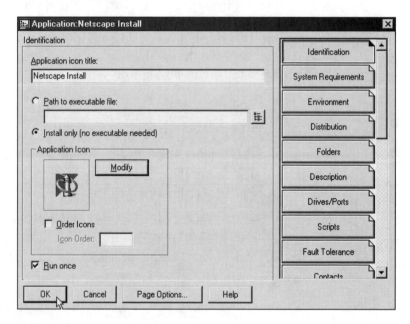

9. Click OK.

I have some older DOS applications that require SET variables, and I am running in a Windows NT environment. How can I make NAL detect my SET variables and run my program?

To enable your DOS applications to recognize SET variables, do the following:

1. Log in as Admin.

2. Run NWADMN32.EXE.

3. Right-click the Application object that requires the SET variable and select Details.

4. Select Scripts and type the SET variables needed for your application in the Run Before Launching windows.

5. Click OK when you have finished.

How does NAL know when to update a file associated with an application?

NAL performs version checking: that is, it checks the internal version numbers of Windows .DLLs, .EXEs, and other system files. Version checking is better than date and timestamp checking because the date and time can easily be changed on files, whereas the version number cannot. To see an example of a file with version stamps, do the following on a Windows 95 or NT machine:

1. Open Explorer.

2. Right-click any program .EXE or .DLL file in Explorer and click Properties.

3. Go to the Version tab and highlight the version in the right pane of the window.

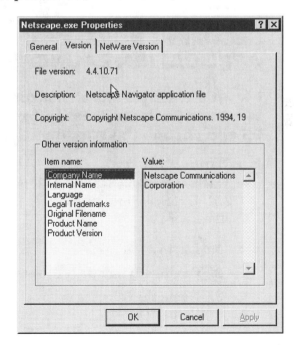

 ### How can I delete a registry key in an Application object?

Currently, Novell does not provide an easy way to delete registration keys. You need to create an .AXT file (if one does not already exist) in the Application object. Next, use a text editor to search for the registry key you want to delete, and then save the file. Finally, create another Application object and use the .AXT file you just modified.

 Note: *Novell supports the addition, deletion, and modification of registry values.*

 ### How can I uninstall an application with NAL?

Novell provides an executable called AOTREV.EXE that will reverse an .AOT object that is used to install a program so that it uninstalls a program. This file is included with the Z.E.N.works Application Toolkit at the following site:

consulting.novell.com/toolkit/zen.html.

SECURING NOVELL APPLICATION LAUNCHER

 ### I want a totally secure desktop. How can I replace the Windows Explorer desktop for Windows NT, 98, and 95 and change the Windows 3.x desktop to NAL?

For Windows NT:

The best way to enable a shell for Windows NT is to use a Z.E.N.works Windows NT user policy. To do this, follow these steps:

1. Log in as Admin.

2. Create a Windows NT user package.

3. Name the NT user policy and check Define Additional Properties.

4. From the Details page, enable NT User System Policy by checking it; then click the Details button.

5. Expand the Windows NT Shell tree.

6. Expand Custom User Interface.

7. Check Custom Shell and enter the path from which NAL will load. For example:

\\SERVERNAME\SYS\PUBLIC\NAL.EXE

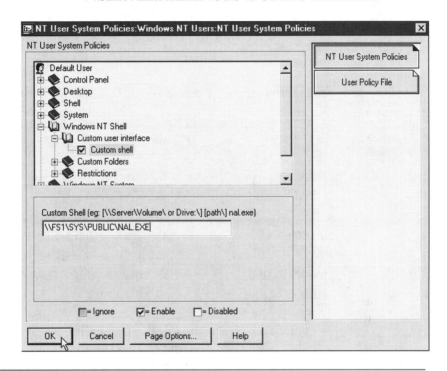

Note: *You must have Novell Workstation Manager loaded on all Windows NT machines that you want to secure and be running Windows NT Service Pack 3 or higher.*

For Windows 95/98:

1. Copy the files listed here from the server's PUBLIC directory to the user's hard disk.

Filename	Directory
NALWIN32.EXE	C:\NOVELL\CLIENT32
NALRES32.DLL	C:\NOVELL\CLIENT32\NLS\ENGLISH
NALBMP32.DLL	C:\NOVELL\CLIENT32\NLS\ENGLISH
NAL.HLP	C:\NOVELL\CLIENT32\NLS\ENGLISH
NAL.CNT	C:\NOVELL\CLIENT32\NLS\ENGLISH
NWAPP32.DLL	C:\NOVELL\CLIENT32

2. To replace the shell, edit the following line in SYSTEM.INI in the [boot] section:

```
shell=c:\novell\client32\nalwin32.exe
```

For Windows 3.x with Novell Client32 Software:

1. Copy the files listed here from the server's PUBLIC directory to the user's hard disk.

Filename	Directory
NALW31.EXE	C:\NOVELL\CLIENT32
NALRES.DLL	C:\NOVELL\CLIENT32\NLS\ENGLISH
NALBMP.DLL	C:\NOVELL\CLIENT32\NLS\ENGLISH
NAL.HLP	C:\NOVELL\CLIENT32\NLS\ENGLISH
NWAPP16.DLL	C:\WINDOWS\SYSTEM
NALCPY16.EXE	C:\WINDOWS

2. To replace the shell, edit the following line in SYSTEM.INI in the [boot] section:

```
shell=c:\novell\client32\nalw31.exe
```

 My organization is running NAL as a secure desktop and users always have to press CTRL-ALT-DELETE to shut down their systems. Can I create an icon for logging out and shutting down?

To provide a user with the ability to log out, you need to customize the launcher configuration with NWADMIN32. Do the following:

1. Click the object you want to modify (an Organizational Unit, Group, or User object) and right-click Details.

2. Go to the Launcher Configuration tab and click Edit.

3. On the General tab, set Allow Users to Exit to Yes.

4. On the Window tab, set Enable Log In to Yes.

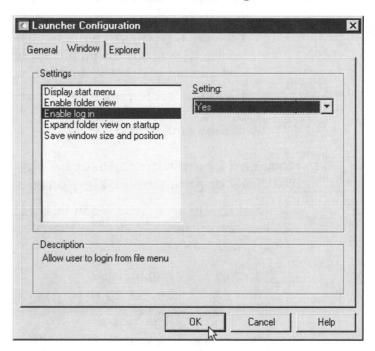

5. Click OK.

6. Now the user can log out and exit. To set Windows 95/98 to shut down when the user closes NAL, run NAL.EXE with the /S switch in your login script.

NOVELL LICENSING SERVICE (NLS)

 ### What is Novell Licensing Service?

Novell Licensing Service (NLS) is a service that helps administrators control licensed applications on a Novell network. NLS objects included the following:

● **License Service Provider (LSP) objects**   LSP is a NetWare Loadable Module (NLM) that interacts with applications that request the licensing service. You can install LSPs on any server in a tree, but you do not need to load it on every server.

● **License Container objects** License Container objects contain one or more license certificates. The names of these objects incorporate the publisher, product, and version. For example, the Novell license lists the name Novell+NetWare 5 Conn SCL+500.

● **License Certificate objects** These objects contain information about the publisher, product name, version, and number of licenses the certificate contains.

● **License Catalog objects** These objects provide catalog services with updated information about licensing information.

 ## How can I generate reports on the number of NetWare connections being used at any given time?

License Manager enables administrators to create reports to determine when they need to upgrade their NetWare licenses. Do the following:

1. Log in as Admin.

2. Go to the SYS:PUBLIC\WIN32 directory and run NLSMAN32.EXE.

3. Double-click your Novell certificate.

4. Click Finish to view the graph.

✦ *Tip:* *You can customize the graph by clicking Action and Customize Graph.*

I currently have a 500-user license on one of my file servers. Can I buy another 500-user license and create a 1,000-user server?

Yes. Each new license certificate is added to the previous certificate to give you a total user count.

JAVA APPLICATIONS

What Java applications come with NetWare and can be run on the server and client?

NetWare 5 comes with the following applications:

- **ConsoleOne**   Used to manage network resources; discussed in Chapter 4 in the section "ConsoleOne and GUI Server Management"
- **Console Manager**   Java graphical remote console
- **JEDITOR**   Java text editor
- **RCONJ**   Java remote console

What advantage does Java give me over C++ programs?

Java is extremely portable. Therefore, you can run applications like ConsoleOne on Unix, OS/2, Macintosh, and Windows workstations.

What platform can these Java applications run on?

Novell supports Java applications on Windows NT only.

Can I view the server's GUI with any of the Java remote-control programs?

At the time of this writing, there are no Java applications to view the server's GUI screens.

My Java applications are slow. What is the problem?

The Java Development Kit version 1.1.5 has a memory leak; this causes the application to slow down and eventually will cause it to crash. Also, Java applications are very demanding on your memory and hardware. Therefore, a Pentium II with 512MB is recommended for these applications.

What Java development tools do I need to develop applications for NetWare 5?

The Metrowerks package CodeWarrior for NetWare will allow you to compile code for Windows 95/98 and Windows NT, as well as for the Macintosh operating system. To obtain this package, contact Metrowerks at 1-800-377-5416.

How can I obtain the Sun Microsystems Java run-time environment for NetWare?

You can download the run-time environment from developer.novell.com/ndk/jre.html.

What is a good development kit that provides a lot of functionality for Novell services?

The best package to obtain is Beans for Novell Services. It can be downloaded from developer.novell.com/ndk/bns.html.

What NLM is needed to run Java on the server?

You need to load JAVA.NLM. Following is a list of parameters this NLM can use for your Java applications.

Parameter	Description
-help	Prints a list of available parameters
-nwhelp	Prints additional parameters specifically for running applications on the server, such as Java Applet Viewer, Java Compiler, and Java Debugger
-version	Displays the version of the applet build
-verbose	Toggles verbose mode
-debug	Enables remote debugging
-noasyncgc	Prevents asynchronous garbage collection
-verbosesegc	Displays a message when garbage collection occurs
-noclassgc	Disables class garbage collection
-ss<number>	Sets the C stack size of a process

Parameter	Description
-oss<number>	Sets the JAVA stack size of a process
-ms<number>	Sets the initial JAVA heap size
-mx<number>	Sets the maximum JAVA heap size
-classpath <directories separated by semicolons>	Sets the directories to the location to search for classes
-prof	Outputs profiling data
-verify	Verifies all classes when read in
-verifyremote	Verifies classes read in over the network
-noverify	Does not verify any class
-d<propetyName=NewValue>	Redefines a property value

Chapter 8

Managing Network Printing

Answer Topics!

● **QUEUE-BASED PRINTING 256**

? Understanding queue-based printing
? The NDS Print Queue object
? Setting up a Print Queue object
? Understanding the Printer object
? Creating a Printer object
? Understanding the Print Server object
? Creating a Print Server object
? Making the three Print objects interact
? Setting up Print object interaction in one operation
? Activating the print server
? Changing the printer assignment from another server
? Configuring a printer attached to a network workstation
? Looking for PCONSOLE
? Using CAPTURE to redirect DOS print jobs
? Trying to use queue-based printing in a Pure IP environment

● **NDPS DEFINITION AND PURPOSE 267**

? Understanding NDPS
? Learning which version of NDPS ships with NetWare 5

? Comparing NDPS 1 and 2
? Comparing NDPS and queue-based printing
? Understanding NDPS hardware requirements

● **MANAGING NDPS 269**

? Understanding NDPS NLMs
? Understanding the NDPS Broker
? Setting up the NDPS Manager object
? Understanding the Printer Agent
? Understanding the printer gateway
? Finding printer gateways
? Comparing public-access and controlled-access printers
? Creating a public-access printer
? Creating a controlled-access printer
? Licensing network printers
? Updating a workstation to NDPS
? Learning whether a newly attached printer will be detected and configured automatically
? Configuring a workstation to print to an NDPS printer
? Finding information about a specific printer or job

- ? Pushing printers or drivers to a workstation automatically
- ? Updating drivers for a specific printer
- ? Installing printers on a workstation automatically
- ? Customizing NDPS print jobs
- ? Understanding bidirectional printing
- ? Controlling print scheduling
- ? Customizing banners

MIGRATING TO NDPS   286

- ? Smoothing the transition to NDPS
- ? Printing to NDPS printers from DOS applications
- ? Choosing a protocol to use with NDPS
- ? Using Pure IP and queue-based printing simultaneously
- ? Using NPRINTER on a workstation
- ? Configuring a workstation-based network printer
- ? Migrating NetWare/IP to NDPS
- ? Advertising printer services without SAP
- ? Using NDPS with no workstation-attached printers
- ? Optimizing NDPS

TROUBLESHOOTING NETWORK PRINTING   291

- ? Correcting NDPSW32.DLL errors during NWADMN32 launch
- ? Correcting NDPSM errors after a server abend
- ? Looking for available gateways
- ? Looking for NDPS printers
- ? Solving NPRINTER print-server-not-found problems
- ? Enabling the Enable Broker button
- ? Looking for drive spooling space
- ? Installing a driver from multiple disks
- ? Reassociating a "lost" NDPS Manager with a volume
- ? Reinstalling NDPS
- ? Serving a remote location with its own broker
- ? Getting an NT driver to communicate with a printer
- ? Trying to service a queue with a public-access printer
- ? Starting RMS on a file server
- ? Resolving slow response on a newly associated Queue object

Managing Network Printing @ a Glance

This chapter addresses printing in NetWare 5. NetWare 5 still provides queue-based printing, using the traditional Print Server, Print Queue, and Printer objects. In addition, it offers the new Novell Distributed Print Services (NDPS). NDPS is a set of distributed, application-layer print services that consist of client, server, and connectivity components that seamlessly link and share printers with applications. In addition, NDPS simplifies administration by reducing the total number of objects that must be maintained to just a single object per printer. For the user, NDPS uses its bidirectional capabilities to provide feedback concerning print jobs sent to an NDPS printer as well as information about the printer itself. Additionally, the user can move or copy print jobs to another printer when, for example, a failure or printer congestion occurs. NDPS is fully backward compatible, allowing gradual migration to NDPS while you continue to use NetWare 4.11 queue-based printers.

- **Queue-Based Printing** answers questions regarding queue printing functions and NetWare queue printing utilities; this section also describes how to create a print queue configuration in your network environment.

- **NDPS Definition and Purpose** discusses the requirements, features, and limitations of NDPS.

- **Managing NDPS** describes strategies for migration from queue-based printers to NDPS and discusses the network impact of NDPS.

- **Migrating to NDPS** discusses migration procedures and alternatives to move your environment to an NDPS printing solution.

- **Troubleshooting Network Printing** explores issues dealing with queue-based printing and NDPS printing with Windows 95/98 and Windows NT.

QUEUE-BASED PRINTING

What is queue-based printing?

Queue-based printing is the same printing environment that was used in previous versions of NetWare. With this method, you can place a printer anywhere in the network, and the printer will be serviced by a server-based print server and print queue. In NetWare 4.*x*, this printing method was enhanced to include logical representations of the Printer objects on the NDS tree for easier management.

What is the function of the Print Queue object?

The Print Queue object is an NDS logical representation of a physical printer queue. Its properties describe the physical location of the queue, who can use and manage the queue, and the current status of the queue. Users use the queue and its associated printer to print. The Print Queue object will typically be placed in the same container as its associated User objects. The physical print queue is a special directory on a file server in which spooled print jobs are stored until they can be serviced by a printer.

 How do I set up a Print Queue object?

To create a Print Queue object, complete these steps from NWADMN32:

1. Select the container in which you want to create the Print Queue object.

2. Click Object, Create, and then Print Queue. This will bring up the Create Print Queue dialog box, shown in the following illustration.

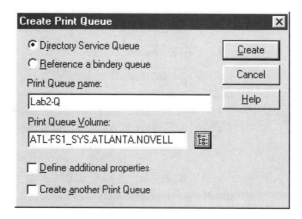

3. Select either Directory Service Queue or Reference a Bindery Queue.

4. Type the name of your print queue (for example, **HPJET1**).

5. Browse for the location of the volume you want to use as the storage location for the print queue volume, select the volume, and click OK.

The print queue will now be available to all users in its container.

 What is a Printer object?

A Printer object is the NDS logical representation of a physical printer. The printer can be connected to the file server or a workstation device or directly to the network using a printer network cable and a printer network interface. Previous versions of NetWare could use the

PCONSOLE utility to create this object. In NetWare 5, this object is created solely through NWADMN32. As with the Print Queue object, the Printer object should be placed in the container that contains the users who will be using the printer.

How do I create a Printer object?

From NWADMN32, follow these steps to create a Printer object:

1. Select the container in which you want to create the Printer object.

2. Click Object, Create, and then Printer (Non NDPS).

3. Type a name for the Printer object.

Tip: *Use a name that describes the printer, such as HP5ACCT_P for an HP5 printer in the Accounting department.*

All users in the container in which you placed the Printer object will automatically become users of the printer.

What is the Print Server object?

A Print Server object is the NDS representation of the server-based process that moves jobs from the print queue to the printer. A single print server can service up to 256 printers, so you don't need to create multiple print servers for the same physical location. For example, you could create on print server for a location that has several NDS containers and queues in several servers at that location. However, if you have a second location, you would typically create another print server at that location, so the print server does not need to cross the WAN to process print jobs for that location.

 How do I create a Print Server object?

To create a print server on your network, complete the following steps in NetWare Administrator and at the server console:

1. From NWADMN32, select the container in which you want to create the Print Server object.
2. Click Object, Create and then Print Server (Non NDPS). Click OK.
3. Type the name of the print server.

How do the three objects I have created (the Printer, Printer Queue, and Print Server objects) interact? Is there more that I should do?

To make the three items you created interact, you must configure certain critical data-fields in each of the objects before the objects can "see" one another.

In NetWare Administrator, double-click the Print Server object and complete the following steps:

1. Click the Assignments button.
2. Click the Add button.
3. Browse to find the context of the Printer object that you want to assign to this print server. Select the correct Printer object from the left pane of the window and then click OK.
4. Click the Users button.
5. Select any additional containers, users, or groups that need access to this printer.
6. Click OK at the bottom of the property page to exit and save your changes.

Double-click the Printer object and complete the following steps:

1. Click the Assignments button.
2. Click the Add button.
3. Browse to find the Print Queue that you want to assign to this printer. Select the printer and click OK.
4. Click the Configuration tab.
5. Set the physical connectivity property fields to correctly identify how this printer is connected to the network.
6. Click OK at the bottom of the property page to exit and save your changes.

Double-click the Print Queue object and check the following properties:

1. Click the Assignments tab. Make sure that the Authorized Print Servers field lists the associated print server and that the Printers Servicing Print Queue field lists the correct print server associated with this queue. An example of this configuration is shown here:

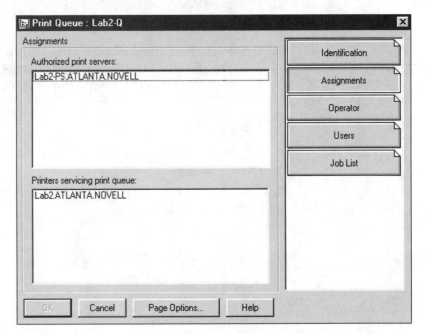

2. Click the Users tab, add any additional containers, users, or groups that need access to this queue.

3. Click OK at the bottom of the property page to exit and save your changes.

At this time, all items are correctly associated with one another. However, for the changes you made to take effect, you must restart the print server at the server console. To do this, follow these steps:

1. Go to the Available Options screen and press ENTER on the Print Server Information option. You will see the following screen:

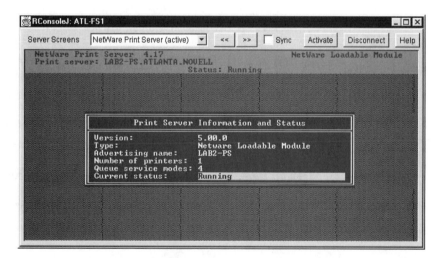

2. Press ENTER again on the Current Status field (which should display Running). This will bring up options to continue running, unload PSERVER, or unload PSERVER after all active jobs have been completed.

3. After choosing a stop option, you will be returned to the command prompt. Type **PSERVER** at the console prompt, press ENTER, and locate the print server in the proper context to start the server.

To guarantee that all the Printer objects have been correctly linked, follow these steps:

1. From NWADMN32, double-click the Print Server object.
2. Click the Print Layout (Non NDPS) tab.
3. An error icon will appear next to any item that is currently not connected or not configured correctly. If this happens, retrace your steps through each of the objects you configured and double-check the functionality and configuration.

The preceding steps are useful for identifying the location of a print failure. For example, if the red exclamation point appears next to the Print Server object, check to make sure that the print server has been activated at the server.

Is there a quicker way to set up the interaction among objects?

Now that you are familiar with the full procedure for setting up the interaction among the Printer, Printer Queue, and Print Server objects, you can try another method that will allow you to complete most of this process in just a single step. Novell identified these steps as troublesome and created a new utility, Printer Services Quick Setup, to perform these steps. This utility is available in NWADMN32.

To use this utility, follow these steps from within NWADMN32:

1. Select the container in which you want to create the various objects.
2. Click Tools and then Print Services Quick Setup (Non NDPS). The dialog box shown next will appear.

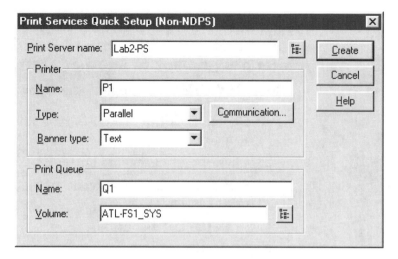

3. Enter all the information in each field as requested.

4. Click Create.

All three items associated with queue-based printing will be created in the container you selected, with all the proper associations between these objects made for you.

How do I activate the print server?

After completing the previous steps of creating and associating Printer objects from within NWADMN32, you then activate the print server at the server console using the following steps:

1. From the server console, type the command **PSERVER** and press ENTER.

2. On the console screen that appears, browse for the context that contains the print server you just created, select the print server, and press ENTER.

The status of your print server will now be Running.

 I want only a single print server for my tree. After using the quick setup method, how do I change the printer assignment to another print server?

From NWADMN32, complete the following steps:

1. Double-click the Printer Server object that you want to modify.

2. Click the Assignments button.

3. Select the Printer you want to remove from this print server.

4. Click the Delete button.

5. Click OK.

6. Double-click the Print Server object that you want to serve the Printer in question.

7. Click the Assignments button.

8. Click the Add button.

9. Browse through the tree and find the Printer object you want to assign to this print server.

10. Select the Printer object and click OK to add the printer to the list of printers served by this print server.

11. Click OK to exit and save your changes.

12. Stop and restart PSERVER at the server console to make the changes take effect.

You now have two Printer objects being served by a single print server. You can safely remove the secondary print server if you have no plans of using it to serve other printers.

 I need to configure a remote printer that is attached to a workstation for network use. How do I do this?

Printers that are attached to a network workstation are addressed by the print server by using NPRINTER. NPRINTER attaches to Printer objects to provide a path for the job to be processed.

There are two methods for activating NPRINTER. A remote printer, such as one attached to a workstation, is considered a manual load printer. Therefore, when you run NPRINTER, you need to specify the Printer object that is to be associated with the remote printer.

To manually configure and activate NPRINTER on a workstation, complete the following steps:

1. Launch NPRINTER for your workstation type. For Windows 95/98, use NPTWIN95.EXE. This file is located in the SYS\PUBLIC\WIN95 directory. The following dialog box will appear:

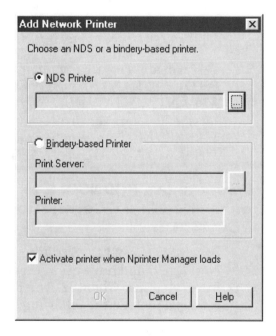

2. Click the NDS Printer browse button and locate the Printer object that will represent the printer attached to the workstation.

3. Select the Printer object in the Available Objects pane and click OK.

   Your printer has now been manually configured to work with the print server. You can close the window at this

time; NPRINTER will continue to operate even with the window closed. If you want to stop NPRINTER, you must clear the connection. To do this, either select the printer you want disconnected and click File and then Remove, or click File and then Remove All to clear all printer connections.

In addition to launching NPRINTER manually, you can automate a printer so that it starts when the workstation is started. This is accomplished by adding the following command in your AUTOEXEC.BAT file following the commands that log you into the network:

NPRINTER [*print server object name*]
[*printer object name*] [*printer number*]

An example of this command is **NPRINTER .CN=LAB1A-PS.OU=ATLANTA.O=NOVELL .CN=LAB1A-PTR.OU=ATLANTA.O=NOVELL**. You could also use a shortened version by using the printer number assigned to the printer in PSERVER: for example, you could enter **NPRINTER .CN=LAB1A-PS.OU=ATLANTA.O=NOVELL**.

 I want to use PCONSOLE to configure a printer on my NetWare 5 Server. How come I can't find PCONSOLE?

Several of the old DOS utilities have been removed from NetWare 5 and have been integrated into NDS objects or integrated into Client32. The printer utilities that have been removed include the following:

PCONSOLE
PRINTCON
PRINTDEF
ENDCAP
PSC
NETUSER
PUPGRADE

 Can I continue to use the CAPTURE command?

Yes. To redirect DOS print jobs, you will still need to use CAPTURE. You can enter this command from the command line or use the graphical version of CAPTURE in the printer properties of the printer you want to capture. Here is an example of this command entered at the command line:

CAPTURE [P=*printer name*] [Q=*queue name*] [L=*LPT#*] [*options*]

Alternatively, this command can be placed in the AUTOEXEC.BAT file after the network connection has been established.

 Can I have a Pure IP environment in NetWare 5 and continue to use the queue-based printing environment?

An environment that uses a true queue-based environment (that is, a connected printer, print queue, and print server) uses SAP broadcasts to advertise the existence of queue-based print objects. Because of this, you cannot have a Pure IP environment and continue to use a true queue-based printing environment.

When a configured print server from NWADMN32 is viewed in a Pure IP environment, the status will be reported as Down.

NDPS DEFINITION AND PURPOSE

 What is NDPS?

Novell Distributed Print Services (NDPS) is a new, centrally managed print environment for NetWare 5. It replaces the traditional Print Queue, Print Server, and Printer objects with a single object in an effort to reduce administration overhead. NDPS also takes advantage of built-in printer

intelligence to manage network printing resources centrally, improve network printing performance, and reduce the hassles of network printing for end users.

Which version of NDPS is included with NetWare 5?

Version 2 is integrated into NetWare 5 and activated by default. Version 1 was released for NetWare 4.11 in September 1997. NDPS 2 is not currently compatible with NetWare 4.11.

What are the differences between NDPS 1 and NDPS 2?

Several enhancements have been made to NDPS in version 2. NDPS now supports native IP, as does NetWare 5. In addition, NDPS 2 provides native support for Windows NT, integration of end-user print tools into the Add Printer Wizard for Windows 95 and Windows NT, and improved remote management of workstation printing configurations. Both versions can interoperate smoothly during a transition. Since NDPS 2 retains backward compatibility, all NDPS 1 clients can continue to print to NDPS 2 Printer Agents.

What are some differences between queue-based printing and NDPS?

Queue-based printing is the method used in NetWare 4.*x* and NetWare 3.*x* in which Print Server, Print Queue, and Printer objects are linked together to form a path by which print jobs are processed. End users can print by specifying either the print queue or the printer.

NDPS enhances this NDS-based printing format by consolidating the aforementioned printing objects into a single object. This reduces the number of possible failure points that exist in traditional queue-based printing. In addition, NDPS provides enhanced notification to alert users and administrators to the status of a printer or print job, including e-mail, pop-up windows, and extensive event logs. Finally, NDPS offers plug-and-print functionality when NDPS-ready printers are plugged into the network.

What are the hardware requirements for NDPS on the server?

NDPS is an integral part of NetWare 5 and is activated by default; therefore, all hardware requirements for NetWare 5 also apply to NDPS. Novell recommendations for a NetWare 5 server are as follows:

- Pentium-based PC or higher
- 64MB of RAM
- 1GB or higher hard disk

More specifically, estimates place the memory requirements of NDPS at 1.5MB of RAM when all NDPS modules are loaded and all brokered services are enabled. In addition, each NDPS printer added to this basic setup will require approximately 30K of additional RAM.

MANAGING NDPS

What NLMs are used to activate NDPS?

NDPS is made up of numerous NLMs, including

- **NDPSM.NLM (206K)** NDPS Manager NLM
- **REGSRVR.NLM (24K)** NDPS Service Registry Service (SRS)
- **NTFYSRVR.NLM (43K)** NDPS Notification Server Service (ENS)
- **RMANSRVR.NLM (154K)** NDPS Resource Manager Service (RMS)
- **PH.NLM (52K)** NDPS Port Handler (Novell gateway)
- **BROKER.NLM (37K)** Main NDPS Broker NLM
- **HPGATE.NLM (243K)** Hewlett-Packard NDPS Gateway

As gateways and certain services are activated, the NDPS Broker automatically loads and unloads needed NLMs into

memory. BROKER.NLM is automatically executed when the server boots.

 What is the NDPS Broker?

The NDPS Broker is a server-based application that is responsible for three functions.

The NDPS Broker contains the Service Registry Service (SRS). SRS is responsible for making public-access printers visible on the network by advertising the device type, device name, address, and other device-specific information once the printer has been registered with this service.

The NDPS Broker also contains the Event Notification Service (ENS). ENS allows NDPS to send specific notifications to users and administrators concerning a job or device status.

In addition, the NDPS Broker contains the Resource Management Service (RMS). RMS is a database that contains all device resources, including printer drivers, definition files, banners, and fonts.

A single NDPS Broker can handle the resources necessary to drive network printing in networks up to three hops away. Therefore, when you install the NDPS Broker on a NetWare 5 server in a network, it will check for the presence of any additional NDPS Broker and determine whether another Broker is necessary.

 What is the NDPS Manager object? How do I set it up?

The NDPS Manager supports Printer Agents that are server based. It is necessary only if a printer does not have its own Printer Agent capabilities. To create an NDPS Manager object, follow these steps:

1. In NWADMN32, select the container in which you want to create the NDPS Manager.

2. Select Object, select Create, click NDPS Manager, and click OK. The property page shown next will appear.

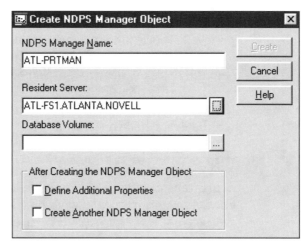

3. Type an NDPS Manager name.

4. In the Resident Server box, browse for and select the server to which you want the NDPS Manager assigned. This can be any server in the NDS tree that does not already have an NDPS Manager assigned to it.

5. Browse for and select the volume in which you want this NDPS Manager to store its database.

6. Click Create.

7. At the server console (or by using a RCONSOLE connection), execute the following command:

NDPSM *distinguished name of NDPS Manager*

 Note: *This command can be entered in AUTOEXEC.NCF for automatic execution during NetWare 5 startup.*

What is a Printer Agent?

The Printer Agent is the heart of NDPS. It combines the functions previously performed by the printer, print queue, print server, and spooler. The location of the Printer Agent depends on the type of printer that is being used. If the

printer is NDPS-aware, the Printer Agent is embedded in the printer's operation software; otherwise, the Printer Agent is located on the NetWare 5 server and represents a local, remote, or other network-attached printer.

Configuration of the Printer Agent depends on whether the printer is a public-access or controlled-access printer; this will be described in detail later.

What is a printer gateway?

A printer gateway is a server-based process that allows clients to communicate with non-NDPS printers. These gateways allow NetWare 5 to directly control a wide variety of printers from the NDS tree.

There are two classifications of printer gateways: third-party gateways and the Novell gateway. Third-party gateways are developed by individual printer manufacturers for use with NetWare 5. Included in NetWare 5 is the Hewlett-Packard gateway for use with HP-brand printers. The advantage of these gateways is that the gateway software can automatically detect and configure a Printer Agent when a gateway-specific printer is plugged into the network (hence, plug-and-print). Additionally, these gateways eliminate the need for utilities designed to configure the network printer before introducing it to the network.

The Novell gateway supports local and remote printers, as well as printers that do not have a specific third-party gateway available yet. This gateway works using two subsystems: the Print Device Subsystem (PDS) and the Port Handler.

The Print Device Subsystem stores printer-specific information in a database. The Port Handler uses various polling methods to ensure that the PDS can communicate with the printer to retrieve device-specific information, including the port that is being used on the printer.

Where can I find printer gateways to support my printer?

As mentioned, HP printers are supported by a gateway built into NetWare 5. At the time of this writing, the only other third-party gateway available is for Xerox printers (available at xerox.networkprinters.com). In time, additional manufacturers will be implementing NDPS gateways for their printers; check the appropriate vendor's Web site for details.

What are the differences between a public-access printer and a controlled-access printer?

As the name implies, a public-access printer is a printer that is visible and available to everyone on the network. As soon as the printer is plugged in and a Printer Agent is assigned to the printer, users are free to use the printer, even if they are not logged into the network. In fact, users do not even need to be represented by an NDS User object to use public-access printers, making these printers ideal for guest and mobile users. In the case of NDPS-aware printers, the printer will automatically be available for use on the network as a public-access printer. A snap-in module for NWADMN32 provides administration of public-access printers. This module is available by clicking Tools and then clicking public-access printers in NWADMN32. No Printer object exists in NDS to represent the printer.

Controlled-access printers, on the other hand, require that the network administrator create Printer objects in the NDS tree so the administrator can control who, how, and when a user can use the printer. In addition, default properties can be assigned to a controlled-access printer, including event and status notifications.

 How do I create a Printer Agent as a public-access printer?

To create a public-access printer, complete the following steps:

1. In NWADMN32, double-click the NDPS Manager you want to manage your new printer.

2. Click the Printer Agent List button on the right side of the dialog box.

3. Click New. This will bring up the following dialog box:

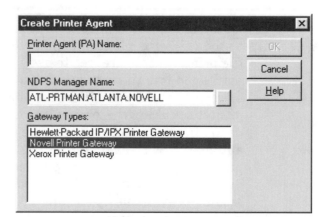

4. Specify a name for the new Printer Agent.

5. Select an appropriate gateway type from the list box.

6. If you select the Novell gateway as your gateway, the following dialog box will appear:

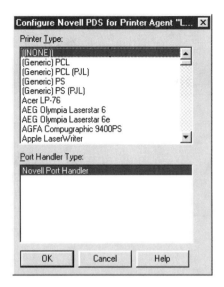

7. Select the printer type and the appropriate port for the connection type that is used by the public-access printer.

8. If you select Hewlett-Packard IP/IPX Printer Gateway, the following dialog box opens:

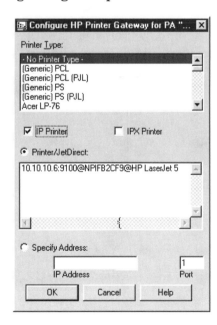

9. Choose the printer type, the protocol, and the Printer/JetDirect listing or specify the address and port of the printer if it is not listed.

10. If you select Xerox Gateway, you will be prompted with the Xerox Setup Wizard; simply follow the prompts to complete the setup process.

11. After you complete these steps, you will have an opportunity to select a printer driver for each type of desktop operating your environment uses. This process will be discussed in detail later in this chapter.

 Note: *No NDS object for the printer will be created using this method.*

How do I create a Printer Agent as a controlled-access printer?

To create a controlled access printer, do the following:

1. In NWADMN32, select the container in which you want to create the NDPS Printer object.

2. Click Object, Create, and then NDPS Printer. Click OK. The following dialog box appears:

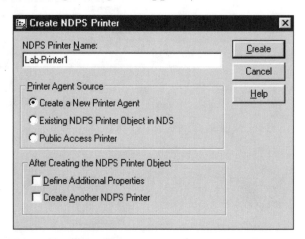

3. Type an NDPS printer name in the appropriate box.

4. Select a Printer Agent source. In this case, choose Create a New Printer Agent for an undefined printer or Existing NDS Printer Object in NDS if you are upgrading an existing queue-based printer.

5. Click Create.

6. You will again be presented with the Printer Gateway dialog box; select the appropriate gateway, click the Browse button under NDPS Manager Name, and select the NDPS Manager object you created previously.

7. Click OK; then configure the printer type and port handler.

8. On the next screen, configure the connection type and port type, click Next, and then complete the remaining configuration entries.

9. Access the Details page for the new Printer object and assign any users, groups, or containers that will need access to the printer.

Does each printer on the network require a license?

A printer configured as a controlled-access printer requires a server license. However, public-access printers do not require a license.

Do I need to update my workstation client to take full advantage of NDPS?

To use NDPS, clients need to be running NetWare Client32 version 2.2 or higher. It is recommended that the client for NetWare 5 be installed as part of the migration process. NetWare Client32 version 3 for Windows 95/98 and Client32 version 4.5 for NT Workstation are included with NetWare 5.

When I attach a network printer to the network, will it automatically be detected and configured?

If the printer is an NDPS-aware network printer, the printer will automatically be configured as a public-access printer when it is plugged in.

How do I configure my workstation to print to an NDPS printer?

Included with NetWare 5 is the NDPS Printer Manager. This utility, named NWPMW32.EXE, resides in the

PUBLIC/WIN32 directory for Windows 95/98 and Windows NT workstations. The Novell Printer Manager is shown here:

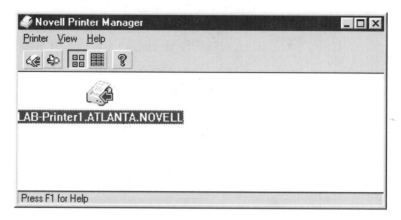

The version for Windows 3.*x* workstations, named NWPMW16.EXE, resides in the PUBLIC directory. To add an NDPS printer manually from the workstation, complete the following steps.

1. In the menu, choose Printer and then click New. The following dialog box appears:

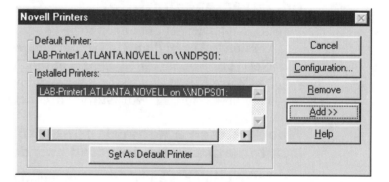

2. From the list of installed printers, select the printer you want to install. If none are listed, use the Browse button to search containers for the printer you want to use. Click Install.

3. After downloading the printer driver, click OK.

4. Click Close.

You will now have access to the printer.

Where do I find information about a specific printer or print job?

Novell Print Manager displays a list of printers currently installed on your workstation. For more information about the configuration of a specific printer, right-click the printer you want to obtain more information about and then click Information. The Printer Information dialog box, shown here, will open, displaying the details of the printer:

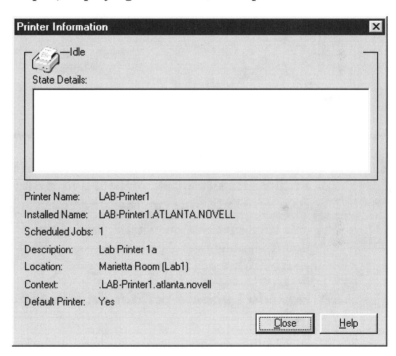

For more information regarding a spooled print job, double-click the printer for which you want job information. This will launch the Novell Job Manager:

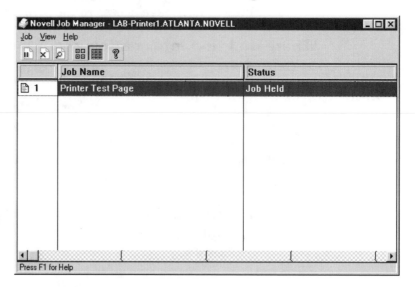

From this dialog box, you can double-click the specific job for even more detailed information regarding the print job.

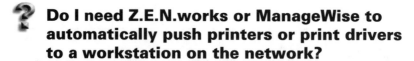

Do I need Z.E.N.works or ManageWise to automatically push printers or print drivers to a workstation on the network?

No, you don't need either. The capability for sending printer assignments and printer drivers is built into NDPS in NetWare 5.

How do I update printer drivers for a specific printer?

Complete the following steps to update or change a printer driver in NDPS:

1. From within NWADMN32, double-click the NDS NDPS Broker object.

2. Click the Resource Management Service (RMS) tab on the right side of the dialog box. The following property page will appear:

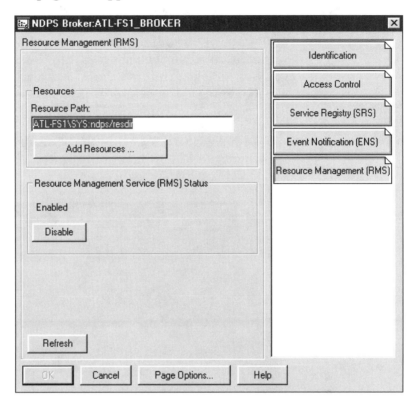

3. In the Resources section of the RMS dialog box, click the Add Resources button.

4. In the Resource Types section of this window, click the appropriate operating system driver you want to add or modify.

5. Click the Add button.

6. Browse to the location of the printer driver's .INF file, select the file, and click OK.

 ## How can I automatically install printers on a user's workstation?

A snap-in utility called NDPS Remote Printer Management is added to NWADMN32 when NDPS is installed. This utility allows the administrator to send a printer to a user workstation when the user logs into the network. In addition, you can remove printers from a user workstations or specify which printer is the default printer. To send a printer to a user workstation, complete the following steps:

1. In NWADMN32, choose the Tools drop-down menu and then select NDPS Remote Printer Management. The following dialog box will appear:

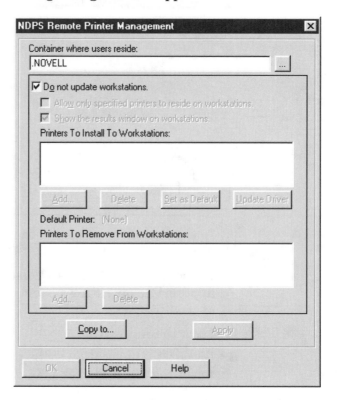

2. Select the container in which the users who are to receive this printer reside.

3. If you want to specify that the users can use only the printers you select, or if you want to show the results to the users as the printers are installed, check the appropriate check boxes.

4. Click Add and select the printers you want the users to receive. You can also choose to update the driver for an existing printer or set a printer as the default for the users at this time.

5. To remove a printer from a user workstation, click the Add button in the Printers To Remove From Workstations box.

When the users log in next time, they will receive or have removed the printers you have selected.

How can I customize NDPS print jobs?

A user can customize NDPS print jobs by accessing the Novell Print Manager. By right-clicking the printer you want to customize and then clicking Configuration, you will be able to change many settings, including priority, banners, media type, job holds, notifications, and drivers.

From NWADMN32, an administrator can access the same configuration information by following these steps:

1. From NWADMN32, double-click the Printer Agent object on the tree that you want to modify.

2. In the printer graphic, click Control; then click Set Defaults.

3. In the Printer Defaults dialog box that appears, make your changes.

In addition to the settings that the user can modify, administrators can determine whether a particular field can be modified or not; the administrator can change a setting and then click the Lock icon next to the field. If the lock is open (or green), the user can continue to modify this field; if the lock is closed (or red), the user can no longer make changes to this field.

The Printer Configuration templates of NDPS can also be modified. The configuration templates are the NDPS equivalent of PRINTCON in previous versions of NetWare. An administrator can create a preset configuration that users can use for specific jobs. To create a printer configuration, follow these steps:

1. From NWADMN32, click the Printer Agent that you want to modify.

2. Double-click the Configuration tab. The following dialog box will appear:

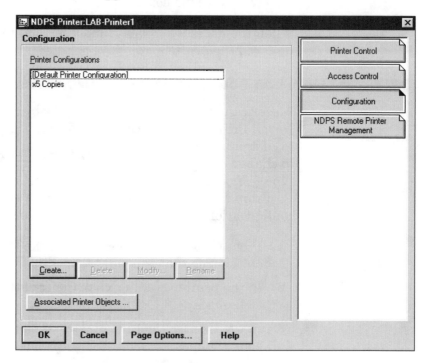

3. Click Create.

4. Name the configuration that you are creating; specify a name that lets users know what this configuration is useful for.

5. In the Printer Configuration dialog box, review the tabs that are available for configuration. Modify the print configuration as you want and then click OK.

For the user, when a printer is installed using Novell Print Manager, a list of print configurations associated with a printer is displayed when the printer is selected. It is then possible to have multiple mappings to the same printer using different configurations. The only requirement is that the user must change the name of the printer to a name relevant to the printer configuration for that mapping.

What is bidirectional printing?

Bidirectional printing is the process that allows printers and clients to communicate with each other in real time. The advantage of this interchange is the availability of real-time information, such as a printer's status, configuration properties, and features. In addition, you can view information on specific jobs, such as scheduling information, job properties, and current status.

How can I control the scheduling of print jobs?

A variety of different configuration options exist for NDPS printers. Follow these steps from NWADMN32:

1. Double-click the printer you want to modify on the NDS tree.

2. On the Printer Control property page, click the Jobs button near the diagram of the printer; then select Spooling Configuration.

3. On the Spooling Configuration property page, choose the type of scheduling you want to use from the Scheduling drop-down box.

NDPS provides several types of scheduling algorithms, including First In, First Out; Smallest Job First; and Minimize Media Changes.

How do I customize banners?

NDPS supports three types of banner files: PCL banners (.PCL extension), PostScript banners (.PS extension), and Generic Text banners (.TXT extension). To create either a

PCL or PostScript banner, you need a working knowledge of PCL and PostScript printer codes. The upper two-thirds of the banner page is available to the administrator for any information the user wants to place there, however, in both circumstances, the lower one-third is reserved for the following information fields: Job Name, Job Owner, Time Printed, and Date Printed.

The third type of banner page, the Generic Text banner, can be created in any printer language and will have no additional information overlaid during printing.

After a customized banner has been created, write the information to the Resource Management Service (RMS) for use with print jobs using the following steps:

1. From NWADMN32, double-click the NDPS Broker object.

2. Select the Resource Management tab.

3. Click the Add Resources button.

4. Select the icon for the type of resource you want to add; in this case, select the banner resource.

5. Click the Add button.

6. Click the Browse button to search for the banner you want to add.

7. After finding the file containing the banner you want to add, select the specific resource to be added in the Resources to Be Added field.

8. Click OK.

After you complete these steps, the banner page will be available for use with print jobs.

MIGRATING TO NDPS

 Other than leaving my printers in queue-based mode as they were in NetWare 4.x, what options do I have after migrating to NetWare 5 and NDPS?

In many circumstances, migration will be gradual, especially in an environment with many network printers. Most

migration activities will be visits to the workstation to change the object being printed to. An interim solution would be to activate all NDPS components on the server and allow the Printer Agents to serve queues. This is achieved using the following steps:

1. From within NWADMN32, double-click a created Printer Agent object that represents the printer that will be printed to.

2. Click the Jobs button and then click Spooling Configuration.

3. At the bottom of the Spooling Configuration dialog box that appears, click Add in the Service Jobs from NetWare Queues section.

4. Browse to and select the queue that you want connected to this NDPS printer.

Over time, you can change workstation printer configurations to print directly to the NDPS Printer Agent rather than to the queue. After all workstations have migrated to the Printer Agent, you will no longer need to maintain the queue assignment in the NDPS spooling properties, and the queue can be removed.

 How do I configure DOS applications to print to an NDPS printer?

There is only one configuration that will allow DOS clients or applications to print to an NDPS printer. Follow the steps described in the preceding section to use queues in combination with NDPS Printer Agents for DOS printing. At the workstation, assign the LPT port to the corresponding queue that you want to print to.

 Which protocol should I use with NDPS?

NetWare 5 offers a variety of print and protocol configurations. NDPS is protocol independent, so it can be used with IP, IPX, or a combination of the two.

 ## Can I use Pure IP in my environment and continue to use queue-based printing?

Yes. Both queue-based printing and NDPS are supported at the same time. Therefore, migration can be on a per-printer basis at a pace that suits your needs.

 ## Do I use NPRINTER on my workstations?

NPRINTER still maintains printing to the workstation in NDPS. The disadvantage to this configuration is that Printer Agents set up as remote printers using the Novell printer gateway use IPX along with SAP to advertise their existence as print servers. NPRINTER will not respond to the Service Location Protocol (SLP) but will respond only to SAP, requiring the Printer Agent object to behave as a print server that sends SAP for NPRINTER's benefit. In addition, some of the detailed information that is available in network-attached Printer Agents is unavailable while using this configuration. It is highly recommended that you migrate your printers from workstation attached to network attached to take advantage of NDPS capabilities when this migration is feasible.

 ## How do I configure a workstation-based network printer?

Workstation-based printing is handled by the Novell printer gateway. After a printer is connected and configured on a workstation, complete the following steps to make the printer available for network use:

1. From within NWADMN32, select the container in which you want to create the NDPS printer, right-click the container object, and click Create.

2. Select NDPS Printer. Click OK.

3. In the Create NDPS Printer dialog box that appears, click the NDPS Printer Name box and enter a name for the printer. Then click Create a New Printer Agent. Click Create.

4. In the Create Printer Agent dialog box that appears, browse for and select the NDPS Manager name on the NDS tree. Select Novell Printer Gateway in the Gateway Type list box. Click OK.

5. Browse through the list of available printer types and select the appropriate printer. Also make sure that Novell Port Handler is selected. Click OK. This will bring up the Configure Port Handler dialog box.

6. In the Connection Type field, select Remote (RPRINTER on IPX), and choose the port that the printer is attached to on the workstation. Click Next.

7. Enter additional information, including the SAP name of the printer and the printer number. Click Next.

8. Choose the printer drivers you want to use with the workstation; then click OK.

9. From the DOS/Windows workstation, activate NPRINTER.

10. Click the Bindery-based Printer box and then click the Browse button next to the Print Server field to display a list of all available print servers. Choose the appropriate print server and attached printer.

Your workstation printer is now ready to receive jobs.

 I have been using queue-based printing in conjunction with NetWare/IP. How do I migrate to NDPS?

The advantage to using NetWare in conjunction with NetWare/IP (NWIP) is that NWIP enables you to print to an LPR-configured print server without using IPX. This opens several possibilities for migration to NDPS.

Several pieces of the NWIP print configuration can be replaced using NDPS components. If workstations that are addressing queues cannot be modified at the present time, back-end components of the print process can be replaced with NDPS components; these include the NWIP Print Server and the NetWare-to-Unix gateway. These can be replaced relatively easily with an NDPS Print Manager,

Printer Agent (which continues to support the original NWIP print queue), and the Novell printer gateway. As time permits, workstations can be reconfigured to print to the Printer Agent instead of the print queue; when the queue is no longer in use, it can be deleted.

Since NetWare 5 no longer uses SAP while in Pure IP mode, how do printers advertise their existence on the network?

Public-access printers configured in NDPS must register their services with a centralized database. This database is the Service Registry Service (SRS). SRS acts as a map to network printing services so that clients can address these services.

For other printer services, the Service Location Protocol (SLP) uses a multicast process to advertise the printer's services on the network.

What is the impact on network traffic of using NDPS with no workstation-attached printers as opposed to using queue-based printing?

Because SAP broadcasts are no longer required to advertise printer services, overall network traffic is reduced.

How can I optimize NDPS?

The most common way to optimize NDPS is to use printers that can support their own processing. In an environment with 50 or more printers, serving a printer can have a serious impact on other file services.

NetWare 5 activation of new NDPS Brokers is a fairly automated process, but some human intervention may be necessary to take certain infrastructure items into consideration. For example, in a WAN environment, although the NDPS Broker can serve printers at both local and remote locations, it may more appropriate to create a second NDPS Broker at the remote site due to low bandwidth between the two locations.

In addition, if printer discovery between two service registries is accomplished using SAP or SLP, any intermediary device, such as a router, between these two service registries that is filtering SAP or SLP packet traffic will prevent the servers from sharing information. All servers on the network must be running the same protocols to synchronize the data they contain about their printers.

TROUBLESHOOTING NETWORK PRINTING

 ### When launching NWADMN32 on Windows 95, I get an error in NDPSW32.DLL. What is causing this?

To view NDPS version 2 objects correctly, you must update your client to Novell Client32 version 3 for Windows 95/98 workstations or Client32 version 4.5 for Windows NT workstations. This will correct this problem.

This problem will also occur if your Windows 95/98 workstation does not have Novell Distributed Print Services installed. To install these print services, right-click the Network Neighborhood icon on your desktop and then click Properties. This will bring up the Network Configuration properties. Check the list of networking components that are installed on your workstation. At the bottom of the list, you should see Novell Distributed Print Services. If you don't, then you need to install it manually. To do so, follow these directions:

1. From the Network Configuration properties page, click the Add button.
2. Click the Service icon. Then click OK.
3. In the Manufacturers pane, click Novell. Then, in the Network Services pane, click Novell Distributed Print Services.
4. Click OK.
5. If necessary, insert the disk that Windows requests.

This should correct the problem.

 After experiencing a server abend, I receive errors when starting NDPSM. What is causing this?

When you start the NDPSM service, if you see the error message "Printer Agent *name* failed to bind to a notification service," you most likely have a corrupted NDPS database.

NDPS contains server-based utilities to provide fault tolerance and permit manual maintenance. To access these utilities, go to the NDPS Manager screen at the server console, select NDPS Manager Status and Control, and press ENTER. Then select the Database Options and press ENTER again. This will bring up the following screen:

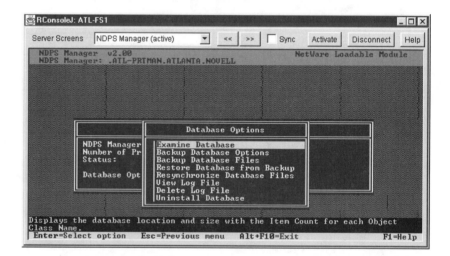

From this location, you have several options for managing the NDPS database. The first option you should try is Resynchronize Database Files. If this does not correct the problem, try Restore Database from Backup. Either of these options temporarily shuts down the NDPS Manager and Printer Agents while the operation runs. The length of time the operation takes depends on the size of the database, which depends on the number of printers and amount of printer activity in your environment.

 ## When I try to create a new Printer Agent, the list of available gateways is empty. Why?

There are three files that make up the list of available printer gateways:

CONFIGHP.PD#
CONFIGPD.PD#
CONFIGPH.PD#

The number (#) field depends on the operating system you used to run NWADMN32. If you are using the 16-bit NWADMN32, the number field of the file extension will be 1. If a 32-bit version of NWADMN32 has been executed, the number will be 2 and the files will be located in the SYS:PUBLIC\WIN32 directory.

If no printer gateways are listed, then the workstation attempting to run NWADMN32 is not able to find these files via a search path. You can either change to the current directory and launch NWADMN32 or map a search drive to the location of these files.

 ## In Windows NT, I cannot see NDPS printers in Explorer. What is wrong?

This is normal. As of release 2 of NDPS, you can see public-access printers and controlled-access printers in Novell Print Manager but not in Explorer on NT systems. However, in Windows 95/98, you can see the printers in both locations.

 ## While loading NPRINTER.EXE, I received an error message reporting that no print server could be found. What is the problem?

The resolution of this problem depends on the printing environment you are using. If you are using a queue-based environment in conjunction with IPX, this error message simply indicates that the print server (PSERVER.NLM) has not been activated on the server.

If you have a Pure IP environment, this message will be displayed every time NPRINTER is launched. This occurs because a print server sends SAP broadcasts, but NPRINTER will not find any print servers in a Pure IP environment.

In NWADMN32, the Enable Broker button is dimmed, even though I am an administrator. What is causing this?

Check to make sure that the Services Registry Service (SRS) is enabled on the NDPS Broker that you are attempting to control. This can be done from the server console.

I am running out of drive space in the volume that my print jobs are spooling to. What are my options?

The best fix in this situation is to move the print job spooling to a drive that has more space available. To do this, follow these steps:

1. In NWADMN32, double-click the printer whose spooling properties you want to modify.

2. On the Printer Control property page, click Jobs and then click Spooling. The Spooling Configuration dialog box appears.

3. From this location, modify the location that print jobs are spooled to. Keep in mind the future storage capabilities of the volume you move your spooling files to.

Alternatively, if the situation is not critical, you can limit the amount of space that the spooling uses on the volume. Reducing the size of a spool file may reduce the speed with which jobs are serviced for this printer. Jobs that exceed the spooling size of the server will be temporarily spooled on the user's workstation until space is made available at the server.

I'm having difficulties installing an updated HP printer driver that came on several disks. What could be causing my problems?

When installing or updating a printer driver for the Resource Management Service (RMS), you must keep in mind that drivers that come on multiple disks may cause an error message stating that the driver cannot be found. To fix this problem, copy the contents of all the disks to a temporary directory on the server and install the driver for RMS from that location instead.

When I click an NDPS Manager object, I see the error message, "The object *name* that was selected is not an NDPS Manager." What is wrong?

This error is the result of a deleted Volume object in NDS. The NDPS Manager object that you are clicking has not been changed to another active volume, and the object is now shown as an unknown object.

To fix this problem, simply associate the NDPS Manager object with an existing Volume object and re-create the printers that are assigned to the NDPS Manager.

I want to reinstall NDPS on my NetWare 5 server. How do I do this?

During the installation of NetWare 5, you are given a choice of whether or not to install NDPS. However, even if NDPS is not installed, the NDS schema is extended to accept NDPS objects. To install NDPS, complete the following steps:

1. Insert the NetWare 5 CD-ROM into the server.
2. Copy the contents of the PRODUCTS/NDPS directory to the root of volume SYS.

3. Open the NDPS directory and unzip all zipped files.

4. Launch NWADMN32 and begin setting up NDPS objects.

In addition, make sure to completely disable the NDPS Broker and NDPS Manager objects before attempting reinstallation.

I want a remote location to be served by its own NDPS Broker rather than to use one across a slow link. Are there any restrictions?

In this release of NDPS, you can create an NDPS Broker object only on a server that has an NDS replica.

When I download a driver for an NT workstation, an error message tells me that the driver cannot be used to communicate with a printer. How do I fix this?

If you manually or automatically install an NDPS printer and receive a driver for that printer on an NT workstation, you may receive an "Error 1797" message when you attempt to use the printer. This is caused by a non-NDPS installation of the printer. You can remove the printer and try downloading the server-based printer again.

Another cause of this problem may be that the NT 4 workstation has received an NT 3.5 workstation printer driver. To determine the type of driver, you need to use Regedit and check the following keys:

```
HKEY_LOCAL_MACHINE \ System \ CurrentControlSet \ Control \
Print \ Environments \ Windows NT x86 \ Drivers \ Version-1
```

and

```
HKEY_LOCAL_MACHINE \ System \ CurrentControlSet \ Control \
Print \ Environments \ Windows NT x86 \ Drivers \ Version-2
```

If the driver appears under the Version-1 key, the driver is installed but is the wrong type. If the driver is under the Version-2 key, the driver is the correct type and version.

Can I use an NDPS public-access printer to service a queue?

No. Only controlled-access printers are allowed to service an existing printer queue.

I can't start the Resource Management Service (RMS) on my file server. What could be the problem?

Any of several conditions may be causing this error. First, check the properties of the directory NDPS\RESDIR. Make sure that the NDPS Broker object has Supervisor rights to the directory. These are necessary for the NDPS Broker to control the Resource Management Service (RMS). Second, the RMS cannot have a directory name that is longer than eight characters or that contains any illegal characters. Make sure that the names are correct everywhere in the path.

I have associated a Print Queue object to be serviced by a Printer object, but when I send a job to the queue, it is never printed.

This could be caused by a Directory Service replication problem. If the problem has not resolved itself in 15 minutes, shut down the Printer Agent and restart it.

Chapter 9

Managing the User Environment

Answer Topics!

● **USER ADMINISTRATION** 300

? Setting up multiple users
? Creating users in NetWare 5
? Creating a user with ConsoleOne
? Creating Template objects
? Renaming a user
? Deleting a user
? Using the Details on Multiple Users option
? Recovering Admin rights
? Assigning specific user rights
? Importing users from an existing database with UIMPORT
? Removing users with UIMPORT

● **LOGIN SECURITY** 311

? Understanding login security
? Setting up Intruder Detection
? Unlocking user accounts locked by exceeding the number of grace logins
? Setting up temporary user accounts
? Setting time restrictions
? Setting password restrictions
? Unlocking user accounts locked because of an expired password

● **MANAGING GROUPS OF USERS** 317

? Understanding Group objects
? Creating Group objects

LOGIN SCRIPTS 319

? Understanding login scripts

? Understanding the four types of login scripts

? Learning the order of login script execution

? Troubleshooting login scripts

? Correcting errors when modifying login scripts

? Executing external commands

? Correcting login script problems with Windows 95 users

? Executing a Windows application from a login script

? Losing the PATH after running login scripts

? Understanding the necessity of login scripts

? Creating a login script

? Setting up profile scripts for users

? Running more than one profile script per user

? Comparing commands and variables

? Learning the NetWare 5 login script commands

? Learning the NetWare 5 login script variables

? Making the login script read a value from the Registry

? Printing login scripts

Managing the User Environment @ a Glance

User administration is one of the most widely used tasks with NetWare 5. The actual creation of users in NetWare 5 is a fairly simple action. However, what happens if you need to create 2,000 users. How can you do this easily? How long will this take? This chapter will answer questions relating to user creation and also present you with tips and tricks to make administration of your network simple. This chapter covers the following:

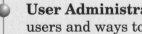

User Administration discusses the methods of creating users and ways to optimize your template for creation of multiple users.

Login Security discusses the security of the network for individuals or groups of users.

Managing Groups of Users shows ways of managing your network more effectively.

Login Scripts answers questions about the different types of login scripts, how they run, and how to optimize them.

USER ADMINISTRATION

 I need to set up several users on the network. What is the best way to do this?

Setting up several users in a short period of time can be done easily with an NDS object called a *template*. For example, imagine that everyone in the marketing department uses SRV1 as their default server. The home directory is located on the SRV1_DATA volume in the USERS directory. Users are required to have a password that is at least six characters long and expires every 60 days. Without a Template object, you would need to go to each individual User object and set up the default server, home directory, and password properties in NetWare Administrator. You can save numerous administrative hours by using a template when creating marketing users. Only the Template object will need to be configured with the desired default server, home directory, and password properties. The Template object is specified during the creation of the user when NDS is instructed to confer all the properties of the Template object to the new User object.

 How do I create a user in NetWare 5?

To create a new User object for each person who needs access to the network, perform the following steps using NetWare Administrator:

1. Log in as Admin.

 Note: *You must be logged in to the network as a user with Create or Supervisor object rights to the container that will hold the new User object. Please refer to the "NDS Security" section in Chapter 12 for more information on NDS Security rights.*

2. Open NetWare Administrator.

3. Click to select the desired container in which the new User object will reside.

 Note: *If you do not see the desired container, select View |
Set Context. Type **[Root]** in the Context field. (Be sure to
include the square brackets [].) Select OK. If you still do not
see the destination container, try double-clicking the container
objects that are displayed until you find it.*

 Tip: *If you cannot see a particular container object, try
highlighting the container that you can see, and then pressing
the BACKSPACE key to go up a level.*

4. Click the Create User Object button on the toolbar.

 Note: *Another way to add a user is to right-click on the
container object and then select Create. Scroll down the
New Object dialog box, and double-click User. Then complete
steps 5–12.*

Create User tool   Browse Template button

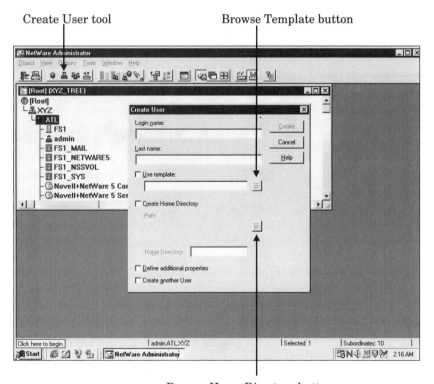

Browse Home Directory button

5. Type the name of the user in the Login Name field. This is the name the user will enter to log in to the network. Remember the name must be unique in the container.

6. Type the last name of the user in the Last Name field.

7. Using a template is optional. Skip to step 10 if you are not using a Template object. Click the Use Template option box if you want to base the new User object on a template.

8. Click the Browse Template button.

9. Click to select the desired template in the Available Objects column, and then click OK.

Note: *If the desired template is not displayed, you may have to scan the tree to find the desired template in the Browse Context column.*

Tip: *Notice the current context is displayed in the upper-left portion of the Select Object dialog box. To change your context back a level, you can double-click the yellow up arrow in the Browse Context column.*

Double-click to move your context back a level

Current context →

Select Object

ATL.XYZ...

Available objects:

ATL_Template

Browse context:

.. ..

Novell+NetWare 5 Conn SCL+5l

Novell+NetWare 5 Server+500

OK

Cancel

Help

Change Context...

Note: *Creation of a home directory is optional. Skip forward to step 11 if you are not creating a home directory for this user. Click the Create Home Directory option box to have a home directory created automatically as the User object is created.*

 Tip: *Use a Template object when creating users if home directories are used. See "How do I create a Template object?" later in this section. Click the Browse Home Directory button.*

10. Click to select the desired home directory in the Available Objects column, then click OK.

 Note: *If the desired directory is not displayed, you may have to scan the tree by double-clicking on the volume object(s) displayed in the Browse Context column.*

By default, the user's new home directory will be named the same as the login name specified in step 5.

 Note: *Skip to step 14 if you are not creating additional users in the selected container.*

11. Click the Create Another User option box to create more users. Then repeat steps 4–12 for each new user.

12. Click OK.

I've heard that you can create a user with ConsoleOne. How is this done?

Users can be created at the server console or at a workstation with ConsoleOne. Perform the following at the server console:

1. Load ConsoleOne at the server by typing **C1START** and pressing ENTER.

 Note: *If the GUI interface is already loaded, you can select the Novell button, and then ConsoleOne.*

2. Double-click the network.

3. Double-click the desired tree.

 Note: *If necessary, you will need to authenticate to the tree as Admin.*

4. Double-click to expand the container in which the User object will reside.

5. Right-click the container in which the User object will reside, select New, and select User.

6. Type the name of the new user.

7. Press TAB.

8. Type the last name of the new user.

9. Click Create.

 ## How do I create a Template object?

Perform the following steps to create a Template object:

1. Log in as Admin and open NetWare Administrator from SYS:PUBLIC\WIN32\NWADMIN32.EXE.

2. Right-click the container in which you want to create the template, and then choose Create.

3. Using the scroll bar, click Template in the Class of New Object dialog box and then click OK to display the Create Template dialog box.

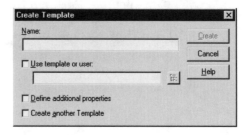

4. Type a name, such as MRKTG_TEMPLATE, for the new object in the Name field.

 Note: *Remember, the name of the new Template object must be unique in the container.*

5. (Optional) To base the template on an existing template or user, check Use Template or User, and then click the Browse button to choose the template or user.

6. Click Create.

 ## How do I rename an existing user?

Renaming a user is a common part of administrating any network. For example, people in your organization may get married or legally change their names. Perform the following steps using NetWare Administrator:

1. Log in as Admin.

 Note: *You must be logged in to the network as a user with Rename or Supervisor object rights to the User object.*

2. Expand the container that holds the User object to be renamed.

3. Click on the User object.

4. Select Object from the menu bar.

5. Select Rename.

6. Type the new name of the user in the New Name field.

 Tip: *Remember the name must be unique in the container. Click the option box for Save Old Name if you would like to have the old user name saved.*

 Note: *This helps users search for the User object by the old name.*

7. Click OK.

 Note: *This procedure does not change the name of the user's home directory in the file system.*

 ## How can I remove a former employee's user ID from the network?

Perform the following using NetWare Administrator.

1. Log in as Admin.

 Note: *You must be logged in to the network as a user with Delete or Supervisor object rights to the User object.*

2. Move to the container that holds the User object to be deleted.

3. Right-click on the User object to be deleted.

4. Click Delete.

5. Click Yes to confirm deletion of the User object.

 Note: *Skip the remaining steps if the user you deleted does not have a home directory.*

6. Steps 1–5 did not delete the user's home directory; therefore, it is necessary to perform the following:

   a. Double-click to expand the Volume object that contains the user's home directory.

   b. If necessary, double-click to expand the directory in which the user's home directory is located (such as USERS).

   c. Right-click on the user's home directory.

   d. Click Delete.

   e. Click Yes to confirm deletion of the user's home directory.

 ## Can I make a change to several users in one step instead of having to go to each individual user and make the change?

Yes. You can use the Details on Multiple Users option to change the properties of many users simultaneously. For

example, suppose the marketing department's phone number has changed. Making this change can be done in only one step using Details on Multiple Users. Without Details on Multiple Users, you would need to change the phone number numerous times by changing the Department Phone Number property for each User object.

To change properties for multiple users simultaneously, perform the following steps in NetWare Administrator:

1. Log in as Admin.

2. Choose the User objects whose properties you want to edit. To choose multiple users, hold down the CTRL key and click on each User object.

Tip: *You can use Template, Group, and container objects with Details on Multiple Users. If you select a Template object instead of a User object in step 2, changes made with Details on Multiple Users will be conferred to all users previously created with that template. If you select a Group object in step 2, changes made with Details on Multiple Users will be conferred to all members of the group. If you select a container object in step 2, changes made with Details on Multiple Users will be conferred to all users whose User objects reside in the selected container.*

3. Click Object on the menu bar, and then choose Details on Multiple Users.

4. Edit the property(s) that you would like changed for each selected user.

Note: *Existing property values are not shown when using Details on Multiple Users. You can only add new values to multivalued properties and replace values of single-valued properties. For example, if you are changing the location from Atlanta to Denver via Details on Multiple Users, you will not see Atlanta. However, entering Denver in the Location property via Details on Multiple Users will replace Atlanta in the Location property.*

5. (Optional) To modify the list of users to which your changes will be applied, choose User List and edit the list, and then click OK.

6. Click OK.

7. Click Yes to confirm the operation. Click the option box to pause if errors occur during the operation. If you choose not to pause on errors, you save and later view any errors when the operation is done.

Users that were not created with a Template object can be added as members of the template with the following steps:

1. Right-click the Template object.

2. Select Details.

3. Select the Members of Template property page.

4. Click Add.

5. Browse to the container holding the User object(s).

6. Press the CTRL key and click each user to be added to the template; then click OK twice.

Now you have allowed the use of the Template object in managing User objects.

 I accidentally deleted my Admin user and have lost supervisor control of the tree. What can I do to get Supervisor rights back?

Several options are available to get your Admin rights back to the root of the tree. The first option is to call Novell Technical Services at (800) 858-4000. For security reasons, you will need to supply proof that you are the administrator of your network. The cost of this service is $200 at the time of this writing.

The second option is to obtain an NLM that is called MAKESU.NLM, which will create a user in your tree with Supervisory access to the [Root]. This program can be purchased for $99 and can be downloaded from the Web at www.dreamlan.com. If this utility creates a concern about security in NetWare 5, you can always use the SECURE CONSOLE command to prevent it from being loaded on the servers. For more information about SECURE CONSOLE, please refer to the question "How can I protect my NetWare server from malicious tampering?" in Chapter 4.

> **_Caution:_** _This program is a third-party product and inserts an object into your tree. Therefore, you should use it with care._

To facilitate administration, I would like to give one of my users rights to change user passwords. Is it possible to assign a user the rights to perform a specific task without the user having Administrator rights?

Yes. This is done through NDS security. Please refer to the "NDS Security" section in Chapter 12.

I have a database that contains all the users I need to add to NDS. Is it possible to import the information in my database into NDS so I don't have to create each user individually?

Yes, you can import users into NDS from an ASCII-delimited text file using the UIMPORT utility that is located in the SYS:PUBLIC directory. First, the actual database file must be exported into ASCII delimited file format. A comma is the default field delimiter. A return (CR/LF) is the default record delimiter.

The second step is to create a separate file called the _control file_ in ASCII format. The control file instructs UIMPORT how the database information is to be imported into NDS—for example, the context the User objects are imported into, the order of fields to be imported into NDS, and so on.

The following is an example of an ASCII-delimited file:

```
John,Doe,101 USA Road,Anytown,GA,30099,7709983322,Senior Sales
Representative,00761
Mary,Smith,102 USA Road,Anytown,GA,30099,7709982211,Vice President Sales,00433
Tom,King,100 USA Road,Anytown,GA,30099,7709986676,Vice President Marketing.00988
```

Jill,Jones,110 USA Road,Anytown,GA,30099,7709987777,Senior Marketing
Representative,00954

The following is an example of an ASCII control file used to import the above information into NDS:

```
Import Control

Name Context=.atl.xyz
Create Home Directory=Y
Home Directory Path=Users
Home Directory Volume= SRV1/VOL1

Fields

Name
Last Name
Mailing Label Information
Mailing Label Information
Mailing Label Information
Mailing Label Information
Telephone
Title
Skip
```

Notice that the control file specifies the following things:

- The context (.ATL.XYZ) that the new users will be imported into.
- The creation of a home directory on SRV1/VOL1.
- The fields or properties that should be imported into NDS (such as Name, Last Name, and so on).

The final step is to use the UIMPORT command to import the information into NDS. The following is an example of the command entered in DOS to import the ASCII file, DB.DAT, into NDS using the CTRL.TXT control file:

```
UIMPORT CTRL.TXT DB.DAT
```

 Can I remove users from NDS using UIMPORT?

Yes. You can use UIMPORT to add, delete, and change single or multiple users in NDS. To set up UIMPORT to delete users, add the following command to the Import Control section of the ASCII control file:

IMPORT MODE = R

LOGIN SECURITY

 ## What is login security?

Login security manages initial access to the network by specifying who can log in, where and when the login can occur, and how login is accomplished. The three divisions of login security are

- User Account Restrictions
- Intruder Detection
- Authentication

User Account Restrictions control when the user can log in to the network, the number of concurrent connections allowed, password requirements, whether or not the account has an expiration date, whether the account is enabled or disabled, and so on.

Intruder Detection prevents someone from guessing another user's password by limiting the number of times a user can incorrectly enter a password. Once the limit has been exceeded, the user account is locked for a specified amount of time.

Authentication is a process used to approve each request made by a user. When a request is made for a network service, authentication locates the object in the tree, verifies that the user has the necessary rights to use the service, and then connects the user to the resource.

 ## How do I set up Intruder Detection to prevent someone from guessing another user's password?

Intruder Detection enhances the security of your network by locking user accounts in which an incorrect password has been entered multiple times. Intruder Detection also logs the node address and time of detection. Log in as Admin and perform the following steps:

1. Open NetWare Administrator.

2. Right-click the container object holding User objects for which you would like to set up intruder detection.

3. Select Details.

4. Click the Intruder Detection button.

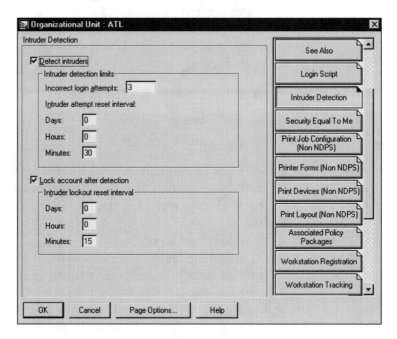

5. Click the Detect Intruders option box to enable intruder detection.

6. Type the desired number of allowable incorrect login attempts in the Incorrect Login Attempts field.

7. Type the number of days, hours, and/or minutes desired in the Intruder Attempt Reset Interval fields. These numbers indicate the time span in which successive failed login attempts can occur and count toward the intruder limit.

8. Click the Lock Account After Detection option box to have the user's account locked automatically.

9. Type the days, hours, and/or minutes desired in the Intruder Lockout Reset Interval fields. This specifies the length of time the user account remains locked after detection has occurred.

10. Click OK.

When my users lock themselves out of the network by incorrectly entering their passwords numerous times, how do I unlock their accounts?

Follow these steps to unlock an account:

1. Log in as Admin.

2. Open NetWare Administrator.

3. Double-click the User object whose account is locked.

4. Click the Intruder Lockout button.

5. Click to unmark the Account Locked option box.

6. Click OK.

I have several temporary employees working on the network. How do I set up user accounts that will automatically expire after a certain date?

Follow these steps to set up temporary user accounts with expiration dates:

1. Log in as Admin or as a user with the necessary rights.

2. Open NetWare Administrator.

3. Double-click the User object.

4. Click the Login Restrictions button.

5. Click the Account Has Expiration Date option box.

6. Type the desired expiration date and time.

7. Click OK.

 Tip: *If the User objects have not been created, first create a Template object and set the account expiration date in the Template object. Use the template when creating the temporary User objects.*

Can I set up my system so that no users are allowed to log in to the network while my daily backup runs?

Yes. You can set user time restrictions using NetWare Administrator. Perform the following steps:

1. Log in as Admin.

2. Select the users or container object(s) holding the users for which you would like to set a time restriction.

3. Select Object from the menu bar, and then select Details on Multiple Users.

4. Click the Login Time Restrictions button.

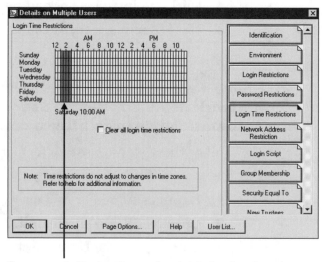

Gray area indicates times of restricted network access

5. Using the mouse, click and drag over the times of day you would like to restrict access to the network.

Note: *If you are having a hard time distinguishing the times of day, perform the following: Point to one cell in the Login Time Restrictions grid. You will see the day of week and time displayed at the bottom of the grid. The restricted times will be displayed in gray. Click and drag over areas that you accidentally marked as restricted to deselect.*

6. Click OK when all time restrictions are set.

7. Click Yes to apply changes to all users.

 Tip: *Create a template and make the above property changes to the Template object. You can then use the template for all new users you add to the network to have these restrictions applied automatically.*

 My company wants to implement a policy requiring all network users to use passwords. The passwords must be changed every 60 days and have a set minimum length. How do I do this?

Setting up password restrictions is a common administrative task in corporate environments. Here's how to do it:

1. Log in as Admin.

2. Open NetWare Administrator.

3. Select all containers holding User objects.

4. Click Object on the menu bar; then select Details on Multiple Users.

5. Click the Password Restrictions button.

6. Click the Require a Password option box.

7. Set the smallest number of characters the user must use for the password in the Minimum Password Length field.

8. Click the option box for Force Periodic Password Change.

9. Type **60** in the Days Between Forced Changes field.

10. (Optional) If you press the TAB key you will see the date that the password will expire.

11. (Optional) Click the Require Unique Passwords option box if the passwords must be unique each time they are changed.

12. To restrict the number of times the user is allowed to log in to the network without changing the password after it has expired, click the Limit Grace Logins option box.

13. Type the number of grace logins you would like the users to have.

14. Click OK to save changes.

15. Click Yes to have the changes applied to all users in the selected container(s).

Tip: *Create a template object with the above properties for all new users added to the network. This will result in less administration on your part and create a set standard of restrictions for any new user created.*

Some of my users receive the following message when their passwords expire because they do not change them: "Your Password has expired and you have exhausted your grace logins. Contact your system administrator." The users then get locked out of the network. How do I unlock a user's account?

A new password must be assigned to the user to unlock the account. Perform the following steps:

1. Log in as Admin.

2. Open NetWare Administrator.

3. Double-click the User object that is locked out of the network.

4. Click the Password Restrictions button.

5. Click Change Password.

6. Type a password in the New Password field.

7. Retype the same password in the Retype Password field.

8. Click OK.

9. Click OK again.

MANAGING GROUPS OF USERS

 ## Do I need to create Group objects?

Container objects act as natural groups since users with similar network needs are typically grouped into the same container. When all users in the container have similar requirements, Group objects are not necessary since the container object can be used to handle the needs of all users in it. For example, granting a container Read and File Scan rights to the DATA:SHARED\COMMON directory gives all users in that container Read and File Scan rights to DATA:SHARED\COMMON.

However, some organizations have a need to further divide the administration of users in a single container. Group objects are needed in these environments to keep network administration for these users simple. For example, the Sales and Marketing departments may be grouped into the same container since they work so closely together. The two departments use many of the same resources except when it comes to the Sales database, which should only be accessed by users in the Sales department. Creating a Sales Group object would greatly reduce administration of the database in this scenario. One way administration would be reduced is that rights to the database could then be managed through the Group object instead of through each individual Sales User object.

 Caution: *Be careful when adding users who exist across WAN connections to the same group. This will cause extra WAN traffic as members of the group are authenticated across the WAN.*

 I have several users in Marketing, Finance, and Human Resources who have similar network access needs. Would creating a Group object assist in administration of these users? How are groups created?

Creating a Group object is an excellent way to administrate these user needs. Follow these steps:

1. Log in as Admin.

 Note: *You must log in to the network as a user with Create or Supervisor object rights to the container in which the Group object will reside.*

2. Open NetWare Administrator.

3. Right-click the desired container in which the new Group object will reside.

4. Double-click Group in the Class of New Object dialog box. The following dialog box will appear:

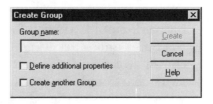

5. Type the name of the new Group object in the Group Name field. Remember that the name must be unique in the container.

6. Click the Define Additional Properties option box and then click Create.

7. Click the Members button and then click Add.

8. Select each user that should be a member of the group.

Note: *To select multiple users simultaneously, hold down the* CTRL *key and click each user. You may have to browse the tree to select users in different containers.*

    9. Click OK to accept all selected users.

    10. Click OK.

LOGIN SCRIPTS

 ### What is a login script?

A login script is simply a set of instructions set up by the network administrator that runs each time a user logs in to the network.

    The purpose of a login script is to establish a user's network environment at login. Typical login script instructions include drive mappings, printer connections, messages, and other commands. The following four types of login scripts are available in NetWare 5:

- Container
- Profile
- User
- Default

 ### What is the purpose of each of the four types of login scripts?

- **Container login script** A container login script is used to set up the network environment for all users whose User objects reside in that container. If the container that holds the User object does not have a login script, then no container script is executed for that user.

- **Profile login script** The purpose of a Profile object is to run a login script for a specific group of users. For example, everyone in the Sales department needs access to the Sales printer and database. You could create a profile named SALES_PROFILE with the necessary login script commands to grant the Sales department users access to the printer and database. A *Profile* is an NDS object created by the network administrator. By default, a user can only run one profile script. The administrator specifies which profile script should be executed through the User object's profile property.

- **User login script** A user login script is used to set up the network environment for a single user at login. Administration of numerous user login scripts is tedious. Therefore, user login scripts are used only when necessary for a single user's unique needs.

- **Default login script** The default login script is contained in the LOGIN.EXE file and cannot be edited. It contains only basic commands, such as a search drive mapping to PUBLIC. The default login script is executed for each user who does not have an individual user login script. Use the NO_DEFAULT command to prevent the execution of the default script.

In what order are the different types of login scripts executed?

The login scripts are executed in the following order:

1. Container
2. Profile
3. User
4. Default (if no user login script is executed)

I'm spending a lot of time troubleshooting problems with login scripts. Are there any troubleshooting tips I can follow when working with or creating login scripts?

Keep the following tips in mind when working with login scripts:

- *Always use uppercase.* This avoids the hassle of accidentally forgetting to enter variables in uppercase.

- *Always group like commands into sections.* That is, group together all mappings of network and search drives.

- *Always remark sections.* This makes it easier for you and other administrators to work with the script.

- *Put a blank line between sections.* This makes reading the script easier. Blank lines do not affect the login script execution.

- *Always use the PAUSE command after WRITE or DISPLAY commands.*

- *Indent IF / THEN statements.* This makes it easier to read the script.

- *Always practice on a test user instead of a whole group of users.* Otherwise, you may accidentally lock everyone out of the network.

- *Try placing a PAUSE command after each section for debugging purposes.* Remove the PAUSE commands when the script is perfected.

- *Use only one command per line.* Start each command on a new line.

- *Ensure that users have the appropriate file system rights to files and directories when troubleshooting map errors.* The user needs to have access to the directories for NetWare to successful map to it.

- *Ensure that users have the appropriate NDS security rights for whichever script that a user needs to execute.* The user must be a trustee of the object and have the Read right to the Login Script property. This is sufficient to run the login scripts. Browse rights are not necessary.

- *Set MAP DISPLAY and MAP ERRORS to ON so errors can be seen when debugging the login script.* These commands can be removed when the script is clean of errors.

- *Avoid syntax and spelling errors.* A majority of problems result from mapping drives and capturing printers. Usually, these problems are due to syntax and spelling errors.

- *Remember the order in which login scripts are executed: Container; Profile; User; and then if no user script exists, the Default login script.* Be sure not to overlap commands. For example, problems occur if you map drive F in the container script, then place a command in the Profile script to map drive F again. The mapping executed from the profile script overwrites the previous mapping made in the container script.

- *Make sure there are no viruses on the computer.* Viruses can cause diverse problems with login scripts that have at one time executed correctly.

- *Edit login scripts with NWADMIN32.* Since NETADMIN and NWADMIN95 are not supported in NetWare 5, you may experience various problems when editing login scripts.

- *Remove any TSR (terminate-and-stay-resident) programs.* Some have been known to cause login problems.

- *Be sure to keep these rules in mind when working with variables:*

  - Type the variable correctly.

  - Enclose environment variables in angle brackets when using them as identifier variables.

  - Identifier variables must be in uppercase letters.

  - A percent sign must precede an identifier variable.

 Note: *The percent sign is only necessary if you want the contents of the identifier variable to be substituted in place of the %*variable *reference in the login script. There are times when you would not include the percent sign, such as when you are checking to see if a variable is equal to a value—for example, IF LOGIN_NAME = "JOHN".*

I'm getting an error when trying to modify a login script. What can I do?

Try opening the login script and making the needed modifications. Copy the contents of the login script to the Clipboard by highlighting all the text and pressing CTRL-C. It's a good idea to paste by pressing CTRL-V and save the contents of the login script to a text file. Then highlight and delete the entire contents of the login script. Save the empty login script. Go back to edit the login script and paste the previously deleted commands back into the login script. You should now be able to save the changes without error.

Complete the following steps if you are in a multiserver environment where several servers hold replicas of the partition in which this Container, Profile, or User object's login script is located:

1. Determine which server is returning the error.
2. Log in to another server that has a replica of the same partition.
3. Run NetWare Administrator.
4. Edit the login script and click OK to save it. The modified login script will be replicated to the other servers holding replicas of the affected partition.

 Note: *Be sure the user has the Read and Write property rights to the object containing the login script.*

I'm having trouble executing an external command on my DOS/Windows 3.1 machines. What can I do?

To troubleshoot this problem, make sure the COMSPEC variable is set in the CONFIG.SYS. Then, make sure LOGIN.EXE is being swapped out correctly.

 One of my Windows 95 users does not run any login scripts. What could be the problem?

Typically, this problem is solved by checking the Run Scripts option box in the GUI Login dialog box. To check this, perform the following steps:

1. Click Start; then select Programs | Novell | NetWare Login.

2. Click the Advance button.

3. Click the Script tab.

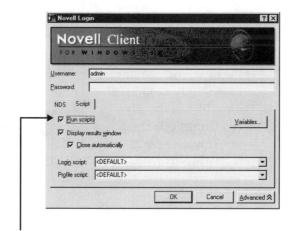

Should be checked to allow scripts to run

4. Be sure there is a check mark in the Run Scripts option box.

5. Enter your login name and password.

6. Click OK.

If this does not correct the problem, check to ensure the user has the sufficient Read property right to the container, profile, or user login script.

I used the @ command in a login script to execute a Microsoft Windows application during login and it didn't work. What is wrong?

Ask yourself the following questions to troubleshoot the problem:

- Is the specified directory or path wrong?
- Does the user have the appropriate file system security rights to execute the application?
- Has the executable file been specified correctly? Do not include the extension of the executable in the path.
- Does the workstation have enough memory available to load the application?
- Have you tried mapping a search drive to the application directory?

I am losing part of the path specified in the AUTOEXEC.BAT after the login script is executed. Why?

Typically, existing path statements are overwritten when drives are mapped with the following command:

MAP S1:=SRV1/VOL1:APPS\DATA

The solution is to use the MAP INS or MAP S16: commands. The following is an example of mapping using INS:

MAP INS S1:=SRV1/VOL1:APPS\DATA

If SET PATH is used in the login script, you can use the %PATH% variable to keep the previous path from being overwritten. For example:

SET PATH=C:\WINDOWS;C:\WINDOWS\SYSTEM;%PATH%

Using this statement places \WINDOWS and \WINDOWS\ SYSTEM in the path without overwriting the previous path assignment.

 Do I need to use login scripts?

No. Except for the default login script, all login scripts are optional. However, login scripts are typically used in most environments to do the following:

● Search and map drives to directories
● Display messages
● Set environment variables
● Execute programs or menus

How do I create a login script?

Perform the following to create a login script.

1. Right-click on the Container, Profile, Template, or User whose login script you want to create or edit.

2. Click Details.

3. Click the Login Script button.

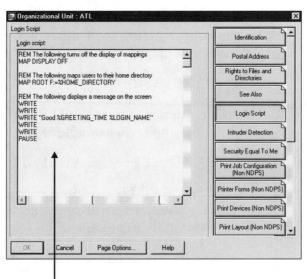

Type login script commands here

4. Enter the desired login script commands.

5. Click OK.

How do I have a profile script run for a user?

Perform the following:

1. Double-click the User object that you would like to run the profile.

2. Click the Login Script button.

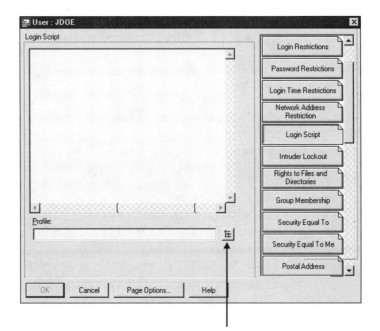

Browse Profile button

3. Click the Browse Profile button.

4. Double-click on the desired profile to be executed for this user.

 Note: *You may have to browse the NDS tree to find the profile if it is not displayed in the Select Object dialog box.*

5. Click OK.

 As a rule, only one profile script can be run per user. How can I run more than one profile script for a user?

Create a Group object and make the user a member of the group. Set up the execution of the first profile script through the User object. Then use the IF/THEN and INCLUDE commands in a container, profile, or user login script to run the second desired profile. The following is an example of using these commands to execute the SALES_PROFILE script:

```
IF MEMBER OF "SALES" THEN
      INCLUDE .SALES_PROFILE.ATL.XYZ
END
```

 What is the difference between a login script command and a variable?

Login script commands perform specific functions and must be written with precise syntax to work properly. For example, the function of the WRITE command is to display a message on the screen at login. The correct syntax for using WRITE is to enter **WRITE**, press the SPACEBAR one time, and enter the message you would like displayed at login in quotes. The following is an example of the syntax that must be used when using WRITE in a login script:

```
WRITE "***** Good Morning! ******"
PAUSE
```

During the login process, the user would see the following displayed on the screen:

```
***** Good Morning! *****
Strike any key when ready . . .
```

 Note: *PAUSE is another login script command used to stop the execution of the login script until a key is pressed.*

The problem with the previous WRITE command is that no matter what time of day a user logs in to the network, it will always say Good Morning. A remedy to this problem is to use identifier variables in order to display more accurate information. The information displayed changes depending on the variable used. The following is an example of using the WRITE command with the %GREETING_TIME variable:

```
WRITE "***** Good %GREETING_TIME! *****"
PAUSE
```

Note: *Identifier variables such as %GREETING_TIME must be written in all uppercase and are preceded by the % sign.*

During the login process, the user would see the following displayed on the screen at night:

```
***** Good Evening! *****
Strike any key when ready . . .
```

whereas in the afternoon, the user would see this:

```
***** Good Afternoon! *****
Strike any key when ready . . .
```

Depending on the variables used, more accurate information is displayed. We can further customize our message by using another variable, %LOGIN_NAME:

```
WRITE "***** Good %GREETING_TIME, %LOGIN_NAME! *****"
PAUSE
```

Now, when John logs in to the network at night, the message will read

```
Good Evening, John!
Strike any key when ready . . .
```

and when Julie logs into the network at night, the message will read

```
Good Evening, Julie!
Strike any key when ready . . .
```

What login script commands are available in NetWare 5?

The login script commands available in NetWare 5, along with code examples and function descriptions, are listed here.

#

CODE EXAMPLE

```
#SRV1/SYS:PUBLIC\CLIENT\SETUP.EXE ACU
```

FUNCTION　Executes an external program and waits until it is finished running before carrying on with other login script commands. You can use this command for either a DOS or a GUI login.

@

CODE EXAMPLE

```
@SALES/VOL1:APPS\GRPWISE5
```

FUNCTION　Executes an external Microsoft Windows program. Must be used with GUI login.

　Note:　*Do not include the extension of the executable filename.*

ATTACH

CODE EXAMPLE

```
ATTACH SRV1/
```

FUNCTION　Establishes a connection to a NetWare 2 or 3 server. Not used to connect to a NetWare 4 or 5 server.

BREAK

CODE EXAMPLE

```
BREAK ON
```

FUNCTION   Allows a user to stop the execution of the login script by pressing CTRL-BREAK immediately after login. BREAK OFF can be used to disallow this action. The default is BREAK OFF.

CLS

CODE EXAMPLE

```
CLS
```

FUNCTION   Clears the workstation's screen during the login process from any previous messages. Used for DOS and OS/2 workstations.

COMSPEC

CODE EXAMPLE

```
COMSPEC=SRV1/SYS:PUBLIC\DOS\COMMAND.COM
```

FUNCTION   Instructs NetWare where the DOS COMMAND.COM file is located. COMSPEC is only needed for users running DOS from a network directory or floppy disk instead of the local hard disk. COMSPEC is used to fix workstation lockups that occur when NetWare cannot locate COMMAND.COM after unloading an application.

CONTEXT

CODE EXAMPLE

```
CONTEXT=.ATL.XYZ
```

FUNCTION   Sets the user's current context at login.

DISPLAY

CODE EXAMPLE

```
DISPLAY SRV1/SYS:PUBLIC\MESSAGE.TXT
```

FUNCTION   Displays the contents of a text file on the workstation's screen during login. The text file can be created

in any text editor and saved to a directory in which the user has Read and File Scan file system rights.

 Note: *Undesirable codes and garbage are displayed if a word processing file is used rather than a text file.*

DOS BREAK

CODE EXAMPLE

```
DOS BREAK ON
```

FUNCTION   Allows a user to terminate a program (other than the login script) by pressing CTRL-BREAK. The default is DOS BREAK OFF.

DOS VERIFY

CODE EXAMPLE

```
DOS VERIFY ON
```

FUNCTION   Ensures that data written to the local hard drive can be read without error by confirming that files copied to the hard disk are not copied to bad sectors. The default is DOS VERIFY OFF.

DRIVE

CODE EXAMPLE

```
DRIVE G:
```

FUNCTION   Changes to the drive letter specified during execution of the login script. The first network drive (typically F:) is used when not specified with the DRIVE command.

ELSE

CODE EXAMPLE

```
IF MEMBER OF "SALES" THEN
     MAP INS S2:=SRV1/VOL1:APPS\SALESDB
ELSE
     MAP INS S2:=SRV1/VOL1:APPS\GENDB
END
```

FUNCTION Only used with the IF and THEN commands. As seen in the previous example, if the user is a member of the Sales group, search drive 2 is mapped to the directory SRV1/VOL1:APPS\SALESDB. Otherwise, if the user is not a member of the Sales group, search drive 2 is mapped to the directory SRV/VOL1:APPS\GENDB.

END

CODE EXAMPLE

```
IF MEMBER OF "SALES" THEN
     MAP INS S2:=SRV1/VOL1:APPS\SALESDB
END
```

FUNCTION Only used with the IF and THEN commands. END specifies the conclusion of the IF statement.

 Note: *END is only needed when the IF / THEN statement exceeds more than one line. For example, END is not needed in the following IF / THEN statement since it is contained on one line:*

```
IF MEMBER OF "SALES" WRITE "HAVE A GOOD DAY!"
```

EXIT

CODE EXAMPLES

```
EXIT
EXIT "WP"
```

FUNCTION Terminates the execution of any login script. For example, if you add EXIT to the end of a container login script, it prevents the execution of other profile, user, and default login scripts. EXIT can also be used to terminate the execution of a login script and execute a program such as a word processor. See the PCCOMPATIBLE command for more information.

 Tip: *Use the NO_DEFAULT command to prevent the execution of only the default login script.*

 Note: *The EXIT command should be at the end of the login script since EXIT stops the execution of the login script.*

FDISPLAY

CODE EXAMPLE

```
FDISPLAY SRV1/SYS:PUBLIC\MESSAGE.DOC
```

FUNCTION Displays the text of a word processing file on the workstation's screen when the user logs in. FDISPLAY filters print commands and garbage so that only the text itself is displayed. FDISPLAY will not display tabs.

FIRE

CODE EXAMPLE (WINDOWS ONLY)

```
FIRE 3 C:\WINDOWS\DINGDING.WAV
```

CODE EXAMPLE (DOS ONLY)

```
FIRE 3
```

FUNCTION Emits a sound to draw attention to the screen. You should specify the number of times you would like the sound executed after the FIRE command.

GOTO

CODE EXAMPLE

```
IF MEMBER OF "SALES" THEN
    MAP INS S2:=SALES/VOL1:APPS\SALESDB
```

```
        GOTO SALES
END

IF MEMBER OF "ACCOUNTANTS" THEN
    MAP INS S2:=SALES/VOL1:APPS\ACCT
    GOTO ACCT
END
SALES:
    CAPTURE Q=SALES_Q NFF NB NT TI=3
    GOTO EXIT

ACCT:
    CAPTURE Q=ACCT_Q NFF NB NT TI=10
    GOTO EXIT

EXIT:
```

FUNCTION   Changes the execution of the login script out of regular sequence. A label is used to indicate where the login script should proceed. For example, in the preceding example, GOTO SALES moves to the SALES: label to continue execution.

 Note: *Problems occur when using GOTO to enter or exit a nested IF / THEN statement.*

IF/THEN

CODE EXAMPLE

```
IF DAY_OF_WEEK = "Friday" AND HOUR24 < "10" THEN
WRITE "Don't forget today's meeting at 9:00am!"
PAUSE
END
```

FUNCTION   Executes an action only under special conditions. The following symbols may be used:

=	Equals
<>	Does not equal
>	Is greater than
<	Is less than
>=	Is greater than or equal to
<=	Is less than or equal to

INCLUDE

CODE EXAMPLES

```
INCLUDE .ATL.XYZ
INCLUDE .JOE.ATL.XYZ
INCLUDE .MRKTG_PROFILE.ATL.XYZ
INCLUDE SRV1/SYS:PUBLIC\SCRIPT.TXT
```

FUNCTION   Executes another login script. The first example shows how INCLUDE can be used to run another container script. The second example shows how INCLUDE can be used to run another user's login script. The third example shows how INCLUDE can be used to run a profile script.

Note: *The user must have the Browse object right and Read property right to the Login Script property of the container, Profile, or User object.*

The fourth example shows how INCLUDE can be used to run a text file written in login script syntax.

INCLUDE can be used to run numerous scripts and is limited only by available memory. In DOS, however, the maximum number of subscript files you can nest is ten.

Note: *The user must have Read and File Scan rights to the file to run the text file script.*

LASTLOGINTIME

CODE EXAMPLE

```
LASTLOGINTIME
```

FUNCTION   Displays the last time the user logged in on the workstation screen.

LOGOUT

CODE EXAMPLE

```
LOGOUT SRV1
```

FUNCTION   Disconnects a user from a particular server while maintaining the connection with other servers.

Note: *The user is logged out of all servers if the LOGOUT command is used by itself.*

MAP

CODE EXAMPLES

```
MAP F:=%HOME _DIRECTORY
MAP
```

FUNCTION   Assigns network drive mappings to network volumes and directories. When the MAP command is used alone, it displays a list of all drive mappings on the user's screen.

MAP DISPLAY OFF

CODE EXAMPLE

```
MAP DISPLAY OFF
```

FUNCTION   Prohibits the display of the results of MAP commands executed during the login procedure.

NO_DEFAULT

CODE EXAMPLE

```
NO_DEFAULT
```

FUNCTION   Prevents the execution of the default login script. This command should be added to the container or profile login scripts.

PCCOMPATIBLE

CODE EXAMPLE

```
PCCOMPATIBLE
```

FUNCTION Used with the EXIT command when a workstation is an IBM-compatible machine that does not have the LONG MACHINE NAME set to IBM_PC.

 Tip: *The LONG MACHINE NAME must be set in the DOS workstation's NET.CFG file.*

 Note: *The PCCOMPATIBLE command must precede the EXIT command.*

PROFILE

CODE EXAMPLE

```
PROFILE .MRKT_PROFILE.ATL.XYZ
```

FUNCTION Overrides a user's assigned profile script. The PROFILE command is used in a container script.

 Note: *The LOGIN username /p profile_object command can also be used when logging in from a DOS prompt to override the assigned profile script.*

REMARK

CODE EXAMPLE

```
REM The following commands map network drives
The following commands capture REM network printers
REM *This is John's User login script
```

FUNCTION Typically used to make login scripts for you or other administrators to read and understand. Text following the REMARK provides interpretation of commands used in the login script. Remarks are not executed and do not appear on the screen during the login process.

SCRIPT SERVER

CODE EXAMPLE

```
SCRIPT_SERVER SALES
```

FUNCTION Sets a home server from which the bindery login script is read for NetWare 2 and 3 users.

SET

CODE EXAMPLE

```
SET PROMPT="$P$G"
```

FUNCTION   Used to set environment variables to a specific value.

Note: *You must use quotation marks (" ") around the values specified.*

SWAP

CODE EXAMPLE

```
SWAP %HOME_DIRECTORY
```

FUNCTION   Used with the # command to move the login utility out of conventional memory onto disk. The login utility goes into extended or expanded memory by default unless the NOSWAP command is used. If you specify a path with the SWAP command, then the login utility swaps to the directory you specified.

TERM

CODE EXAMPLE

```
TERM 000
```

FUNCTION   Stops execution of the login script and returns an error code. Typically used with the NetWare Application Launcher (NAL).

TREE

CODE EXAMPLE

```
TREE XYZ_TREE /.cn= JOHN.ou=ATL.o=XYZ;userpassword
```

FUNCTION   Directs the login script to refer to resources in another tree. TREE is used in multiple tree environments only.

 Note: *Use caution when including passwords in a login script. It is more secure to eliminate the password.*

 ## What login script variables are available in NetWare 5?

The following table shows the available login script variables in NetWare 5.

Variable	Function
DAY	Day number 01–31.
DAY_OF_WEEK	Name of the day of the week, such as Monday.
MONTH	Number of the month 01–12. For example, 01 would display for January.
MONTH_NAME	Name of the month, such as January.
NDAY_OF_WEEK	Number of the weekday. Sunday =1. For example, 2 would display for Monday.
SHORT_YEAR	Last two digits of the year, such as 98, 99.
YEAR	Four-digit year, such as 1998, 1999.
AM_PM	Night or day (A.M. or P.M.).
GREETING_TIME	Time of day as Morning, Afternoon, and Evening.
HOME_DIRECTORY	Path to a user's volume/home directory.
HOUR	Hour on a 12-hour scale.
HOUR24	Hour on a 24-hour scale.
MINUTE	Minutes 00–59.
SECOND	Seconds 0–59.
CN	User's full NDS login name.
FULL_NAME	The value of the FULL NAME property of a User object.
LAST_NAME	The value of the Last Name property of a User object.
LOGIN_CONTEXT	Context of User object.
LOGIN_NAME	The value of the LOGIN NAME property of a User object. Note: This will only allow up to eight characters when used to map a user's home directory.
MEMBER OF "GROUP"	Group to which user is assigned.
NOT MEMBER OF "GROUP"	Group to which the user is not assigned.

Variable	Function
PASSWORD _EXPIRES	Number of days before the expiration of the user's password.
REQUESTER_ CONTEXT	Original context when login started.
USER_ID	Number assigned to each user.
FILE_SERVER NETWORK_ ADDRESS	NetWare server name and network address. The network address represents an eight-digit hexadecimal number assigned to the cabling segment. Also called the IPX External network number.
MACHINE	Computer type (e.g., IBM_PC.).
NETWARE_ REQUESTER	VLM version number.
OS	Operating system used on workstation (for example, DOS).
OS_VERSION	Version of the operating system on the workstation.
P_STATION	A 12-letter hexadecimal number of the workstation's network card.
PLATFORM	Operating system of the workstation (for example, Windows 95 or DOS).
SHELL_TYPE	Version of workstation shell.
SMACHINE	Short machine name of workstation.
STATION	Connection number of workstation. Number varies depending on login order.
WINVER	Version of Windows running on the workstation.
DIALUP	1 if using NetWare Mobile client. 0 if not using NetWare Mobile Client.
OFFLINE	0 if connected. 1 if not connected.
<VARIABLE>	Any DOS variable can be used as long as it is inside angle (<>) brackets.
ACCESS_SERVER	True = Access Server is functional. False = Access Server is not functional.
ERROR_LEVEL	Error number. 0=no error.
%n	Allows the user to enter variable parameters as part of login. The login script can take different actions depending on what the first variable (%2), second variable (%3), and so on, are. The user's login name is typically %1.

Variable	Function
PROPERTY NAME	Property values of NDS objects can be used as variables, such as %HOME_ DIRECTORY, %LOGIN_NAME, %FULL_NAME, %GIVEN_NAME, or %DEFAULT_SERVER.

Is it possible to have the login script read a value from the Registry?

Yes. You can use the new REGEAD login script command with the version 3 and 4.5 or higher client. The syntax for REGREAD is as follows:

REGREAD *"HIVE,KEY,VALUE"*

Note: HIVE *is HKLM, HKCU, HKU, and so on. KEY is the path to the value—for example, Network\Novell\System Config\NetWare DOS Requester\Name Context. The* VALUE *parameter can be left blank unless you want to read a value other than the default value.*

How do I print a login script?

There are several ways to print a login script. Below are two simple methods to do this within Windows and in DOS.

Windows-Based Workstation Steps

Perform the following steps to copy the login script into Notepad and print it out:

1. Right-click the object containing the login script and select Details.

2. Click the Login Script button.

3. Highlight all desired text.

4. Press CTRL-C to copy the highlighted text to the Clipboard.

5. Click OK to close the Details dialog box.

6. Open Notepad.

7. Press CTRL-V to paste the information from the Clipboard into Notepad.

8. Select File from the menu bar.

9. Select Print.

 Tip: *Login scripts can become corrupted or accidentally deleted. Therefore, it is a good idea to keep a printed copy of all login scripts.*

Steps for DOS Workstations Running 3.3 or Above

To print a login script from the DOS command line, you can use the NLIST command and redirect the output to a file or a printer. You must be in the object's context to see and print the login script of that object.

 Note: *You may need to use the CX command to change your workstation's current context. For more information on CX, refer to "How can I browse the NDS tree at a DOS prompt?" in Chapter 12.*

Type the following at a DOS prompt to print a user's login script to the LPT1 port:

NLIST user-*username* show "login script">LPT1

For example,

```
NLIST USER =JDOE SHOW "LOGIN SCRIPT">LPT1
```

Type the following at a DOS prompt to print a container's login script to the LPT1 port:

NLIST "organizational unit" = "*ou name*" show "login script">LPT1

For example,

```
NLIST "organizational unit" = ".ATL.XYZ" show "login script">LPT1
```

 Note: *Any object that includes a space in its name must be enclosed in quotes when using the NLIST command.*

 Tip: *Be sure you have Read property rights to the object's Login Script property.*

Chapter 10

Managing FastTrack Web Server

Answer Topics!

OVERVIEW 346

? Understanding minimum client/server requirements

? Preparing for installation

? Differences between FastTrack Server and Enterprise Server

? Updating the Netscape browser

? Comparing an intranet and the Internet

? Understanding firewalls

? Understanding HTTP

? Understanding URLs

INSTALLATION 349

? Installing FastTrack Server

ADMINISTRATION 352

? Logging in to Netscape Server Administration

? Understanding types of access controls

? Configuring User-Group access through NDS

? Understanding Lightweight Directory Access Protocol (LDAP)

? Configuring LDAP services

? Comparing LDAP and NDS

? Loading and unloading FastTrack Server remotely

? Supporting ODBC drivers in FastTrack

? Using FastTrack to date-stamp Web pages

TROUBLESHOOTING 356

? Configuring FastTrack for faster client request processing

? Changing the document directory path

? Getting back into the FastTrack Server after being locked out

? Using Microsoft FrontPage Server Extensions

Managing FastTrack Web Server @ a Glance

Web servers play a major role in the success of the Internet. Novell has recently teamed up with Netscape to form a new division of Novell called Novonyx. This division's major product is its FastTrack Web Server for NetWare, which tightly integrates NDS within FastTrack. The typical administrator can use FastTrack to set up an intranet environment for coworkers or bring FastTrack out on the Internet for the entire world to use. Here are the areas explored in this chapter:

- **Overview** covers the requirements for FastTrack Server and definitions of important Internet terms.

- **Installation** defines a path for installing FastTrack Server.

- **Administration** answers questions dealing with everyday tasks in FastTrack Server.

- **Troubleshooting** discusses problem solving of complications that can be encountered with FastTrack Server.

OVERVIEW

 I have a server that I would like to set up as a Web server using FastTrack Server. What are the minimum requirements for client and server?

Below is a list of minimum requirements for FastTrack Server, which ships with NetWare 5. These are the minimum requirements just for installation of the server, not for optimal performance. The server requirements are as follows:

- NetWare 4.11 or above
- IP configuration
- CLIB 411J installed and running (CLIB411J will be installed during the FastTrack Server install if necessary.)
- Intel x486 and higher
- 32MB RAM minimum (64MB recommended and mandatory if server is running Oracle 8 and FastTrack Server.)
- 100MB hard disk space
- Long name space installed (Long name space will be installed during the FastTrack Server install if necessary.)
- Novell's NLDAP gateway installed (only needed if integrating users and groups into NDS with the Administration server)

The requirements for the client machine performing the FastTrack installation are as follows:

- Windows 95 or NT
- Current version of Novell's Client32
- Netscape 4.x or above browser
- 100MB free disk space
- CD-ROM for installation from CD

❓ I will be installing FastTrack Server. What do I need to do prior to the installation?

Before installing FastTrack Server you must have some key information available when prompted during the installation. Make sure you have the following before you begin the installation of the FastTrack Server:

- Administrative rights to the SYS volume in which FastTrack will be installed
- IP address information or DNS host name
- Subnet mask for IP address
- Default IP gateway address
- DNS host name for server in which FastTrack will be installed
- DNS server that will provide IP address resolution for the Web server

❓ When should I upgrade my FastTrack Server to Enterprise Server? What are the differences?

Enterprise Server is intended for more complex Web installations in which more extensive tools are needed for creating and managing Web content and infrastructure. You should consider upgrading to Enterprise Server when one or more of the following situations occur:

- Multiple users publish to the same server.
- End users want search capabilities on the server.
- End users need a way to manage their content (for example, through Enterprise Server's NetShare capabilities).
- Multiple servers need to be centrally administered.
- The server will need to run a high-performance database (such as Oracle or Sybase) or distributed applications.

FastTrack Server contains a proper subset of the capabilities in Enterprise Server. The following features are not found in FastTrack Server, but are included in Enterprise Server:

- End-user content management
- NetShare, which includes Web publishing, revision control, access control, link management, and agent services
- Search capabilities
- Custom views
- Centralized administration
- Cluster management (managing multiple servers simultaneously)
- SNMP-based monitoring
- Native database connectivity to Oracle and Sybase (FastTrack provides ODBX connectivity only.)

How can I update my Netscape browser that came with NetWare 5 to the latest version?

You can go to home.netscape.com to download the latest version of Netscape Navigator.

What is the difference between an intranet and the Internet?

An intranet can be a LAN or WAN that uses technologies found on the Internet such as browser software (for example, Netscape Communicator or Internet Explorer), FTP, DNS/DHCP, e-mail, and Web servers. The difference between an intranet and the Internet is that information on an intranet is accessed within the boundaries of an organization and is not open for public access on the Internet. Intranets are typically used to publish internal information such as job postings, health benefit information, employee information, and more.

What is a firewall?

A company's intranet is kept secure from public access over the Internet by *firewalls*. Firewalls can be hardware or software combinations. An intranet that has been made open to the Internet community is called an *extranet*.

What is HTTP?

Hypertext Transfer Protocol (HTTP) is what makes Web server and Web browser communication possible by ensuring that the server and browser both speak the same language. Web servers speak HTTP to specify what kind of information is sent between the Web server and browser.

What is a URL?

A Uniform Resource Locator (URL) must be used to look up information on the Internet and is typed into the browser's location field. For example, www.novell.com is the URL for accessing the Novell Web site.

INSTALLATION

How do I install the FastTrack Server?

Check the server and workstation hardware and software requirements before performing the FastTrack Server installation. For workstation and server requirements, see the first question in this chapter.

Perform the following steps to install FastTrack Web Server.

1. Insert the NetWare 5 Operating System CD in the workstation CD-ROM.

2. Click the Start button; then select Run. Browse to the CD-ROM drive. Change to the \PRODUCTS\WEBSERV directory and type **SETUP.EXE**. Click Finish after reading the workstation requirements.

3. Click Next at the Welcome screen.

4. Click Yes to accept the license agreement.

5. Click Browse and select the network drive that is mapped to the destination server's SYS volume. (This is typically the F: drive.)

6. Click Next.

7. Enter the correct IP address and host name. Confirm that the correct IP address is displayed in the IP Address field, and then enter the desired host name for this server in the Host Name field.

 Tip: *It's a good idea to write down the IP address and host name for future reference.*

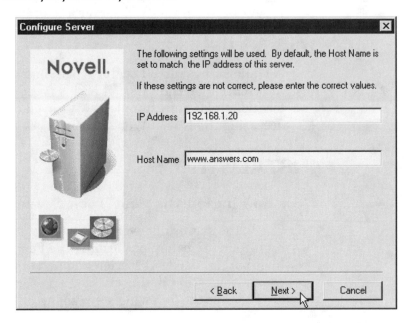

8. Click Next.

9. To accept the default port of 80, click Next. Otherwise, enter the desired port in the Server Port field, and then click Next.

10. Accept the default Web server's administrator port number. The Web server installation will generate a number for you, which you should accept unless you have a reason to specify your own. It's a good idea to write down this number, because you'll need it later to access the administration server.

 Tip: *For future reference and administration of the Web server, it's important to write down the port entered on this screen. You will see an information screen indicating that the administration port number entered is necessary for administration of the Web server. If you need to change the port number assigned in step 10, click the Back button. Click OK to continue the install.*

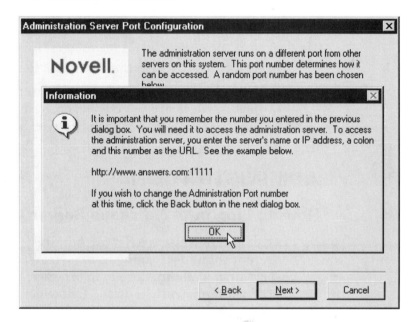

11. The default user name for Web server administration is Admin. You can enter a different user name for the Web server admin in the Username field.

12. Enter the password that you would like to use each time you administrate the Web server.

13. Retype the password entered in step 12.

14. Click Next.

15. Read the information about Lightweight Directory Access Protocol (LDAP) and click the Next button.

16. Update the AUTOEXEC.NCF file. Click the "Change the AUTOEXEC.NCF" radio button if you would like to have

the FastTrack installation program update the file to
have the Web server automatically started each time the
server is restarted. Otherwise, select the "Do not change
the AUTOEXEC.NCF file" radio button.

17. Click Next.

18. Review the summary of all previously selected items.

 Note: *You may want to write down this information for
future referral.*

19. Click Next to begin the FastTrack Server file copy.

20. Click Finish when all files have been copied and the
option boxes are selected as desired to view the
README file and launch the Web server.

ADMINISTRATION

 ### How do I log in to Netscape Server Administration?

Logging in to Netscape Server Administration is much
different than just logging in to a NetWare server because
everything is administered via browser. To log in to Netscape
Server Administration, do the following:

1. Start Netscape Navigator.

 Note: *You must have Netscape Navigator 4 or greater to
successfully administer the server.*

2. Next, you must enter your site address and port number
in the Netsite field. The site address is the IP address of
your NetWare server with FastTrack loaded. The port
number is the number that was generated during the
Web server installation.

 Note: *If you have DNS resolving your IP address, you can use your host name instead of the IP address.*

3. Now you should have a window requesting your username and password. Once again, enter the username and password you specified in the installation process.

What type of access controls can I place on my FastTrack Server?

There are two types of access controls you can set. The first control is the User-Group control, which requires a user to enter a username and password to get access to the Web site. The user and password list can be stored in a Lightweight Directory Access Protocol (LDAP) database or a native NDS. Using LDAP, you can manage access control through Netscape. Using NDS, you can manage access through the Novell file system trustees.

The second type of access control is the Host-IP. This option restricts users from your Web site who don't have a specific IP address or host name. For example, if a user attempts to access your Web site using 192.1.2.3 and you have only authorized 192.1.2.4, that user will be denied access. This option is good for administrators who want seamless access to their Web sites.

Caution: *You must be using DNS on your network to use Host-IP access control.*

 I want to configure FastTrack to do User-Group access through native NDS. Where can I configure this option?

If you want to configure FastTrack to use native NDS for User-Group authentication, do the following:

1. Log on to Netscape Server Administration.

2. Under General Administration, select Global Settings.

3. You should now see a Configure Directory Service setting and three radio button options. Choose Novell Directory Services. At this point, you should see a message telling you that you are about to switch to NDS mode. Click OK and select Save Changes.

4. Set the Search Context, select Save Changes, and unload FastTrack NLMs. Then load the NLMs back to make changes effective.

 What is LDAP?

The Lightweight Directory Access Protocol (LDAP) is based on the X.500 specification and provides access to management and browser applications that offer read/write interactive access to the X.500 Directory. LDAP is becoming the standard across the Internet. However, this protocol is in its early stages and NDS is still the better choice in directory services since LDAP currently does not support replication or scalability. This may change as this protocol matures. To obtain more information about LDAP, go to the Web site www.FreeSoft.org/CIE/RFC/Orig/rfc1777.txt.

 I want to configure LDAP on my FastTrack server. How can I do this?

Novell has a support document at www.novell.com that explains how to install LDAP on your server. The Technical Information Document (TID) is 2938227.

Which is better to use: LDAP or NDS?

NDS is much easier to set up than LDAP. However, LDAP is very flexible about implementing access control. NDS is able to access users in a large tree faster than LDAP, but LDAP will eventually be standardized across network operating systems. Your choice should be based on the environment you are running in.

How can I remotely unload and load FastTrack after making changes?

When you log in to Netscape Server Administration you should see three buttons on the bottom of the page that look like this:

Clicking the FastTrack Server off and on will unload and load FastTrack from your NetWare server.

Can FastTrack support ODBC drivers for database queries?

Novonyx has stated that it is supporting ODBC and ODBX drivers in NetWare 5.

I would like FastTrack to place the current date on each page on my Web site. How can I do this?

FastTrack gives you several options for date stamping on Web pages. To access this feature, do the following:

1. Log on to Netscape Server Administration.

2. Select your server by clicking the icon with your server name.

3. Click Content Management.

4. Select Document Footer in the left panel.

5. Select the directory you wish to start date stamping.

6. Select your date format and click OK.

TROUBLESHOOTING

 It takes a long time to process client requests from my FastTrack Server. What could be the problem?

There could be a couple of problems in this scenario. One possible problem might be the overall performance of your hardware. Is the processor utilization too high? Is disk I/O extremely heavy? If hardware is not the problem, maybe the setting for client requests in your server is too low. Reconfigure the Maximum Simultaneous Requests setting by doing the following:

1. Log on to Netscape Server Administrator.

2. Click your server name.

3. Select Performance Tuning.

4. Change the Maximum Simultaneous Requests setting to a higher number. You are going to have to play with this option to optimize your system correctly.

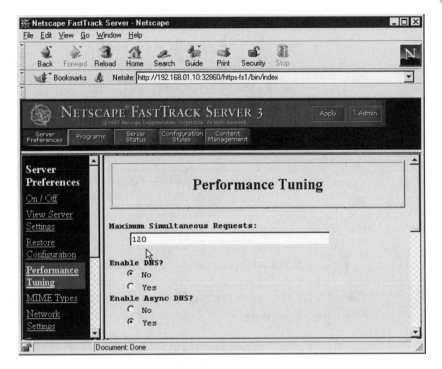

You can also check to see if DNS lookups can be slowing you down. Typically, DNS lookups cause the FastTrack Server to resolve the IP address to the host name of every client making a request. This is a nice feature for administrators to look at in their logs but it can degrade performance on your server.

 I am running out of room on the SYS volume. How do I change my document directory for my Web site?

You can set a path in the FastTrack server to any directory you want. By default, the primary document directory is

located in SYS:NOVONYX\SUITESPOT\DOCS. For example, if someone tries to access a Web page on your server, he or she would type the following:

http://*hostname*/readme/readme.html

which translates to this:

```
SYS:\NOVONYX\SUITESPOT\DOCS\README\README.HTML
```

To change the primary document setting, go to the Server Manager screen and click the server icon. This will bring you to the server settings. Select Content Management, enter your new directory, and click OK. Now, instead of mapping all your URLs to another directory, you have just moved the directory onto another volume.

I am locked out of my FastTrack Server! How can I get back in?

The user account/password for the FastTrack Server, before binding LDAP to NDS, only exists in the server code. If you bind LDAP to NDS, the FastTrack Server will look to NDS to find the "user" account. Now, *which* user account is the question. Because the NDS Admin account is in a different context than the objects for the FastTrack server, if you enter the User/Password for authenticating to the Web server, you will be denied. The workaround is to create an Alias object in the context of the Web server's objects that points to your NDS User object. Now, when LDAP consults NDS, it "finds" the User object.

Is there a way of getting Microsoft FrontPage Server Extensions to work on a Novell FastTrack Server?

According to Novell, since there is no NLM for FrontPage Server Extensions, it cannot be supported.

Chapter 11

Managing DHCP and DNS Services

Answer Topics!

● **DHCP SERVER OVERVIEW   362**

? Understanding the purpose of DHCP

? Learning how much traffic DHCP requests create on a network

? Using DHCP on Windows NT 4 or NetWare servers

? Allowing DHCP across subnets

? Meeting requirements for the DNS/DHCP Management Console utility

● **DHCP INSTALLATION   364**

? Installing the DNS/DHCP Management Console utility on a workstation

? Installing and configuring a NetWare 5 DHCP server

? Learning what the Locator object is

● **TROUBLESHOOTING A DHCP SERVER   370**

? Learning what happens when DHCP cannot access the Locator object

? Running the DNS/DHCP Management Console

? Confirming the IP address on a workstation

● **DHCP ADMINISTRATION   372**

? Importing earlier DHCP databases into NetWare 5

? Excluding an IP address from assignment by the DHCP server

? Preventing your DHCP server from distributing an address already in use

? Having multiple DHCP servers service the same subnet

? Making sure your DHCP server is working

? Assigning multiple subnets to the same network segment

? Preventing redundancy in a DHCP server scheme

? Learning about supernetting

DNS SERVER OVERVIEW 377

? Understanding the purpose of a DNS server

? Understanding the differences between a primary and a secondary DNS server

? Learning how secondary name servers keep up to date with primary name servers

? Understanding the DNS process

? Learning about DNS domains and subdomains

? Understanding DNS zones

DNS INSTALLATION 382

? Installing and configuring a DNS Server in NetWare 5

DNS ADMINISTRATION 388

? Importing DNS records from NetWare 4.11 into NetWare 5

? Making DNS database changes active

? Load-balancing different Web servers using DNS's round-robin support

? Multihoming with DNS

? Learning about DNS BIND compliance

? Learning what rights are needed to administer DNS

Managing DHCP and DNS Services @ a Glance

The evolving standard of TCP/IP in corporate environments has brought DNS and DHCP into the foreground in NetWare 5 and the upcoming Microsoft Windows NT 2000 release. Both of these services are used extensively in NetWare 5, and administrators need to know the structure of how these services work. This chapter will cover the following:

DHCP Overview defines what DHCP is and how it works in an enterprise environment.

DHCP Installation covers the installation and configuration of DHCP.

Troubleshooting a DHCP Server answers questions dealing with DHCP IP delivery and DHCP stability issues.

DHCP Administration explores ways to effectively optimize your DHCP environment.

DNS Server Overview covers the purpose and process flow of DNS.

DNS Installation discusses setup methods with the DNS server and the workstations that will be communicating with DNS.

DNS Server Administration covers ways to import other DNS databases and discusses the rights needed to manage DNS.

DHCP SERVER OVERVIEW

 ## What is the purpose of a Dynamic Host Configuration Protocol (DHCP) server?

In traditional non-DHCP TCP/IP network environments, administrators have to go to each device and manually configure it with its own unique IP address and accompanying IP configuration information. The purpose of a DHCP server is to automate dynamically the allocation of IP address and configuration parameters for workstations on your network, thereby eliminating the need to configure each workstation individually.

DHCP uses the following process to automate the assignment of IP address information:

● A workstation makes a request for IP address information by sending a broadcast packet out on the wire so that any listening DHCP server will hear the request.

● The DHCP server responds with the requested IP information by determining which network segment the request came from. If the DHCP server has the configuration information for that network segment, it will respond with the requested information.

A NetWare 5 DHCP server can allocate IP address assignments in one of three ways.

● **Dynamic allocation**   The DHCP server assigns an IP address for a given length of time. Using dynamic allocation, the IP address is leased by a host.

● **Automatic allocation**   The DHCP server gives a permanent IP address to a host.

● **Manual allocation**   The network administrator assigns a permanent IP address to a host.

In addition to the allotment of IP address information, a DHCP server can assign default NDS tree and context information to clients.

 Will DHCP requests from workstations create heavy traffic on my network?

Network traffic in a DNS/DHCP environment is minimal because once the information is requested from a workstation, it is cached in the DHCP/DNS server's RAM. In addition, DHCP requests are broadcasts that are not forwarded to other network segments by routers. Therefore, if a DHCP server does not physically reside on the same segment from which the DHCP request is made, the DHCP server will never respond to the request, nor will the request be forwarded to other network segments.

 I have several Microsoft Windows NT 4 servers currently running DHCP. Is it necessary to have Novell DHCP service for connection to a NetWare 5 server running TCP only?

No, DHCP is a standard, and Microsoft Windows NT DHCP will work just fine in a Novell 5 environment. However, Novell's DHCP has more DHCP options, such as POP3 and NNTP information distribution, which NT currently does not have.

Can I allow a workstation on one network segment to receive IP address information from a DCHP server on another network segment?

To allow a DHCP server to respond to DHCP requests from a workstation on a separate network segment, you must use a *relay agent*. A relay agent is a router software that forwards DHCP requests to the DHCP server and then returns the answer to the workstation.

BOOTPFWD.NLM is a Novell relay agent. If you have a workstation that must route through a NetWare server in order to get to your DHCP server, you must load the BOOTPFWD.NLM on the NetWare server and configure it to forward DHCP requests to your DHCP server.

 What are the requirements for the DNS/DHCP Management Console utility?

The DNS/DHCP Management Console on a client workstation requires the following:

- 64MB of memory (recommended), 32MB minimum
- 5MB of free disk space
- Novell Client software shipped with NetWare 5 (or later) installed

DHCP INSTALLATION

How do I install the DNS/DHCP Management Console utility on my workstation?

Do the following to install to a workstation:

1. In Windows 95 or Windows NT, click Start and select Run. In DOS/Windows, select File | Run.

2. Select Browse and highlight SETUP.EXE from the SYS:PUBLIC\DNSDHCP directory. Click Open and then click OK.

3. At the Welcome screen click Next.

4. Accept the default destination by selecting Next.

5. Make sure the Copy Snapin Files box is checked.

Note: *Keeping this option checked will allow you to open the DNS/DHCP Management Console utility from within the NetWare Administrator utility.*

6. Click Next.

7. Select Browse to select the snapin file directory.

8. Change to the SYS:PUBLIC\WIN32 directory. Then click OK.

9. Click Next.

10. Select No to view the Readme file.

11. Click OK.

How do I install and configure a NetWare 5 DHCP server?

Log in as Admin and use the following steps to install and configure NetWare 5 DHCP services.

Extending NDS Schema

To extend an NDS schema:

1. Type **DNIPINST** at the server console and press ENTER.
2. Authenticate yourself as a user with Supervisor object rights to the [Root] of the tree. In the Administrator Name field, type the distinguished name of your admin user (that is, cn=admin.o=*xyz*) and press ENTER. Type the password for the admin user in the Password field and press ENTER. Press ENTER on the "Press <ENTER> to Login to NDS" option.
3. Enter the context where you would like the DNS/DHCP Locator, Group, and RootServerInfo Zone objects. Then press ENTER on the "Press <ENTER> to Create Objects" field.
4. Press ENTER to continue.

Installing the DNS/DHCP Management Console

See the previous question, "How do I install the DNS/DHCP Management Console utility on my workstation?"

Creating the DHCP Server Object

Follow these steps to create the Server object:

1. Start the DNS/DHCP Management Console utility by double-clicking on the DNS/DHCP shortcut provided on the desktop.
2. Be sure the correct tree name is displayed in the Launch Novell DNS/DHCP Management Console dialog box. Select Launch.
3. Click the DHCP Service tab. The following box is displayed:

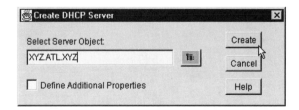

4. Select the Create button.

5. Click DHCP Server. Then click OK.

6. Browse to the container where your NetWare server is located.

7. Select the Server object you would like to have as a DHCP server and click OK. (The new DHCP Server object name you just created will begin with DHCP_ and end with the name of your NetWare server.)

8. Click Create. You will see the new DHCP server in the bottom part of the DNS/DHCP Management Console window. A red line will appear across the DHCP server icon until the DHCP service is actually loaded on the NetWare server.

Creating and Configuring the DHCP Subnet Object

Create and configure the Subnet object as follows:

1. If not opened already, use the shortcut provided on the desktop to launch the DNS/DHCP Management Console utility with the correct tree name.

2. Click the DHCP Service tab.

3. Select the Create button on the toolbar.

4. Double-click the Subnet option, and the following dialog box is displayed:

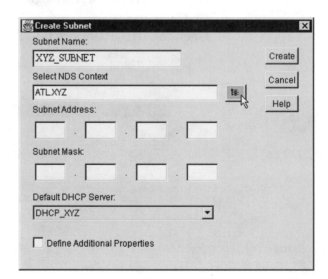

5. In the Subnet Name field, type the NDS Name that you would like to appear in your tree for the new Subnet object. (For example, you might use the name of the group this subnet will service, such as Mrktg_Subnet, or the subnet number itself, like the name of the DHCP server or XYZ_Subnet.) Each Subnet object in your tree must have a unique NDS name; otherwise, the Subnet object creation will fail.

6. In the Select NDS Context field you may type in or browse to the NDS context where you would like this Subnet object to reside in your tree. For example, as shown in Figure 11-1, if you wanted your Subnet object to reside in the MRKT container of the following tree, the context would be .MRKT.ATL.ABC.

Note: *The subnet name should not be included in the context.*

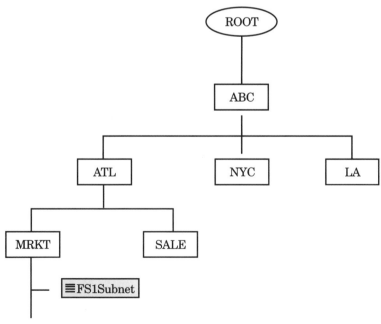

Figure 11-1 Example NDS tree

7. Type the subnet address for this DHCP server in the Subnet Address field (such as 192.168.2.0). A subnet address can only exist once in the NDS tree; otherwise, the Subnet object creation will fail.

8. Type the subnet mask for this DHCP server in the Subnet mask field (for example, 255.255.255.0).

9. The name of your DHCP server should be displayed in the Default DHCP Server field. Click on the down arrow to select your server if it is not shown.

10. Click Create. The new Subnet object will appear with the name you specified in step 5. Double-click the new Subnet object and notice the two automatic assignments that were made.

Creating and Configuring a DHCP Subnet Range Object

11. If not opened already, launch the DNS/DHCP Management Console utility with the correct tree name.

12. Click the DHCP Service tab.

13. Highlight the Subnet object that the range will occupy.

14. Select the Create button.

15. The following dialog box is displayed. Highlight Subnet Address Range object and click OK.

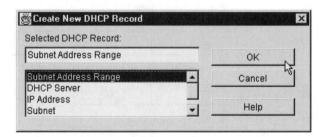

16. Type in a name for the Subnet Address Range object.

17. Enter the Start and End Address information. For example, if my assigned IP address was 206.113.247.0 with a subnet mask of 255.255.255.0, I could enter 206.113.247.50 for the start address and 206.113.247.100 for the end address. That would allow for up to 50 IP addresses to which the DHCP server could assign hosts in that subnet. The start and end address range of the Subnet Address Range object cannot overlap or the creation process will fail.

18. Click Create.

Starting the DHCP Server

To start the DHCP server, type **DHCPSRVR** at the server console and press ENTER.

Configuring the Workstation for DHCP

Follow these steps to configure your workstation:

1. In Windows 95 select Start and click Settings | Control Panel.

2. Double-click Network.

3. In the Configuration folder, select the TCP/IP network component for your network card. Then select Properties.

4. The IP Address folder should be active. Select the "Obtain an IP Address automatically" radio button. Click OK twice.

5. Answer Yes to Restart the computer.

What is the Locator object ?

The Locator object contains a list of DHCP and DNS Server objects, Subnet objects, Zone objects, DHCP global defaults, and excluded MAC addresses. The Locator object and the DNS/DHCP Group object should reside high in the NDS tree.

The objects can reside anywhere in the tree, as long as they are accessible by all DNS and DHCP servers in the tree.

TROUBLESHOOTING A DHCP SERVER

What happens if DHCP cannot access the Locator object when loading?

The DHCP server will still be able to load without having access to the DNS/DHCP Locator object. Nevertheless, the first time the DHCP server loads, it does require access to the DNS/DHCP Locator object in order to acquire a copy of global configuration information. A copy of the global configuration is saved in SYS:\ETC\DHCP\DHCPLOC.TAB.

The DHCP server will try to obtain the global configuration information from the DNS/DHCP Locator object whenever loaded. If the information is not available in subsequent loads, it is read from the last saved copy of SYS:\ETC\DHCP\DHCPLOC.TAB.

I am unable to run the DNS/DHCP Management Console. What can I check to fix the problem?

If you are unable to run DNS/DHCP Management Console you might want to try these techniques:

- You must first log in to the NDS tree you want to administer before launching the DNS/DHCP Management Console.

- You must have Read and Write rights to the container object where the DNS/DHCP Group and Locator objects are located.

- You must have Read and Write rights to the specific container you want to administer.

- Has the NDS schema been extended? If not, please see "How do I install and configure a NetWare 5 DHCP server?" earlier in this chapter.

 How do I confirm that my workstation received a valid IP address from my DHCP server?

To see if your workstation received a valid IP address:

1. In Windows 95, 98, and NT, select Start, then Run.

2. Type **WINIPCFG** for Windows 95 and 98 and press ENTER. Type **IPCONFIG** for Windows NT and press ENTER.

 Note: *IPCONFIG will work in both Windows NT and Windows 98.*

3. The IP Configuration dialog box will display the IP address and subnet mask that was assigned to the workstation.

4. Select the More Info button to see the IP address of the DHCP server that fulfilled the request, as shown here:

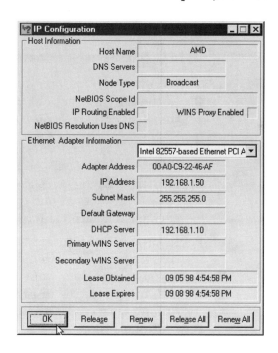

DHCP ADMINISTRATION

 Is it possible to import my previous NetWare DHCP 2 database into NetWare 5's DHCP 3 database?

Yes. First the information must be in a DHCP 2 or 3 file format in order to be imported. Complete the following steps while logged in as Admin.

1. Open the DNS/DHCP Management Console utility by double-clicking on the shortcut located on your desktop andselect the tree you wish to administrator. If the DNS/DHCP Management Console utility has not been installed on your workstation, see "How do I install the DNS/DHCP Management Console utility on my workstation?" earlier in this chapter for installation instructions.

2. Click the Import Database button.

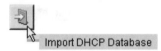

3. In the DHCP File field, type or browse to the path where the DHCP file to be imported is located.

4. Click Next and the Import DHCP-Subnet list dialog box is displayed.

5. Highlight each desired subnet and click Add. To add several subnets at one time, hold down the CTRL key and click each desired subnet, then click Add.

6. In the Subnet Context field, type in or browse to the context where you would like the imported Subnet objects to reside in your tree. For example, look at the example NDS tree in Figure 11-1. If you wanted the Subnet objects you are importing to go into the MRKT container; then you would enter **MRKT.ATL.ABC** in the Subnet Context field.

7. When the context is set and all chosen subnets are listed in the right column, click the Next button.

8. The Import dialog box is then displayed summarizing the context and subnet(s) you have chosen. If the information displayed is correct, click Import; otherwise, you will need to select Back and redo steps 5–7.

9. Select a DHCP server to manage the configuration you are importing for each Subnet object listed.

10. Click Finish once the transfer is complete.

I have a few IP addresses that I do not want assigned by my DHCP server. How do I do this?

Open the DNS/DHCP Management Console utility by double-clicking on the shortcut located on your desktop and Launch with the correct tree name selected. If the DNS/DHCP Management Console utility has not been installed on your workstation, see "How do I install the DNS/DHCP Management Console utility on my workstation?" earlier in this chapter for installation instructions.

1. Select the DHCP Service tab.

2. Click to select the Subnet object where the excluded IP address resides.

3. Click the Create button on the toolbar.

4. Double-click the IP Address option and follow dialog box displayed.

6. In the IP Address field, enter the IP address to be excluded from assignment by the DHCP server.

7. Be sure the Assignment Type reads Exclusion.

8. Click Create.

Is there a way to prevent my DHCP server from distributing an address that may already be in use without knowing what the address is?

Yes, we have previously discussed ways of excluding addresses that may be permanent static addresses. But what

happens if two DHCP servers have overlapping IP addresses in a subnet address range or a user decides to get his or her PC a static IP address? Novell has an option called Ping Enabled. This option allows the DHCP service to ping for an address first before it leases one out. This type of functionality prevents a DHCP server from leasing an address that is already in use. To enable this option, do the following:

1. Open DNS/DHCP Management Console utility and select your tree.

2. Select the DHCP tab.

3. Click your DHCP service and click the Options tab.

4. Scroll down to the bottom of the page and click Ping Enabled.

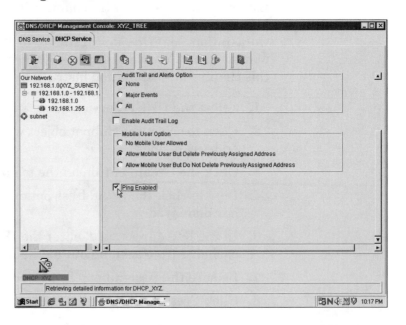

Can multiple DHCP servers service the same subnet, and if so, how?

Yes. Multiple DHCP servers can exist on the same physical segment. However, they must be configured to service separate ranges of IP addresses. Multiple DHCP servers

cannot distribute the same IP addresses. Draft RFCs (Request for Comments) do address this issue.

You can also logically split up a subnet so that multiple DHCP servers service the same logical subnet. You must assign each DHCP server its own range of IP addresses. When you configure a Subnet object, you must provide a default DHCP server to assign to this subnet. The default DHCP server refers to the server that will service BOOTP requests. Therefore, one Address Range object should be configured to service BOOTP clients. Other Address Range objects should be configured to service DHCP clients only. By configuring the address range to service DHCP clients only, you can change the default DHCP server for that address range and assign that range to a different DHCP server.

How can I make sure that my DHCP server is working?

NetWare allows you to load DHCPSRVR with the –d (debug) option to see what packets are going back and forth from your server concerning DHCP. To load in debug mode, type **DHCPSRVR -d** at the server console.

How do I assign multiple subnets to the same physical network segment?

Log in as Admin and perform the following to assign multiple Subnet objects to the same physical network segment.

Creating a Subnet Pool Object

First, create the Subnet Pool object as follows:

1. Open the DNS/DHCP Management Console utility by double-clicking on the shortcut located on your desktop and select the tree you wish to administer.
2. Click the DHCP Service tab.
3. Click the Create button on the toolbar.
4. Double-click the Subnet Pool option.
5. Type a name for the new Subnet Pool object.
6. Type or browse to the NDS context where the new Subnet Pool object should reside.
7. Click Create.

Assigning Subnet Objects to the Subnet Pool Object

Then assign Subnet objects to your Subnet Pool object as follows:

1. Click the Subnet Pool object you just created.

2. Click Add.

3. Select the Subnet objects you want to assign to the Subnet Pool object by pressing the CTRL key and then clicking on each Subnet object.

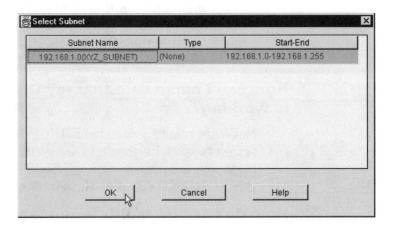

4. When all desired Subnet objects are highlighted, click OK. You should see the selected Subnet object names displayed in the Subnet Pool folder.

5. Click the Save Data to NDS button on the toolbar.

What type of DHCP server scheme will be supported with the first release of DNS/DHCP to prevent redundancy?

Most often, two DHCP servers are set up to service the same subnet with each server distributing a different range of addresses.

If the DHCP server goes down for some reason, it is possible to change the Default DHCP Server setting to another DHCP server. One problem with this method is with the DHCP server's log files. The log files keep track of the updates to NDS (DHCPTRAN.LOG, DHCPSYNC.LOG, DHCPLOG.LOG). When the original DHCP server goes down, addresses may have been assigned to clients that were updated to NDS. When the backup DHCP server is loaded, it contacts NDS for all of the configuration information and addresses that have been assigned. Consequently, there may be clients using addresses that the backup DHCP server is unaware of. Enable PING ahead on the backup DHCP server to resolve this problem.

 Note: *If the backup DHCP server is not a DHCP production server, you can copy the log files from the original DHCP server to the backup DHCP server. If the backup DHCP server is a production DHCP server, then the log files already exist.*

What is supernetting, and does DHCP 3 support it?

Not yet. Supernetting is a way to get more addresses out of a class C address range. This is done by manipulating the subnet mask and using the third octect as part of the node address. DHCP 3 allows you to configure and perform supernetting. The TCP/IP version that ships with NetWare 5 does *not* support this, but future support packs will.

DNS SERVER OVERVIEW

What is the purpose of a DNS server?

The Domain Name System (DNS) is used on the Internet to translate alphanumeric host names to numeric IP addresses. For example, when you type the alphanumeric **www.novell.com** host name in your Internet browser, it is a Domain Name Server (DNS) that translates that host name into the necessary numeric 192.215.81.66 IP address. This is advantageous since host names such as www.novell.com are easier to remember than their numeric IP address equivalents.

DNS servers, also called *name servers*, respond to browser requests by supplying the host name to IP address conversion. The *resolver* portion of the DNS server will ask another name server for the information when it does not have the information locally in its database. When a server does not have to resolve an address, it is said to be an *authoritative server* for that zone.

❋ *Note:* *A Novell client is also considered a resolver.*

What is the difference between a primary (master) and secondary (replica) DNS server?

In traditional DNS systems, there are two types of DNS servers: primary and secondary name servers. The primary name server, also called the *master name server*, stores DNS configuration information locally in a Master Bind file. The Master Bind is kept up to date by the administrator and enables the primary server to resolve domain names into numeric IP addresses.

Secondary name servers, also called *replica servers*, hold copies of the Master Bind file. Secondary servers are necessary in order to share the processing load of the primary server and create a fault-tolerant environment in case the primary server becomes unavailable.

NetWare 5 servers have to be made *designated* servers in order to perform the tasks of primary or secondary name servers.

How do secondary name servers keep up to date with primary name servers?

A secondary name server periodically checks to make sure that its Master Bind file or replica is up to date. If the secondary name server's replica is not up to date, it obtains a new copy from master files stored on the primary name server. The secondary server then saves the updated information locally. These configuration updates to the secondary name server replica are called *zone transfers*.

A NetWare 5 server has to be made a *designated server* in order to perform the tasks of a secondary or replica name server. A designated secondary server periodically receives updated information from a primary or master server whose information is not stored in NDS. (Such as a primary or master server that may be provided by your Internet service provider.) The updated information is then placed in NDS, where it can be used to more quickly resolve names into IP addresses.

How does the DNS server process work?

The workstation is a type of DNS client called a *resolver*. A resolver requests an address in much the same way you may call directory assistance for a phone number. The operator may provide the phone number or connect you to another operator who provides the number.

DNS works in a similar manner. The resolver starts with knowledge of at least one name server. If the host name http://www.novell.com is requested, the COM domain must be located first. If the known name server is unable to fulfill the request for COM, it will forward the request to another name server. The COM name server is then queried for the NOVELL.COM domain. The NOVELL.COM name server will then query for www.novell.com. In order to speed up this process, some address information is cached in the DNS server's memory and therefore will not need to be queried each time.

What is a DNS domain and subdomain?

Users enter domain names like www.novell.com to connect to a particular host or Web site, instead of the more complicated IP address (192.215.81.66) used by the Internet. Domain names are reserved by organizations to guarantee that the name will be resolved to the correct IP address. To reserve a domain name on the Internet, an organization must submit a request to the Network Information Center (NIC). Some Internet service providers will also provide DNS registration service for you. For more information on registering a domain name, go to internic.net.

The domain name space shown in Figure 11-2 is arranged like an upside-down tree with the ROOT residing at the top.

Immediately below the ROOT are common top-level *domains*. Common top-level domains include COM for commercial organizations, EDU for educational institutions, and GOV for government agencies. Organizations can further divide domains into *subdomains* like NOVELL.COM. The NOVELL.COM domain is further divided into subdomains such as SUPPORT.NOVELL.COM and DEVELOPER. NOVELL.COM.

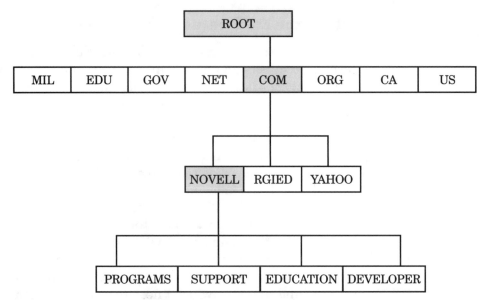

Figure 11-2 Domain name structure

In DNS, every node on the tree is called a domain. Everything below a node falls into its domain. Domains at the end of the branches represent individual addressable host computers on the Internet. Therefore it is important to note that the SUPPORT host computer is part of the .NOVELL domain as well as the COM domain.

A domain name can be up to 255 characters.

 Note: *A host is defined here to mean any addressable entity on a TCP/IP network.*

 ## What is a DNS zone?

Since the Internet is so large, it would be impossible for one DNS server to locally store a complete database of *all* Internet hosts to IP address information. Therefore, DNS servers only store information locally about specific parts of the domain name space. These portions of the domain name space are called *zones*. Zones represent logical divisions of the Internet. A DNS server that stores a complete database of a portion or division of the domain name space is said to be

authoritative for that particular portion or zone. One DNS server could contain authoritative information, or complete databases, on one or more zones.

For example, the NOVELL.COM domain could be divided into multiple zones as shown in Figure 11-3.

In this example, the NOVELL.COM zone contains a complete authoritative database on the SUPPORT and DEVELOPER subdomains. The NOVELL.COM zone contains a reference to another authoritative DNS server for information on the EDUCATION.NOVELL.COM zone.

Zones are created and maintained by network administrators. Zones are necessary in some environments to break up management of the domain into independent administrative sections. Therefore, Novell administrators are responsible for administrating the DNS portion of the NOVELL.COM domain and its subdomains on the Internet, and may elect to break up the domain's administration by

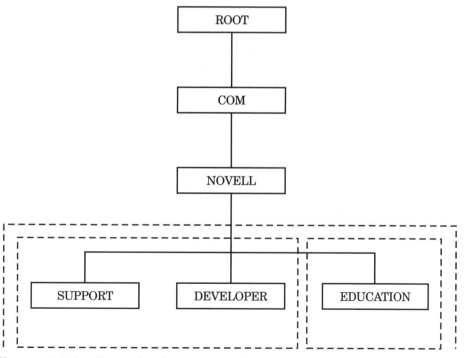

Figure 11-3 Example of possible DNS zones

creating multiple zones. A zone starts at a designated domain and extends down the domain name space until an end node is reached or another subzone begins. If no subdomains were created under the NOVELL.COM domain, then it would be both a domain and a zone.

There are three basic zone types that can be created in NetWare 5:

● A new zone, which contains records to resolve domain names into numeric IP addresses.

● An IN-ADDR.ARPA zone, which maps the numeric IP address to the alphanumeric domain name.

● The IP6.INT zone, which supports the next-generation IP addressing scheme when it is released. The IP6.INT zone will be used to resolve domain names into IPv6 addresses.

A DNS server must be configured as a primary or secondary *designated server* to service one of the three types of zones.

NetWare 5 stores zone data within NDS, allowing it to be replicated around the network, therefore making it available in multiple locations around the network. Thus, a benefit of DNS/NDS integration is that a fault-tolerant environment is created, so if one DNS server goes down, the zone data is still available.

DNS INSTALLATION

 How do I install and configure a DNS server in NetWare 5?

Log in as Admin and use the following steps to install DNS services:

Creating the DNS Server Object
Create the DNS Server object as follows:

1. Open the DNS/DHCP Management Console utility by double-clicking on the shortcut located on your desktop and launch with the correct tree name selected. If the DNS/DHCP Management Console utility has not been installed on your workstation, see "How do I install the DNS/DHCP Management Console utility on my workstation?" earlier in this chapter for installation instructions.

2. Click the DNS Service tab.

3. Highlight the ALL ZONES virtual object.

4. Click the Create button.

5. Click on DNS Server to display the following dialog box.

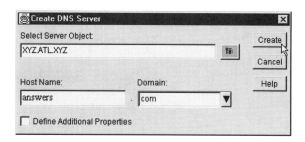

6. Browse to and select the container where the NDS Server object you want to designate as a DNS Server object is located.

7. In the Host Name field, type the name you would like your DNS Server object to have in its domain. Typically the name of the server is used.

8. In the Domain field, type the domain that your DNS server will reside in. The domain you specify may or may not be part of your current NDS tree. (For example, the MMM company has been given the domain name MMM.COM, therefore the DNS server's domain may be specified as MMM.COM.)

9. Click Create.

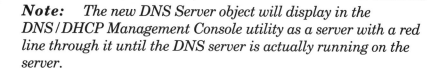

Note: *The new DNS Server object will display in the DNS/DHCP Management Console utility as a server with a red line through it until the DNS server is actually running on the server.*

Creating a DNS Zone

Now create a DNS zone as follows:

1. Open the DNS/DHCP Management Console utility by double-clicking on the shortcut located on your desktop and launch with the correct tree name selected. If the DNS/DHCP Management Console utility has not been installed on your workstation, see "How do I install the DNS/DHCP

Management Console utility on my workstation?" earlier in this chapter for installation instructions.

2. Select the DNS service folder.

3. Highlight the ALL ZONES virtual object.

4. Click the Create button.

5. Double-click the Zones option and the following dialog box is displayed.

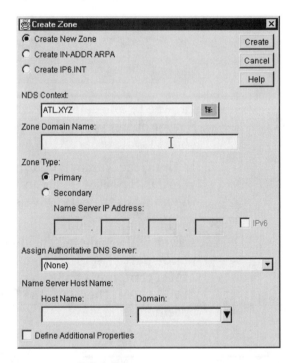

6. First select the type of zone you are creating. (that is, New Zone, IN-ADDR.ARPA, or IP6.INT.) See the previous question for zone type information.

7. In the NDS Context field, type or browse to the NDS context in which you would like the Zone object to reside.

8. In the Zone Domain Name field, type the desired zone domain name.

9. Click Create.

10. Select OK after reading the confirmation and reminder to create the proper A and PTR resource records.

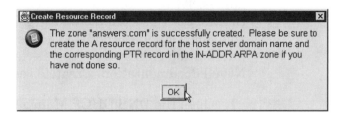

Designating a DNS Server to Service Your DNS Zone

Use the following steps to designate a DNS server for your zone:

1. Open the DNS/DHCP Management Console utility by double-clicking on the shortcut located on your desktop and launch with the correct tree name selected. If the DNS/DHCP Management Console utility has not been installed on your workstation, see "How do I install the DNS/DHCP Management Console utility on my workstation?" earlier in this chapter for installation instructions.

2. Select the DNS service folder.

3. Click on the desired DNS Zone object.

4. In the right pane of the DNS/DHCP Management Console screen, the Attributes folder should be selected. In the Available DNS Servers field highlight the server that will service the zone selected in step 3.

5. Click Add. You will see the server displayed in the Authoritative DNS Servers field.

6. Click the Save Data to NDS button.

7. Click Yes.

Creating a Resource Record

A resource record is simply data associated with domain names. These records are divided into different types of classes. For this example we are going to use a Class A record, which is a standard name to address mapping. For more information on resource records classes, please refer to the Novell documentation. Create a resource record as follows:

1. Open the DNS/DHCP Management Console utility by double-clicking on the shortcut located on your desktop and launch with the correct tree name selected. If the DNS/DHCP Management Console utility has not been installed on your workstation, see "How do I install the DNS/DHCP Management Console utility on my workstation?" earlier in this chapter for installation instructions.

2. Select the DNS service folder.

3. Click the Create button.

4. Double-click Resource Record.

5. The Class A radio button should remain selected.

6. Type the name of your server in the Host Name field.

7. Type in the IP address of your DNS server under the Resource Record Data field.

8. Click Create.

Starting the DNS Server

To start the DNS server, type **NAMED** and press ENTER at the server console.

Configuring the Workstation to Use DNS Services

Use the following steps to configure a Windows 95 workstation:

1. Click Start; then select Settings | Control Panel.

2. Double-click Network.

3. Click to highlight TCP/IP for your network card under "The following Network Components are installed."

4. Select Properties.

5. Click the DNS Configuration folder.

6. Select the radio button for Enable DNS if not already selected.

7. In the Host field, type your workstation name.

Note: *If you do not know the name of your workstation, you will need to click Cancel to exit the TCP/IP Properties dialog box. Click the Identification folder. The Computer Name field shows the name of your workstation. Now click on the Configuration folder and repeat steps 3–7.*

8. Type the desired domain for this workstation.

9. Enter your DNS server's IP address in the DNS Search Order field.

10. Click Add.

11. Click OK twice.

12. Answer Yes to restart your computer.

Use the following steps to configure a Windows NT workstation:

1. Click Start, the select Settings | Control Panel.

2. Double-click Network.

3. Select the Protocols tab.

4. Click TCP/IP Protocol.

5. Select Properties.

6. Click the DNS folder.

7. In the Host field, type your workstation name.

Note: *If you do not know the name of your workstation, you will need to click Cancel to exit the TCP/IP Protocol Properties dialog box. Click the Identification folder. The Computer Name field shows the name of your workstation. Now click on the Protocols folder and repeat steps 4–7.*

8. Type the desired domain for this workstation.

9. Under the DNS Service Search Order field, click Add.

10. Enter your DNS server's IP address in the DNS Server field.

11. Click Add.

12. Click OK twice and close the Network dialog box.

13. Answer Yes to restart your computer. You may have to click Start, select Shut Down, close all programs, and log on as a different user. Answer Yes and press CTRL-ALT-DEL to restart your computer.

DNS ADMINISTRATION

 Is it possible to import my NetWare 4.11 DNS database into the NetWare 5 DNS database?

Yes. First you need to run DNSCNVRT.NLM. This utility converts the Btrieve DNS files, used in previous NetWare DNS, into a BIND file format so it can be imported into NDS, which Novell uses for its DNS service. When running this utility, DNSCNVRT looks for two files:

sys:\etc\dns\hosts.db (Master DNS database)
sys:\etc\dns\hostsrev.db (PTR record database)

Then this utility converts these files to BIND format and renames the files as follows:

sys:\etc\dns\h.dat
sys:\etc\dns\hr.dat

You can then use the DNS/DHCP Management Console utility to import a BIND file into NetWare's DNS database. If the DNS/DHCP Management Console utility has not been installed on your workstation, see "How do I install the DNS/DHCP Management Console utility on my workstation?" earlier in this chapter for installation instructions.

Log in as Admin and perform the following instructions after you have obtained the master NetWare DNS BIND file.

1. Open the DNS/DHCP Management Console utility by double-clicking on the shortcut located on your desktop and launch with the correct tree name selected.

2. Select the DNS tab.

3. Click the Import DNS Database button.

4. Type in or browse to the location of the formatted BIND file.

5. Click Next.

6. Type or browse to the NDS context in which you would like the DNS Zone object to reside.

7. Click Next.

8. Click the DNS server that you would like to manage the imported zone.

9. Click Next.

10. The Import DNS dialog box is then displayed summarizing the context and DNS server you have chosen. If the information displayed is correct, click Import; otherwise, you will need to select Back two times and redo steps 6–9.

11. Click Finish when the transfer is complete.

When do DNS database changes become active?

Every minute DNS runs a maintenance thread. DNS will make the updates active when the SOA serial number has been modified. Unloading and loading NAMED.NLM will also make all changes active.

Can NetWare's DNS support round robin?

Yes, NetWare's DNS can support round-robin configurations. Round robin simply lets you load-balance different Web servers. For more information, refer to TID: 2941333.

Does the new directory-enabled DNS handle multihoming (multiple IP interfaces on the same server)?

Yes. *Multihoming* is when a DNS server has more than one network interface card installed in the server. A DNS response is sent out to the same interface from which the request was received.

What version of BIND is the new DNS compliant with?

DNS is BIND 4.9.6 compliant. DNS was tested and found compatible with BIND 8.1.1.

What rights do administrators need to manage the DNS/DHCP?

To create new configuration objects and modify existing objects, the following NDS rights are needed:

DNS/DHCP Objects	Object Rights	All Property Rights
Locator object	Browse	Supervisor
Group object	Browse	Supervisor
Existing DNS/DHCP objects	Supervisor	Supervisor

To create or delete IP addresses, ranges of addresses, or resource record sets, the following rights are needed:

DNS/DHCP Objects	Object Rights	All Property Rights
Locator object	Browse	Read
Group object	Browse	Read
Existing DNS/DHCP objects	Supervisor	Delete Supervisor

To view DNS/DHCP configuration, the following rights are needed:

DNS/DHCP Objects	Object Rights	All Property Rights
Locator object	Browse	Read
Group object	Browse	Read
Existing DNS/DHCP objects	Supervisor	Read

Chapter 12

NDS and Tree Design

Answer Topics!

NDS BASICS   394

? Defining NDS

? Browsing the NDS tree

? Contrasting context and current context

? Setting current context

? Comparing distinguished and relative distinguished names

? Using trailing periods

? Setting your users' current contexts at login

? Understanding the purpose of the [Root] object

? Understanding container objects

? Renaming the NDS tree

TROUBLESHOOTING NDS   406

? Diagnosing Unknown objects

? Checking NDS versions on a network

? Upgrading DS.NLM

? Running a full, unattended repair

? Troubleshooting NDS

? Coping with Error 625

? Changing a server's internal IPX address

? Upgrading server hardware and NDS

? Deciding whether to remove NDS for long-term shutdown

? Forcefully removing NDS

? Deciding how frequently to run a full, unattended repair

CATALOG SERVICES   415

? Learning about Catalog Services

? Installing Catalog Services

? Creating a catalog for Contextless Login

? Understanding Slave Catalogs

? Locating catalogs on a server

? Trying to move catalogs to a different volume

WAN TRAFFIC MANAGER   422

? Defining WAN Traffic Manager (WTM)

? Understanding types of traffic managed by WTM

? Determining cost factor

? Starting WTM

? Getting WTM to check for changed settings automatically

? Disabling WTM logging

? Enabling WTM policies

? Viewing traffic messages with WTM

? Managing WTM policies in one location

PARTITION/REPLICA MANAGEMENT   427

? Defining partition and replication

? Comparing replica types

? Making a read/write or read-only replica a Master replica

? Encountering Error -666 when removing a Master replica

? Trying to "communicate with server name"

SCHEMA MANAGER   432

? Defining Schema Manager

? Performing tasks with Schema Manager

? Recognizing base schema modifications

? Contrasting object classes and attributes

? Adding object attributes to existing objects

NDS DESIGN   435

? Avoiding poor tree design

? Designing upper and lower layers

? Avoiding single-purpose containers

? Establishing associations with Application objects

? Setting workstation import policies

? Designing partitions and replicas

TIME SYNCHRONIZATION   445

? Changing time on the server

? Comparing customizing and default time synchronization

? Customizing time synchronization in a mixed IP/IPX environment

NDS SECURITY   447

? Defining inheritable rights

? Limiting a password administrator's rights

? Creating an intruder lockout administrator

? Creating container administrators

? Creating exclusive container administrators

NDS and Tree Design @ a Glance

Novell Directory Services (NDS) is the heart of NetWare 5. Novell has recently made a big push to get NDS integrated with other third-party vendors like Cisco, Lucent, and Microsoft. This type of integration gives you the advantage in managing not only

NetWare-specific environments, but other environments as well. Imagine being able to administer routers, internal phone systems, NT user administration, and NetWare in one high-speed, concise database. This chapter will cover the following areas of NDS:

- **NDS Basics** answers questions on the fundamentals of NDS and specific tasks administrators need to know when administering NDS.

- **Troubleshooting NDS** covers issues relating to removing servers from NDS, repairing NDS after corruption, and other troubleshooting techniques related to maintaining an NDS environment.

- **Catalog Services** discusses what catalogs do and how they can make an administrator's life easier.

- **WAN Traffic Manager** addresses ways to reduce NDS traffic across your network.

- **Partition/Replica Management** covers how read and write replicas work and troubleshooting tips when problems occur.

- **Schema Manager** explores what an NDS schema is and how the Schema Manager can help administrator effectively organize the network.

- **NDS Design** discusses different ways to design a tree according to your particular environment.

- **Time Synchronization** answers questions about keeping track of time across wide area networks (WANs)

- **NDS Security** explores how administrators can divide their NDS maintenance to multiple users without giving up administrator security.

NDS BASICS

 What is NDS?

NDS stands for Novell Directory Services. NDS has two major functions. First, NDS is a database of all network

resources such as users, groups, containers, printers, servers, volumes, and organizational roles. Therefore, any time an administrator adds a new user or printer to the network, they are adding the user and/or printer to the NDS database.

NDS replaces the NetWare 3.*x* bindery. The bindery is also a database of a server's resources such as users, groups, and printers. The bindery is *local*, not global, meaning that a NetWare 3 server's bindery, or database, only contains information about that server's resources, as illustrated here:

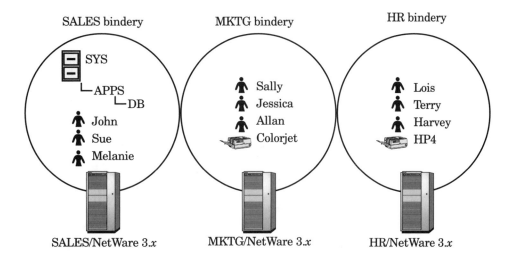

Each of the pictured NetWare 3 servers has its own bindery located in its SYS:SYSTEM directory. Therefore, the SALES server's bindery has no information on the users, printers, groups, and volumes located on the MKTG or HR servers. If Sally from MKTG needs to use a database application located on the SALES server, the administrator must add Sally as a user on the SALES server and grant her the necessary file system rights. This means that the administrator must add the Sally user twice. Sally must be added as a user once on the MKTG server and again on the SALES server. A lot of time is needed to administer the NetWare 3 bindery.

The following illustrates how NDS replaces the NetWare 3 bindery, easing NetWare administration:

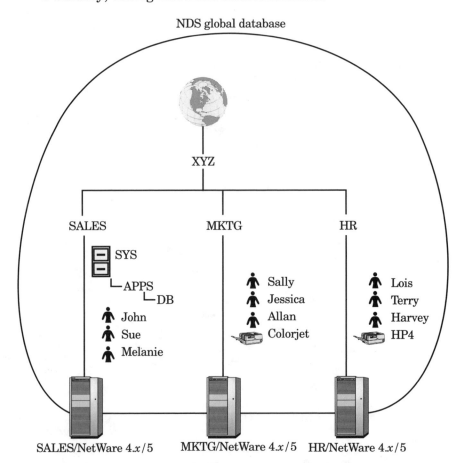

NDS global database

This illustration shows how NDS is *global,* meaning every server knows which resources are available on every other server in the tree. For example, the SALES server has information about its own resources and about MKTG and HR servers resources. Now, only file system rights must be granted for Sally to have access to the SALES database. The administrator does not need to add Sally as a user to the SALES server because Sally is an NDS *network* user. Her User object only needs to be created once in the NDS database. Any server recognizes Sally, since all servers have access to the same NDS database.

Note: *Except for the server and volume object, NDS does not contain information on the file system.*

NDS allows for *partitioning,* which is the process of dividing the database. Partitioning is useful because the NDS database can contain information on thousands of objects and become very large. For example, an 800MB NDS database can be partitioned, or divided. Let's say, for example, we partition our 800MB database into four parts of approximately 200MB each. Each 200MB portion can then be *replicated,* or copied, on various servers throughout our organization. Let's say our organization has 20 servers. Partitioning and replication allow us to have multiple copies of our database portions (200MB) on different servers. If one server goes down, another server still provides the information needed to keep that portion of the database functional, creating a fault-tolerant environment. Since the Directory is divided (partitioned) and copied (replicated) to multiple servers, NDS is said to be a *distributed* database.

Note: *Refer to the question "What is Partitioning and Replication?" later in this chapter, for more information on partitioning and replication.*

The second function of NDS is to process requests for network resources. A good analogy of this is the Directory Assistance Operator. You dial the operator and request the phone number for Joe Johnson. The Operator looks up the number, verifies that it is correct, and can even dial the number (connect) for you. In NDS a user requests a network resource, such as printing a document on the HP LaserJet 5 printer. It is NDS, like the operator, that processes the print request by locating the Printer object, verifying that the user has permission to use the printer, and finally, connecting the user to the printer.

Note: *The NDS database is also called the Directory. The NDS Directory is capitalized to differentiate it from a file system directory.*

 How can I browse the NDS tree at a DOS prompt?

You can use the CX command. If you type **CX** and press ENTER, you will see the current context of your workstation. To move to another context, type **CX**, press the SPACEBAR one time, and type the distinguished name of the context you would like to move to. CX /R moves you to the [Root] of the NDS tree.

 Note: *You can also use CX . to move back one level of the current context. CX .. moves back two levels of the current context.*

 How is context different than current context?

The *context* is an *object's* position, or location, in the tree. For example, you add the User object John to the ATL container in the following tree:

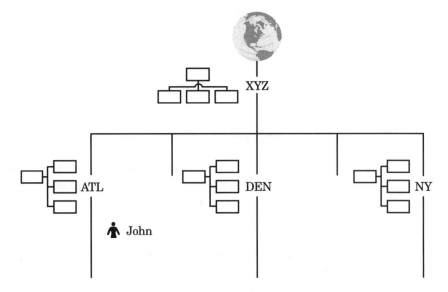

The John User object's context, or location, is .ATL.XYZ. The *current context* is your workstation's current view of the tree, much like your current directory in DOS describes your workstation's current view of the file system.

The current context is typically set to the container that holds the network resources the user accesses most often.

The network administrator can set up a workstation's current context when the station boots. Using the tree illustrated as an example, let's say that John's workstation has been set to the .ATL.XYZ current context. Now let's say we change the workstation's current context by exiting to a DOS prompt, typing **CX /R**, and pressing ENTER. By executing the CX /R command, we changed the workstation's current context from .ATL.XYZ to the [Root]. However, John's context is still .ATL.XYZ. Therefore, the current context can be changed with the CX command and is workstation-specific, whereas the context is object-specific and cannot be changed.

What is the difference between a distinguished name and a relative distinguished name?

A *distinguished name* is the name of the object (or common name), combined with the object's entire path of containers holding that object up to the [Root]. The distinguished name begins with a leading period. For example, the distinguished name of the User object Kathy in the following illustration is .KATHY.ATL.XYZ.

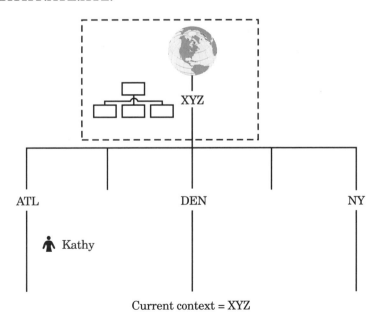

Current context = XYZ

The entire path of the User object Kathy begins with a leading period, includes the name of the User object (Kathy), a period, followed by the container that holds the User object, a period, and all the containers up to the [Root].

A distinguished name always exactly identifies an object and always works, since all the information NDS needs to locate the object (the entire path) is entered explicitly.

A *relative distinguished name* is *not* the entire path of an object. Instead, it is the path of an object up to the current context. A relative distinguished name does not start with a leading period. Periods are used to separate objects in the name. Therefore, for a workstation with a current context of .XYZ, the relative distinguished name for the Kathy User object in the illustrated figure is

KATHY.ATL

Notice that the relative distinguished name does not start with a leading period, nor does it list the entire path of the object. It only lists the object and containers up to the current context. Therefore KATHY.ATL is all that is needed, since the current context illustrated is XYZ. When the path does not begin with a leading period, NDS knows to place the current context at the end of the relative distinguished name, which in essence builds an object's distinguished name. Here is an example of how a relative distinguished name is understood in NDS:

Relative Distinguished Name	Current Context	Consequent Distinguished Name
KATHY.ATL	XYZ	.KATHY.ATL.XYZ

Relative distinguished names are used by network users when logging in to the network. For example, we would set up Kathy's workstation to have a current context of ATL.XYZ. Therefore, when Kathy logs in to the network, all that is needed at the GUI login dialog box is the relative distinguished name, Kathy, and a password. Since a beginning period was not entered, NDS knows that a relative distinguished name was entered. NDS then takes the current context, ATL.XYZ, and places it at the end of KATHY to build a distinguished name of KATHY.ATL.XYZ from it.

 Note: *For more information on setting up contexts, refer to the question "How do I set my users' current contexts at login so they don't need to be trained to use distinguished names?," coming up in this chapter.*

Relative distinguished names can use trailing periods whereas distinguished names cannot. Refer to the following quistion, "How do trailing periods work?" for more information.

Distinguished and relative distinguished names are used by administrators in dialog boxes, scripts, and at the command-line prompt.

How do trailing periods work?

Trailing periods can be used with relative distinguished names. We will use the following tree to illustrate trailing periods:

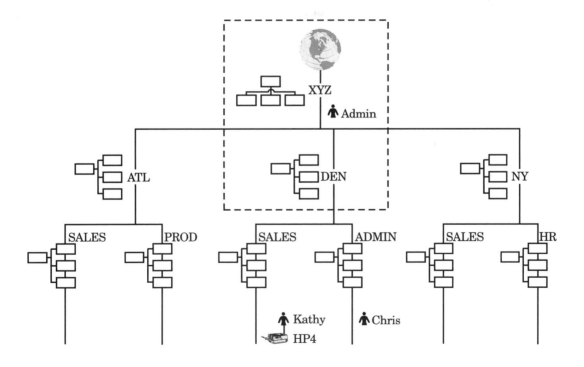

Let's say that you want to log in to the network as ADMIN.XYZ using a relative distinguished name. If your current context is DEN.XYZ, you can use the trailing period method by logging in as

ADMIN.

You cannot use a simple relative distinguished name such as Admin here, because the User object you want to use (ADMIN) is higher in the NDS tree than your current context. The trailing period(s) allows you to reference higher levels in the tree with a relative distinguished name.

Each trailing period instructs NDS to remove one object name from the left of the current context. In our example, only one period is used, therefore the DEN container is removed from the current context, leaving XYZ. As indicated earlier, a relative distinguished name is the path of an object up to the current context; but by using the trailing periods, you can remove portions of the path from your current context.

How do I set my users' current contexts at login so they don't need to be trained to use distinguished names?

Perhaps the easiest method of setting a workstation's current context is through the Z.E.N.works Starter Pack. To set the current context for a group of workstations, you must first install the Z.E.N.works Starter Pack on your server and create a workstation policy. For more information on creating workstation policies, refer to Chapter 5.

Perform the following after the workstation policy is created:

1. Open NWADMN32.EXE.

2. Right-click the workstation policy object and select Details.

3. Ensure that the Policies page is displayed and check the Novell Client Configuration option box.

4. Click Details.

5. Click the Settings page and then click the Configure button.

6. You now should see the Novell Client Configuration window. This window may seem familiar because this is the exact window used to configure the client at the workstation. Click the Client tab.

7. Enter the desired current context in the Name context field. Make sure you verify the Preferred server and Preferred tree information. Otherwise, the workstation might not be connected to the desired server and tree.

8. Click OK.

The final step is to associate and schedule the policy to the workstations, organizational units, and/or organizations you wish to enable. For more information on association and scheduling of a policy, refer to Chapter 5.

You can also set a workstation's current context using Network Neighborhood in Windows 95/98. The following must be performed at each Windows 95/98 or NT workstation installed with the NetWare 5 Client:

1. Right-click on Network Neighborhood.

2. Select Properties.

3. Select Novell NetWare Client and then click Properties.

4. Click the Client tab if necessary.

5. Type the desired context in the Name Context field. Note that the typeless distinguished name can be entered in the Name Context field with or without a leading period.

6. Click OK twice.

7. Click YES to restart the computer and have the changes take effect.

Finally, you can also set the current context in a login script with the CONTEXT command. To set the context in a login script use the following command in a container, profile, or user login script.

CONTEXT *distinguished name*

An example of a CONTEXT defined login script is CONTEXT .ATL.XYZ

 ## What is the purpose of the [Root] object in NDS?

The [Root] object is a placeholder only. It contains no information. Each NDS tree only has one [Root] object that is always at the top of the NDS tree. The [Root] object is created when the first server is installed in a new tree. You cannot move, delete, or rename the [Root] object, and it is always represented in square brackets [ ].

Often the [Root] object is used to grant global rights. For example, if every user in the NDS tree will use the same e-mail server, the administrator could grant the [Root] object the necessary file system rights to use the e-mail program. Because of inheritance, this would give all users in the tree access to e-mail.

Note: *The [Root] is not a container object, although it is often referred to as a container.*

What is the purpose of container objects?

Container objects help the administrator organize the NDS tree to fit particular organizational needs. For example, let's say you work for the XYZ company. The XYZ company has three locations in Atlanta, Denver, and New York City. Sales and production are located in Atlanta. Sales, Administration, and R&D are located in Denver. Sales and Marketing are located in New York. Using container objects you might create an NDS tree as follows:

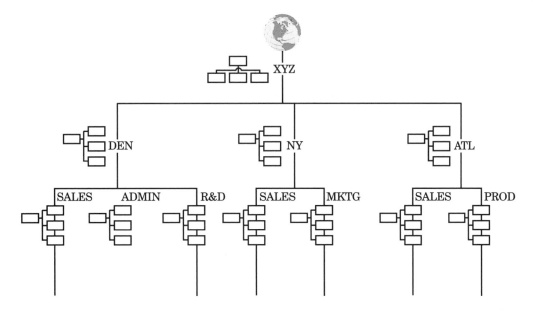

This illustration demonstrates how container objects can be used to organize network resources *logically*. Container objects also ease administration of network resources. If all Sales users in the XYZ company needed access to the Marketing database in the MKTG container, the administrator need only grant the SALES container rights to the MKTG database, which would give all users in the SALES container rights to the MKTG database.

There are three types of container objects: Organization, Organizational Units, and Country containers. Only the Organization container is mandatory.

 ## How do I rename my NDS tree?

Use DSMERGE.NLM on the server holding the Master replica of the [Root] partition to rename the NDS tree. Perform the following at the server console:

1. Type **DSMERGE** and press ENTER.
2. Select Rename this tree.

3. Log in to the tree by entering the full distinguished name of the Admin user and the associated password.

4. Type the name of the new tree and press F10.

You can also run the LIMBER process to expedite the tree's synchronization of the name change. To do this, perform the following commands at the server console prompt and press ENTER after each step.

1. SET DSTRACE=ON.

2. SET DSTRACE=+LIMBER.

3. SET DSTRACE=L.

4. SET DSTRACE=*H.

Press CTRL-ESC to toggle to the Directory Services screen and watch the LIMBER process occur.

Note: *Consider the following when changing the tree name: Ensure that time is in sync on all servers before changing the tree name. Resolve any DS errors in DSTRACE. Ensure that DS.NLM is latest version on all servers. Install the latest server patches on all servers. Perform the change on the server holding the Master replica of the [Root] partition. Change any workstations that have preferred tree statements. Change any backup servers that run a script to backup the tree. Edit any login scripts that refer to the old tree name.*

TROUBLESHOOTING NDS

 After performing a NetWare 5 upgrade, I notice several Unknown NDS objects. The objects have question marks in front of them. I try to delete them but they keep coming back. What is wrong?

This occurs in mixed environments (NetWare 4 and 5) or in a LAN/WAN environment in which communication is not stable. Perform the following to correct the problem:

● Check time synchronization. You can use DSREPAIR.NLM on the server to check Time synchronization.

● Ensure that each server in the replica ring is running the same version of the DS.NLM.

● Make sure that all the replicas for the partition in question are in the On state. You can use DSREPAIR.NLM on the server holding the Master replica of the [Root] partition to check the replica state. Load DSREPAIR at the server console and select Advanced Options, then Replica and Partition Operations. Select the replica in question and press ENTER. Select View Replica Ring. This will show you the status of the replicas.

● Make sure that the server holding the Master replica is accessible to all other servers.

● Delete all Unknown objects. To search for Unknown objects, log in as Admin and enter the following at a DOS prompt:

NLIST UNKNOWN /S /R

You can also load DSREPAIR by entering **DSREPAIR -A** at the server console and selecting Advanced Options Menu, Replica and Partition Operations, and Delete Unknown Leaf Objects.

How do I check the NDS versions running on my network?

One way to check the NDS version(s) running on your network is with NDS Manager. Perform the following at a workstation running the NetWare 5 Client software:

1. Open SYS:PUBLIC\WIN32\NDSMGR32.EXE.

2. Select Object from the menu bar.

3. Select NDS Version, then View. The dialog box shown next will appear.

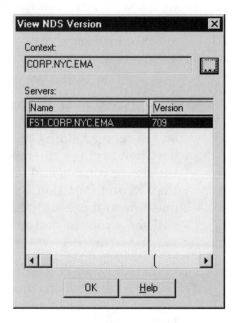

 Note: *You may have to use the Browse button to enter the context in which the Server object resides.*

Another way to check NDS versions on your network is with DSDIAG.NLM. DSDIAG is a new utility that ships with NetWare 5. You can generate the Check NDS Versions option of DSDIAG.NLM to allow you to see which versions of NDS are running on servers in an NDS tree. Perform the following at the server console:

1. Type **DSDIAG** and press ENTER at the server console.

2. Select Generate a Report and press ENTER.

3. Select Check NDS Versions and press ENTER.

4. Accept the default options and press F10 to generate the report.

 Note: *For further information on the DSDIAG utility, refer to the 411_UPG.TXT file in the PRODUCTS\411_UPG directory on the NetWare 5 Operating System CD-ROM.*

 Note: *You can also use DSREPAIR at the server console to check NDS version information.*

 I need to update NDS on all my NetWare 4.11 servers before installing NetWare 5. What is the best way for me to do this?

Use the NetWare 5 DSDIAG.NLM utility to generate a report to see which versions of NDS are running on the servers in your tree. Then perform the following to update NDS where needed:

1. At the server console, type **LOAD INSTALL.NLM**.
2. Select Products Options and select Install a Product Not Listed.
3. Specify the path to the Novell Directory Services version 5.99a or later for NetWare 4.11 files.
4. Press F3, BACKSPACE to remove the reference to drive A:, and enter the path.
5. Select Novell Directory Services version 6 or later for NetWare 4.11.
6. After verifying that the check box is checked, press F10.
7. Use NDS Manager to distribute files.

You can also manually copy files from the NetWare 5 Operating System CD-ROM to the NetWare 4.11 server. However, if the NDS tree has multiple NetWare 4.11 servers, use NDS Manager version 1.25 to deploy DS.NLM and ROLLCALL.NLM throughout the entire NDS tree quickly. Perform the following at a workstation running the NetWare 5 Client:

1. Select the Server object that you copied the updated files to.
2. Select Object from the menu bar.
3. Select NDS Version | Update | Settings | Entire Subtree; then click OK. You should note that if Update is grayed out, you have selected a container instead of a Server object.

4. From the Name window, select the servers you want to update. Using the RIGHT ARROW, move these server names into the Target Servers to Be Updated field.

5. Click OK.

How can I run a full, unattended NDS repair without having to manually unload DSREPAIR after the process is complete?

To do this, type **DSREPAIR -U** and press ENTER at the server console. This will run a full, unattended repair and exit DSREPAIR automatically when the operation is complete.

What are the standard troubleshooting steps I should take when troubleshooting NDS problems?

The following is a list of standard troubleshooting steps to take when experiencing NDS problems:

● Be sure all the latest patches have been installed on your server(s). When updating DS.NLM, be sure all servers in the replica ring are updated. The patches will not take effect until all servers in a replica ring are updated.

● Check time synchronization on the server. You can go to each server's console, type **TIME**, and press ENTER. If you see time is *not* synchronized to the network, you must resolve this first. You can also use DSREPAIR.NLM to check network time synchronization.

● Delete Unknown objects and re-create them.

● Run a full unattended repair using DSREPAIR.

● Check the DSTRACE screen for errors and resolve those errors. At the server console, type **SET DSTRACE=ON** and press ENTER. Press CTRL-ESC and select the menu option for Directory Services.

● If you are experiencing NDS errors in NetWare Administrator or NDS Manager, try rebooting the workstation and reloading these utilities. Rebooting the workstation flushes the cache.

● Check Synchronization by loading DSREPAIR; then select Report Synchronization Status. Resolve any synchronization errors.

 Note: *Novell recommends running a full, unattended repair twice a week as a maintenance precaution.*

 ## What can I do about a 625 (FD8F) Transport Failure NDS error?

A 625 error indicates that a server tried to contact another server to synchronize and was not able to reach the server using the internal IPX network address. Try checking the following:

● When you receive a 625 error, it is almost always a LAN issue. Check cabling and LAN card, and the LAN driver. For example, one problem could be a LAN driver is loaded, but the actual physical network cable is not connected to the network card.

● You can also check for SAP filtering of the DS SAP types of 0004 (server), 26B, (Time Synchronization), and 278 (NDS). You can use IPXCON, Services, and Display Entire Services Table. If you can see the server (0004 packet) and your specific tree (0278 & 026b packet), then you are not being filtered at the router level.

● Make sure that you can RCONSOLE to the target server from a workstation.

● Be sure the most current NIC patches have been applied to all LAN cards.

● Look for high utilization that would cause communication delays.

● Try the following DSTRACE commands at the server console, as described here:

SET DSTRACE=*	Resets DS.NLM: unloads then reloads DS.NLM. This can take some time on large directories.
SET DSTRACE=*U	Tells the server to set all server status to up; in effect makes the server try harder to communicate.
SET DSTRACE=*H	Heartbeat process; schedules immediate synchronization.

Perform the preceding commands at both the problem server and the other server. Do they connect? If the servers connect, then *U might have fixed the problem. If it connects and then disconnects, there might be more to troubleshoot, such as two servers with the same internal IPX address. You can use the DISPLAY NETWORKS command to check the IPX number. Then down the server and use the DISPLAY NETWORKS command at another server console. If the IPX number is still in the list, then identical IPX numbers are being used. Change one of the server's IPX numbers.

Some servers might report different IPX numbers in the SAP tables. To correct this, run DSREPAIR, select Advanced Options, and select Servers Known to This Database. Select the server, and select Repair All Network Addresses. This verifies that the IPX internal numbers for the Server object are correct. If this method fails, try these other troubleshooting tips:

● Type **RESET ROUTER** and press ENTER at the server console. Then type **SET DSTRACE=*U** and press ENTER at the source server to flag all servers as UP and retry communicating with them.

● Try running a full, unattended DSREPAIR.

● Make sure that all routers between the two servers are functional.

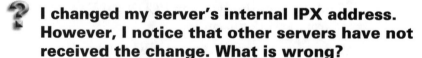 **I changed my server's internal IPX address. However, I notice that other servers have not received the change. What is wrong?**

Changing a server's internal IPX address might cause this, since it can take up to 30 minutes before other servers in the replica ring detect the change and reestablish connections with the server that has a new address.

You can force an update by executing the following console commands:

SET DSTRACE = *U

SET DSTRACE = *H

 I am going to upgrade my server's hardware. Is there anything I should do to NDS?

Yes. Use NWCONFIG to save the local NDS database prior to the hardware upgrade. Perform the following at the server console. If the server plays a critical role in time synchronization (for example, if it is a Reference, or Single Reference time provider), you need to reassign the time server functions and responsibilities to another server before running NWCONFIG.

1. Type **NWCONFIG** and press ENTER.
2. Select Directory Options.
3. Select Directory Backup and Restore Options. The Directory Backup and Restore option provides the same functionality as NetWare 4.1's DSMAINT.NLM.
4. Select Save Local DS Information Prior to Hardware Upgrade.

This locks the NDS database so it cannot be accessed again. You should use this option only if you restore the database to new hardware.

 Tip: *Before you run NWCONFIG, perform and verify a current backup of the entire server. When you select the Save Local DS Information Prior to Hardware Upgrade option, NWCONFIG creates a file called BACKUP.NDS in the server's SYS:SYSTEM directory. BACKUP.NDS stores all of the NDS information for the server, including replica information. Include this file in the backup. The Save Local DS Information Prior to Hardware Upgrade option locks and disables the NDS database. This prevents data changes and user authentication. To users and other servers, the server appears to be down. Therefore, perform this operation during nonbusiness hours.*

> *Caution:* *NDS partition and replica information should remain unchanged during the entire upgrade process. For example, no replicas should be added or removed, nor should any replica or partition types be changed during this time.*

I've heard that I should remove NDS if I will be downing the server for maintenance procedures, such as adding a new hard disk. Is this true?

At times, it is necessary to remove a NetWare Server object from the NDS tree for a brief period of time. It is in these circumstances that NDS is removed from the server. Removing NDS from the server not only removes the Server object from the NDS tree, it also removes all other references to the Server object. For more information on removing a server from NDS, refer to the question "I have an old 486 server that I would like to remove permanently from my NetWare 5 tree? What is the best way to do this?" in Chapter 4. As stated in the previous question and answer, the NetWare 5 NWCONFIG.NLM utility includes options to help preserve Novell Directory Services (NDS) information and integrity when the server will be down for maintenance procedures.

Some server maintenance procedures or upgrades do not affect the server as an NDS object (for example, upgrading the hard disk containing the SYS volume). You do not need to remove NDS from the server for this procedure. Instead, you can use NWCONFIG to save NDS information in preparation for the hardware upgrade. You then restore the NDS information to the server with NWCONFIG following the upgrade.

> *Note:* *A brief shutdown is considered less than 6–8 days. If the shutdown is less than 6–8 days, it is suggested that you down the server, perform the necessary maintenance tasks, and bring it back online without removing NDS (presuming nothing else will be changing). For any time period longer than 6–8 days, follow the suggestions listed.*

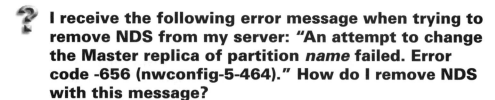 **I receive the following error message when trying to remove NDS from my server: "An attempt to change the Master replica of partition *name* failed. Error code -656 (nwconfig-5-464)." How do I remove NDS with this message?**

Type **NWCONFIG -DSREMOVE** and press ENTER at the server console to force the removal of NDS.

How often should I run a full unattended repair using DSREPAIR.NLM?

Novell recommends running a full unattended repair twice a week as a maintenance precaution.

CATALOG SERVICES

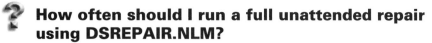 **What are Catalog Services?**

Catalog Services allow administrators to store a subset of information about NDS objects, creating faster searches for other services like LDAP, Contextless Login, NDS White Pages, and others. Catalog Services uses an NLM loaded on a server that will update the catalog at scheduled times. This service eliminates the need for applications that need to search an NDS tree and reduces processor utilization on the server.

Catalogs are created through NWADMN32, along with the NCP Server object.

How do you install Catalog Services?

Catalog Services can be installed during the installation of NetWare 5 or through NWCONFIG on the server after installation. Catalog Services must be installed when no one is using NWADMN32, since this installation will extend the schema with additional objects.

How can I create catalogs for Contextless Login?

Contextless Login allows users to browse through catalogs within one or more containers. Contextless Logins depend on

catalogs to browse for NDS objects. Do the following to create a catalog and configure Contextless Logins:

1. Once Catalog Services is installed, go to the server console prompt, type **DSCAT.NLM**, and press ENTER. This NLM is called the Catalog Services Dredger. The dredger's main purpose in life is to scan and update catalogs at predetermined intervals.

2. Log in as Admin and launch NWADMN32.

3. Create a Master Catalog by right-clicking the organization unit, select Create, choose NDSCat:Master Catalog, and click OK.

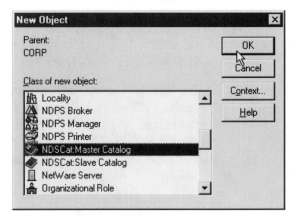

4. Give the catalog a name (e.g., USER_CATALOG), click additional properties, and click Create.

5. Double-click on the new Catalog object to access the Details page.

6. Browse at the Host Server field, select the server in which you loaded DSCAT.NLM in step 1, and click OK.

7. Next, Browse the Security Equal field, select an object that has rights to browse the tree, and click OK.

8. Select New under Label to create Primary and Secondary labels. A label lets you further identify the catalog. Applications and administrators can use the label to identify which catalog to use. Enter the label names and click OK.

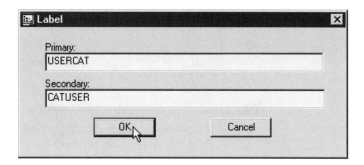

9. Go to the Filter button and type **"Object Class" = "User"**. This will create a catalog of users within NDS. You can use Server or Printer for your object class as well.

10. Go to Scope, browse the Context Limits field, and select the container you want to limit your search.

 Note: *You can have multiple Context Limits in a catalog.*

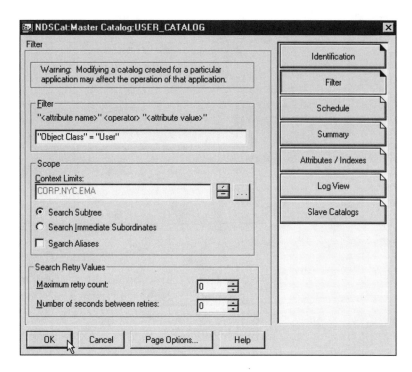

11. Go to the Schedule button and determine when the catalog should be updated. Automatic will update the catalog at a scheduled time and frequency that you define.

 Note: *If you change the schedule, you must unload DSCAT.NLM and load it back.*

12. Go to the Attribute/Index page, choose Selected Attributes, and Select Attributes. Select Full Name, click Add, and then click OK.

13. Go to Select Indexes, highlight Full Name, click Add, and then click OK.

14. Click OK to save changes.

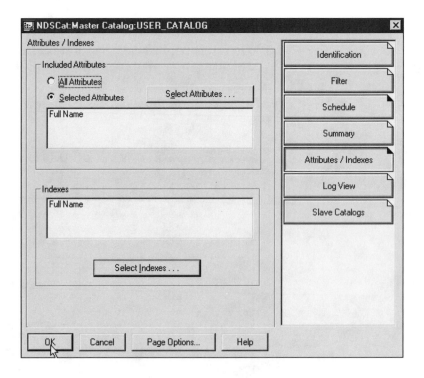

15. Go to the parent container of the Catalog object and right-click it. Select Trustees of This Object and grant your Catalog object the Create object right and the Read and Compare property rights; then click OK.

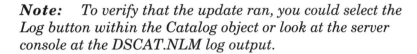

16. Right-click your Catalog object and choose Details, Schedule, and Update Now to update the catalog.

Note: *To verify that the update ran, you could select the Log button within the Catalog object or look at the server console at the DSCAT.NLM log output.*

17. To test your catalog, go to the Summary button within your Catalog object, review your settings, select Query Catalog, and then select Query on the next page. You should see results on your query in the large windows. If not, check your filter and verify that it is correct. If you have to change the filter, you *must* unload DSCAT.NLM and load it back to read the new settings.

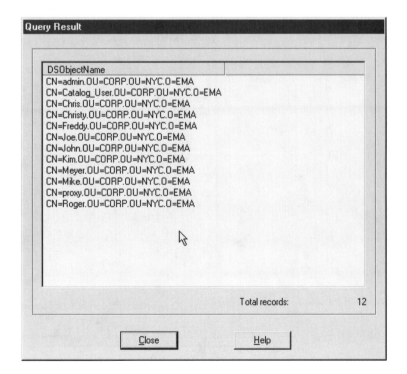

For Windows 95/98 systems, you must now set the Contextless Login for your clients.

1. Go to the Control Panel and click Network. Highlight Novell NetWare Client and click Properties.

2. Click Contextless Login and check the Enabled box.

3. Next, go to the Tree field, enter your tree name, tab to Catalog, enter the distinguished name of your Catalog object, and click Add.

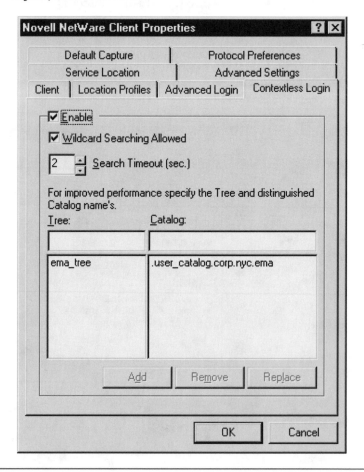

 Note: *Wildcard Searching Allowed will let a user type a partial name, and the catalog will deliver the closest matches it can find.*

4. Finally, reboot your machine and press TAB at the User Login prompt.

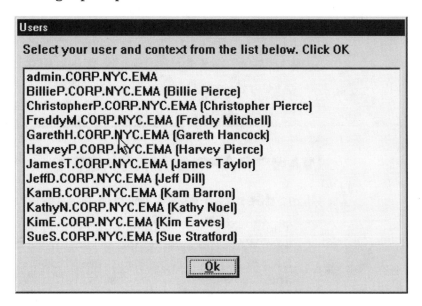

Users

Select your user and context from the list below. Click OK

```
admin.CORP.NYC.EMA
BillieP.CORP.NYC.EMA [Billie Pierce]
ChristopherP.CORP.NYC.EMA [Christopher Pierce]
FreddyM.CORP.NYC.EMA [Freddy Mitchell]
GarethH.CORP.NYC.EMA [Gareth Hancock]
HarveyP.CORP.NYC.EMA [Harvey Pierce]
JamesT.CORP.NYC.EMA [James Taylor]
JeffD.CORP.NYC.EMA [Jeff Dill]
KamB.CORP.NYC.EMA [Kam Barron]
KathyN.CORP.NYC.EMA [Kathy Noel]
KimE.CORP.NYC.EMA [Kim Eaves]
SueS.CORP.NYC.EMA [Sue Stratford]
```

[Ok]

Tip: *It is strongly recommended that you use Z.E.N.works to populate Contextless Login settings to all of your clients.*

What does a Slave Catalog do?

A Slave Catalog serves the same purpose as NDS partitions and replicas. Its primary function is to hold a copy of the master catalog and accept replication changes as they come. Using Slave Catalogs, which are optional, will save bandwidth and allow DSCAT.NLM to search in one area. To configure a Slave Catalog, launch NWADMN32, create an NDSCat:Slave Catalog, and assign the catalog to the Master Catalog object.

Caution: *Do not delete catalogs that were created by other applications (e.g., LDAP Services for NetWare).*

Where are my catalogs kept on the server?

The catalogs are located in the SYS:_NETWARE\CATALOG directory. You must use RCONSOLE to view this directory. Refer to the question "If my SYS volume must have TTS and

not be an NSS volume and I want to make it as small as possible, how should I calculate the minimum size for my SYS Volume?" in Chapter 6 for more information on viewing this hidden directory.

 ### Can I move my catalogs to a different volume?

At the time of this writing, there is no option for placing the catalog onto a different volume. Catalogs are closely integrated with NDS and therefore cannot be moved easily.

WAN TRAFFIC MANAGER

 ### What does the WAN Traffic Manager do?

The WAN Traffic Manager allows you to control NDS traffic over WAN links using policies within NDS. It can control the time of day that replication takes place, the type of traffic, and the assigning of the cost of traffic. WAN Traffic Manager works with NDS and NLMs on the NetWare 5 servers. Here is an example of how the WAN Traffic Manager works:

NDS Server 1

1. Receives synchronization request

2. Queries WAN Traffic Manager

Don't send

NDS Server 2

Checks policies

Do send

 What types of traffic does WAN Traffic Manager control?

WAN Traffic Manager controls several areas of NDS traffic. Listed are the different types of NDS traffic that can exist in a WAN environment:

- **Replica synchronization** is a process done by NDS to synchronize changes to all replicas of the partition.
- **Schema synchronization** is similar to replica synchronization, except that the schema is updated across the network.
- **Heartbeat** is when the servers communicate with each other for updates.
- **Limber** makes sure the replica pointers are consistent across the network.
- **Backlink** is a verification process of external references within NDS.
- **Connection management** establishes a secure virtual connection for transferring NCP packets and for schema synchronization and backlink.
- **Server status check** is when a server without a replica establishes a connection to the nearest server that holds a writeable replica partition.

 What is a cost factor?

A cost is used by WAN policies based on the expense of WAN traffic. Cost factors also let WAN Traffic Manager compare the cost of traffic with other destinations that are managed through WAN policies.

 How do you start WAN Traffic Manager?

To create a WAN Traffic Manager, you must do the following:

1. Login as Admin.
2. Run NWADMN32.

3. Right-click the server you want to control your NDS traffic, and select Details.

Note: *You must load WTM.NLM on each server whose traffic you wish to control.*

4. Select WAN Policies.

Note: *If you do not see the WAN Policies, make sure you have installed WAN Traffic Manager through NWCONFIG.NLM or your NetWare GUI on your server.*

5. Select a Predefined Policy group. For this example, we will select 1–3 A.M. This policy will restrict schema synchronization, external references, login restriction, and backlink checking from 1:00 A.M. to 3:00 A.M.

6. Select Load Group to set the policy, and verify that there are no errors.

7. Click OK.

8. Load WTM.NLM, or if WTM is already loaded, check the status and verify that the policy took effect.

How can I get WTM.NLM to check settings that have changed at certain time intervals?

There is a program called WANMAN.NLM that works in conjunction with WTM.NLM. To set a refresh interval for WTM, enter the following at the server console prompt:

WANMAN REFRESH INTERVAL = *number of minutes before refresh*

Tip: *To update the policy, immediately type* **WANMAN REFRESH IMMEDIATELY**.

How can I turn off the logging of WAN Manager?

At the server console, type **WANMAN LOGFILE = OFF**.

Can I enable a policy direct from the server console?

Yes. To enable a policy at the server console, type the following:

WANMAN POLICY ENABLE = *policy name*

Tip: *If you want to load multiple policies, you can use wildcards with the policy name. For example, WANMAN POLICY ENABLE = POL*.*

How can I view WAN Traffic messages with WAN Traffic Manager?

To view traffic messages, perform the following at the server console:

1. Type **DSTRACE** and press ENTER.
2. Type **DSTRACE SCREEN** and press ENTER. (This will dump NDS information to the screen.)
3. Type **SET DSTRACE = +WANMAN** and press ENTER.
4. Press CTRL-ESC and enter the DSTRACE option number to view messages.

I have several servers in the same location and would like to set the same policies on all servers. How can I set one policy to affect all the servers in one location?

The best way to optimize WAN Traffic Manager across multiple servers is to use the LAN Area object. To create a LAN Area object, do the following:

1. Log in as Admin.
2. Right-click on your Organizational Unit object, select Create, and select LAN Area.

3. Give your LAN Area a name and check Define Additional Properties.

4. Click on Servers Belonging to LAN Area and add your servers.

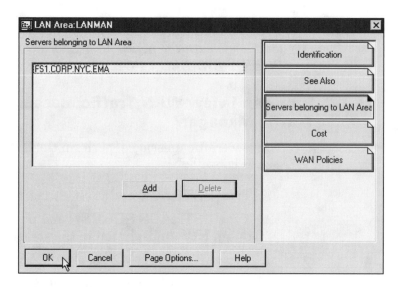

5. Click WAN Policies, define the policy or policy groups you wish to use, and load them.

6. Click OK twice.

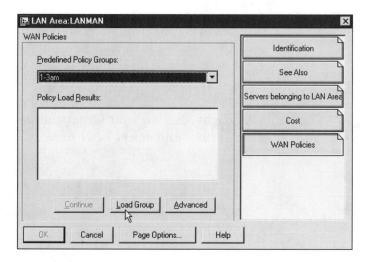

 Note: *You can customize what you would like to happen with that specific policy by selecting Advanced and actually edit the commands that WTM.NLM will use to control traffic.*

PARTITION/REPLICA MANAGEMENT

 ## What is partitioning and replication?

Partitioning is the process of dividing the NDS database. Since NDS can contain information on thousands of objects, it can become very large. Partitioning occurs along the boundaries of container objects.

Replicas are copies of the actual data for objects within the boundaries of a partition. Replicas are stored on the server's SYS volume. There are four types of replicas, or copies of a partition, in NetWare: Master, read-write, read-only, and subordinate references.

Let's use the phone book as an example of partitioning. If you live in a large city, more than likely the phone book has been divided, or partitioned, into different parts—for example, the yellow pages, the business pages, and the resident pages. Why is the phone book broken up into multiple sections? Because breaking it up into sections makes it easier to manage and use. Can you imagine trying to find a phone number in a phone book that was not partitioned, or divided, into different *logical* sections? It would take longer to find a number in such a large book.

Partitioning serves the same purpose on a NetWare 5 network. By logically dividing NDS into different portions or parts, you can more easily manage the database, and user requests are processed much more quickly.

Taking a very simplistic approach, we will say that our entire NDS database is approximately 1GB and we have a total of 30 servers in our organization. Since NDS is stored on the SYS volume, this would mean that without partitioning, each of the 30 servers in our organization that stored the NDS database would need to have a SYS volume of at least 1.5GB just to run NetWare! In addition, it would take a lot more time for a user just to log in to the network with such a

large database. However, if we partition the database into logical sections and replicate those partitions on different servers, then we have divided and distributed the NDS processing load across multiple servers.

Let's say that we divide the database into eight main sections of approximately 125MB each. Users will be logged in to the network much more quickly with a smaller (125MB) database than the 1GB database. In addition, our SYS volume will not need to be as large as 1.5GB for each server in our organization.

Perhaps one of the greatest reasons to partition and replicate is for fault tolerance—meaning that if we replicate our database on multiple servers, it is not a catastrophe if one server goes down, since another server contains the information needed to keep that portion of the database functional.

 ## What are the differences between Master, read-only, read/write, and subordinate reference replicas?

Initially, A Master replica is the original copy of a partition and is created at the same time the partition is created. There is only one Master replica, whereas you can have multiple read-write, read-only, and subordinate reference replicas. A Master replica is a complete copy of a partition and can be used to perform any partition operation or object change.

Note: *Partition operations include creating a partition, merging a child partition into its parent partition, and moving a container, as well as replica operations.*

A *read/write* replica is a complete copy of a partition. Multiple read/write replicas can exist on a partition and can be placed on servers by the administrator. A read/write replica can only fulfill object change requests, such as adding a User object to a partition. The read/write replica cannot complete partition operations; instead, it forwards partition operations to the Master replica. If a Master replica is lost or damaged, a read/write replica can be upgraded to Master replica status.

Note: *Only Master and read/write replicas support authentication. Therefore, if a user logs in to a server that contains only a read-only replica of the partition that holds his or her User object, it will direct the login request (authentication) to a server holding a Master or read/write replica.*

Note: *Only Master and read/write replicas support bindery services.*

A *read-only* replica is also a complete copy of a partition. Multiple read-only replicas can exist for a partition and are placed on servers by the administrator. A read-only replica cannot fulfill object change requests, such as adding a User object to a partition. A read-only replica forwards object change requests to Master and read/write replicas. A read-only replica cannot fulfill partition operations; instead, it forwards partition operations to the Master replica.

Note: *You can use NDS Manager to change a read/write or read-only replica into a Master replica. A read-only replica can also be changed to a read/write replica.*

Note: *Only Master, read/write, and read-only replicas support the viewing of NDS objects.*

A *subordinate reference* is not a complete copy of a partition. No object data is contained in a subordinate reference. Subordinate references only point to replicas that contain information about a partition. Subordinate references are created by NDS on servers that hold a Master, read/write, or read-only replica of a parent partition, but do not contain a

Master, read/write, or read-only replica of that parent's child partition(s). For example, look at the following tree:

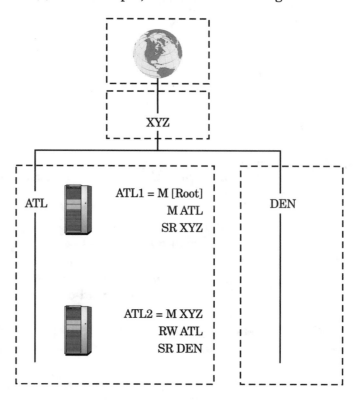

The ATL1 server contains Master replicas of the [Root] and ATL partitions. The [Root] partition is a parent partition to the XYZ child partition. However, XYZ is not replicated as a Master, read-only, or read/write replica on server ATL1. Therefore, NDS will automatically place a subordinate reference replica to the XYZ partition on the ATL1 server.

Therefore the phrase "where the parent is and the child is not" is often used to state how subordinate references are placed on servers.

 ### The server holding the Master replica crashed, and I need to turn one of my read/write replicas into a Master. How is this done?

You can turn a read/write or read-only replica into a Master replica by using NDS Manager. Perform the following if the

server's original Master replica is corrupt or unrecoverable, the server's hard disk that held the SYS volume crashed, or the server lost its data integrity.

1. Log in as Admin at a workstation.

2. Open SYS:PUBLIC\WIN32\NDSMRG32.EXE.

3. Browse to the partition holding the server and the read/write or read-only replica.

4. Click to select the partition.

5. Select Object from the menu bar.

6. Select Partition Continuity.

7. Click to select the server holding the read/write or read-only replica.

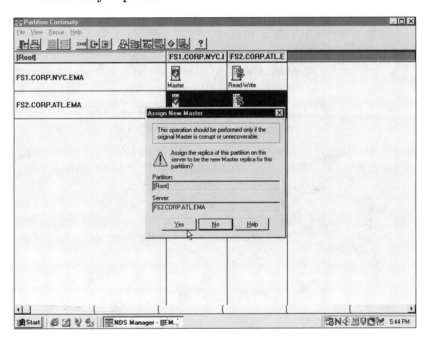

8. Select Repair from the menu bar.

9. Select Assign New Master replica.

10. Click Yes twice.

11. Click Close.

 Note: *You can change a read/write or read-only replica to a Master in NDS Manager by selecting the partition. Right-click and select Change Type. Select the radio button for Master and click OK. Use this option if the server holding the Master replica is intact but you would like to move the Master to another server.*

 While trying to change a Master replica from a NetWare 5 server to a NetWare 4.11 server, the -666 error appears. Also, the NetWare 5 server that holds the Master replica of the partition cannot be uninstalled because there is no other NetWare 5 server to pass the Master replica to. What is wrong?

This is working as designed. NetWare 5 does not allow a Master replica to be changed from a NetWare 5 server back to a 4.11 server.

 I'm getting the following error, even though NDS replication is working fine: "Unable to communicate with *server name*." What is wrong?

This can occur when the Master replica of a partition is on a server with both IP and IPX protocols, and a read-write replica of the same partition is on a server with either IP-only or IPX-only protocol support. Prior to NetWare 5, NDS required all servers in a replica ring to communicate. In a mixed protocol environment, this isn't possible. The Transitive Synchronization feature ensures correct replication in NetWare 5.

SCHEMA MANAGER

What is the schema?

When using NetWare Administrator (NWADMN32.EXE) to add an object or modify an object's properties, you are selecting an object class (User, Group, container) from the NDS schema. The *schema* defines what can become an object (such as users, printers, and groups) in the NDS tree. The

schema also outlines which information is mandatory and which information is optional when creating an object.

The schema that originally shipped with NetWare is called the *base schema*. Once the base schema has been modified in any way, such as adding a new class or a new attribute, it is considered the *extended schema*.

 Note: *Some third-party applications add to the base schema during installation (for example, Intel Landesk, Cheyenne ArcServe 6, Z.E.N.works, GroupWise, and NAL).*

What kinds of things can I do with Schema Manager?

Schema Manager allows users with Supervisor rights to a tree to customize the schema. The Schema Manager utility now allows you to extend the base schema in NDS to meet your organization's needs. For example, you might want to extend the base schema to include information such as a user's social security number. Using the Attribute Wizard in Schema Manager, you can create a new attribute, or field, for Social Security Number and then add it to the User class.

The following are other functions of Schema Manager:

- Viewing schema classes and attributes
- Comparing the schemas of two trees and printing the results
- Creating a report on a selected class, attribute, or schema
- Deleting an object class
- Deleting an attribute
- Identifying and resolving schema problems

Schema Manager is accessed from the Object menu in the NDS Manager utility (SYS:PUBLIC\WIN32\NDSMGR32.EXE) after you select a partition.

How do I know if my server's base schema has been modified?

You can quickly assess whether or not the base schema has been modified by opening Schema Manager. The illustration that follows points to the icon that represents an extension to the base schema. The question mark icon indicates that this object class is an addition to the base schema.

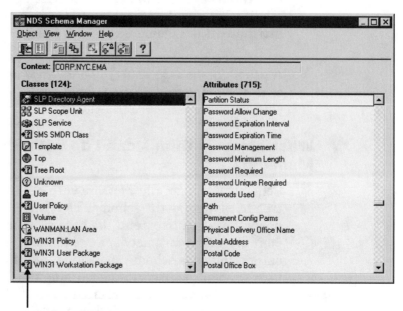

Indicates an extension to the base schema

What is the difference between an object class and an object attribute?

A Directory object, such as the user NDS object, is a class. The User object class is just a skeleton that contains no data. When selecting a new object to add to NDS, such as a User object, a class is selected by the administrator. Attributes are the blank fields in a class (such as telephone or department). A Class object contains *attributes,* or fields, for potential data. You can use the Class Wizard to create a new Class object and the Attribute Wizard to create attributes.

I want to add a social security number to my user properties in NetWare Administrator. Can I do this?

There are currently only two methods for adding attributes to an existing object's properties. The first method is to extend the NDS schema and then create a snapin .DLL file. To create the snapin .DLL, download the NetWare Software Developers Kit (SDK) at developer.novell.com.

The second method is much easier if you do not have strong software development skills. You can use a recently released utility called ScheMax by Netoria. ScheMax guides you through creating snapin DLLs using wizards. ScheMax requires no coding skills, and files can be created very quickly. Download an evaluation copy of ScheMax at www.netoria.com.

NDS DESIGN

 What are the consequences of a poorly designed tree?

Poorly designed NDS trees create many undesirable and unnecessary problems for your network. Some of the consequences of a poorly designed NDS structure are high utilization problems for the server processor, high WAN traffic, network slowdown, potential database loss, and cumbersome administration and use. Although there is no one right way to design an NDS tree that works for every network, it is important to follow some proven techniques and guidelines to avert such undesirable consequences.

What are the general guidelines for designing the upper- and lower-layer containers of my NetWare 5 NDS tree?

Although there is no one right way to design a tree for every network, there are some general guidelines that should be followed.

It is a good idea to create a naming standard first to indicate how objects are named in your organization. For example, you might set a standard in your organization for User objects such that User objects will be named by their first initial and last name (e.g., JDOE or MSMITH). The naming standard may also include which properties of information should be entered when creating new objects. For example, User objects must always have a first and last name, title, home directory, and phone number. You might also indicate whether uppercase or lowercase letters are permitted.

Note: *The upper layers of the tree typically represent the regions and locations in which a company operates. For example, a company with offices in New York and Chicago should have a separate container for each location. These containers are placed under an organization container to represent the company, and they form the upper layer of the company's NDS tree. A small NDS tree representing a single location typically does not have this level of containers in the NDS. The lower layers typically represent departments or work groups. For example, within the Chicago office, there might be an Accounting department and a Marketing department. Containers below Chicago for ACCT and MKTG represent the lower layers of this company's tree.*

The following outlines some general design concepts for upper- and lower-layer container placement in the NDS tree:

- Upper layers should be designed so that they will not ever need to be changed, if possible. They will remain intact. It is the lower layers that may change as the network grows and evolves. Consider that the first two to three layers are upper-layer containers, while the remaining are lower-layer containers. The [Root] is not counted as a layer.

- Use a single organization container under the [Root].

● After container placement is complete, the tree should resemble a pyramid. Few containers will occupy the upper layers, while most container objects are placed in the lower layers of the tree.

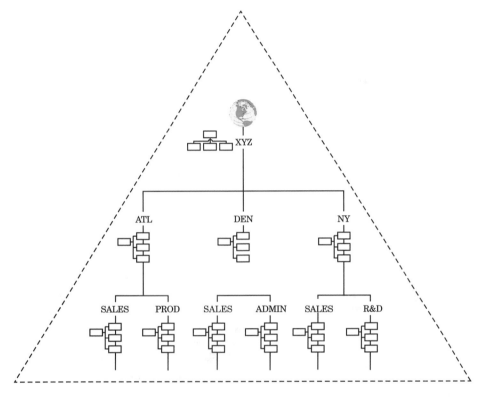

● The upper-layer containers should resemble the network infrastructure.

● Create one upper-layer container for each location in WAN environments (for example, one container for the Denver location and another container for the New York location). Upper-layer containers can represent each department or division in your organization if your network is small, has no WAN connections (or is in one location), and has less than 250 users.

● When creating the upper-layer containers, you might need to use regional containers if your organization has many WAN locations (10–15 subcontainers).

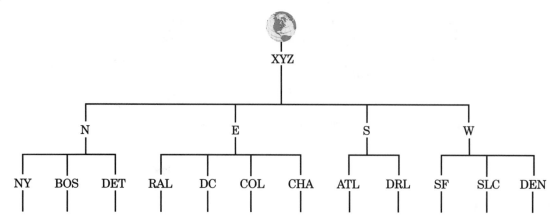

- If your organization has dial-up lines to different locations, do not include the dial-up locations as part of the main tree.

- Create lower-layer containers to hold users that have similar access needs. For example, every one in the Sales and Marketing departments uses the same printers, applications, and database. Therefore, create one container for all Sales and Marketing users. Typically, the tree's lower layers correspond to a company's organizational chart or department structure. By grouping users who have similar network access needs into the same container, you can effectively reduce administration time.

- Create the Group object in the same container as the associated users or the Application object to which you are granting the group members access.

- Limit the number of group members to a maximum of 1,000–1,500.

- If possible, keep the users in the group in the same partition to minimize external references and associated network traffic.

● Do not give users access to Application objects across the WAN in remote partitions.

● Do not create one Application object for your entire network if it will be accessed from multiple locations across the WAN.

● Do not create a Group leaf object that has users that exist in different locations or across a WAN link.

Can I make containers for single groups?

Do not create single-purpose containers. The following bottom layer of the NDS tree (under OU=LOCATION) is not recommended:

OU=LOCATION (or SITE)

OU=USERS

OU=SERVERS

OU=PRINTERS

OU=GROUPS

OU=ORG_ROLES

OU=APPLICATIONS

OU=POLICIES

OU=WORKSTATIONS

Although this design might work if all the containers are in the same partition, Novell does not recommend designing your NDS tree using these single-purpose containers for these reasons:

● It reduces user speed of access.

● It causes the bottom of the tree to become inflexible.

- It reduces scalability at the bottom of the tree.
- It creates a need to further partition containers (which reduces performance).
- These problems are heightened if the site or location grows to thousands of objects.

What's the best way to establish associations with Application objects?

For the best performance, use the following guidelines for establishing associations with Application objects:

- Set the searching to 0 or 1. This will turn off searching or localize the search just to the user's local container.
- Set the searching to 2 if the parent and parent's parent are local to the user. Local means in the containers on the same LAN, not across the WAN network.
- Use the -1 (search to top of tree) setting sparingly. -1 should be used only on LAN-only networks.
- If user access is across the WAN, restrict the searching of groups. The group searching can be turned off.
- Use the Application object's Schedule property page to let you control when applications are delivered to users. For example, you may not want applications delivered at 8:00 A.M. when users are logging in to the network.

How should I set workstation import policies?

Workstation import policies define where workstation objects are created in your NDS tree. Therefore, you should consider the following design guidelines:

- Create the workstation objects in the same container as associated User objects, assuming the total number of objects does not exceed the partition number guidelines (1,500 to 3,500). This will keep the design of NDS flexible and efficient.

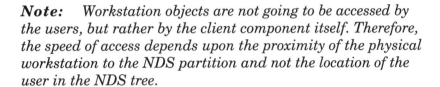

- Creating the workstation objects in a single-purpose container, such as WORKSTATIONS, has limitations. However, in a decentralized administration environment, this type of design will enable you to assign, certain network administrators access to manage just workstation objects. As the number of objects in the current partition grows, you can later partition off just the WORKSTATIONS container as its own partition.

Note: *Workstation objects are not going to be accessed by the users, but rather by the client component itself. Therefore, the speed of access depends upon the proximity of the physical workstation to the NDS partition and not the location of the user in the NDS tree.*

- Place Policy Package objects close to the users or workstations that will be accessing them.
- Create the Container Policy Package at the highest level of the tree as is necessary.
- Create the User Policy Package in the same container as the users that will access it.
- If user access to the Policy Package is across the WAN, the group searching should be turned off using the search policy.
- Your organization's network administration approach may impact the design of the NDS tree. For example, in organizations in which network management is performed by different administrators, the tree will have numerous lower layers. However, the tree will have fewer lower layers when administration is performed by a single group of administrators. Why? Because when only a few administrators are managing the network, you want the tree to be as simple as possible with fewer layers to administer. When numerous administrators are managing the network, then typically more containers are created and customized by each individual administrator.

● If your organization needs to implement Bindery Services in order to provide backward compatibility to NetWare 2 and 3, you may have to plan container placement carefully. Bindery Services will allow only up to 16 containers to be placed in the bindery context. If services are needed in more than 16 containers, you may have to group containers and services together so you do not exceed the 16-container limit.

● Typically, no container should hold more than 3,500 objects. If a container exceeds more than 3,500 objects, consider creating another container.

Note: *Some objects used only for administration purposes, such as DNS/DHCP, can be placed in their own containers for partitioning and replication. This will not affect user access.*

How do I design partitions and replicas?

You may not need to create a partition/replication strategy if all of the following criteria are met:

● Your organization exists in one location (no WAN links).

● There are less than 15 servers that will be holding replicas.

● Novell recommends less than 1,500 objects per partition, especially if your server's hardware is a Pentium 100+MHz with 64MB of RAM. In extreme circumstances, Novell recommends the 3,500-object limitation if your server's hardware is Pentium Pro 200+MHz, with 128MB of RAM.

If any of the above items are not met, Novell recommends that you carefully design a partition/replication strategy for your organization, as follows:

● Create fewer upper-layer partitions. Create more partitions in the tree's lower layers. If the tree was created with a pyramid design, this guideline will be easy to implement.

● Create partitions for each physical location (or by WAN infrastructure).

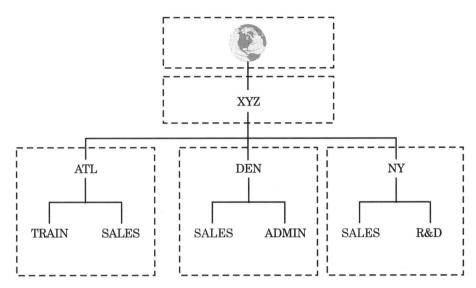

● Create smaller partitions if WAN bandwidth is a problem. Also create fewer replicas for each partition. This will effectively reduce synchronization traffic across the WAN.

● Be sure that a partition contains objects from a single location. Don't span the WAN when creating partitions.

● Partitions should contain less than 1,500 objects. Create another partition if more objects are needed in a single partition.

● Novell recommends three or more replicas for each partition in the tree for fault tolerance. It is a good idea to store one replica off site if possible.

● Replicate the [Root] partition three or more times. The [Root] is the most important partition in the tree. If the [Root] partition becomes corrupted, you will lose access to the tree.

● To keep synchronization traffic to a minimum, no more than 10 replicas should exist for a partition and no more than 20 replicas should exist on a server.

● The number of replicas on any server depends on how long it takes for synchronization processes to be completed. Synchronization should be completed in 30 minutes or less. The following factors affect the time it takes to complete synchronization: CPU speed of the replica server, number of replicas, number of objects in each replica, size of each replica ring, location of replicas in the replica ring (whether local or remote over a WAN link), speed of the WAN links connecting remote replicas (including bandwidth and round trip time), RAM available on the replica server, and frequency of inbound replica synchronization.

● Be sure to place replicas on servers that are physically close to the users who access that partition's resources. Users should have a read/write or Master replica containing their context on a server physically near them to minimize network traffic authentication. Place replicas of a partition in the location of greatest access by users, groups, and services.

● Keep Master replicas close to the administrator who will be performing partition operations. For example, you might consider placing all Master replicas in one location to avoid excessive traffic across the WAN during partition operations.

● Use WAN Traffic Manager if NDS synchronization creates excessive server-to-server WAN traffic.

● Each parent partition should have no more than 10–15 subordinate reference partitions. With the enhancements to NDS discussed in Chapter 2, this general guideline might change. Now that subordinate reference replicas are no longer involved in the synchronization process, Novell might recommend new guidelines to subordinate replicas after enough testing is completed. However, if you have a mixed NetWare 4 and 5 environment, subordinate references are involved in the synchronization process; therefore the 10–15 subordinate reference guideline should be followed.

● Partition only when necessary. Avoid creating too many partitions, since this increases synchronization traffic.

Volume SYS Size Recommendation for NDS Design

You should plan your SYS volume disk size to accommodate for growth in future years. Since NDS resides on the SYS volume, Novell recommends that you create a SYS volume of at least 4GB to accommodate future growth. This recommendation assumes that network printing does not exist on the SYS volume. If printing does reside on the SYS volume, the disk space requirement will increase.

TIME SYNCHRONIZATION

 I noticed that the time on one of my servers is incorrect. How do I properly change a server's time?

You should first check the replica timestamps to see if they are ahead of the actual time. Perform the following at the server console:

1. Type **DSREPAIR** and press ENTER.
2. Select Advanced Options.
3. Select Replica and Partition Operations.
4. Select a replica.
5. Select Display Replica Information.
6. Review the timestamp.

Now view the server's current time by typing **TIME** and pressing ENTER at the server console. If the time on a single reference server is earlier than the actual desired time, set the time forward to the correct time by downing the server and changing the DOS clock.

If the time on a single reference server is less than one week ahead of the actual time, perform one of the following:

● Shut down the server during nonbusiness hours to allow the actual time to catch up with the future timestamps.

● Refrain from performing replica/partitioning operations until actual time catches up with the future timestamps.

If the timestamp is more than one week ahead, avoid synthetic time by not setting the time. Synthetic time occurs when timestamps are ahead of the actual time on a replica of a partition on a server. Because replica synchronization depends on timestamps, synthetic time may cause problems with NDS.

Correct synthetic time by using DSREPAIR. You could, however, *severely damage* your tree if this procedure is not done correctly. Call Novell Technical Services to have them help you with the process.

When should I create a custom time synchronization strategy?

You can keep the default setting for time synchronization when you have an IPX-only protocol environment (no IP), your environment has fewer than 30 servers, and you have no WAN links. Otherwise, it's a good idea to create a time synchronization strategy to optimize time synchronization and reduce network traffic.

I set up a customized time synchronization strategy in my NetWare 4.11 environment. I am now migrating to a Pure IP environment with NetWare 5. How is time synchronization accomplished in a Pure IP or mixed IPX/IP environment?

Network Time Protocol (NTP) and TIMESYNC.NLM are used to synchronize time in a Pure IP or mixed IPX/IP environment. Using an external Internet time source, NTP provides timestamps for time synchronization. When NTP.NLM is loaded on an IP server, it becomes the time source for IP and IPX servers. Therefore, all IPX servers must be set to secondary time source types. TIMESYNC.NLM is loaded automatically on all NetWare 5 servers running IP, IPX, or both IP and IPX protocols.

Note: *NTP.NLM is located in the SYS:ETC directory and must be loaded manually. TIMESYNC.NLM is automatically loaded. NTP is an open IP standard defined in RFC 1305.*

When NTP.NLM is loaded, it reads the NTP.CFG configuration file located in the SYS:ETC directory. The NTP.CFG file is similar to the TIMESYNC.CFG file found in traditional NetWare 4.*x* IPX networks. NTP.CFG specifies the mode that the time synchronization subnet will operate and the time server host name or address. When the server is configured in server address mode (a Single Reference or Reference server), it will allow the local server to be synchronized to a remote server; however, the remote server *cannot* be synchronized to the local server.

Note: *When no Internet access is available, server mode allows the server to use its own clock as the reference by using the 127.127.1.0 address.*

When the server is configured in a peer address mode (a single reference or reference server), it will allow the local server to be synchronized to the remote server or the remote server to synchronize to the local server. This is beneficial if either the local or remote server is a good time source.

Note: *When more than one time source is specified in the NTP.CFG file, the time servers will be loaded in reverse order.*

Since NTP gets time from an external Internet time source, that time is always considered accurate; and, therefore, no voting or negotiation for time is performed. Secondary servers always adjust their time to correspond to the NTP server's time.

Note: *Prototypical NTP configurations also use multiple redundant servers and different network paths to achieve high accuracy and reliability.*

NDS SECURITY

What is an inheritable right in NDS security?

Inheritable rights allow administrators to assign users or groups to manage different parts of NDS such as e-mail

addresses and phone numbers. This feature is great for administrators who want to delegate their tasks to others without giving up security.

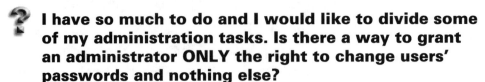

I have so much to do and I would like to divide some of my administration tasks. Is there a way to grant an administrator ONLY the right to change users' passwords and nothing else?

Yes. Using NDS Security, NetWare 5 allows you to grant only the password management Write right to a user. Perform the following to give a user only the rights necessary to change other users' passwords:

1. Log in as Admin.

2. Open SYS:PUBLIC\WIN32\NWADMN32.EXE.

3. Right-click the container that holds the User objects whose passwords will be administered, and select Trustees of this Object.

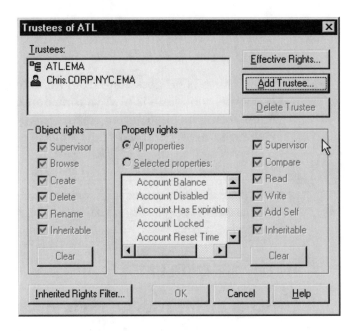

4. Click Add Trustee.

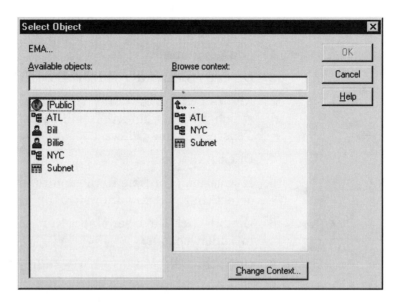

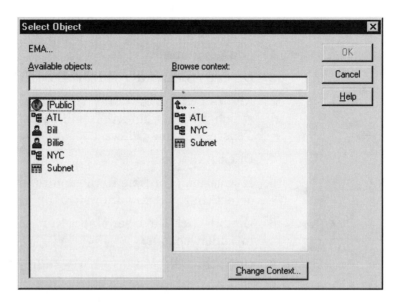

5. If necessary, browse to the container that holds the User object that will be administrating user passwords.

6. Double-click the User object that will administrate user passwords.

7. Click the Selected Properties radio button.

8. Use the scroll bar under Selected Properties and click Password Management.

9. Click the Read, Write, and Inheritable property rights option boxes.

10. Click OK.

Now the user can use NWADMN32.EXE to administer passwords of users in the selected container.

 Is it possible to grant a user ONLY the right(s) necessary to unlock a user's account when the user has repetitively entered an incorrect password?

Yes. NetWare 5 allows you to grant a user the NDS rights necessary to unlock user accounts that have been locked by

intruder detection. Perform the following to give a user only the rights necessary to unlock user accounts:

1. Log in as Admin.
2. Open SYS:PUBLIC\WIN32\NWADMN32.EXE.
3. Right-click the container that holds the User objects in which intruder detection will be administered, and select Trustees of this Object.
4. Click Add Trustee.
5. If necessary, browse to the container that holds the User object that will be administrating intruder lockout.
6. Double-click the User object that will administrate intruder lockout.
7. Click the Selected Properties radio button.
8. Use the scroll bar under Selected Properties and click Account Lock.
9. Hold down the CTRL key and click Account Reset Time.
10. Use the scroll bar under Selected Properties to find Incorrect Login Attempt, press CTRL, and click to select Incorrect Login Attempt. (Three properties should be selected at this point: Account Lock, Account Reset Time, and Incorrect Login Attempt.)
11. Continue pressing CTRL and then click the Read, Write, and Inheritable property rights option boxes.
12. Click OK.

 ### How do I give a user all administration rights to a container and *not* the entire NDS tree?

The most common way to give a user administration rights to a container is to make the user a *container administrator* using an Organizational Role object. Perform the following to create the organization role with the appropriate administration rights to manage a container:

1. Log in as Admin.
2. Open NWADMN32.EXE.

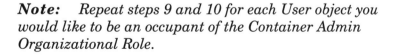

3. Right-click the container to be administered, and select Create.

4. Use the scroll bar to find the Organizational Role object and then double-click the Organizational Role object to select it.

5. Type **Container Admin** in the Organizational Role name property.

6. Click the Define Additional Properties option box; then click Create.

7. Select the Occupant Browse button.

8. Click Add in the Occupant dialog box shown here:

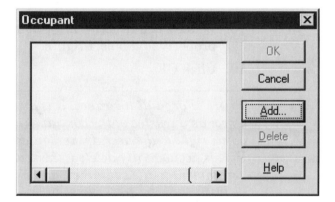

9. Browse to the container holding the User object that you wish to administer the container.

10. Double-click the User object to add it as an occupant of the Container Admin Organizational Role.

Note: *Repeat steps 9 and 10 for each User object you would like to be an occupant of the Container Admin Organizational Role.*

11. Click OK twice.

12. Right-click the container that the Organizational Role object will administer.

13. Select Trustees of this Object.

14. Click Add Trustee.

15. Browse to the container holding the Organizational Role object.

16. Double-click the Organizational Role object to add it as a trustee of the container.

17. Click the Supervisor object right to grant supervisor rights to the container. For fault tolerance, it is a good idea to select all Object and Property rights option boxes. If Supervisor is blocked by an IRF lower in the tree structure, all other rights will still be available.

18. Be sure the Inheritable option boxes are selected for both property and object rights.

19. Click OK.

Tip: *For fault tolerance, it is a good idea to also add a User object as a trustee of the container and grant the Supervisor object right to the user. If the Container Admin Organizational Role is accidentally deleted, there will still be a supervisor assignment to the container, and Supervisor rights will not be lost.*

Caution: *The preceding steps give the container administrator Supervisor rights to the file system. To prevent Supervisor rights to the file system, create an IRF on the Server object that blocks the Supervisor right.*

 ### How can I ensure that I am the only user with Supervisor administration rights to my container?

NDS security allows you to effectively block all users' inherited Supervisor rights to containers by using an Inherited Rights Filter (IRF). It is very important, however, to ensure that at least one user has an explicit trustee assignment to the container with Supervisor rights before implementing an IRF to block inherited Supervisor rights.

When a user is given an explicit rights assignment at a higher level in the tree, those rights are inherited to, or flow down to, the lower levels in the tree. To illustrate the concept of inheritance, we will use the following tree:

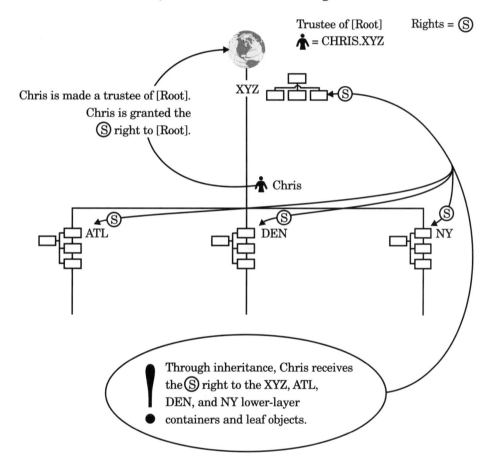

Trustee of [Root]   Rights = Ⓢ
🧍 = CHRIS.XYZ

Chris is made a trustee of [Root].
Chris is granted the
Ⓢ right to [Root].

XYZ

🧍 Chris

ATL   DEN   NY

Through inheritance, Chris receives the Ⓢ right to the XYZ, ATL, DEN, and NY lower-layer containers and leaf objects.

Therefore, to make yourself an exclusive container administrator, you should use an IRF to block inherited rights.

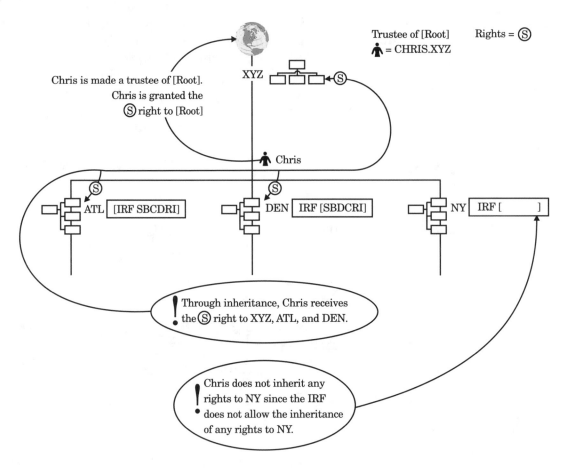

Trustee of [Root]   Rights = Ⓢ
= CHRIS.XYZ

Chris is made a trustee of [Root].
Chris is granted the
Ⓢ right to [Root]

XYZ

Chris

ATL [IRF SBCDRI]

DEN IRF [SBDCRI]

NY IRF [   ]

Through inheritance, Chris receives
the Ⓢ right to XYZ, ATL, and DEN.

Chris does not inherit any
rights to NY since the IRF
does not allow the inheritance
of any rights to NY.

Perform the steps in Parts 1 and 2 to block inherited rights.

Part 1

Ensure that there is at least one User object with an explicit
supervisory trustee assignment to the container on which you
will be placing the IRF. Log in as Admin and perform the
following:

1. Open NWADMN32.EXE.

2. Right-click the container on which you will be placing an
    IRF, and select Trustees of this Object.

3. Look in the Trustee portion of the dialog box for your User object, and click to select your User object. If you do not see your User object listed in the Trustee list, perform the following: Click Add Trustee, browse to the container holding your User object, double-click your User object, be sure all Object rights option boxes are marked (Supervisor, Browse, Create, Delete, Rename, and Inheritable should have a check mark next to them), and all Property rights option boxes are marked (Supervisor, Compare, Read, Write, Add Self, and Inheritable should have a check mark next to them). Click OK. Otherwise, you could lose supervisor control of the container.

4. Ensure that your User object has all object and property rights (Supervisor, Browse, Create, Delete, Rename, Inheritable, Compare, Read, Write, and Add Self should have check marks next to them).

5. Look at the trustee list of the container for other unwanted user assignments that are listed with supervisor rights. Delete unwanted trustee assignments.

6. Click OK when you have confirmed that you have all rights to the container and all unwanted assignments have been deleted.

Note: *Many NetWare 5 installations use the Organizational Role object to grant container Administrator rights. It's a good idea to have both the Organizational Role object and a User object as trustees of the container with Supervisor rights. This provides a backup administrator, in case the Organizational Role object is accidentally deleted.*

Tip: *It is a good idea to create an additional User object and grant the user Supervisor rights to the container. Write the username and password on paper and keep it secure by locking it in a safe place.*

Part 2

Place an IRF on the container to block unwanted Supervisor rights. You should still be logged in as Admin with NetWare Administrator running. Perform the following:

1. Right-click the container in which the IRF will be placed.
2. Select Trustees of This Object.
3. Click the Inherited Rights Filter button.
4. Remove check marks next to each right that you do not want to be inherited in the container.

Note: *Keep the Browse and Read rights if you would like other users and administrators to see the container in the tree.*

Caution: *The Supervisor right will need to be restored if partitioning operations are needed at a later time.*

5. Click OK twice.

Appendix A

Web Resources

NOVELL SITES

- **Novell Developer Kit** An excellent site where developers can download the latest Novell Software Development Kit (SDK), along with numerous documents, add-ons, sample code, and downloads

  developer.novell.com/ndk/

- **NetWare 5 search** NetWare 5 Knowledgebase

  support.novell.com/products/nw5/

- **NetWare 5 Online Documentation** Complete online documentation for NetWare 5 (will change as NetWare 5 continues to mature)

  www.novell.com/documentation/en/nw5/nw5/docui/index.html

- **Year 2000 testing verification for third-party products incorporated in Novell products** Provides information about third-party products included in NetWare 5 that have been Y2K tested

  www.novell.com/year2000/third_party.html

- **Novell Consulting Toolkit** Includes useful tools for Z.E.N.works, NetWare 5, and other Novell-related products

  consulting.novell.com/toolkit/tkhome.html

- **Z.E.N.works Cool Solutions home page** Chock full of updates, hints, and tips about Z.E.N.works and Novell Application Launcher (NAL)

  www.novell.com/coolsolutions/zenworks

- **NetWare 5 white papers** In-depth technical specifications and writings about NetWare 5

  www.novell.com/whitepapers/nds4nt/twhitepaper.html

- **NetWare 5 technical presentations**   A library of technical PowerPoint and Real Video presentations on NetWare 5.

  www.novell.com/passport/technical/techprod.html

- **Novell Education**   Contains the latest information on NetWare 5 courseware and exam listings

  education.novell.com

NETWARE-RELATED MAGAZINES AND JOURNALS

- **NetWare Connection**   An online magazine devoted to the Novell product line

  www.nwconnection.com

- **AppNotes (Novell Application Notes)**   A free 12-month technical online journal for network design, implementation, administration, and integration for Novell's product line

  developer.novell.com/research/appnotes.htm

- **Novell Developer Notes**   A free 12-month technical journal for network software development (also a great resource for advanced network administrators)

  developer.novell.com/research/devnotes.htm

- **Inside NetWare**   In-depth monthly articles that provide NetWare administration tips from Ziff-Davis (a subscriber-only site)

  www.zdjournals.com/inw/

NETWARE-ORIENTED FORUM RESOURCES

- **Novell Forums**   Official newsgroup forums for the complete Novell product line

  Log in to the newsgroup server: nntp://forums.novell.com

- **CNE Net**   Product-oriented Novell forums for Novell certified professionals

  cnenet.novell.com

NETWORK PROFESSIONAL ASSOCIATIONS

- **Network Professional Association (NPA)**   A site dedicated to advancing the network computing profession (formerly known as the CNEPA)

  www.npa.org

- **NetWare Users International (NUI)**   An association of NetWare computing professionals sponsored and supported by Novell

  www.novell.com/nui

- **CNE Net**   A virtual community for Novell certified professionals only

  cnenet.novell.com

THIRD-PARTY BACKUP PRODUCTS FOR NETWARE

- **Seagate Software**   Developer of Backup Exec (NetWare backup software)

  www.seagatesoftware.com/homepage/

● **Computer Associates** Developer of ARCserve (NetWare backup software)

www.cai.com

OTHER THIRD-PARTY NETWARE SITES

● **Netoria** Developer of utilities for coexistence between Windows NT and Novell, as well as other useful utilities for NetWare 5

www.netoria.com

● **PowerQuest** Developer of ServerMagic, which allows you to expand and decrease DOS and NetWare partitions

www.powerquest.com

● **Ontrack** Developer of data recovery utilities for NetWare and other operating systems

www.ontrack.com

● **Avanti Technology** Provider of network management utilities for NetWare

www.avanti-tech.com

● **enMasse** Developer of Mass User Management (MUM) software for NDS

www.enmasse.com

● **Vinca** Provider of data protection clustering and server mirroring solutions for NetWare servers

www.vinca.com

● **Simware** Developer of REXXWARE, a migration utility for NetWare

www.simware.com

- **Network Associates** Provider of virus protection products for NetWare servers using NLM technology

  www.nai.com

- **Command Software Systems** Developer of Command AntiVirus product for NetWare

  www.commandcom.com

OPERATING SYSTEM SERVICE PACK AND PATCH SITES

- **Minimum Patch List** NetWare service packs and patches

  support.novell.com/misc/patlst.htm

- **Support Online** Microsoft Windows 95/98/NT service packs and patches

  support.microsoft.com/support/downloads/

USEFUL NOVELL SHAREWARE PROGRAM SITES

- **Dave's Novell Shareware** www.novellshareware.com
- **DreamLAN Network Consulting (NDS Toolkit for NetWare 5)** www.dreamlan.com
- **Net-Utils.com** www.net-utils.com

Index

A

Abend, 108–109
Access controls, FastTrack
  Server, 353–354
Across-the-Wire Migrations,
  33–35, 48
Active Directory Services
  (ADS), 1–6
Admin rights
  to a container, 450–452
  getting back after losing,
  12, 308
ALIAS command, 125–126
Application Explorer, 230
Application Fault Tolerance, 232
Application Load Balancing, 232
Application management,
  228–253
Application objects
  associating, 440
  creating, 240–241
  NAL and, 234–246
  registry key, 246
  removing drives and ports, 235

Application support
  enhancements, NetWare 5,
  24–27
Application version checking,
  245
Applications
  installing after invoking
    NAL, 243–244
  stopped working, 73–74
  uninstalling, 246
ASCII control file, 310
ASCII delimited file, 309
Associations with Application
  objects, 440
At (@) command in a login script,
  325, 330
ATTACH login script command,
  330
Attribute (object)
  adding, 435
  explained, 434
Attribute replication, ADS and
  NDS, 5
Attribute requests, 142

Attribute Wizard (Schema
  Manager), 433
Authentication, 311
Authoritative server, 377,
  380–381
AUTOEXEC.BAT path, losing
  with login scripts, 325
AUTOEXEC.NCF, 90
Automatic allocation (of IP
  addresses), 362
Automatic Client Upgrade
  (ACU), 170–173

B
Backing up and restoring, ADS
  vs. NDS, 4
Backup, NetWare 5
  enhancements, 28
Backup programs
    with NSS, 222, 461–462
    third-party, 129
Backup rights, 130
Backup strategies, 129, 131
Banner files (NDPS), 285
Banners, customizing, 285–286
Base schema
    assessing modification to,
      433–434
    explained, 433
Bidirectional printing, 285
BIND file, 388
BIND version, 390
Bindery, NetWare 3.x, 395–396
Bindery emulation, 121

Bindery Gateway, 74
Bindery services, or NDS,
  176–177
Block suballocation, 71–72, 195
Boot files, editing, 115–116
Booting
    from DOS, 46
    having IP load first, 97
    will not boot, 104–105
BREAK login script command,
  330–331
Bringing down a server
  permanently, 87
Browse Home Directory, 301
Browse Template, 301
B-trees, 205

C
Cache buffers, 117, 184,
  218–219
Cache hits, and need for
  RAM, 116
CAPTURE command, 267
Catalog Services, 415–422
Catalogs
    ADS vs. NDS, 3–4
    context limits in, 417
    for contextless login,
      415–421
    on the server, 421–422
CD volume commands, 187
CD volumes, 187
CDINST.NLM, 51
CDROM command, 187

CD-ROM support, NetWare 5, 18
Certificate authorities (CAs), 132
Class object, 434
Clean Up Network
    Resources, 236
Client support
        ADS and NDS, 4–5
        NetWare 5, 24
Clock (workstation), getting in
    synch, 177
CLS login script command, 331
Common Layer Interface
    (CLI), 206
Communication protocol
    support, 178
Compatibility Mode, 12–13,
    76, 96
Compatibility Mode drivers
    (CMD), 12, 74, 96
Compression (file), 123,
    196–201
        changing, 199–201
        setting, 71–72
        statistics for a NWFS
        volume, 197–198
COMSPEC, 323, 331
Configuration boot files, editing,
    115–116
Configuration information
        getting, 108
        saving, 28
Connections, reporting on, 250
Console command history,
    126–127

Console command shortcuts,
    125–126
Console commands, new
    NetWare 5, 17–18
Console enhancements, NetWare
    5, 17–19
ConsoleOne utility, 21
        bringing up, 94
        creating users with,
        303–304
        for editing boot files,
        115–116
        memory for, 93–94
        mouse movement, 94
        and NDS tree, 94
        on a workstation, 95
Consumers (NSS), 205
Container administrator,
    creating, 450–452
Container login scripts, 320
Container objects
    (containers), 317
        administration rights to,
        450–452
        explained, 404–405
        single-purpose, 439–440
        types of, 405
Context, vs. current context, 398
Context limits in a catalog, 417
CONTEXT login script
    command, 331
Contextless login, 176
        catalogs for, 415–421
        setting for clients, 420

Controlled Access printers, 23, 273, 276–277
Core dump, 106–107
Core dump image, saving, 106–107
Core dump results, viewing, 107
Corrupted NSS volume, recovering, 224–226
Country (container) object, 64, 68
Crashed server, 104–105
Create User object, 301
Current context
    explained, 398–399
    setting, 402–404
Current tree, setting up, 175–176
Cursor movement table, 50–51
Custom device modules (CDMs), 55
CX command, 398

D
DATA volume block size, 77
Date stamping Web pages, 356
Daylight Savings Time, 62
Debugging commands, 107–108
Default login scripts, 320
Designated servers, 378, 382, 385
Desktop, secure, 246–248
Details on Multiple Users, 306–307
Device driver setup, 54–58

DHCP administration rights, 390–391
DHCP enhancements, NetWare 5, 22
DHCP Server, 362–377
    administration, 372–377
    checking working of, 375
    installation, 364–370
    overview, 362–364
    preventing redundancy, 376–377
    starting, 369
    subnet service, 374–375
    troubleshooting, 370–371
    workstation configuration, 369
DHCP Server object, creating, 365–366
DHCP Subnet object, creating, 366–368
DHCP Subnet Range object, creating, 368–369
DHCP 2 database, importing to DHCP 3, 372–373
Directories
    managing, 180–226
    not copied by Migration Wizard, 71
Directory agents (DA), 140–141
Directory attribute replication, ADS and NDS, 5
Directory Service replication, 297

Disk allocation block size, setting, 71–72
Disk drivers, 16, 209
Disk thrashing, 102
DISPLAY ENVIRONMENT command, 114
DISPLAY login script command, 331–332
DISPLAY MODIFIED ENVIRONMENT command, 115
DISPLAY NETWORKS command, 112, 412
DISPLAY SERVERS command, 112
Distinguished name, 399–401
Distributed database, 397
DNS domain and subdomain, 379
DNS enhancements, NetWare 5, 22
DNS Server object, creating, 382–383
DNS servers, 377–391
  administration, 388–391
  administration rights to, 390–391
  designating, 385
  installing, 382–388
  multihoming, 390
  overview of, 377–382
  starting, 386
  types of, 378

DNS services
  importing NetWare 4.11, 388–389
  workstation configuration, 386–388
DNS zones
  creating, 383–385
  example, 381
  explained, 380–382
  types of, 382
DNS/DHCP environment network traffic, 363
DNS/DHCP Management Console, 373–374, 382–385
  installing, 364
  requirements, 363–364
  will not run, 370
Document directory, Web site, 357–358
Documenting the system, 28
Domain name space, 379
Domain name structure, 380
Domain names, 379
Domains, 379–380
DOS, booting from, 46
DOS applications
  printing to NDPS printer, 287
  SET variables for, 244–245
DOS BREAK login script command, 332
DOS clients, and Pure IP, 98
DOS FAT commands (NSS), 216–217

DOS partition, setting up, 44–45
DOS utilities, 45
DOS VERIFY login script
    command, 332
DOS version, 45
DOS volume mount, NSS
    and, 192
DOS workstations
    backing up, 131
    printing login scripts, 343
    trouble with executing
        commands, 323
DRIVE login script command,
    332
Drive mapping to the server, 92
DSDIAG.NLM, 408–409
DSK driver standard, 51
DSMERGE.NLM, 405
DS.NLM versions, 47–48
DSREPAIR -U command, 410
DSREPAIR.NLM, 407, 410, 415
DSTRACE, 411
Dynamic allocation (of IP
    addresses), 362
Dynamic Host Configuration
    Protocol (DHCP), 22, 362. *See
    also* DHCP Server

E
EDIT.NLM, for editing boot files,
    116
ELSE login script command, 333
Enable Broker button dimmed,
    294

Encryption, 23, 131–134
Encryption features,
    NetWare 5, 23
END login script command,
    333
Enhanced SBACKUP, 222
Enterprise Server, vs. FastTrack
    Server, 347–348
Ethernet frame types, loading
    multiple, 73
Event Notification Service
    (ENS), 270
EXIT login script command,
    333–334
Extended schema, 433
Extranet, 349

F
FastTrack (Web) Server, 22
    access controls, 353–354
    configuring LDAP on, 354
    date stamping Web pages,
        355–356
    document directory, 357–358
    vs. Enterprise Server,
        347–348
    installing, 349–352
    locked out of, 358
    managing, 344–358
    minimum requirements,
        346
    and ODBC drivers, 355
    pre-installation, 347
    remote load/unload, 355

slow processing requests, 356–357

troubleshooting, 356–358

Fault Tolerance (application), 232

FDISPLAY login script command, 334

File Allocation Table (FAT), 216–217

File compression, 123, 196–201

File system. *See* NWFS (NetWare File System)

File system maintenance, 222–226

File system security, 220–222

File system support enhancements, NetWare 5, 24

File system volume setup, 60–61

FILER.EXE, 188, 198

Files, managing, 180–226

FIRE login script command, 334

Firewalls, 348

FLAG utility, 199–200

Forums, NetWare-oriented, 461

486 server, removing, 87

Free blocks, adequate, 124–125

Free space, minimum needed, 37

Free storage space, pool of, 201

G

Garbage collection, 128

Gateways, 272–273, 293

GOTO login script command, 334–335

Graphical installation, hanging during, 70

Group objects
creating, 318–319
need for, 317

Groups of users, managing, 317–319

GUI screen
changing the background, 96
disabling, 94–95

GUI server management, 93–96

H

Hardware device driver setup, 54–58

Hardware enhancements, NetWare 5, 16–17

Hardware requirements, NetWare 5 server, 36–38

Hardware upgrades, and saving NDS database, 413

HELP, 125

Host adapter modules (HAMs), 55

Host name, 350

Host-IP control (FastTrack Server), 353

Hot Fix feature (NetWare), 40

HotPlug Support Module (HSM), 16, 40, 55

HP printer driver, installing, 295

Hung server, 70, 104

Hypertext Transfer Protocol (HTTP), 349

I

Icon for logging out and shutting
  down, 248–249
IF/THEN login script command,
  335
iMac Pure IP support, 98
Import policies (workstation),
  440–442
Importing a DHCP 2 database to
  DHCP 3, 372–373
Importing NetWare 4.11 DNS
  services, 388–389
Importing users into NDS,
  309–310
INCLUDE login script
  command, 336
Inheritable rights in NDS
  security, 447–448
Inheritance, ADS vs. NDS, 3
Inherited Rights Filter (IRF),
  220, 452–456
Inherited supervisor rights,
  blocking, 452–456
INI files, importing/exporting
  with NAL, 231
In-Place Upgrades, 32–33,
  207–208
Installation enhancements,
  NetWare 5, 16–17
Installations. *See also*
  Upgrading
    of Catalog Services, 415
    of DHCP server, 364–370

of DNS server, 382–388
and Ethernet frames, 73
FastTrack Server
  pre-installation, 347
license, 78–81
of multiple servers, 38
of NetWare License Services
  (NLS), 66
non-GUI, 48
of Novell Application
  Launcher (NAL), 230
of Novonyx FastTrack
  Server, 349–352
of NSS, 207–212
of 100 servers, 47
of other products, 67–68
post-installation, 73–78
pre-installation, 9–10, 32–50
of printers automatically,
  282–283
server, 30–81
server hanging during, 70
server-to-server, 51
and setting block allocation,
  71–72
and storage device failures,
  68–70
using Novell's install,
  52–68
of Z.E.N.works Starter Pack,
  151–152
INSTALL.BAT, 32
INSTALL.NLM, 49

Intelligent I/O (I$_2$O), 16, 103
Internet Group Management
Protocol (IGMP), 140
Internet (the), 348
Intranet, 348
Intruder Detection, 311–313
IP
having it load first, 97
migrating from IPX to, 21
NetWare vs. Pure, 98
running without UDP
traffic, 98–99
IP addresses, 38, 350
assignments, 362
confirming receipt of, 371
excluding from assignment,
373–374
IP Configuration dialog box, 371
IP segments, NetWare 5 with, 46
IP TimeSync utility, 20
IP-only feature of Novell Client,
21, 178
IPX
migrating to IP, 21
removing, 77
IPX address (server), changing,
412
IPX Compatibility driver, 13,
74, 96
IPX connectivity, 96
IPX number, customizing during
installation, 71
IPX Router, remote, 100

IPX segments, NetWare 5
with, 46
IPX servers, viewing,
76–77
I$_2$O support, 16, 103

J
Java applications,
251–253
Java GUI Server console, 21
Java Runtime Environment
(JRE), 92
Java support, NetWare 5, 21
JAVA.NLM application
parameters, 252–253

K
Kernel design changes, NetWare
5, 17
Key Material object, 131
Keyboard locking, 127

L
LAN Area object, creating,
425–426
LAN drivers, 38
LAN traffic, reducing with
Z.E.N.works, 167–168
Large Internet Packet (LIP),
118–119
LASTLOGINTIME login script
command, 336

Launcher Configuration (NAL), 234–246
LDAP
  configuring, 134–137
  configuring on FastTrack Server, 354
  vs. NDS, 355
  software that supports, 137
LDAP catalog, 9, 44
LDAP client, troubleshooting, 140
LDAP server, and Outlook Express, 137–139
Least recently used (LRU) sitting time, 117
License Catalog objects, 250
License Certificate objects, 250
License certificates, 250
License connections, maximum, 92–93
License Container objects, 250
License installation, 78–81
License objects, moving, 93
License Service Provider (LSP) objects, 249
License Services (NLS), installing, 66
Licenses, printer, 277
Lightweight Directory Access Protocol (LDAP), 134, 353–354
LIMBER process, 406
LOAD command, 19

Load Balancing (application), 232
Loadable Storage Subsystem (LSS), 205
Local bindery, 395
Location profile, 175
Locator object, 369–370
Locking the server keyboard, 127
Log out and shut down icon, creating, 248–249
Logically dividing NDS, 427–428
Logically organized network resources, 405
Login script commands
  list of, 330–339
  vs. variables, 328–329
Login script variables, 322–323, 328–329, 340–342
Login scripts, 319–343
  @ command in, 325
  creating, 326
  error when modifying, 323
  explained, 319
  and losing AUTOEXEC.BAT path, 325
  migration and, 46–47
  need for, 326
  order of execution, 320
  printing, 342–343
  reading Registry values, 342
  for registering workstations, 156

for setting current context, 404

troubleshooting, 321–322

types of, 319–320

will not run, 324

Login security, 311–317

LOGIN.EXE, 323

LOGOUT login script command, 336–337

Long filenames, 112–113, 196

M

Magazines, NetWare-related, 460

Maintenance, file system, 222–226

MAKESU.NLM, 308

Managed object, 202

Manual allocation of IP addresses, 362

MAP commands, 325, 337

MAP DISPLAY OFF login script command, 337

Master Bind file, 378

Master catalog, creating, 416

Master License Agreement (MLA), 81, 93

Master name server, 378

Master replica, 104, 428

changing, 432

recovering crashed, 430–431

Maximum Simultaneous Requests, 356

Media Access Layer (MAL), 203

MEMORY command, 114

Memory needs, 116–117, 119–120

MAP login script command, 337

Microsoft Active Directory Services (ADS), 1–6

Microsoft Client, 169–170

Microsoft Management Console (MMC), 3

Migration

from Banyan VINES, 47

from IPX to IP, 21

login scripts and, 46–47

to NDPS, 286–291

of NetWare 3.12 users, 48

of NWIP queue-based printing to NDPS, 289

passwords and, 46

from Windows NT 4, 6–7, 50

Migration Agent, 74

loading, 72

server display, 97

Migration Wizard, directories not copied by, 71

MLA vs. NLS license, 93

MONITOR utility, 97, 113, 119–120

Mounting NSS volumes, 215

Mouse setup and configuration, 53–54, 78, 111

MSBATCH, 173

Multihoming, 390

Multiple processor support, 103
Multiple servers, installing, 38
Multiple users
    changing, 306–308
    setting up, 300
Multiport serial cards, 144
Multi-processing Kernel (MPK),
    103

N

NAL (Novell Application
    Launcher), 24–27, 230–249
    access to C drive, 233
    vs. Application Explorer, 230
    and Application objects,
        234–246
    application version checking,
        245
    Auto Verify feature, 237
    changing the background,
        233
    hiding the Welcome screen,
        232–233
    installation and tips, 230
    installing an application
        after invoking, 243–244
    Launcher Configuration,
        234–246
    roaming profile support, 232
    securing, 246–249
    uninstalling an application,
        246

user refreshes, 234–235
user upgrade prompt, 236
and Windows 98, 234
on Windows 95/98 Start
    menu, 231–232
in Windows 3.x startup
    group, 230
Name servers, 377
Name space support, NSS
    volumes, 188
NCCPPR32.EXE, 234
NCIMAN.EXE, 171
NDIR command, 198
NDPS Broker, 270, 290
NDPS database, corrupted, 292
NDPS Manager, setting up,
    270–271
NDPS (NetWare Distributed
    Print Service), 23, 267
    banner files, 285
    client updates for, 277
    customizing print jobs,
        283–285
    defined, 267–268
    errors when starting, 292
    hardware requirements, 269
    managing, 269–286
    migrating NWIP
        queue-based printing, 289
    migrating to, 286–291
    NLMs used to activate,
        269–270

optimizing, 290–291

Printer Configuration templates, 284

purposes, 268

and queue-based printing, 268

reinstalling, 295–296

versions, 268

NDPS 1 vs. NDPS 2, 268

NDPS Printer Manager, 277

NDPS printers

    Explorer and, 293

    printing DOS applications to, 287

    printing to, 277–279

NDPS protocols, 287

NDPS Volume object, deleted, 295

NDPSW32.DLL, error in, 291

NDS configuration, 63–66

NDS database, saving prior to upgrades, 413

NDS Directory, 397

NDS enhancements, NetWare 5, 19–20

NDS network user, 396

NDS (Novell Directory Services), 1, 19, 392–456

    vs. ADS, 1–6

    basics, 394–406

    or bindery services, 176–177

    explained, 1, 394

    global, 396

    importing users into, 309–310

    vs. LDAP, 355

    logically dividing, 427–428

    removing from the server, 414

    removing users from, 310–311

    Root object, 404

    troubleshooting, 406–415

    updating where needed, 409–410

NDS schemas, 365, 432

NDS security, 447–456

NDS Template object, 300

NDS tree design, 367, 435–445

NDS tree example, 367

NDS tree name, 63

NDS trees

    browsing at DOS prompt, 398

    design guidelines, 435–439

    example, 367

    NSS volumes added to, 210–211

    objects with question marks, 406–407

    object's position in, 398

    poorly designed, 435

    removing NSS volumes from, 211

    renaming, 405–406

NDS version, checking running,
407–408
NDSDIR, 191
NDSMGR.EXE, 49
NETADMIN, 21
Netscape Navigator
    installing, 240–241
    scheduling access to,
        241–242
    snapshot of, 237–240
    updating, 348
Netscape Server Administration,
    352–356
NetWare Administrator,
    300–311
NetWare Distributed Print
    Service. *See* NDPS
NetWare 5, new in, 14–28
NetWare 4.*x* tree,
    pre-installation of NetWare 5,
    9–10
NetWare License Services
    (NLS), 79–80, 92–93, 249–250
    Installation Kit, 80–81
    installing, 66
    vs. MLA license, 93
Netware Loadable Modules. *See*
    NLMs
NetWare OS new server
    installation, 52–53
NetWare partition setup, 58–59

NetWare Support Packs, 76
NetWare 3.12 users, migration
    template, 48
NetWare 3.*x* bindery, 395–396
NetWare 2.2 server
    upgrading, 46
NetWare/IP (NWIP), 6, 98, 289
NetWare-oriented forums, 461
NetWare-related magazines, 460
Network Board driver, 57
Network configurations,
    preventing changes to,
    164–165
Network Information Center
    (NIC), 379
Network Neighborhood, setting
    current context, 403
Network printer
    adding, 264–266
    attaching, 277
    finding, 175
Network printing
    managing, 254–297
    troubleshooting,
        291–297
Network professional
    associations, 461
Network Time Protocol (NTP),
    20, 446
NIAS (Novell Internet Access
    Server), 144–146

NLMs (Netware Loadable
Modules), 58, 249
  Java application
    parameters, 253
  and long filenames, 112–113
  memory needed for running,
    119–120
  remote loading of, 126
  server-based, 103
  used to activate NDPS,
    269–270
NLS (NetWare License
Services), 79–80, 92–93,
249–250
  Installation Kit, 80–81
  installing, 66
  vs. MLA license, 93
NLS objects, creating, 80
NO_DEFAULT login script
command, 337
Novell Application Launcher.
See NAL
Novell Client
  automatic upgrade, 170–173
  functions, 174–176
  installation and upgrades,
    169–174
  vs. Microsoft Client,
    169–170
  need for upgrade, 7
  NetWare 5 features, 27

passwords, 174–175
troubleshooting, 176–177
version, 174
Y2K compliance, 7, 169
Novell Client for Windows 95/98
  troubleshooting, 177
  uninstalling, 173
Novell Client32 secure desktop,
248
Novell Desktop Management
icon access, 166–167
Novell Directory Services. See
NDS
Novell Distributed Print
Services. See NDPS
Novell encryption, 131–134
Novell gateway, 272
Novell Internet Access Server
(NIAS), 144–146
Novell Job Manager, 280
Novell Licensing Services
Installation Kit, 80–81
Novell Licensing Services (NLS),
79–80, 92–93, 249–250
Novell Print Manager, 283–284
Novell printer gateway, 288
Novell Printer Manager,
278–279
Novell Public Key Infrastructure
Services (PKIS), 23,
133–134

Novell shareware program sites,
  463
Novell SMS, 130
Novell Storage Services. *See*
  NSS
Novell Upgrade Wizard, 33,
  35–36, 70–71
Novell Upgrade Wizard project,
  creating, 70–71
Novell web sites, 459–460
Novell Workstation Manager,
  156, 247
Novonyx FastTrack Server. *See*
  FastTrack (Web) Server
NPRINTER command, 264–266,
  288, 293–294
NSDIAG.NLM, 49
NSS Administration menu,
  214
NSS architecture, 203–207
NSS architecture drawing,
  204
NSS command-line utilites,
  215–218
NSS commands, 215–218
  cache buffer optimizing,
    218–219
  DOS FAT commands,
    216–217
  information only, 216
  load commands, 216
  Salvage, 215–216

NSS components, vs. NWFS
  components, 201
NSS components drawing, 202
NSS (Novell Storage Services),
  24, 183–185
  administration utilities,
    212–220
  and backup programs, 222
  DOS volume mount, 192
  limitations of, 189–192
  new capabilities of, 183–184
  vs. NWFS, 185–186
  salvage by volume, 188
  on a server-by-server basis,
    187
  storage devices supported,
    203
  and system performance,
    184
  upgrade options, 207–208
NSS partition, 202
NSS volumes, 42, 202
  added to NDS tree, 210–211
  creating, 184, 209–210
  deleting, 219–220
  managing, 212–220
  mounting, 215
  name space support, 188
  vs. NWFS volumes, 185–186
  print queues, 187
  recovering corrupted,
    224–226

removing from NDS tree, 211

resizing, 211–212

transferring data to, 208

NTP (Network Time Protocol), 20, 446

NWADMN95, 21

NWBACK32, 28

NWBACKUP, 130

NWCONFIG, 75, 80, 116, 209, 212, 413

NWFS components, vs. NSS components, 201

NWFS (NetWare File System), 185

    features of, 192–201

    vs. NSS, 185–186

    user space limits, 192–194

NWFS volumes

    compression settings, 199–201

    compression statistics, 197–198

    vs. NSS volumes, 185–186

NWInst Automated Server Installation, 47

NWIP (NetWare/IP)

    migrating queue-based printing, 289

    print configuration, 289

    vs. Pure IP, 6, 98

NWPMW32.EXE, 277

O

Object administration, ADS vs. NDS, 3

Object attributes, 434–435

Object class, 434

Object Engine, 205–206

Object naming, ADS vs. NDS, 2

Open Database Connectivity (ODBC) drivers, 164, 356

Operating system service pack and patch, 463

Optimizing the server environment, 113–125

Oracle 8 for NetWare, 27

Outlook Express, with LDAP server, 137–139

P

Packet Burst Protocol, 117–118

Partitioning, 397, 427–432

Partitions

    designing, 442–445

    NetWare, 58–59

    NSS, 202

Password restrictions for users, 315–316

Password rights, granting only, 448–449

Passwords

    migration and, 46

    preventing guessing of, 311–313

Patches (installed), finding, 108
PCCOMPATIBLE login script command, 337–338
PCI HotPlug Support Module (HSM), 16, 40, 55
PCONSOLE command, 266
Percent sign (%), in login script variables, 322–323, 329
PKIS (Public Key Infrastructure Services), 23, 133–134
Platform Support Module (PSM), 40, 54
Pool of free storage space, 201
Port Handler, 272
Port number, 351
Ports, TCP and UDP, 99
Post-installation issues, 73–78
Preferred server, setting up, 175–176
Pre-installation of FastTrack Server, 347
Pre-installation (server), 32–50
    items to gather, 39–42
    into NetWare 4.x tree, 9–10, 48–50
Pre-upgrade procedures, 7–9, 42–44
Primary name server, 378
Print Device Subsystem (PDS), 272
Print job spooling, moving to another drive, 294

Print jobs
    customizing, 283–285
    getting info about, 280
    scheduling, 285
    spooling, 294
Print Queue object, 256–257, 260
Print queues, NSS volume, 187
Print server
    activating, 263
    creating, 259
    reassigning, 264
Printer Agent, 271–272
    controlled-access printer, 276–277
    public-access printer, 274–276
Printer Configuration templates (NDPS), 284
Printer drivers
    copying with Z.E.N.works, 167
    NT workstation, 296
    pushing to a workstation, 280
    updating, 280–281
Printer gateways, 272–273, 293
Printer Information dialog box, 279
Printer licenses, 277
Printer object, 257–258, 260, 262
Print Server object, 258–259

Printer Services Quick Setup,
    262–263
Printers (network)
    adding, 264–266
    attaching, 277
    configuring remote, 264–266
    controlled-access, 276–277
    finding on the network, 175
    getting info about, 279
    installing automatically,
        282–283
    public vs. controlled-access,
        273
    public-access, 274–276
    pushing to a workstation,
        280
    registering public-access,
        290
    using bindery emulation,
        121
Printing DOS applications to
    NDPS printer, 287
Printing features, NetWare 5, 23
Printing login scripts, 342–343
Printing (network)
    managing, 254–297
    troubleshooting, 291–297
    bidirectional, 285
    queue-based, 256–267
    workstation-based, 288–289
Printing object interactions,
    259–263

Processor exception, 109
Processor utilization, lowering,
    120–125
Processors, 17, 102–103
Product installation,
    67–68
Professional associations, 461
Profile login scripts, 320,
    327–328, 338
Profile object, 320
Protecting a server, 87–88
Protocol configuration, 61–62
Protocol management,
    96–100
Protocols, 61–62, 96–100, 287
Protocols window, 61
Providers (NSS), 203–204
PSERVER command, 263
PSM (Platform Support Module),
    40, 54
Public Access printers, 23
Public Key Infrastructure
    Services (PKIS), 23,
    133–134
Public key security, 131–134
Public-access printers, 273
    creating, 274–276
    registering, 290
Pure IP
    vs. NetWare/IP, 6, 98
    and queue-based printing,
        267, 288

 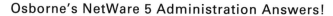

Q

Queue-based printing, 256–267, 297
    migrating, 289
    NDPS and, 268
    Pure IP and, 267, 288

R

RAM needs, 116–117, 119–120
RCONAG6, 91–92
RCONJ.EXE, 88, 92
RCONSOLE, 88–89
RCONSOLE function keys, 91
RCONSOLEJ connections, setting up, 89–90
Read-only replica, 429
Read/write replica, 428–429
Rebooting remotely, 90
REBUILD, 224–226
Redundancy, preventing, 376–377
REG files, importing/exporting with NAL, 231
Registered IP address, 38
Registering workstations, 156, 158–159
Registry key, Application object, 246
Registry values, reading, 342
REGREAD login script command, 342
Reinstalling a product, 75
Relative distinguished name, 400–402

REMARK login script command, 338
Remote Access Services (RAS)
    installing, 75
    uninstalling, 74–75
Remote IPX Router, 100
Remote printer, configuring, 264–266
Remote rebooting, 90
Remote server management, 88–92
Remote TCP/IP host, 99–100
Removing a user, 306
Removing users from NDS, 310–311
Renaming the NDS tree, 405–406
Renaming a user, 305
Replica servers, 378
Replicas
    designing, 442–445
    explained, 427
    types of, 428–429
Replication, 397, 427–432
Reporting on NetWare connections, 250
Requirements, NetWare 5 server, 36–38
RESET ENVIRONMENT command, 114
RESET SERVER command, 18
Resolver (DNS client), 377, 379
Resource Management Service (RMS), 270, 281, 286, 297

Resource process requests, 397
Resource record, creating, 386
RESTART SERVER command, 90–91
Restore Database from Backup, 292
Resynchronize Database Files, 292
REXXWARE Migration Toolkit (RMT), 34–36
Rights
    blocking inherited Supervisor, 452–456
    container, 450–452
    DNS server administration, 390–391
    getting back after losing, 12, 308
    in NDS security, 447–448
    password only, 448–449
    to unlock user accounts, 449–450
Root object (in NDS), 404
RSA algorithm, 133
RSA security, 133
Run scripts, 324

S

Salvage by volume (NSS), 188
Salvage (NSS command option), 188, 215–216
SAP (Service Advertising Protocol), 22, 142
SAVE ENVIRONMENT command, 115
SAVE MODIFIED ENVIRONMENT command, 115
Scheduling print jobs, 285
Schema Manager, 432–435
Schemas (NDS), 432
SCMD.NLM, 74
Screen saver, 19, 127–128
SCRIPT SERVER login script command, 338
Secondary name server, 378
Secure Authentication Services (SAS), 23
SECURE CONSOLE command, 95, 308–309
Secure desktop, 246–248
Secure Sockets Layer (SSL), 132
Securing NAL, 246–249
Securing a server, 87–88
Security, 131–134
    ADS vs. NDS, 2–3
    file system, 220–222
    login, 311–317
    NDS, 447–456
Select Object dialog box, 302
Semantic Agent (SA), 205–206
Server base license, 92
Server crash, 104–105
Server environment optimization, 113–125
Server installation, 30–81

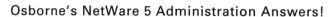

Server keyboard locking, 127
Server maintenance, 87–88
Server management, 82–146
Server processors, 102–103
Server shortcuts, 125–127
Server time configuration, 62
ServerMagic (Powerquest), 45
Service Advertising Protocol (SAP), 22, 142
Service agents (SA), 140–141
Service registration/deregistration, 141
Service Registry Service (SRS), 270, 290
Service requests, 141–142
SERVMAN.NLM, 18
SET login script command, 339
SET parameters for file compression, 199–200
SET variables, enabling for DOS applications, 244–245
Shareware program sites, 463
SHELL32.DLL, 231
Shut down icon, creating, 248–249
SHUTDOWN command, 91
Shutdown (brief), 414
Single-purpose containers, 439–440
Slave catalog, 421
SLP (Service Location Protocol), 22, 74, 140–141, 178, 290
vs. SAP, 142

Scope Container object, 143
settings, 142–144
Snapshot of Netscape Navigator, 237–240
Software exception, 109
Software requirements, NetWare 5 server, 36–38
Space limits (user), 192–194
Startup. *See* Booting
Static IP address, 38
Storage deposit, 201
Storage devices, NSS-supported, 203
Storage group, 201–202
Storage management, 129–130
Storage Management Services (SMS), 130, 222
Storage objects, deleting, 219–220
Storage space, pool of free, 201
Storage-device installation failures, 68–70
Suballocation block, 195
Suballocation block size, 125
Subdomains, 379
Subnet objects, assigning to subnet pool, 376
Subnet Pool object
assigning Subnet objects to, 376
creating, 375
Subnet service, DHCP Server, 374–375

Subordinate Reference replica, 104

Subordinate references, 104, 429–430

Summary screen, 67

Supernetting, 377

Supervisor rights
blocking, 221
blocking inherited, 452–456
getting back after losing, 12, 308

Swap file, virtual memory, 100–101

SWAP login script command, 339

Symmetrical multiprocessing (SMP), 103

SYS volume, 41
minimum, 47
and NSS, 189
setup, 58–59
sizing, 190–191, 445

System, documenting, 28

System requirements, NetWare 5 server, 36–38

T

Target Service Agents (TSAs), 130–131

TCP Defend Land Attacks, 99

TCP Defend SYN Attacks, 99

TCP ports, 99

TCP/IP, 98

TCP/IP host, remote, 99–100

Technical Information Documents (TID), 120

Technical Services assistance, 28

TECHWALK.NLM, 28

Template object (NDS), 300, 304–305

Temporary users with expiration, 313

TERM login script command, 339

Third-party backup programs, 129, 222, 461–462

Third-party NetWare Web sites, 462–463

Third-party printer gateways, 272

Time configuration, 62

Time restrictions for users, 314–315

Time (server), changing, 445–446

Time synchronization, 20, 445–447

TimeSync in IP environment, 20

TIMESYNC.NLM, 446

Traffic. *See* WAN Traffic Manager

Trailing periods, 401–402

Transport failure (NDS error), 411

Tree. *See* NDS trees

TREE login script command, 339

Troubleshooting
    DHCP Server, 370–371
    FastTrack Server, 356–358
    login scripts, 321–322
    NDS (Novell Directory
        Services), 406–415
    network printing, 291–297
    Novell Client, 176–177
    the server, 104–113
Trustee assignments, managing,
    221–222
Trustee rights, 220

U

UDP ports, 99
UIMPORT command, 309–310
Uniform Resource Locator
    (URL), 349
Uninstalling
    an application with NAL,
        246
    Novell Client for Windows
        95/98, 173
    RAS (Remote Access Server),
        74–75
    Z.E.N.works Starter Pack,
        168–169
Unlocking a user account, 313,
    316–317
Unlocking user accounts, rights
    to, 449–450
Updating NDS where needed,
    409–410

Updating Netscape Navigator,
    348
Upgrade prompt for users, 236
Upgrade Wizard, 33, 35–36,
    70–71
Upgrading. See also
    Installations
        from NetWare 4.x or 3.x, 32
        a NetWare 2.2 server, 46
        to NSS (Novell Storage
            Services), 207–212
        pre-upgrade procedures,
            7–9, 42–44
        saving NDS database prior
            to, 413
        using Novell's install, 52–68
User Account Restrictions, 311
User accounts. See Users
User administration, 65,
    300–311
User agents (UA), 140–141
User environment, managing,
    298–343
User licenses, 250
User login scripts, 320, 324. See
    also Login scripts
User object rights, 221
User password, preventing
    guessing of, 311–313
User password restrictions,
    315–316
User profile scripts, running,
    327–328

User space limits, NWFS, 192–194
User upgrade prompt, 236
User-Group control (FastTrack Server), 353–354
Users
    changing multiple, 306–308
    creating, 300–303
    creating with ConsoleOne, 303–304
    importing into NDS, 309–310
    managing groups of, 317–319
    removing, 306
    removing from NDS, 310–311
    renaming, 305
    setting up multiple, 300
    temporary with expiration, 313
    time restrictions for, 314–315
    unlocking, 313, 316–317

V

Variables, login script, 322–323, 328–329, 340–342
Version checking (NAL), 245
Video card resolution configuration, 112
Video card setup, 111–112
Virtual area network (VAN), 178

Virtual memory, 100–102
Virtual memory swap file, 100–101
Virus scan, 160–163
Volume object in NDPS, deleted, 295
VREPAIR utility, 222–223

W

WAN Traffic Manager, 19, 422–427
    cost factor, 423
    loading policies, 425
    optimizing, 425–426
    starting, 423–424
    turning off logging, 424
    viewing messages, 425
WANMAN.NLM, 424
Warm boot, 18
Web page date stamping, 356
Web resources, 458–463
Web Server. *See* FastTrack (Web) Server
Web site document directory, changing, 357–358
Web sites
    Novell, 459–460
    Novell shareware, 463
    OS service pack and patch, 463
    third-party NetWare, 462–463

Wildcard searching (catalog), 420
Windows 95 User system policy, 165
Windows 95/98 secure desktop, 247–248
Windows NT 4, migrating from, 6–7, 50
Windows NT secure desktop, 246–247
Windows NT Service Pack 3, 247
Windows NT user policy (Z.E.N.works), 246–247
Windows NT workstation printer driver, 296
Windows 3.1, trouble executing commands, 323
Windows 3.x secure desktop, 248
Windows warning, removing, 88–89
Windows workstations, printing login scripts, 342–343
Workstation clock, getting in synch, 177
Workstation current context, setting, 402–404
Workstation import policies, 440–442
Workstation information, exporting, 164
Workstation object, creating, 153
Workstation-based printing, 288–289

Workstations
importing, 153–155, 157
need for upgrade, 7
registering, 156, 158–159
updating, 158
WSIMPORT, scheduling, 157–158
WTM.NLM, 424

Y
Y2K compliance, 7, 169

Z
Z.E.N.works, 150–169
copying a printer driver, 167
policies, 168
reducing LAN traffic, 167–168
versions, 168
Windows NT user policy, 246–247
vs. Z.E.N.works Starter Pack, 10–12
Z.E.N.works scheduler, 157–158
Z.E.N.works Starter Pack, 10–12, 24, 150–169
installing, 151–152
setting current context, 402–403
uninstalling, 168–169
Zone transfers, 378
Zones (DNS), 380–385